Win32 Perl Scripting:
The Administrator's Handbook

Dave Roth

Win32 Perl Scripting:
The Administrator's Handbook

by Dave Roth

Copyright © 2001 by New Riders Publishing

FIRST EDITION: November, 2000

International Standard Book Number: 1-57870-215-1

Library of Congress Catalog Card Number: 00-100521

05 04 03 02 01   7 6 5 4 3 2 1

Interpretation of the printing code: The rightmost double-digit number is the year of the book's printing; the rightmost single-digit number is the number of the book's printing. For example, the printing code 01-1 shows that the first printing of the book occurred in 2001.

Composed in Sabon and MCPdigital by New Riders Publishing

Printed in the United States of America

Trademarks

Warning and Disclaimer

Publisher
David Dwyer

Associate Publisher
Al Valvano

Executive Editor
Stephanie Wall

Managing Editor
Gina Brown

Product Marketing Manager
Stephanie Layton

Publicity
Susan Petro

Acquisitions Editors
Karen Wachs
Leah Williams

Development Editor
Katherine Pendergast

Project Editor
Lori Lyons

Copy Editor
Chuck Hutchinson

Indexer
Sharon Shock

Manufacturing Coordinators
Chris Moos
Jim Conway

Book Designer
Louisa Klucznik

Cover Designer
Aren Howell

Proofreader
Debbie Williams

Composition
Amy Parker

Contents At a Glance

Contents

About the Author

Dave Roth is the contributor of various popular Win32 Perl extensions, including Win32::ODBC, Win32::AdminMisc, Win32::Daemon, and Win32::Perms. He has been providing solutions to the Perl community for difficult-to-solve problems since 1994. Dave has been a speaker at the O'Reilly Perl Conferences as well as the USENIX LISA-NT conferences. He has also contributed to the *Perl Journal* and is the author of *Win32 Perl Programming: The Standard Extensions* (New Riders Publishing, 1999).

Dave has been programming since 1981 in various languages, from assembler to C++, LPC, and Perl. His code is used by organizations such as Microsoft, the U.S Department of Defense, Disney, Lucus Films, Digital Paper, Hewlett-Packard, Metagenix, Radcom, the state of Michigan, and various colleges and universities, among many others. Dave helped assemble and administer a statewide WAN for the state of Michigan and has designed and administered LANs for Michigan State University and Ameritech.

About the Technical Reviewers

These reviewers contributed their considerable hands-on expertise to the entire development process for *Win32 Perl Scripting: The Administrator's Handbook*. As the book was being written, these dedicated professionals reviewed all the material for technical content, organization, and flow. Their feedback was critical to ensuring that *Win32 Perl Scripting: The Administrator's Handbook* fits our reader's need for the highest quality technical information.

Joseph Casadonte (joc@netaxs.com) is the lead software architect for Global Logistics Technologies, with 15 years professional programming experience in C, C++, Java, Perl, and most recently, Lisp. In his spare time he enjoys creating large programs (usually in Perl) to automate frivolous tasks, such as cataloging his growing Grateful Dead CD collection. He has recently taken to writing Lisp to customize his new favorite editor, Emacs. His Perl for Win32 page is at http://www.netaxs.com/~joc/perlwin32.html, where you can also link to his CD collection and Emacs pages.

Jutta M. Klebe is an Engineer and a Microsoft Certified Professional (MCP) with 15 years of programming and operating system experience. After finishing the polytechnic as a mechanical engineer (Dipl.-Ing. in Germany), she has worked since 1990 as a system administrator. Jutta is responsible for the installation process of Windows NT computers and troubleshooting user problems in a heterogeneous network with UNIX servers, Windows NT servers, and Windows NT Workstations. In her spare time, she administers Web servers and develops Internet and intranet applications using technologies like ActiveX/COM, (D)HTML, Perl, C/C++, VB, VBScript, and JavaScript. Jutta lives with her boyfriend in Hannover, Germany. She also does some biking in her spare time.

Dedication

This book is dedicated to my late grandfather. He has been a silent guiding force in my life. His suggestion that I "ride the wave" was right on, and I can only assume that he had some divine knowledge that I did not. Even though he never programmed, he did play a mean violin and was a wonderful example of how to be when I eventually grow up. Yes, this book is a technical reference, but in spirit it follows suit to those that he has written.

Acknowledgments

I would like to give a word of thanks to the two people who have worked with me by providing simply indispensable technical reviews of my work— Joe Casadonte (www.netaxs.com/~joc/perlwin32.html) and Jutta Klebe (www.bybyte.de/jmk). Without these two working as hard as they did, this book would be an absolute mess. Thank you both for your attention to detail and working through monotonous pages of code!

Next in line to thank are my editors; and do they need a thank you! Karen Wachs, Leah Williams, Katie Pendergast, Lori Lyons, Chuck Hutchinson, and everyone else related to this project deserve a good raise! Without your patience and professionalism, the final chapters may have never seen the light of day, let alone be printed. Thank you for sticking with it as deadlines slipped.

I do want to acknowledge those who gave me flack for working on yet another book. You know who you are: Zu, Chris, Chris, Kris, Chadd, Larry, Susan, Heather, Anton, Toshi, Bushia, Laura, Grandma, Mom, Ttootty, Greg, Gwen, Andy, Alex, Audrey, Anne ve Baba, Dilek, Leila, Harlan, Bill...the whole gang. Thanks to your unrelentless antagonism, I was able to muster the perserverence to carry on—even though it may have been out of simple spite. You can stop asking, "So, are you done with the book yet?" Now on to the next book!

And finally, I am honored to thank Nazli, my reassuring wife. Your ability to maintain a calm while I stressed and laugh when I scowled has made this journey bearable. You have brought a joy to my soul unlike anything I have ever felt. I thank you for your love and compassion. My dear, you are the world to me. Thank you.

Tell Us What You Think

As the reader of this book, you are the most important critic and commentator. We value your opinion and want to know what we're doing right, what we could do better, what areas you'd like to see us publish in, and any other words of wisdom you're willing to pass our way.

As the Executive Editor for the Networking team at New Riders Publishing, I welcome your comments. You can fax, email, or write me directly to let me know what you did or didn't like about this book—as well as what we can do to make our books stronger.

Please note that I cannot help you with technical problems related to the topic of this book, and that due to the high volume of mail I receive, I might not be able to reply to every message.

When you write, please be sure to include this book's title and author as well as your name and phone or fax number. I will carefully review your comments and share them with the author and editors who worked on the book.

Fax: 317-581-4663
Email: nrfeedback@newriders.com
Mail: Stephanie Wall
            Executive Editor
            New Riders Publishing
            201 West 103rd Street
            Indianapolis, IN 46290 USA

Introduction

All administrators need tools to correctly perform their job. These tools can range from books and programs to programming languages. For a network administrator, one of the greatest tools is a good scripting language.

Depending on whom you ask, the preferred scripting language of choice differs. Some like Java and some like Visual Basic. Others prefer Rexx and yet others use Python. Then there is the ubiquitous Perl language, the king of scripting languages. Perl is a jack-of-all-trade language. It can be used to perform almost any possible task. It is easy to learn and fun to use. Perl brings a network administrator not only a tool, but an entire toolset.

Win32 administrators, however, are usually not familiar with Perl. This unfamiliarity could be because Perl originated in the UNIX world. Or it could be that Microsoft promotes Visual Basic as the scripting language of choice for Win32 machines. This is too bad because Perl will quickly become a Win32 system administrator's best friend.

Generally speaking, Win32 administrators focus on looking for full-blown solutions to problems. They like to buy some off-the-shelf software that is designed to perform some administrative task. It is quite easy to install some software package and have it automatically solve some problem. However, this approach becomes costly as the number of problems increases.

Solving problems with Perl, however, is cheap—especially when you consider that one script can be adapted to fix other problems. Not only is this a reasonable way to solve problems, but it is also the foundation for automating your network.

Every network administrator will, at one point, be inundated with work. Likewise, every administrator will have to quickly solve emergencies. And while both of these things are happening to the administrator, new issues will arise that feed back into this cycle. At that point, a server will go down and chaos will ensue. This result is typical and should be expected.

But these situations are manageable. Fires can be extinguished, and problems can be rectified. The only serious problem is that doing so takes time. An administrator's time usually is so taken up with the chaos of daily problems that there is never time to consider how to solve major problems and issues. This is where scripting comes in.

When an administrator leverages the power of a good scripting language, processes can be automated. This means that daily reports can be generated, servers can be monitored, and routine maintenance can be automated. Implementing such activities can be the stepping-stone to achieving a better-implemented network.

When I was a network administrator for the state of Michigan, I automated almost every possible aspect of my job. Every day, log files were created on my servers and Web pages were generated by automatically merging data from databases into template files. I found that by creating automated processes, I was able to perform my daily tasks in one-fourth the time it took my peers in other departments. This free time I could spend solving bigger problems and implementing solutions that no one else had time for.

Why This Book?

The goal of this book is not to attempt to teach you how to run a Win32 network. Enough books are available to do that. Instead, this book introduces different techniques for monitoring events, quickly resolving problems, and proactively preparing for inevitable catastrophes.

You should read these chapters if you're looking for techniques to simplify your work. Tasks such as discovering which users are disabled or locked out of their accounts (Chapter 2) or killing a process on a remote machine (Chapter 9)—these are tasks that are of benefit to any administrator.

This book is divided into nine chapters, each one focusing on a different topic.

Chapter 1: Perl and the Admin

This chapter discusses the various aspects of what an administrator needs to know when introducing the Perl language to a network. This is a good place to start for those who have never played with Perl. For those well-seasoned Perl gurus, you may find some interesting Win32-specific tricks to help make the best use of Perl on Windows 2000, NT, ME, 98, and 95.

Chapter 2: Account Maintenance

The purpose of this chapter is to break free of the GUI application bonds that Win32 administrators have found themselves subject to. Here you will discover scripts that will enable you to manage your Win32 accounts from a command line without ever having to lift the mouse. These scripts also provide an effective way to automate account maintenance.

Chapter 3: Tools

What administrator would be caught dead without the proper tools? Unfortunately, most Win32 administrators, that's who. Not that it is anyone's fault, but there is a definite lack of affordable utilities that can solve tasks.

In this chapter, you can find tools that are more than just handy; they can be used in everyday tasks. Tools for discovering shared directories (including hidden shares), discovering NTFS alternate data streams, discovering file information, reading permissions, setting the owner on files and Registry keys, and setting a machine to automatically log on a particular user.

Chapter 4: Crisis Management

Every network goes through some sort of crisis—some more than others. In this chapter, you will learn some simple and effective techniques to prepare for the inevitable. Recovering COM-based documents, forcing users to disconnect from a shared resource and backing up and restoring user accounts, and using file permissions and network shares are just a few of the topics covered.

Chapter 5: Monitoring and Reporting

Just how does an administrator go about preemptively addressing problems? The answer is pretty simple: by proactively monitoring networked machines. Sure, this is easy to say, but just how do you do it? Chapter 5 discusses the various aspects of monitoring the Win32 events, such as the event log.

After events have been monitored, they need to be reported so that your administration team can respond. Various reporting methods are discussed, ranging from sending out network messages and emails to paging.

Chapter 6: Logon Scripts

Logon scripts are those little programs that run when a user logs on to a domain. They are usually overlooked, but they can be used to update user files and reconnect to network resources. What's even more interesting is how you can leverage these scripts to perform routine maintenance and even perform new computer configurations.

Chapter 7: Processes

Creating and managing processes are not as straightforward as they were under UNIX. Not only does Win32 Perl inherit all of its UNIX-like, process-creating functionality, but it adds some Win32-specific ones as well. Mixing these flavors, however, can cause some painful programming. This chapter discusses which functions should be avoided and which other ones should be promoted.

Here you will also learn how to use Perl to examine the list of processes and how to go about killing individual tasks.

Chapter 8: Win32 Services

UNIX administrators call them daemons, and Win32 administrators call them services. Either way, they both refer to a program that runs on its own. Yes, Win32 Perl scripts can be run as a service, but it is not as simple as you may think. This chapter discusses techniques to run Perl scripts as services.

Chapter 9: ADSI and WMI

The two acronyms that can cause even the most seasoned Win32 administrator to panic are ADSI and WMI. These are two fairly new technologies that provide an incredible wealth of information and control. Every administrator will eventually have to face these technologies. This chapter exposes them by describing what they are and how they work.

Let's face it, Win32 machines are not simple, nor are they simple to manage. Creating a new user account, making the user's home directory, and then applying correct permissions can be quite tedious. This book assumes that you understand these concepts of administering a network. It simply provides a series of tools that enable you to perform your job quickly and more efficiently.

Enjoy the read.

Perl and the Admin

If you are reading this book, chances are that either you are a system administrator who needs to automate administrative tasks, or you have an extraordinary sense of curiosity. Either way, you are embarking on a journey that will take you to the far reaches of administering Win32 machines.

As a system administrator, I quite often found myself having to automate tasks that my colleagues were content to do by hand. For some reason, they felt that adding tens of users at a time to a domain was best accomplished using the User Manager application. The closest they came to automating was using a batch file that deleted temporary files from the temp directory. If they ever needed to make environmental modifications on a wide scale (say, across thousands of machines), they would rather walk to each box, log on, and make the necessary modifications. I, on the other hand, found that approach simply an unacceptable waste of my time. In the time it would take me to modify two or three machines, I could have written a Perl script that would scurry across the network and make the necessary modifications on all the machines. The total turnaround time to hit all the computers on the network was in the scope of minutes, whereas my peers would require an entire weekend or more.

Scripting—whether in Perl, JavaScript, Visual Basic, Python, or any of a dozen other languages—is a tremendous way to automate, thus saving time, effort, and, in the end, money. In my mind, a system administrator must be able to effectively use a scripting language; otherwise, he is simply a knowledgeable computer user. You can follow this logic back to the UNIX platform, where scripting was necessary to keep a machine configured properly. It is not untypical to see a UNIX box littered with shell, Perl, and other types of scripts. For some unfortunate reason, Win32 has departed from that trend. Win32 administrators far too often look to some third-party application that will magically perform some type of configuration or automation without having to write any code. Whereas such products ease the burden of administrating, it usually results in far fewer options for the administrator.

A Note About This Book

You should consider this book to be just a leaping point into administration using Win32 Perl. The information held within these pages is just a guide. Consider it a guide from a system administrator who has learned a few things. Almost all the extensions that I have authored have been to solve problems that I have encountered while managing Windows networks.

The sample scripts are designed to be functional and illustrate how particular problems can be resolved. The emphasis is on the latter more than the former. For example, many scripts use third-party extensions, such as Win32::Lanman. Even though this extension is not yet part of the standard library, it provides a wonderful interface to the Win32 Lan Manager application programming interface (API). Other scripts, however, use the ever handy Win32::API to access functions that Win32::Lanman exposes. You might be confused why one script uses Win32::Lanman for some function but Win32::API for the same function in a different script. This is done on purpose. You should understand that Win32 Perl is much like Perl in general in that "there is more than one way to do it."

You will find that some scripts are useful but could be expanded to include some additional functionality. This is true; however, these scripts can consume much time in development, so to avoid "feature creep" (as well as "time creep"), some functionality has been ignored. Feel free to mangle these scripts to fit your particular need. I also hope that you will not only use the scripts, but study and learn the concepts behind them. These concepts can be indispensable when you're solving other similar, but different, problems.

Reusing Code

Having come from a C and assembler background, I have found that the ability to structure Perl scripts into discrete, reusable code chunks has made my life much easier. As a matter of fact, most coders feel the same way. Evidence of this can be found at any Comprehensive Perl Archive Network (CPAN) site, such as www.perl.com, where entire directories of donated chunks of code are available. Most of them are in the form of Perl extensions and modules—reusable code that others find beneficial.

It is this benevolence that characterizes the core of the Perl community. The availability of reusable code is great for most coders; however, system administrators are a different breed. For many reasons—some of which include system integrity, security, and corporate politics—many administrators refuse to use code that has been prepackaged by someone they do not know. I found times when it was easier to write my own modules than to attempt to understand the how's and why's of someone else's code.

Often I have found that one module was built on another module that was, in turn, built on yet another module. This is, after all, the foundation of reusable code. However, it poses a problem: If one of those modules fails, the entire project fails. When all your code depends on layer upon layer of reusable code modules, just locating, debugging, and fixing problems can become quite time-consuming.

Such concerns led me to write a considerable amount of my own modules and extensions. For the sake of community, much of this code was donated to the public domain under the GNU license. This way, other users can use the code and catch bugs that I overlooked. However, I found that more and more of my time was spent on documenting and fielding questions. This is one of the nonglamorous aspects of donating code to the public forum. It did, however, lead me to a belief that even though most Perl programmers mean well, it is inevitable that many will attempt to use modules and extensions without understanding the code, logic syntax, structure, or concepts. Consider, for example, the ODBC modules such as `DBD::ODBC`, `Win32::ODBC`, `iODBC`, and `ODBCTable`. These wonderful extensions provide access to databases; however, unless users understand what ODBC does and how it works, a flurry of questions, complaints, and constructive criticisms will inevitably arise.

Regardless, simple mistakes will be made when a programmer does not fully understand an extension or module. It becomes obvious that thorough documentation must be created in addition to the software. A lack of this documentation may not be a problem for those of us who routinely walk through the source code to understand it. Even though documentation may exist for some software, many of us still examine the source (you would not believe how many undocumented features can be found).

Perl

Perl has been around for quite a while and has found itself a home in virtually every operating system, from Linux to the Macintosh and from VMS to DOS. The Win32 platform is no exception and has begun to gather quite a following of Perl coders. This actually makes sense because Win32 lacks a reasonable scripting language. Since the first version of Win32, the only way to script was to use batch files; this approach was rife with problems and not much different from its DOS origins. To be fair, the Win32 command processor (which batch files stem from) is far superior to the DOS command processor; however, it still falls terribly short on automation capabilities.

With NT 4.0, Microsoft introduced the Windows Scripting Host (WSH) technology, which facilitates different scripting engines such as PerlScript, JavaScript, and VBScript. This technology enables you to execute scripts that provide functionality far beyond the reach of the command processor's batch files.

WSH was a separate download for NT 4.0, but ships with Windows 2000. A scripting language must be designed as a COM server that is WSH-engine compliant. Perl not only does this, but also enables you to use it as a command-line application, meaning that you don't need to register a COM server, nor do you need to have WSH installed at all.

Running Perl Scripts from a Command Line

Years ago, I was working with a friend who was a system administrator for a Solaris box. Every time he wanted to run a Perl script, he had to laboriously type in the full path to the Perl executable. I don't know why he didn't just add the Perl bin directory to the path. Each time he typed in the full path, I would sigh with anticipation—especially when he mistyped something and had to delete, fix it, and then retype the rest of the path. At that point, it occurred to me that not everyone adds Perl to the system path.

When you add the perl\bin directory to the system path, running a Perl script is easier because you don't have to specify the full path to PERL.EXE. You can simply run a script (such as an imaginary FOO.PL script) by entering the following:

```
perl foo.pl
```

Some administrators prefer to add this line only to a user path, but I find that is far more useful to add it to the system path so that all processes can utilize it.

You can use many tricks to get a Perl script to execute without having to type in something like this:

```
c:\perl\bin\perl.exe c:\perl\scripts\myscript.pl
```

By far the easiest way is to use a simple, three-step method that makes Perl scripts run simply and efficiently. The following steps work with Windows NT/2000 but, unfortunately, not with Windows 95/98. For Windows 95/98, there is no simple way to achieve the same results.

1. Associate the .PL extension with Perl by using the `assoc` command:

   ```
   assoc .pl=PerlFile
   ```

2. Register the `PerlFile` file type with the Perl binary by using the `ftype` command:

   ```
   ftype PerlFile=c:\perl\bin\perl.exe "%1" %*
   ```

   Notice that the `%1` is surrounded by double quotes. This is important, especially if you expect to reference a Perl script that has embedded spaces in its filename.

3. Add the .PL extension to the list of executable extensions. Windows 2000 uses an environment variable called `PATHEXT`, which is a list of file extensions that are considered executable. An example could look like this:

   ```
   PATHEXT=.COM;.EXE;.BAT;.CMD;.VBS;.VBE;.JS;.JSE;.WSF;.WSH
   ```

   Simply add the `.PL` extension to this list:

   ```
   PATHEXT=.PL;.COM;.EXE;.BAT;.CMD;.VBS;.VBE;.JS;.JSE;.WSF;.WSH
   ```

4. (Optional) Place Perl's `bin` directory in the path.

After you complete these steps, you can run a Perl script by using only its filename:

```
myscript.pl
```

This will result in Perl executing the script.

If the script ends with a `.PL` (or whatever extension you specified in the `assoc` command), *and* you are running on a Windows 2000 machine with the extension added to the `PATHEXT` variable, you can call a script by using only its name, without an extension:

```
myscript
```

You can pass parameters into the script as well. However, if you need to pass in some flag, such as `-d` or `-w`, you need to perform the optional fourth step and modify the system path. You then can either reference the entire command line, including `perl.exe`, as in

```
perl -d c:\temp\myscript.pl
```

or, alternatively, add the flags to the "sha-bang" line in the beginning of the script, as in Example 1.1.

Example 1.1   *Backticks and File Associations*

```
01. #!perl -w -d
02. my @Output = `c:\\temp\\perltest.pl`;
03. print @Output;
```

Example 1.2 uses these steps to set up a computer for Perl use. Notice that some lines use the `Win32::AdminMisc` environment variable functions. This point is important because if you simply use the `%ENV` hash to set the variables, they are lost the moment the script terminates.

Example 1.2   *Configuring a Machine for Perl*

```
01. use Win32::AdminMisc;
02. $TIMEOUT = 30;
03. $PERL_DIR = $^X;
04. $PERL_EXTENSION = '.pl';
05. # Check that the path is accurate
06. if( -d $PERL_DIR )
07. {
08.   if( ! -f "$PERL_DIR\\bin\\perl.exe" )
09.   {
10.     print "WARNING: You are missing your Perl executable.\n";
11.   }
12. }
13. else
14. {
15.   print "WARNING: You are missing your Perl directory.\n";
16. }
17. # Before anything, set the file extension association
18. print "Associating $PERL_EXTENSION to perl...";
19. `assoc $PERL_EXTENSION=PerlFile`;
20. print "done\n";
21.
22. # Now link the association with Perl
23. print "Linking the perl extension to perl executable...";
24. $Command ='%PERL%\bin\perl.exe %1 %*';
25. `ftype PerlFile=$Command`;
26. print "done.\n";
27.
28. # Set the Perl variable
29. print "Setting Perl environment variable...";
30. if( $Result = ModifyVar( 'Perl', $PERL_DIR ) )
31. {
32.   print ( ( 0 < $Result )? "successful\n":"wrote over previous value\n" );
33. }
34. else
35. {
36.   print "failure\n";
37. }
38.
39. # Add Perl to the system path...
```

```perl
40. print "Setting path...";
41. if( $Result = ModifyPath( 'Path', '%PERL%\bin' ) )
42. {
43.   print ( ( 0 < $Result )? "successful\n":"already set\n" );
44. }
45. else
46. {
47.   print "failure\n";
48. }
49.
50. # Add .pl to the path extension list
51. print "Setting path extensions...";
52. if( $Result = ModifyPath( 'PATHEXT', $PERL_EXTENSION ) )
53. {
54.   print ( ( 0 < $Result )? "successful\n":"already set\n" );
55. }
56. else
57. {
58.   print "failure\n";
59. }
60.
61. sub ModifyVar
62. {
63.   my( $VarName, $VarValue ) = @_;
64.   my $PrevValue = Win32::AdminMisc::GetEnvVar( $VarName, ENV_SYSTEM );
65.   my $Result = Win32::AdminMisc::SetEnvVar( $VarName,
66.                                             $VarValue,
67.                                             ENV_SYSTEM,
68.                                             $TIMEOUT );
69.   $Result *= -1 if( defined $PrevValue );
70.   return( $Result );
71. }
72.
73. sub ModifyPath
74. {
75.   my( $VarName, $VarValue ) = @_;
76.   my $Result = -1;
77.   my $Path = Win32::AdminMisc::GetEnvVar( $VarName, ENV_SYSTEM );
78.   if( defined $Path )
79.   {
80.     my $RegexValue = $VarValue;
81.     $RegexValue =~ s/([.$%@()\[\]\\\/])/\\$1/g;
82.     if( $Path !~ /$RegexValue/i )
83.     {
84.       $Path .= ";$VarValue";
85.       $Path =~ s/;+/;/;
86.       $Result = Win32::AdminMisc::SetEnvVar( $VarName,
87.                                              $Path,
88.                                              ENV_SYSTEM,
89.                                              $TIMEOUT );
90.     }
91.   }
92.   else
```

continues ▶

Example 1.2 *continued*

```
93.  {
94.    $Result = 0;
95.  }
96.  return( $Result );
97. }
```

Using Perl over a Network

Ideally, an administrator would install Perl on each machine in a network. By doing so, she can guarantee that each computer can run Perl for logon scripts, services, and scheduled batch jobs, or by user scripts.

Having Perl on each desktop can be remarkably empowering. However, not all machines can handle it. Even though drive space is becoming less and less expensive, many shops have older equipment and no budget to upgrade. This can place a couple of megabytes of drive space at a premium.

One rather simple way around this problem is to copy Perl onto a file server and share its directory. This solution is pretty simple. When someone wants to call a Perl script, he can simply access the shared Perl directory on the file server. This solution, however, has its own issues to consider.

As I mentioned earlier in this chapter, you can add Perl's `bin` directory to the path for easy access to Perl. Doing so is an absolute must, in my opinion. However, if you are accessing Perl remotely on a file server's shared directory, what do you put in the path? There are two answers to this question.

First, you can map a drive letter to the shared directory. After you do so, you can modify the path environment variable to include the `perl\bin` directory on the mapped drive. Doing so requires that you can reliably map a specific drive to the share. As silly as it may seem, some applications out there still require you to use a specific drive letter. So, depending on your organization's needs, you might have to think about which drive is available. Another issue to contend with is a user accidentally deleting the mapped drive. When this is done, Perl won't run, and chances are the user won't tell you this has happened.

The second and more desirable approach is to refer to Perl's `bin` directory as a universal naming convention (UNC). This means adding the UNC to the path. Here is a little trick: When you add the UNC to the path, make sure to add it at the end. For example, if your path is

```
C:\winnt;c:\winnt\system32
```

you should add the Perl UNC to the end of the path like this:

```
C:\winnt;c:\winnt\system32;\\server1\perlshare\bin
```

Positioning the UNC in the beginning or middle of the path can be a problem. If the share is removed, the remote server goes offline, or the network has problems, then *all* programs that are run may temporarily pause when first starting. The pause would occur due to Win32 waiting to timeout on the request to access the UNC.

On an NT machine (or Windows 2000), a user has his own set of environment variables, including his own personalized path. When the user logs on to an NT machine, his user path variable is appended to the system path variable. This means that if you locate the Perl UNC at the end of the system path, it ends up being in the middle of the user's path variable. You should consider this issue when configuring your network for Perl use: It is ideal to add the Perl UNC to the end of the user's path variable.

By now, the issue of adding a remote Perl share to your path is not as simple as you might have first assumed. Now let me toss in another problem. Say that you have a network with 1,000 users. Also, assume that each user has a Perl-based logon script, and you have configured each user to access Perl from a network share. At 8:00 a.m. on Monday, you have 1,000 users all logging on to their machines. Imagine the network traffic as all users are accessing Perl's binaries and assorted libraries and packages. Ideally, you would set up a shared Perl directory for each subnet, therefore minimizing traffic across routers. This means that each machine needs to know which server on the subnet contains the Perl shared directory.

Now consider these two issues together. If you add the Perl UNC to the end of the user path variable, and each machine has to know which specific server to connect to, alas—you have a problem: A user can log on to a machine on any subnet. Therefore, hard-coding the Perl UNC in the user's path variable could cause Perl access to travel across routers. This problem, too, has a solution. You can create a system variable called PERLDIR on each machine. This new variable contains the UNC to the shared Perl directory on the local subnet. Now all you have to do is add %PERLDIR% to the end of the user's path variable. For example, you can set the *system* PERLDIR variable to the following:

```
PERLDIR = \\server1\perlshare
```

Then you can append the variable to the *user's* path variable like this:

```
PATH = c:\Program Files\Foo;%PERLDIR%\bin
```

This is the ideal solution.

Minimizing Network Bandwidth Use

Win32 tries to minimize memory usage. Considering that the operating system is a multitasking environment, one process may need more memory at one time, whereas another process may require less. Because a machine has only a finite amount of memory, Win32 swaps blocks of memory in and out of RAM. For example, if you're editing a TIFF graphic in Photoshop, Windows may temporarily move a Word document from RAM to a swap file on the hard drive. This frees up RAM for Photoshop to use. When you go back to Word to continue editing the document, the operating system may move Photoshop's TIFF file data to the swap file and reload the Word document back into RAM. As a result, you may often experience disk thrashing when you have many applications running.

Win32 also uses another way of managing memory. When an application runs (such as Photoshop, Excel, or Perl), the operating system has to load the program's code into RAM to execute. This process can take up quite a bit of memory. Just like a TIFF file or Word document, code memory can be swapped out of RAM.

Why should you fill up the swap file with this code when it is already stored on the hard drive in its .EXE or .DLL file? The answer is that there is no reason. This is precisely why some programs and libraries are marked as DISCARDABLE. If code is marked as purgable, it is purged from RAM when more memory is needed by another process. This means it is removed from RAM but not stored in the swap file. When the code is needed again, it is simply reloaded from the .EXE or .DLL file. This process works remarkably well. Well, almost remarkably well.

A problem arises when you are accessing Perl over a network or from a CD-ROM. If Win32 purges the Perl program code, it has to travel across the network or start to spin up the CD to reload the code later when it is needed. This burdens both the network with excess traffic and the user in terms of latency.

You can mark executables and libraries so that they "run from a swap file." This means that when the .EXE or .DLL file is loaded, all of its image is loaded into RAM. Therefore, if any pages are swapped out of memory, they go into the pagefile on the hard drive instead of being purged from RAM altogether.

Typically, neither Perl nor any of its libraries are marked for this type of forced loading into memory. However, if you are compiling Perl yourself using Microsoft Visual C++ (MSVC), you can tell the linker to set the header flags such that network and/or CD-ROM access forces the file image to fully load into RAM. If, however, you are not compiling Perl, you can still set the flags by using a binary image header editor utility, such as EDITBIN.EXE (which comes with Microsoft's Visual C++).

You can set the appropriate flags (for network or CD-ROM access) by using the following command:

```
editbin perl.exe /swaprun:net /swaprun:cd
```

Of course, only specify the switch you want (or both if need be). To remove the flags, use the following command:

```
editbin perl.exe /swaprun:!net /swaprun:!cd
```

The following three files should be configured with the swaprun flags for Perl 5.005:

```
perl.exe
perlcore.dll
perlcrt.dll
```

And for Perl 5.6 (a.k.a. 5.006), you use these files:

```
perl.exe
perl56.dll
```

Likewise, you might want to set the flags on any extension DLL that is used often, especially if they are large, such as Win32::GUI, Win32API::Registry, Win32::ODBC, and Win32::WinError.

The list of files loaded by Perl can be determined using the modules.pl script (Example 7.17), which is discussed in Chapter 7, "Processes."

Extensions

Many extensions are available for Win32 Perl. These extensions provide an absolute wealth of functionality that makes Perl very powerful. Because extensions are written by people who have different needs, it is common to find an extension that exposes some functionality identical to that found in other extensions. For example, the Win32::Lanman extension provides a function called NetServerEnum() that returns a list of servers; the Win32::NetAdmin extension also provides a similar function called GetServers(). Fundamentally, there is no difference between the two because they both end up calling the same Win32 API function, but there is a difference in how each of the functions is called.

So, why would you want to use one function as opposed to another? There is no easy answer to this question; the choice may totally depend on the programmer and the situation. For example, if I am writing a script that makes extensive use of `Win32::Lanman`, I would probably use its `NetServerEnum()` function instead of loading the `Win32::NetAdmin` extension just for a call to its equivalent `GetServers()` function. Another reason to consider is the simplicity or completeness of one extension's function, such as creating a new account. The `Win32::Lanman::NetUserAdd()` function, for example, takes the place of both the `Win32::NetAdmin::CreateUser()` and `Win32::AdminMisc::UserSetMiscAttributes()` functions.

One simple criterion that is commonly used in deciding what extensions to use has to do with an extension's availability. Because `Win32::NetAdmin` comes with ActivePerl as a part of the standard library, it is more likely that machines with Win32 Perl installed will have that extension. Using `Win32::Lanman`, however, requires that someone download and install it.

Consistency

Keep in mind that Perl extensions are full of inconsistencies. Even though many of the Win32 extensions call the same Win32 API functions (as we saw in the previous section), they may expose these functions differently. For example, to add a user to a local group, the `Win32::NetAdmin` extension uses

```
LocalGroupAddUsers( $Server, $GroupName, @Users );
```

However, `Win32::Lanman` uses

```
NetLocalGroupAddMembers( $Server, $Group, \@UserSID );
```

The first difference here is the name of the function. If you are a C programmer or a seriously hard-core VB or Delphi coder, using the `Win32::Lanman` version of this function makes sense because its name is identical in the Win32 API. The second difference is that the former version of the function accepts an array of username strings. The latter function accepts an array of user security identifiers (SID).

These mini-issues come up quite often when you're programming Win32 Perl. If you decide to use one extension over another, you might have to implement a different strategy than if you used the other extension.

Administration and Computer Languages

Most UNIX administrators know several programming languages, such as C, Perl, Java, Python, sed, awk, and the various shells. I have seen UNIX administrators laugh in the faces of Windows administrators when they admit that they only know how to write batch files. I suppose this revelation quickly leads into a platform flaming war, but I do want to make a point here. Just because a platform is easy to use does not mean anyone can be an effective administrator.

UNIX administrators normally know several languages because they have to. It is almost impossible to install and maintain a network of UNIX boxes without writing RC scripts or modifying shell scripts. Win32 administrators can usually get away with knowing only batch files because so much of the platform is automated. This fact I find quite disheartening.

Unless your department is just bursting at the seams with money, obtaining all the tools you need to fully automate your systems is not easy. Even if you can afford to buy the latest and greatest software tools to administer your network, you'll inevitably encounter a problem for which a tool has yet to be written that will solve it. For these reasons, knowing how to solve such problems using a programming language, such as Perl, is imperative.

However, because Perl itself is written in C, you can easily make the argument that you should know C or C++. I would not debate you there. The real reason for this intimate knowledge of the C language is actually driven more out of the need for documentation than anything else.

Because dependable Perl documentation is hard to find and the Internet is full of misinformation, it is incredibly useful to walk through Perl's or an extension's source code yourself to understand exactly what it does. When I wrote *Win32 Perl Programming: The Standard Extensions*, this is exactly what I did. At the time, most of the extensions were either not documented or inaccurately documented. To fully understand what a funtion's parameters represent, I read the source code. While doing so, I also located a few bugs that I was able to correct. All in all, reading the source code is good for everyone. To be sure, I am not suggesting that administrators enroll in a four-year college to earn a degree in programming. However, a casual understanding is incredibly useful.

Even if you are not ready to read source code, an understanding of C is useful for interacting with the Win32 extensions. Many of them directly expose the Win32 API, such as Win32::Lanman and Win32::API. An understanding of how each function works can be absolutely invaluable.

Most Useful Extensions

After you wrestle with Win32 Perl for any duration of time, your appreciation for certain extensions will begin to grow. You'll find yourself automatically thinking in terms of solving problems with a particular extension instead of considering others.

Of all the Win32 extensions I have either used or written, I have to confess that these five (in alphabetical order) have proven to be the most useful:

```
Win32::API
Win32::Daemon
Win32::Lanman
Win32::OLE
Win32::Registry
```

There are many other extensions that are more than just useful, but for my administration needs, these particular extensions have solved the most problems. If you are not familiar with them, you should be. This book uses them quite extensively, and having a grasp of what they do and how they work is incredibly beneficial. Refer to the section "Modules Used in This Book," in Appendix A to find out how to obtain these extensions.

Conclusion

As a network administrator, you are entering a brave new world of Perl coding. No matter how good you are as an administrator or how many exams you have passed, you are about to embark in a journey that will do wonders for you.

Whether you have coded in Perl before or are a novice, this book walks you through many of the more obnoxious problems that you will face. And by leveraging the flexibility of Perl, you will quickly see how your network can benefit from your use of this language.

To be sure, Perl itself can be confusing—especially because it is Open Source software. Anyone can make his own extensions and modules and post them on the Internet—usually without documentation. But with due diligence and a bit of careful study, Perl coding can be tamed and mastered.

2

Account Maintenance

At the heart of a Win32 network are the accounts. For any process to start, an account must be associated with it. Even automatic processes, such as services, are started by some logged-on user. In some cases, this user is a normal user; in others, it may be a special user whose account has been granted specialized privileges.

Most users are familiar with accounts because they have to use them to log on to a machine. As administrator, however, you know that several types of accounts are available: user, group, machine, and domain trust accounts. You have to know these various types of accounts because you have the burden of managing them.

Creating Accounts

You can easily create an account by using the GUI-based User Manager or Microsoft Management Console (MMC) snap-in. Basically, you point and click, fill in some information, and then click OK. This task is pretty simple. However, when you're in a rush or you need to work on multiple accounts, doing it programmatically can often be easier. For example, creating 30 accounts by hand can be quite tedious, but when you use a script, it's a snap.

Using GUI applications requires more effort than simply creating the account. After you create the account, you still need to add the new user to various groups. Having done that, you need to create the user's home directory as well as apply any security permissions to the directory tree. On the bright side, when a script is set up to do those things, as you'll see in Example 2.1, it's no longer a burden.

Unfortunately, writing scripts that create accounts programmatically is more burdensome than using a GUI because a script has to deal with some aspects of an account that someone using a GUI never sees. For example, a script needs to know if the account is a user, machine, or domain trust account; GUI applications typically assume you are referring to a user account.

Example 2.1 creates a user account in a specified domain (or specified machine), adds the user to various specified groups, and creates and applies permissions to the user's home directory. To use this code, you need to change some variables to match your own network.

You should modify the %PATH hash so that the home key (line 8) reflects the path to your user's home directories. The profile key (line 9) reflects the path to your user's profiles. The script key (line 10) is the path to a logon script. The logon script path is relative to the logon script's directory on the domain controller (DC) that authenticates the user. See Chapter 6, "Logon Scripts," for more details.

Additionally, you can change the permission masks in the %Permission hash to suit your needs (lines 14–23). The hash contains sub-hashes, one per user or group. (the key for the sub-hash is a user or group account name). One key, called <user>, is replaced by the account's name for which the directory is being created. Lines 159–172 actually apply the permissions, depending on how the hash is constructed: File permissions are applied if a file hash key exists, and directory permissions are applied if a dir hash is defined.

The %Account hash in lines 58–76 defines how the account will be created. Here, you can tweak the attributes of the account. By default, the password is a lowercase version of the account name. Table 2.1 explains some of the other, more obscure attributes.

Table 2.1   Meanings of the Keys in Example 2.1's %Account Hash

Key	Description
usr_comment	This attribute specifies a comment about the user account. Nobody sees it except those who examine the account at a low level, such as the script in Example 2.2. Even if an administrator uses the User Manager, this attribute is not displayed. It is typically not used; however, it might contain a comment about the state of the account, such as `Temporarily disabled until further notice`
params	This attribute should be left empty. It is modified by certain programs to store configuration information. Additionally, Microsoft stores Remote Access Services (RAS) and other configuration information here.
workstations	This attribute represents the machines the account is allowed to log on to in a comma-separated list, such as `server1,server2,JimsComputer` If this attribute is empty, the account is permitted to log on to any machine in the domain.

Key	Description
`acct_expires`	This attribute indicates the time when the account expires. After the account expires, the user is locked out and cannot log on. An administrator must unlock the account through the User Manager or with Example 2.6 (shown later).

Even though the script uses several hard-coded configuration options, some user-specific attributes can be specified from the command line. These particular attributes are user-specific rather than domain-specific hard-coded options. Table 2.2 describes the command-line switches that can be specified.

Table 2.2   Command-Line Switches for Example 2.1

Switch	Function
`-m Machine`	Specifies the computer where the account is located.
`-d Domain`	Specifies the domain where the account is located. It overrides any `-m` switch.
`-c Comment`	Contains the user account's comment.
`-f FullName`	Specifies the user's full name.
`-g Group`	Indicates a group that the user will be made a member of. It can be either a global or local group.
	Multiple `-g Group` switches can be specified.

If neither domain nor machine names are specified, the script defaults to the current domain of the user running the script.

An example of using this script is:

```
perl AddUser.pl -d MyDomain -c "Joel's Account" -f "Joel Smith" -g Users -g "Domain
Users" Joel
```

In this particular example, the user is creating a new user account called `Joel` in the `MyDomain` domain. The account has become a member in both the `Users` and `Domain Users` groups.

After you run this script, you should perform a domain synchronization. Refer to the "Synchronizing Domain Controllers" section in this chapter.

Example 2.1   *Creating Accounts*

```
01. use Win32;
02. use Getopt::Long;
03. use Win32::Perms;
04. use Win32::Lanman;
05.
06. # Change these values to match your network
07. %PATH = (
08.   home  =>  "\\\\server\\Home\$",
```

continues ▶

Example 2.1   *continued*

```
09.   profile => "\\\\server\\Profiles\$",
10.   script  => "logon.pl",
11. );
12.
13. # Change these values to match your needs
14. %Permission = (
15.   '<user>'    =>  {
16.     dir   => CHANGE_DIR,
17.     file  => CHANGE_FILE,
18.   },
19.   administrators  =>  {
20.     dir   => FULL_CONTROL_DIR,
21.     file  => FULL_CONTROL_FILE,
22.   },
23. );
24.
25. %Config = (
26.   flags   => UF_SCRIPT | UF_NORMAL_ACCOUNT,
27.   priv  => USER_PRIV_USER,
28.   machine => Win32::NodeName(),
29. );
30.
31. Configure( \%Config );
32. if( $Config{help} )
33. {
34.   Syntax();
35.   exit();
36. }
37.
38. if( "" ne $Config{domain} )
39. {
40.   Win32::Lanman::NetGetDCName( '',
41.                               $Config{domain},
42.                               \$Config{machine} );
43. }
44. elsif( "" eq $Config{machine} )
45. {
46.   Win32::Lanman::NetGetDCName( '',
47.                               Win32::DomainName(),
48.                               \$Config{machine} );
49. }
50.
51. print "Creating $Config{machine}\\$Config{name}...";
52. CreateAccount( \%Config );
53.
54. sub CreateAccount
55. {
56.   my( $Config ) = @_;
57.   my $Result = 0;
58.   my %Account = (
59.     name     => $Config->{name},
60.     password => lc $Config->{name},
```

```
61.     home_dir   =>   "$PATH{home}\\$Config->{name}",
62.     comment    =>   $Config->{comment},
63.     usr_comment =>  '',
64.     flags      =>   $Config->{flags},
65.     params     =>   '',
66.     script_path =>  $PATH{script},
67.     full_name  =>   $Config->{fullname},
68.     workstations=>  "",
69.     profile    =>   "$PATH{profile}\\$Config->{name}",
70.     acct_expires=>  -1,
71.     # logon_hours is a binary bitmap where each bit represents an
72.     # hour in a week (168 bits).
73.     logon_hours =>  pack( "b168", "11111111" x 21 ),
74.     home_dir_drive  => "Z:",
75.     password_expired=> 1,
76.   );
77.
78.   if( Win32::Lanman::NetUserAdd( $Config->{machine}, \%Account ) )
79.   {
80.     my( $Domain, $Sid, $SidType );
81.
82.     print "Success\n";
83.     next unless( Win32::LookupAccountName( $Config->{machine},
84.                              $Config->{name},
85.                              $Domain,
86.                              $Sid,
87.                              $SidType ) );
88.     $Result = 1;
89.     foreach my $Group ( @{$Config->{groups}} )
90.     {
91.       # First try the global group...
92.       if( ! Win32::Lanman::NetGroupAddUser( $Config->{machine},
93.                            $Group,
94.                            $Config->{name} ) )
95.       {
96.         # Global group failed try local group...
97.         Win32::Lanman::NetLocalGroupAddMember( $Config->{machine},
98.                                     $Group,
99.                                     $Sid );
100.      }
101.     }
102.
103.     MakeDir( $Account{profile} );
104.     if( MakeDir( $Account{home_dir} ) )
105.     {
106.       # The home directory exists, apply permissions...
107.       if( ApplyPermissions( "$Config{machine}\\$Account{name}",
108.                        $Account{home_dir} ) )
109.       {
110.         print "success\n";
111.       }
112.       else
113.       {
```

continues ▶

Example 2.1   *continued*

```
114.          print "failed to apply permissions.\n";
115.        }
116.      }
117.    }
118.    return( $Result );
119. }
120.
121. sub MakeDir
122. {
123.    my( $Dir ) = @_;
124.    my @DirList;
125.    my $DirCount;
126.    my $Result = 1;
127.    my( $Root, $Path )
128.      = ( $Dir =~ /^(\w:\\?|\\\\.+?\\.+?\\|\\\)?(.*)$/ );
129.
130.    return( 1 ) if( -d $Dir );
131.    @DirList = split( /\\/, $Path );
132.    $Path = $Root;
133.
134.    while( $Result && scalar @DirList )
135.    {
136.      $Path .= ( shift @DirList ) . "\\";
137.
138.      next if( -d $Path );
139.      $Result = mkdir( $Path, 0777 );
140.    }
141.    return( $Result );
142. }
143.
144. sub ApplyPermissions
145. {
146.    my( $User, $Path ) = @_;
147.    my $Perm = new Win32::Perms( $Path ) || return( 0 );
148.    my $Result = 0;
149.
150.    $Perm->Remove( -1 );
151.
152.    $Perm->Owner( $User );
153.    foreach my $Account ( keys( %Permission ) )
154.    {
155.      my $UserName = $Account;
156.      $UserName = $User if( "<user>" eq $Account );
157.
158.      # Apply file permissions
159.      if( defined $Permission{$Account}->{file} )
160.      {
161.        $Perm->Allow( $UserName,
162.                      $Permission{$Account}->{file},
163.                      FILE );
164.      }
165.
```

```
166.      # Apply dir permissions
167.      if( defined $Permission{$Account}->{dir} )
168.      {
169.        $Perm->Allow( $UserName,
170.                       $Permission{$Account}->{dir},
171.                       DIR );
172.      }
173.    }
174.    print "Applying permissions to '$Path'...";
175.    $Result = $Perm->Set();
176.    return( $Result );
177. }
178.
179. sub Configure
180. {
181.    my( $Config ) = @_;
182.
183.    Getopt::Long::Configure( "prefix_pattern=(-|\/)" );
184.    $Result = GetOptions( $Config,
185.                  qw(
186.                     machine|m=s
187.                     groups|g=s@
188.                     domain|d=s
189.                     fullname|f=s
190.                     comment|c=s
191.                     help|?
192.                  )
193.                );
194.
195.    $Config->{help} = 1 if( ! $Result );
196.    if( "" ne $Config->{machine} )
197.    {
198.      $Config->{machine} = "\\\\$Config->{machine}";
199.      $Config->{machine} =~ s/^(\\\\)+/\\\\/;
200.    }
201.    $Config->{name} = shift @ARGV;
202.    $Config->{help} = 1 if( "" eq $Config->{name} );
203. }
204.
205. sub Syntax
206. {
207.    my( $Script ) = ( Win32::GetLongPathName( $0 ) =~ /([^\\\/]*?)$/ );
208.    my( $Line ) = "-" x length( $Script );
209.    my( $WhiteSpace ) = " " x length( $Script );
210.
211.    print <<EOT;
212.
213. $Script
214. $Line
215. Create an account.
216.
217. Syntax:
218.      perl $Script AccountName [-d Domain | -m Machine][-c Comment]
```

continues ▶

Example 2.1 *continued*

```
219.        $WhiteSpace [-f FullName] [-g Group]
220.        -c.........Specify the account's comment.
221.        -f.........Specify the account's full name.
222.        -g.........A group the account is a member of.
223.                   This is only applicable to user accounts.
224.                   Specify this switch as many times as needed.
225.        -m Machine..Specify a machine where the user account will live.
226.        -d Domain...Specify a domain where the user account will live.
227.        AccountName.The name of the account (the userid).
228. EOT
229. }
```

Examining Accounts

When a user complains that her account is not working correctly, you can run the User Manager or some equivalent program to check on the account. This process, however, involves moving a mouse around and negotiating a GUI. Instead, you can do the same thing quite quickly from the command line. Example 2.2 does exactly this: You pass in the account name and out comes an exhaustive dump of the account's configuration. You can even use it for groups and domain trust accounts.

Figure 2.1 shows the configuration of the administrator account on a machine called Server1. Notice that the account flags are broken out into flag names. These are the same names you would specify when creating an account or modifying the `flags` attribute.

All the values displayed reflect the account's attributes for the machine displayed on the first line. If the account is a member of a domain, certain values apply only to the domain controller listed. These attributes are

```
last logon
last logoff
num logons
bad pw count
```

For example, the last logon date displayed is May 15, 2000, at 8:31 a.m.; however, the user may have logged on to a different domain controller at a later time. The only way to know for sure is to query each domain controller in the domain and compare to see which attribute is later. Likewise, the bad password count should be the total number of passwords across each domain controller. Refer to Example 2.5, later in this chapter, for an example of querying across all domain controllers in a domain for an accurate account of these attributes.

```
C:\> dumpaccount.pl -m Server1 administrator
Displaying \\ServerFoo\administrator:
       acct expires:    No date specified
       auth flags:      AF_OP_ACCOUNTS
                        AF_OP_PRINT
                        AF_OP_SERVER
       bad pw count:    0
       code page:       0
       comment:         Built-in account for administering the computer/domain
       country code:    0
       flags:           UF_SCRIPT
                        UF_SETTABLE_BITS
                        UF_NORMAL_ACCOUNT
                        UF_DONT_EXPIRE_PASSWD
       full name:       Mr. Administrator
       home dir:        \\server1\home$\administrator
       home dir drive:  Z:
       last logoff:     No date specified
       last logon:      Mon May 15 08:31:30 2000
       logon hours:     Sunday: 00-23
                        Monday: 00-23
                        Tuesday: 00-23
                        Wednesday: 00-23
                        Thursday: 00-23
                        Friday: 00-23
                        Saturday: 00-23
       logon server:    \\*
       max storage:     Unlimited storage
       name:            administrator
       num logons:      209
       parms:           m  `````á````` @@@` d nPdop fx
       password:        <Unknown>
       password age:    1 Years 64 Days 04 Hours 51 Minutes
       password expired: 0
       primary group id: 512
       priv:            USER_PRIV_ADMIN
       profile:
       script path:     administrators\logon.pl
       units per week:  168
       user id:         1001
       usr comment:
       workstations:
```

Figure 2.1 *The administrator account's configuration.*

Example 2.2 *Displaying an Account's Configuration*

```
01. use Win32;
02. use Getopt::Long;
03. use Win32::NetAdmin;
04. use Win32::AdminMisc;
05. use Win32::API::Prototype;
```

continues ▶

Example 2.2   *continued*

```
06.
07. %FLAGS = (
08.    eval UF_TEMP_DUPLICATE_ACCOUNT        => "UF_TEMP_DUPLICATE_ACCOUNT",
09.    eval UF_NORMAL_ACCOUNT                => "UF_NORMAL_ACCOUNT",
10.    eval UF_INTERDOMAIN_TRUST_ACCOUNT     => "UF_INTERDOMAIN_TRUST_ACCOUNT",
11.    eval UF_WORKSTATION_TRUST_ACCOUNT     => "UF_WORKSTATION_TRUST_ACCOUNT",
12.    eval UF_SERVER_TRUST_ACCOUNT          => "UF_SERVER_TRUST_ACCOUNT",
13.    eval UF_DONT_EXPIRE_PASSWD            => "UF_DONT_EXPIRE_PASSWD",
14.    eval UF_SETTABLE_BITS                 => "UF_SETTABLE_BITS",
15.    eval UF_SCRIPT                        => "UF_SCRIPT",
16.    eval UF_ACCOUNTDISABLE                => "UF_ACCOUNTDISABLE",
17.    eval UF_HOMEDIR_REQUIRED              => "UF_HOMEDIR_REQUIRED",
18.    eval UF_LOCKOUT                       => "UF_LOCKOUT",
19.    eval UF_PASSWD_NOTREQD                => "UF_PASSWD_NOTREQD",
20.    eval UF_PASSWD_CANT_CHANGE            => "UF_PASSWD_CANT_CHANGE",
21. );
22.
23. %AUTH_FLAGS = (
24.    eval AF_OP_PRINT        => "AF_OP_PRINT",
25.    eval AF_OP_COMM         => "AF_OP_COMM",
26.    eval AF_OP_SERVER       => "AF_OP_SERVER",
27.    eval AF_OP_ACCOUNTS     => "AF_OP_ACCOUNTS",
28. );
29.
30. %PRIVILEGES = (
31.    eval USER_PRIV_GUEST      => "USER_PRIV_GUEST",
32.    eval USER_PRIV_USER       => "USER_PRIV_USER",
33.    eval USER_PRIV_ADMIN      => "USER_PRIV_ADMIN",
34. );
35.
36. @WEEKDAYS = qw(
37.    Sunday
38.    Monday
39.    Tuesday
40.    Wednesday
41.    Thursday
42.    Friday
43.    Saturday
44. );
45.
46. # Vicious hack to get the time zone
47. if( ApiLink( 'kernel32.dll',
48.        'DWORD GetTimeZoneInformation( PVOID pTZInfo )' ) )
49. {
50.    my $pTZInfo = NewString( 200 );
51.    my $Result = GetTimeZoneInformation( $pTZInfo );
52.    if( 0 == $Result || 2 == $Result )
53.    {
54.      $TZOffset = unpack( "l", $pTZInfo ) / 60;
55.    }
56. }
```

```
57.
58. Configure( \%Config );
59. if( $Config{help} )
60. {
61.   Syntax();
62.   exit();
63. }
64.
65. if( "" ne $Config{domain} )
66. {
67.   # Find the primary domain controller for the specified domain.
68.   $Config{machine} = "";
69.   Win32::NetAdmin::GetDomainController( '',
70.                                         $Config{domain},
71.                                         $Config{machine} );
72. }
73. elsif( "" eq $Config{machine} )
74. {
75.   # Find the primary domain controller for the current domain.
76.   $Config{machine} = "";
77.   Win32::NetAdmin::GetDomainController( '',
78.                                         Win32::DomainName(),
79.                                         $Config{machine} );
80. }
81.
82. # Expand any user account wildcards
83. foreach my $Account ( @{$Config{accounts}} )
84. {
85.   if( $Account =~ /\*$/ )
86.   {
87.     my( $Prefix ) = ( $Account =~ /^(.*)\*$/ );
88.     my @Users;
89.     Win32::AdminMisc::GetUsers( $Config{machine}, $Prefix, \@Users );
90.     push( @AccountList, @Users );
91.   }
92.   else
93.   {
94.     push( @AccountList, $Account );
95.   }
96. }
97.
98. $~ = Attributes;
99. foreach my $Account ( sort( @AccountList ) )
100. {
101.   my %Info;
102.   print "Displaying $Config{machine}\\$Account:\n";
103.   if( Win32::AdminMisc::UserGetMiscAttributes( $Config{machine},
104.                                                $Account,
105.                                                \%Info ) )
106.   {
107.     foreach $Key ( sort( keys( %Info ) ) )
108.     {
109.       $Value = $Info{$Key};
```

continues ▶

Example 2.2   *continued*

```
110.      ( $DisplayKey ) = ( ( lc $Key ) =~ /^.*?_(.*)/i );
111.      $DisplayKey =~ s/_/ /g;
112.      if( $Key =~ /_age/i )
113.      {
114.        # Break apart the C timestamp into years, days,
115.        # hours and minutes
116.        # There are 31536000 seconds in a year...
117.        # There are 86400 seconds in a day...
118.        # There are 3600 seconds in an hour...
119.        # And of course 60 seconds in a minute.
120.        my $Time = $Info{$Key};
121.        my $Years   = int( $Time / 31536000 );
122.        my $Days    = int( ( $Time % 31536000 ) / 86400 );
123.        my $Hours   = int( ( ( $Time % 31536000 ) % 86400 )
124.                        / 3600 );
125.        my $Minutes = int( ( ( ( $Time % 31536000 ) % 86400 )
126.                          % 3600 ) / 60 );
127.        $Value = sprintf( "%01d Years %02d Days %02d Hours %02d Minutes",
128.                    $Years, $Days, $Hours, $Minutes );
129.      }
130.      elsif( $Key =~ /LAST/i || $Key =~ /ACCT_EXPIRES/i )
131.      {
132.        if( 1 > $Value )
133.        {
134.          $Value = "No date specified";
135.        }
136.        else
137.        {
138.          $Value = scalar localtime( $Info{$Key} );
139.        }
140.      }
141.      elsif( $Key =~ /AUTH_FLAGS/i )
142.      {
143.        # Break apart the flags attribute into individual flag strings
144.        $Value = DecodeBits( $Value, \%AUTH_FLAGS );
145.      }
146.      elsif( $Key =~ /FLAGS/i )
147.      {
148.        # Break apart the flags attribute into individual flag strings
149.        $Value = DecodeBits( $Value, \%FLAGS );
150.      }
151.      elsif( $Key =~ /PASSWORD$/i )
152.      {
153.        $Value = "<Unknown>";
154.      }
155.      elsif( $Key =~ /PRIV$/i )
156.      {
157.        $Value = $PRIVILEGES{$Value};
158.      }
159.      elsif( $Key =~ /MAX_STORAGE$/i )
160.      {
```

```
161.        if( -1 == $Value )
162.        {
163.          $Value = "Unlimited storage";
164.        }
165.        else
166.        {
167.          # Format the number to include commas as in 123,456,789
168.          while( $Value =~ s/^(-?\d+)(\d{3})/$1,$2/ ){};
169.          $Value .= " bytes";
170.        }
171.      }
172.      elsif( $Key =~ /LOGON_HOURS/i )
173.      {
174.        # Determine which hours on what days of the week this user has
175.        # permission to logon
176.        my $DayIndex = 0;
177.        my $BinaryHours = $Value;
178.        my $HourString = unpack( "b*", $BinaryHours );
179.        $Value = "";
180.
181.        # We need to offset the logon hours string by the number
182.        # of hours we are either before or after GMT.
183.        if( 0 > $TZOffset )
184.        {
185.          $TZOffset *= -1;
186.          $HourString =~ s/^(.*)(.{$TZOffset})$/$2$1/;
187.        }
188.        else
189.        {
190.          $HourString =~ s/^(.{$TZOffset})(.*)$/$2$1/;
191.        }
192.
193.        # Now walk through each day and determine what
194.        # hours the user is allowed to log on.
195.        foreach my $Day ( $HourString =~ /.{24}/g )
196.        {
197.          my @Hours;
198.          my $Display = "";
199.          my $Index = 0;
200.
201.          $Day .= "0";
202.          foreach my $HourValue ( split( "", $Day ) )
203.          {
204.            if( $HourValue )
205.            {
206.              if( "" eq $Display )
207.              {
208.                $Display = sprintf( "%02d", $Index );
209.              }
210.            }
211.            else
212.            {
213.              if( "" ne $Display )
```

continues ▶

Example 2.2 *continued*

```
214.                {
215.                  if( $Display < $Index - 1 )
216.                  {
217.                    $Display .= sprintf( "-%02d", $Index - 1 );
218.                  }
219.                  push( @Hours, $Display );
220.                  $Display = "";
221.                }
222.              }
223.              $Index++;
224.            }
225.            $Value .= sprintf( "%- 50s", "$WEEKDAYS[$DayIndex++]: "
226.                      . join( ",", @Hours ) ), "\n";
227.          }
228.        }
229.      write;
230.    }
231.  }
232.  else
233.  {
234.    print "failure: ";
235.    print Win32::FormatMessage( Win32::AdminMisc::GetError() );
236.  }
237.  print "\n";
238. }
239.
240. sub DecodeBits
241. {
242.   my( $Bits, $FlagList ) = @_;
243.   my $Result = "";
244.
245.   foreach my $Flag ( keys( %{$FlagList} ) )
246.   {
247.     # Add spaces so that the format breaks lines (formats will not
248.     # break lines on carriage returns)
249.     $Result .= $FlagList->{$Flag} . " " x 40 . "\n" if( $Bits & $Flag );
250.   }
251.   return( $Result );
252. }
253.
254. sub Configure
255. {
256.   my( $Config ) = @_;
257.
258.   Getopt::Long::Configure( "prefix_pattern=(-|\/)" );
259.   $Result = GetOptions( $Config,
260.                 qw(
261.                   machine|m=s
262.                   domain|d=s
263.                   help|?
264.                 )
265.               );
```

```
266.
267.    $Config->{help} = 1 if( ! $Result );
268.    if( "" ne $Config->{machine} )
269.    {
270.      $Config->{machine} = "\\\\$Config->{machine}";
271.      $Config->{machine} =~ s/^(\\\\)+/\\\\/;
272.    }
273.    push( @{$Config->{accounts}}, @ARGV );
274.    $Config->{help} = 1 if( ! scalar @{$Config->{accounts}} );
275. }
276.
277. sub Syntax
278. {
279.    my( $Script ) = ( Win32::GetLongPathName( $0 ) =~ /([^\\\/]*?)$/ );
280.    my( $Line ) = "-" x length( $Script );
281.
282.    print <<EOT;
283.
284. $Script
285. $Line
286. Displays an account's configuration.
287.
288. Syntax:
289.      perl $Script [-d Domain | -m Machine] Account [Account2 ...]
290.            -m Machine..Specify a machine where the user account lives.
291.            -d Domain...Specify a domain where the user account lives.
292.            Account.....The name of the account (the userid).
293.                        This account can end with a * char to indicate
294.                        all accounts that begin with the specified string.
295.            If no domain or machine is specified then the current domain
296.            is used.
297. EOT
298. }
299.
300. format Attributes =
301.    @<<<<<<<<<<<<<<<< ^<<<<<<<<<<<<<<<<<<<<<<<<<<<<<<<<<<<<<<<<
302.    "$DisplayKey:",   $Value
303. ~                   ^<<<<<<<<<<<<<<<<<<<<<<<<<<<<<<<<<<<<<<<<
304.                      $Value
305. ~                   ^<<<<<<<<<<<<<<<<<<<<<<<<<<<<<<<<<<<<<<<<
306.                      $Value
307. ~                   ^<<<<<<<<<<<<<<<<<<<<<<<<<<<<<<<<<<<<<<<<
308.                      $Value
309. ~                   ^<<<<<<<<<<<<<<<<<<<<<<<<<<<<<<<<<<<<<<<<
310.                      $Value
311. ~                   ^<<<<<<<<<<<<<<<<<<<<<<<<<<<<<<<<<<<<<<<<
312.                      $Value
313. ~                   ^<<<<<<<<<<<<<<<<<<<<<<<<<<<<<<<<<<<<<<<<
314.                      $Value
315. ~                   ^<<<<<<<<<<<<<<<<<<<<<<<<<<<<<<<<<<<<<<<<
316.                      $Value
317. ~                   ^<<<<<<<<<<<<<<<<<<<<<<<<<<<<<<<<<<<<<<<<
318.                      $Value
```

continues ▶

Example 2.2   *continued*

```
319. ~                    ^<<<<<<<<<<<<<<<<<<<<<<<<<<<<<<<<<<<<<<<<<<
320.                      $Value
321. ~                    ^<<<<<<<<<<<<<<<<<<<<<<<<<<<<<<<<<<<<<<<<<<
322.                      $Value
323. ~                    ^<<<<<<<<<<<<<<<<<<<<<<<<<<<<<<<<<<<<<<<<<
324.                      $Value
325. .
```

Disabling Accounts

When you need to make an account temporarily unusable, you can disable it. Some administrators feel that disabling accounts is a waste of time and instead should be deleted. However, disabling can be a time-saver. For example, if a manager leaves a company, you could disable her account instead of deleting it. This way, when a replacement is hired, you only need to enable and rename the account to reflect the new manager. The alternative would be to create a new account, but doing so entails not only reconfiguring the account but also walking through each file, directory, and share to reapply permissions for that particular manager. Depending on the configuration of the domain, this task can be quite unreasonable.

The script in Example 2.3 accepts lists of user accounts, so you can disable multiple accounts at once. For example, the following line disables both the Joel and Betty accounts:

```
perl Disable.pl joel betty
```

Additionally, you can specify an asterisk wildcard (*) to disable passwords for all users whose usernames begin with the specified string. For example, the following command disables all accounts that begin with Test, such as Test, Testuser1, Testuser2, and Testaccount:

```
perl disable.pl test*
```

The three switches in the following table can be passed in:

Switch	Function
-m Machine	Specifies the computer where the account is located.
-d Domain	Specifies the domain where the account is located. It overrides any -m switch.
-e	Enables the specified accounts. Use this if the account is already disabled and you want to enable it.

If neither domain nor machine names are specified, the script defaults to the domain of the user running the script.

After you run this script, you should perform a domain synchronization. Refer to the "Synchronizing Domain Controllers" section in this chapter.

Example 2.3   *Disabling an Account*

```
01. use Win32;
02. use Getopt::Long;
03. use Win32::NetAdmin;
04. use Win32::AdminMisc;
05.
06. Configure( \%Config );
07. if( $Config{help} )
08. {
09.   Syntax();
10.   exit();
11. }
12.
13. if( "" ne $Config{domain} )
14. {
15.   # Must first assign some value to the machine key otherwise
16.   # GetDomainController() will fail.
17.   $Config{machine} = "";
18.   Win32::NetAdmin::GetDomainController( '',
19.                                       $Config{domain},
20.                                       $Config{machine} );
21. }
22. elsif( "" eq $Config{machine} )
23. {
24.   # Must first assign some value to the machine key otherwise
25.   # GetDomainController() will fail.
26.   $Config{machine} = "";
27.   Win32::NetAdmin::GetDomainController( '',
28.                                       Win32::DomainName(),
29.                                       $Config{machine} );
30. }
31.
32. foreach my $Account ( @{$Config{accounts}} )
33. {
34.   if( $Account =~ /\*$/ )
35.   {
36.     my( $Prefix ) = ( $Account =~ /^(.*)\*$/ );
37.     my @Users;
38.     Win32::AdminMisc::GetUsers( $Config{machine}, $Prefix, \@Users );
39.     map
40.     {
41.       $AccountList{lc $_} = 1;
42.     } ( @Users );
43.   }
44.   else
45.   {
46.     $AccountList{lc $Account} = 1;
47.   }
48. }
```

continues ▶

Example 2.3   *continued*

```
49.
50. # Notice that we use a hash (%AccountList) to track the users we
51. # are working on. This is a simple hack to prevent us from
52. # processing the same user more than once (if the user passed
53. # in the same account name multiple times).
54. foreach my $Account ( keys( %AccountList ) )
55. {
56.   print ( ( $Config{enable} )? "Enabling" : "Disabling" );
57.   print " '$Config{machine}\\$Account'...";
58.   if( Win32::AdminMisc::UserGetMiscAttributes( $Config{machine},
59.                                                $Account,
60.                                                \%Attrib ) )
61.   {
62.     my $Flag;
63.     if( $Config{enable} )
64.     {
65.       $Flag = $Attrib{USER_FLAGS} & ~UF_ACCOUNTDISABLE;
66.     }
67.     else
68.     {
69.       $Flag = $Attrib{USER_FLAGS} | UF_ACCOUNTDISABLE;
70.     }
71.
72.     $Result = Win32::AdminMisc::UserSetMiscAttributes(
73.                             $Config{machine},
74.                         $Account,
75.                         USER_FLAGS => $Flag );
76.   }
77.
78.   if( $Result )
79.   {
80.     print "successful.\n";
81.   }
82.   else
83.   {
84.     my $Error =  Win32::FormatMessage( Win32::NetAdmin::GetError() );
85.     $Error =~ s/\r|\n//g;
86.     print "failed to delete ($Error)\n";
87.   }
88. }
89.
90. sub Configure
91. {
92.    my( $Config ) = @_;
93.
94.    $Config->{enable} = 1;
95.    Getopt::Long::Configure( "prefix_pattern=(-|\/)" );
96.    $Result = GetOptions( $Config,
97.                 qw(
98.                   machine|m=s
99.                   domain|d=s
```

```
100.                    enable | e
101.                    help | ?
102.                 )
103.                );
104.    $Config->{help} = 1 if( ! $Result );
105.    $Config->{enable} = ! $Config->{enable};
106.    if( "" ne $Config->{machine} )
107.    {
108.      $Config->{machine} = "\\\\$Config->{machine}";
109.      $Config->{machine} =~ s/^(\\\\)+/\\\\/;
110.    }
111.    push( @{$Config->{accounts}}, @ARGV );
112.    $Config->{help} = 1 if( ! scalar @{$Config->{accounts}} );
113. }
114.
115. sub Syntax
116. {
117.    my( $Script ) = ( $0 =~ /([^\\\/]*?)$/ );
118.    my( $Line ) = "-" x length( $Script );
119.
120.    print <<EOT;
121.
122. $Script
123. $Line
124. Disables an account.
125.
126. Syntax:
127.     perl $Script [-e] [-m machine | -d domain] Account [ Account2 ... ]
128.        -e.........Enables a disabled account.
129.        -m Machine..Specify a machine where the user account lives.
130.        -d Domain...Specify a domain where the user account lives.
131.        Account.....The name of the account (the userid).
132.                    This account can end with a * char to indicate
133.                    all accounts that begin with the specified string.
134.     If no domain or machine is specified then the current domain
135.        is used.
136. EOT
137. }
```

Deleting Accounts

Sometimes you simply need to delete an account rather than disable it. Of course, you should consider disabling the account (refer to the section "Disabling Accounts" earlier in this chapter), but if the account will never be used again, removing it from the accounts database is a good idea. This is especially true if there is a high account turnaround such that new user accounts are created, used, and then abandoned.

Deleting an account is a drastic measure because it is literally removed from the accounts database. This may result in permission settings on objects such as files, Registry keys, and network shares showing a `deleted` account entry. If neither domain nor machine names are specified, the script defaults to using the current domain of the user running the script.

Example 2.4 quickly deletes accounts. The script accepts lists of user accounts, so you can delete multiple users at once. For example, the following line deletes the accounts of both the users Joel and Betty:

```
perl DelUser.pl joel betty
```

Additionally, you can specify an asterisk wildcard (*) to delete all users whose usernames begin with the specified string. For example, the following command deletes all users whose names begin with Test, such as Test, Testuser1, Testuser2, and TestAccount:

```
perl DelUser.pl test*
```

The two switches described in Table 2.3 can be passed into Example 2.4.

Table 2.3   Switches for Example 2.4

Switch	Function
-m Machine	Specifies the computer where the account is located.
-d Domain	Specifies the domain where the account is located. It overrides any -m switch.

If neither domain nor machine names are specified, the script defaults to the domain of the user running the script.

After you run this script, you should perform a domain synchronization. Refer to the "Synchronizing Domain Controllers" section in this chapter.

Example 2.4   *Deleting Accounts*

```
01. use Win32;
02. use Getopt::Long;
03. use Win32::NetAdmin;
04. use Win32::AdminMisc;
05.
06. Configure( \%Config );
07. if( $Config{help} )
08. {
09.   Syntax();
10.   exit();
11. }
12.
13. if( "" ne $Config{domain} )
14. {
15.
16.   # Must first assign some value to the machine key otherwise
17.   # GetDomainController() will fail.
```

```perl
18.    $Config{machine} = "";
19.    Win32::NetAdmin::GetDomainController( '',
20.                                           $Config{domain},
21.                                           $Config{machine} );
22. }
23. elsif( "" eq $Config{machine} )
24. {
25.    # Must first assign some value to the machine key otherwise
26.    # GetDomainController() will fail.
27.    $Config{machine} = "";
28.    Win32::NetAdmin::GetDomainController( '',
29.                                           Win32::DomainName(),
30.                                           $Config{machine} );
31. }
32.
33. foreach my $Account ( @{$Config{accounts}} )
34. {
35.    if( $Account =~ /\*$/ )
36.    {
37.      my( $Prefix ) = ( $Account =~ /^(.*)\*$/ );
38.      my @Users;
39.      Win32::AdminMisc::GetUsers( $Config{machine}, $Prefix, \@Users );
40.      map
41.      {
42.        $AccountList{lc $_} = 1;
43.      } ( @Users );
44.    }
45.    else
46.    {
47.      $AccountList{lc $Account} = 1;
48.    }
49. }
50.
51. foreach my $Account ( keys( %AccountList ) )
52. {
53.    print "Account '$Config{machine}\\$Account'...";
54.    if( Win32::NetAdmin::UserDelete( $Config{machine}, $Account ) )
55.    {
56.      print "deleted.\n";
57.    }
58.    else
59.    {
60.      my $Error =  Win32::FormatMessage( Win32::NetAdmin::GetError() );
61.      $Error =~ s/\r|\n//g;
62.      print "failed to delete ($Error)\n";
63.    }
64. }
65.
66. sub Configure
67. {
68.    my( $Config ) = @_;
69.
70.    Getopt::Long::Configure( "prefix_pattern=(-|\/)" );
```

continues ▶

Example 2.4   *continued*

```
71.   $Result = GetOptions( $Config,
72.                           qw(
73.                                machine | m=s
74.                                domain | d=s
75.                                help | ?
76.                           )
77.                         );
78.
79.   $Config->{help} = 1 if( ! $Result );
80.   if( "" ne $Config->{machine} )
81.   {
82.     $Config->{machine} = "\\\\$Config->{machine}";
83.     $Config->{machine} =~ s/^(\\\\)+/\\\\/;
84.   }
85.   push( @{$Config->{accounts}}, @ARGV );
86.   $Config->{help} = 1 if( ! scalar @{$Config->{accounts}} );
87. }
88.
89. sub Syntax
90. {
91.   my( $Script ) = ( $0 =~ /([^\\\/]*?)$/ );
92.   my( $Line ) = "-" x length( $Script );
93.
94.   print <<EOT;
95.
96. $Script
97. $Line
98. Deletes an account.
99.
100. Syntax:
101.     perl $Script [-m machine | -d domain] Account [ Account2 ... ]
102.           -m Machine..Specify a machine where the user account lives.
103.           -d Domain...Specify a domain where the user account lives.
104.           Account.....The name of the account (the userid).
105.                         This account can end with a * char to indicate
106.                         all accounts that begin with the specified string.
107.           If no domain or machine is specified then the current domain
108.           is used.
109. EOT
110. }
```

Last Logon and Logoff

Example 2.2 (shown earlier), which displays a user account's configuration, shows all attributes related to the account. Two of these attributes are the last time the user logged on to and off the domain. These values, however, can be quite misleading. Notice that in Figure 2.1, the *last logoff* time was No date specified. So, how can a user log on to the domain but never log off? There are two possible answers to this question: Either the user never formally logged off (for example, the machine crashed, the network became disconnected, and so forth), or a different DC processed the logoff event.

When a user logs on to a network, a DC must process the logon. This machine is responsible for authenticating the user's password and checking whether the account is disabled, the password has expired, the user is allowed to log on using the machine he is on, and a host of other things. Just as with logging on, when the user logs off the domain, a DC processes this activity as well. However, there is no guarantee that the same DC will process both the logon and logoff events.

Because any number of different DCs can process logon and logoff requests, the *last* logon and logoff times may be scattered among DCs. Therefore, the appropriate technique to determine the last logon and logoff times for a given user is to query each DC in the domain and compare the logon and logoff times. Whichever controller reports the most recent time is the one you're interested in. You must query each controller for each attribute because different controllers could have processed the logon and logoff events.

Two other attributes fall into a similar predicament: the logon count and the bad password count. These values represent the total number of times the user successfully logged on to the domain and the number of times an attempt to log on to the domain failed because of an incorrect password. The true value of these attributes consists of the sum of each DC's value. Therefore, each controller is queried, and its result is added to the value.

Figure 2.2 illustrates the use of this technique. In this particular instance, the administrator account is being queried for the domain MyDomain. Two DCs were discovered for this domain: \\server1 and \\server2. The various domain-wide attributes are processed and displayed. You run this query by using Example 2.5.

```
C:\>perl lastlogon.pl -d MyDomain administrator
Querying \\server1
Querying \\server2
administrator (Mr. Administrator):
        Last logon: Sat May 20 19:00:00 2000 ( \\server1 )
        Last logoff: Sat May 20 19:00:00 2000 ( \\server2 )
        Total number of bad password attempts: 0
        Total number of logons: 471
```

Figure 2.2 *Displaying the last logon time.*

The code in Example 2.5 can process any number of accounts. In this script, as with many other scripts in this chapter, you can supply an asterisk as an account's suffix to indicate that all accounts matching that name are to be displayed. For example, the following line results in the processing of the Testuser1, Testuser2, Testusertemp, and Joel accounts for the MyDomain domain:

```
perl lastlogon.pl -d MyDomain testuser* joel
```

This script accepts the command-line switches described earlier in Table 2.3, with the exception that you can specify multiple machine names. This allows you to purposely query specific machines for the last logon times.

If neither domain nor machine names are specified, the script defaults to the current domain of the user running the script.

Example 2.5   *Determining the Last Logon and Logoff Times*

```
01. use Getopt::Long;
02. use Win32::NetAdmin;
03. use Win32::AdminMisc;
04.
05. Configure( \%Config );
06. if( $Config{help} )
07. {
08.   Syntax();
09.   exit();
10. }
11.
12. if( "" ne $Config{domain} )
13. {
14.   # Must first assign some value to the machine key otherwise
15.   # GetDomainController() will fail.
16.   $Config{machine} = "";
17.   Win32::NetAdmin::GetDomainController( '',
18.                                        $Config{domain},
19.                                        $Config{machine} );
20.   Win32::NetAdmin::GetServers( $Config{machine},
21.                                $Config{domain},
22.                                SV_TYPE_DOMAIN_CTRL| SV_TYPE_DOMAIN_BAKCTRL,
23.                                \@MachineList );
24. }
25. else
26. {
27.   if( 0 == scalar @{$Config{machine_list}} )
28.   {
29.     # Must first assign some value to the machine key otherwise
30.     # GetDomainController() will fail.
31.     $Config{machine} = "";
32.     Win32::NetAdmin::GetDomainController( '',
33.                                          $Config{domain},
34.                                          $Config{machine} );
35.     push( @{$Config{machine_list}}, $Config{machine} );
```

```
36.    }
37.    push( @MachineList, @{$Config{machine_list}} );
38. }
39.
40. # Notice that we use a hash (%AccountList) to track the users we
41. # are working on. This is a simple hack to prevent us from
42. # processing the same user more than once (if the user passed
43. # in the same account name multiple times).
44. foreach my $Account ( @{$Config{accounts}} )
45. {
46.    if( $Account =~ /\*$/ )
47.    {
48.      my( $Prefix ) = ( $Account =~ /^(.*)\*$/ );
49.      my @Users;
50.      Win32::AdminMisc::GetUsers( $Config{machine}, $Prefix, \@Users );
51.      map
52.      {
53.        $AccountList{lc $_} = 1;
54.      } ( @Users );
55.    }
56.    else
57.    {
58.      $AccountList{lc $Account} = 1;
59.    }
60. }
61.
62. foreach my $Machine ( @MachineList )
63. {
64.    ( $Machine = "\\\\$Machine" ) =~ s/^\\+/\\\\/;
65.    print "Querying $Machine\n";
66.
67.    foreach my $Account ( sort( keys( %AccountList ) ) )
68.    {
69.      my %Attrib;
70.      if( Win32::AdminMisc::UserGetMiscAttributes( $Machine,
71.                                                   $Account,
72.                                                   \%Attrib ) )
73.      {
74.        my $Data = $Result{$Account} = {};      \%{$RESULT{$ACCOUNT}};
75.        $Data->{fullname} = $Attrib{USER_FULL_NAME};
76.        if( $Data->{lastlogon}->{value} < $Attrib{USER_LAST_LOGON} )
77.        {
78.          $Data->{lastlogon}->{value} = $Attrib{USER_LAST_LOGON};
79.          $Data->{lastlogon}->{machine} = $Machine;
80.        }
81.        if( $Data->{lastlogoff}->{value} < $Attrib{USER_LAST_LOGOFF} )
82.        {
83.          $Data->{lastlogoff}->{value} = $Attrib{USER_LAST_LOGOFF};
84.          $Data->{lastlogoff}->{machine} = $Machine;
85.        }
86.        $Data->{badpwcount} += $Attrib{USER_BAD_PW_COUNT};
87.        $Data->{logons} += $Attrib{USER_NUM_LOGONS};
88.      }
```

continues ▶

Example 2.5 *continued*

```
89.   }
90. }
91. foreach my $Account ( sort( keys( %Result ) ) )
92. {
93.    print "$Account ($Result{$Account}->{fullname}):\n";
94.    print Report( "Last logon", $Result{$Account}->{lastlogon} ), "\n";
95.    print Report( "Last logoff", $Result{$Account}->{lastlogoff} ), "\n";
96.    print "\tTotal number of bad password attempts: ";
97.    print "$Result{$Account}->{badpwcount}\n";
98.    print "\tTotal number of logons: $Result{$Account}->{logons}\n";
99.    print "\n";
100. }
101.
102. sub Report
103. {
104.   my( $Field, $Data ) = @_;
105.   my $Date = scalar localtime( $Data->{value} );
106.   my $Location = "( $Data->{machine} )";
107.
108.   $Date = "Not available" if( 0 == $Data->{value} );
109.   $Location = "" if( 0 == $Data->{value} );
110.   return( "\t$Field: $Date $Location" );
111. }
112.
113. sub Configure
114. {
115.     my( $Config ) = @_;
116.
117.     Getopt::Long::Configure( "prefix_pattern=(-|\/)" );
118.     $Result = GetOptions( $Config,
119.                         qw(
120.                             machine_list|m=s@
121.                             domain|d=s
122.                             help|?
123.                         )
124.                     );
125.
126.     $Config->{help} = 1 if( ! $Result );
127.     push( @{$Config->{accounts}}, @ARGV );
128.     $Config->{help} = 1 if( ! scalar @{$Config->{accounts}} );
129. }
130.
131. sub Syntax
132. {
133.     my( $Script ) = ( $0 =~ /([^\\\/]*?)$/ );
134.     my( $Line ) = "-" x length( $Script );
135.
136.     print <<EOT;
137.
138. $Script
139. $Line
```

```
140. Displays the last logon and logoff time for a specified account.
141.
142. Syntax:
143.    perl $Script [-m Machine | -d domain] Account [Account2 ...]
144.        -m Machine..Specify a machine the accounts live on.
145.        -d Domain...Specify the domain the accounts live in.
146.        Account.....The name of the account (the userid).
147.                    This account can end with a * char to indicate
148.                    all accounts that begin with the specified string.
149. EOT
150. }
```

Unlocking Accounts

Some domains implement policies that prevent abuses of accounts. For example, a policy may force a user to change her password every 90 days. Another policy may prevent the user from reusing the same password. Several policies can be leveraged to help secure a domain.

One of these policies, however, can lead to very frustrated users. This policy locks out a user account if too many logon attempts are made using the incorrect password. Such locking prevents the user from logging on, even with the correct password. It is very similar to a disabled account, with the exception that an account cannot be placed manually in the locked-out state; it must violate particular policies (such as too many bad logon attempts). It is locked so that you know the account was disabled due to policy violation.

The only correct way to change the state of a locked-out account is to have an administrator unlock the account. This is normally done by using the User Manager or MMC and deselecting the Account Locked Out check box. However, by using the script in Example 2.6, you can quickly unlock accounts from the command line.

The script can take any number of accounts to process. In this script, as with many other scripts in this chapter, you can supply an asterisk as an account's suffix to indicate that all accounts matching that name are to be displayed. For example, the following line results in the unlocking of the Testuser1, Testuser2, Testusertemp, and Joel accounts for the MyDomain domain:

```
perl unlock.pl -d MyDomain testuser* joel
```

This script accepts the command-line switches described earlier in Table 2.3.

If neither domain nor machine names are specified, the script defaults to the domain of the user running the script.

After you run this script, you should perform a domain synchronization. Refer to the "Synchronizing Domain Controllers" section in this chapter.

Example 2.6   *Unlocking an Account*

```
01. use Getopt::Long;
02. use Win32::NetAdmin;
03. use Win32::AdminMisc;
04.
05. Configure( \%Config );
06. if( $Config{help} )
07. {
08.   Syntax();
09.   exit();
10. }
11.
12. if( "" ne $Config{domain} )
13. {
14.   # Must first assign some value to the machine key otherwise
15.   # GetDomainController() will fail.
16.   $Config{machine} = "";
17.   Win32::NetAdmin::GetDomainController( '',
18.                                        $Config{domain},
19.                                        $Config{machine} );
20. }
21. else
22. {
23.   if( "" eq $Config{machine} )
24.   {
25.     # Must first assign some value to the machine key otherwise
26.     # GetDomainController() will fail.
27.     $Config{machine} = "";
28.     Win32::NetAdmin::GetDomainController( '',
29.                                          Win32::DomainName(),
30.                                          $Config{machine} );
31.   }
32. }
33.
34. foreach my $Account ( @{$Config{accounts}} )
35. {
36.   if( $Account =~ /\*$/ )
37.   {
38.     my( $Prefix ) = ( $Account =~ /^(.*)\*$/ );
39.     my @Users;
40.     Win32::AdminMisc::GetUsers( $Config{machine}, $Prefix, \@Users );
41.     map
42.     {
43.       $AccountList{lc $_} = 1;
44.     } ( @Users );
45.   }
46.   else
47.   {
48.     $AccountList{lc $Account} = 1;
```

```
49.   }
50. }
51.
52. # Notice that we use a hash (%AccountList) to track the users we
53. # are working on. This is a simple hack to prevent us from
54. # processing the same user more than once (if the user passed
55. # in the same account name multiple times).
56. foreach my $Account ( keys( %AccountList ) )
57. {
58.   my %Attrib;
59.   print "$Config{machine}\\$Account ... ";
60.   if( Win32::AdminMisc::UserGetMiscAttributes( $Config{machine},
61.                                                $Account,
62.                                                \%Attrib ) )
63.   {
64.     my $Flags = $Attrib{USER_FLAGS};
65.     if( $Flags & UF_LOCKOUT )
66.     {
67.       $Flags &= ~UF_LOCKOUT;
68.       if( Win32::AdminMisc::UserGetMiscAttributes( $Config{machine},
69.                                                    $Account,
70.                                                    USER_FLAGS => $Flags ) )
71.       {
72.         print "success.";
73.       }
74.       else
75.       {
76.         print "failed: " . Error();
77.       }
78.     }
79.     else
80.     {
81.       print "not locked out.";
82.     }
83.   }
84.   else
85.   {
86.     print "can not query account: " . Error();
87.   }
88.   print "\n";
89. }
90.
91. sub Error
92. {
93.     return( Win32::FormatMessage( Win32::AdminMisc::GetError() ) );
94. }
95.
96. sub Configure
97. {
98.   my( $Config ) = @_;
99.
100.   Getopt::Long::Configure( "prefix_pattern=(-|\/)" );
101.   $Result = GetOptions( $Config,
```

continues ▶

Example 2.6   *continued*

```
102.                        qw(
103.                           machine | m=s
104.                           domain | d=s
105.                           help | ?
106.                        )
107.                     );
108.
109.    $Config->{help} = 1 if( ! $Result );
110.    if( "" ne $Config->{machine} )
111.    {
112.       $Config->{machine} = \\\\$Config->{machine};
113.       $Config->{machine} =~ s/^(\\\\)+/\\\\/;
114.    }
115.    push( @{$Config->{accounts}}, @ARGV );
116.    $Config->{help} = 1 if( ! scalar @{$Config->{accounts}} );
117. }
118.
119. sub Syntax
120. {
121.     my( $Script ) = ( $0 =~ /([^\\\/]*?)$/ );
122.     my( $Line ) = "-" x length( $Script );
123.
124.     print <<EOT;
125.
126. $Script
127. $Line
128. Unlocks a locked account.
129.
130. Syntax:
131.     perl $Script [-m Machine | -d Domain] Account [Account2 ...]
132.         -m Machine..Specify a machine the accounts live on.
133.         -d Domain...Specify the domain the accounts live in.
134.         Account.....The name of the account (the userid).
135.                     This account can end with a * char to indicate
136.                     all accounts that begin with the specified string.
137. EOT
138. }
```

Expiring Passwords

You can configure an account so that the next time the user logs on he is forced to change his password. This is typically performed automatically when you set a password age for accounts. When an account's password grows older than is allowed, the account password is automatically *expired*.

To manually expire an account, you must set a flag on the account. Not only does the password expire when it has grown older than is allowed, but you also can purposely expire the account by setting this flag. The User

Manager (or the Computer Management MMC snap-in) enables such expiration by exposing the User must change password at next logon flag.

Example 2.7 expires an account's password by setting the password expiration flag. The script first removes the "user cannot change password" (UF_PASSWD_CANT_CHANGE) flag if it has already been set. This is required; otherwise, the next time the user logs on, he will be forced to change the password, but the flag will prevent him from doing so. Next, the "password never expires" (UF_DONT_EXPIRE_PASSWD) flag is cleared if it has already been set. This flag must not be set before an attempt is made to expire the password. Finally, the "user must change password at next logon" (USER_PASSWORD_EXPIRED) attribute is set to either true or false, depending upon whether or not the -u switch was passed in.

Another flag, at first glance, would appear to be a problem. If the password never expires flag is set, it seems as though the password cannot be expired. However, when the script expires the password, Win32 automatically removes the password never expires flag.

Keep in mind that after the user resets his password, the user cannot change password and password never expires flags are *not* set. As administrator, you might need to change the password flags after the user changes his password.

Example 2.7 accepts lists of user accounts, so you can expire multiple users' passwords at once. For example, the following line forces the users Joel and Betty to change their passwords the next time they log on:

```
perl expire.pl joel betty
```

Additionally, you can specify an asterisk wildcard (*) to expire passwords for all users whose usernames begin with the specified string. For example, the following command expires passwords for all users whose names begin with Test, such as Test, Testuser1, Testuser2, and TestAccount:

```
perl expire.pl test*
```

You can also un-expire accounts by passing in the -u switch as in:

```
perl expire.pl test* -u
```

The following three switches can be passed in:

Switch	Function
-m Machine	Specifies the computer where the account is located.
-d Domain	Specifies the domain where the account is located. It overrides any -m switch.
-u	Causes each account to un-expire the password. Therefore, the next time the user logs on, he will not be forced to change his password.

If neither domain nor machine names are specified, the script defaults to the domain of the user running the script.

After you run this script, you should perform a domain synchronization. Refer to the "Synchronizing Domain Controllers" section in this chapter.

Example 2.7   *Expiring an Account's Password*

```
01. use Getopt::Long;
02. use Win32;
03. use Win32::NetAdmin;
04. use Win32::AdminMisc;
05.
06. Configure( \%Config );
07. if( $Config{help} )
08. {
09.     Syntax();
10.     exit();
11. }
12.
13. if( "" ne $Config{domain} )
14. {
15.   $Config{machine} = "";
16.   Win32::NetAdmin::GetDomainController( '',
17.                               $Config{domain},
18.                               $Config{machine} );
19. }
20. elsif( "" eq $Config{machine} )
21. {
22.     $Config{machine} = "\\\\" . Win32::NodeName();
23. }
24. else
25. {
26.   $Config{machine} = "\\\\$Config{machine}";
27.   $Config{machine} =~ s/^\\+/\\\\/;
28. }
29.
30. # Notice that we use a hash (%AccountList) to track the users we
31. # are working on. This is a simple hack to prevent us from
32. # processing the same user more than once (if the user passed
33. # in the same account name multiple times).
34. foreach my $Account ( @{$Config{accounts}} )
35. {
36.   if( $Account =~ /\*$/ )
37.   {
38.     my( $Prefix ) = ( $Account =~ /^(.*)\*$/ );
39.     my @Users;
40.     Win32::AdminMisc::GetUsers( $Config{machine}, $Prefix, \@Users );
41.     map
42.     {
43.       $AccountList{lc $_} = 1;
44.     } ( @Users );
45.   }
```

```
46.   else
47.   {
48.     $AccountList{lc $Account} = 1;
49.   }
50. }
51.
52. foreach my $Account ( sort( keys( %AccountList ) ) )
53. {
54.   my %Attrib;
55.   my $Result = 0;
56.   my $Flag = 0;
57.
58.   print ( ( $Config{expire} )? "Expiring" : "Unexpiring" );
59.   print " password for '$Account'...";
60.   if( Win32::AdminMisc::UserGetMiscAttributes( $Config{machine},
61.                                                $Account,
62.                                                \%Attrib ) )
63.   {
64.     $Flag = $Attrib{USER_FLAGS};
65.     # If we are expiring the password AND the account does not allow
66.     # the password to change then modify it so that it DOES allow the
67.     # password to change.
68.     if( ! $Config{unexpire} )
69.     {
70.       $Flag &= ~UF_PASSWD_CANT_CHANGE;
71.
72.       # If the account does not allow the account to expire then
73.       # temporarily allow it...
74.       if( $Flag & UF_DONT_EXPIRE_PASSWD )
75.       {
76.           $Flag &= ~UF_DONT_EXPIRE_PASSWD;
77.       }
78.     }
79.
80.     if( $Flag != $Attrib{USER_FLAGS} )
81.     {
82.       Win32::AdminMisc::UserSetMiscAttributes( $Config{machine},
83.                                                $Account,
84.                                                USER_FLAGS => $Flag );
85.     }
86.
87.     # Force the account to expire and reset the flags...
88.     $Result = Win32::AdminMisc::UserSetMiscAttributes(
89.                     $Config{machine},
90.                     $Account,
91.                     USER_PASSWORD_EXPIRED => !$Config{unexpire} );
92.   }
93.
94.   if( $Result )
95.   {
96.     print "successful.\n";
97.   }
98.   else
```

continues ▶

Example 2.7 *continued*

```
99.   {
100.        my $Error = Win32::FormatMessage( Win32::GetLastError() );
101.        $Error =~ s/\r|\n//g;
102.        print "failed to ";
103.        print (($Config->{unexpire})? "unexpire" : "expire" );
104.        print ": ($Error)\n";
105.   }
106. }
107.
108. sub Configure
109. {
110.   my( $Config ) = @_;
111.
112.   Getopt::Long::Configure( "prefix_pattern=(-|\/)" );
113.   $Result = GetOptions( $Config,
114.                         qw(
115.                             machine|m=s
116.                             domain|d=s
117.                             unexpire|u
118.                             help|?
119.                         )
120.                       );
121.   $Config->{help} = 1 if( ! $Result );
122.   if( "" ne $Config->{machine} )
123.   {
124.     $Config->{machine} = "\\\\$Config->{machine}";
125.     $Config->{machine} =~ s/^(\\\\)+/\\\\/;
126.   }
127.   push( @{$Config->{accounts}}, @ARGV );
128.   $Config->{help} = 1 if( ! scalar @{$Config->{accounts}} );
129. }
130.
131. sub Syntax
132. {
133.   my( $Script ) = ( $0 =~ /([^\\\/]*?)$/ );
134.   my( $Line ) = "-" x length( $Script );
135.
136.   print <<EOT;
137.
138. $Script
139. $Line
140. Expires an account forcing the user to change passwords at next logon.
141.
142. Syntax:
143.     perl $Script [-u] [-m machine | -d domain] Account [ Account2 ... ]
144.         -u.........Un-expire the account.
145.         -m Machine..Specify the machine the accounts lives on.
146.         -d Domain...Specify the domain the accounts live in.
147.         Account.....The name of the account (the userid).
148.                     This account can end with a * char to indicate
149.                     all accounts that begin with the specified string.
150. EOT
151. }
```

Renaming Accounts

It is not uncommon for human events to impose themselves into the realm of the network administrator. For example, if a user gets married, you might need to change that user's account name to reflect the new name. The ability to rename accounts comes in quite handy at this point.

Example 2.8 enables you to rename a user account from the command line. For example, the following command line renames the user account OldUser to NewUser in the MyDomain domain:

```
perl rename.pl -d MyDomain OldUser NewUser
```

The account remains intact; only the name changes. Therefore, all permissions and groups reflect the name change automatically.

This script accepts the command-line switches described earlier in Table 2.3.

If neither domain nor machine names are specified, the script defaults to the domain of the user running the script.

After you run this script, you should perform a domain synchronization. Refer to the "Synchronizing Domain Controllers" section in this chapter.

Example 2.8   *Renaming User Accounts*

```
01. use Getopt::Long;
02. use Win32::NetAdmin;
03. use Win32::AdminMisc;
04.
05. Configure( \%Config );
06. if( $Config{help} )
07. {
08.   Syntax();
09.   exit();
10. }
11.
12. if( "" ne $Config{domain} )
13. {
14.   # Must first assign some value to the machine key otherwise
15.   # GetDomainController() will fail.
16.   $Config{machine} = "";
17.   Win32::NetAdmin::GetDomainController( '',
18.                                         $Config{domain},
19.                                         $Config{machine} );
20. }
21. else
22. {
23.   # Must first assign some value to the machine key otherwise
24.   # GetDomainController() will fail.
25.   if( "" eq $Config{machine} )
26.   {
27.     $Config{machine} = "";
```

continues ▶

Example 2.8   *continued*

```
28.     Win32::NetAdmin::GetDomainController( '',
29.                                    Win32::DomainName(),
30.                                    $Config{machine} );
31.   }
32. }
33.
34. print "Renaming '$Config{machine}\\$Config{name}' to ";
35. print "'$Config{machine}\\$Config{new_name} ... ";
36. if( Win32::AdminMisc::RenameUser( $Config{machine},
37.                                  $Config{name},
38.                                  $Config{new_name} ) )
39. {
40.   print "successful.\n";
41. }
42. else
43. {
44.   my $Error =  Win32::FormatMessage( Win32::AdminMisc::GetError() );
45.   $Error =~ s/\r|\n//g;
46.   print "failed to rename: $Error\n";
47. }
48.
49. sub Configure
50. {
51.   my( $Config ) = @_;
52.
53.   Getopt::Long::Configure( "prefix_pattern=(-|\/)" );
54.   $Config->{machine} = Win32::NodeName();
55.   $Result = GetOptions( $Config,
56.                         qw(
57.                             machine|m=s
58.                             domain|d=s
59.                             help|?
60.                          )
61.                       );
62.
63.   $Config->{help} = 1 if( ! $Result );
64.   if( "" ne $Config->{machine} )
65.   {
66.     $Config->{machine} = "\\\\$Config->{machine}";
67.     $Config->{machine} =~ s/^(\\\\)+/\\\\/;
68.   }
69.   $Config->{name} = shift @ARGV;
70.   $Config->{new_name} = shift @ARGV;
71.   $Config->{help} = 1 unless( "" ne $Config->{name}
72.                              && "" ne $Config->{new_name} );
73. }
74.
75. sub Syntax
76. {
77.     my( $Script ) = ( $0 =~ /([^\\\/]*?)$/ );
78.     my( $Line ) = "-" x length( $Script );
```

```
79.
80.    print <<EOT;
81.
82. $Script
83. $Line
84. Renames an account.
85.
86. Syntax:
87.    perl $Script [-m Machine | -d Domain] Account NewAccount
88.        -m Machine..Specify the machine the account lives on.
89.        -d Domain...Specify the domain the accounts live in.
90.        Account.....The name of the account (the userid).
91.        NewAccount..The new name of the account.
92. EOT
93. }
```

Privileges

In Win32, a privilege is something that an administrator grants to an
account. A privilege dictates what account is permitted to perform what
actions. For example, the SE_BACKUP_NAME privilege enables an account to
back up files and directories bypassing security permissions placed on the
files and directories. For an account to shut down a computer remotely, it
requires the SE_REMOTE_SHUTDOWN_NAME privilege. An account has to be specifically granted these permissions by an administrator.

Privileges can be assigned to either a user account or a group. Assigning a
privilege to a group can be very useful, especially if groups of user accounts
share a particular purpose. Consider, for example, the ability to take ownership of objects such as files, directories, and Registry keys. This powerful
privilege renders all security useless because a user with this privilege can
simply become the owner of any object (and therefore have full permissions
to manipulate it). It stands to reason that such a powerful ability should be
bestowed upon network administrators. If your domain has several administrators, you might find yourself assigning this privilege to each administrator user account. A more efficient method would be to assign the privilege
to the Administrators and Domain Admins groups. This way, user accounts
assigned to either of these groups have this privilege.

Normally, you would have to run the User Manager or MMC to assign
privileges (also known as *user rights*). Sometimes these privileges are
assigned automatically for the administrator, such as when an account other
than local system is chosen to log on for a service. Example 2.9, shown
later, is a full-privilege management script that enables you to query which

privileges are assigned to a group or user and which groups and users have a particular privilege. You can also add and remove privileges from users and groups. Additionally, this script prints all the different privileges that are available.

Displaying Available Privileges

Example 2.9 contains a few different syntax variations. To dump a list of available privileges, you can use this syntax:

```
perl priv.pl -p
```

This command displays all privileges in a format illustrated in Figure 2.3. The figure also illustrates what a part of the output looks like. The first line of each privilege is the privilege constant name (such as SE_ASSIGN_ PRIMARYTOKEN_NAME). Win32 internally uses the display name to represent the privilege. For the sake of this script, you can specify either of these names; they are synonymous. However, programmers who program the Win32 API are advised to use constant names because they are guaranteed not to change as Windows versions change.

Some of the privilege entries in the figure have comment lines. They simply describe what the privilege is used for—which is welcome information, especially when you try to decipher the meaning from the privilege name. Not all privileges have comment lines because Win32 does not supply them.

```
C:\>perl priv.pl -p
SE_ASSIGNPRIMARYTOKEN_NAME:
        Display name: SeAssignPrimaryTokenPrivilege
        Comment: Replace a process level token

SE_AUDIT_NAME:
        Display name: SeAuditPrivilege
        Comment: Generate security audits

SE_BACKUP_NAME:
        Display name: SeBackupPrivilege
        Comment: Back up files and directories

SE_BATCH_LOGON_NAME:
        Display name: SeBatchLogonRight
```

Figure 2.3   *Displaying available privileges.*

Displaying Who Has a Privilege

Another syntax the script Example 2.9 takes is to show all the groups and accounts that have a particular privilege. This is useful to determine the scope of who has a particular ability. The script does so by specifying the show privilege assignment (-s) option:

```
perl priv.pl -s Privilege1 Privilege2
```

The list of privileges can either be fully formatted privilege constants (for example, SE_BATCHLOGON_RIGHT) or display names (for example, SeBatchLogonRight). The script is flexible enough to handle *mangling* of either. Mangling is done by specifying the root of the privilege, such as BATCHLOGON.

The script displays all users and groups who have each of the specified privileges, as shown in Figure 2.4. Notice that the first privilege specified is the full display name, but the second is only the root of a privilege name.

```
C:\>priv.pl -s SeBatchLogonRight restore
SE_BATCH_LOGON_NAME (SeBatchLogonRight):
        MyDomain\Administrator
        MyDomain\Daemons
        MyDomain\Mail Users
        MyDomain\MailServices

SE_RESTORE_NAME (SeRestorePrivilege):
        BUILTIN\Backup Operators
        BUILTIN\Server Operators
        BUILTIN\Administrators
        MyDomain\BackupService
```

Figure 2.4 *Displaying who has particular privileges.*

Displaying and Modifying User and Group Privileges

User and group privileges are powerful only as long as they can be modified. This is the default operation of the script. If you specify neither the -s nor the -p switch, the parameters passed in are assumed to be user or group names. The privileges assigned to each of these users and groups are displayed. Displaying them is a simple and easy way to discover who has what privileges. Figure 2.5 shows the result of a simple query on the BackupService account.

```
C:\>priv BackupService
MyDomain\BackupService:
    SE_AUDIT_NAME                Generate security audits
    SE_BACKUP_NAME               Back up files and directories
    SE_RESTORE_NAME              Restore files and directories
    SE_TCB_NAME                  Act as part of the operating system
    SE_INTERACTIVE_LOGON_NAME
    SE_SERVICE_LOGON_NAME
```

Figure 2.5   *Displaying a user's privileges.*

You can specify as many users and groups as needed. The script also accepts the * wildcard for user accounts. It expands into all user accounts that match the string before the asterisk.

In this mode, the script accepts privilege names to be either added (prefixed with a +) or removed (prefixed with a -) from all the specified accounts and groups. The order of execution is as follows: privileges are first added, then subtracted, and finally, the end result is displayed.

Figure 2.6 demonstrates adding and removing privileges on particular accounts. Notice that in addition to the Joel and Betty accounts, the user has specified all user accounts that begin with test. Various privileges have been added to the specified user accounts, and one privilege has been removed.

```
C:\>perl priv.pl +batch_logon +backup -tcb +security
+SE_take_ownership_name +secreatetokenprivilege test* joel betty
MyDomain\Test_Guest:
    SE_BACKUP_NAME               Back up files and directories
    SE_SECURITY_NAME             Manage auditing and security log
    SE_TAKE_OWNERSHIP_NAME       Take ownership of files or other objects
    SE_CREATE_TOKEN_NAME         Create a token object
    SE_BATCH_LOGON_NAME

MyDomain\Test_Guest2:
    SE_BACKUP_NAME               Back up files and directories
    SE_SECURITY_NAME             Manage auditing and security log
    SE_TAKE_OWNERSHIP_NAME       Take ownership of files or other objects
    SE_CREATE_TOKEN_NAME         Create a token object
    SE_BATCH_LOGON_NAME

MyDomain\joel
    SE_BACKUP_NAME               Back up files and directories
    SE_SECURITY_NAME             Manage auditing and security log
    SE_TAKE_OWNERSHIP_NAME       Take ownership of files or other objects
    SE_CREATE_TOKEN_NAME         Create a token object
    SE_BATCH_LOGON_NAME
```

Figure 2.6   *Adding and removing privileges to accounts.*

When you're specifying which privileges to remove, the * character indicates to remove *all* privileges, as you can see in Figure 2.7.

```
C:\>perl priv.pl -* test*
MyDomain\test2_:

MyDomain\Test_Guest:

MyDomain\Test_Guest2:

MyDomain\testuser:
```

Figure 2.7 *Removing all privileges from accounts.*

When modifications are made to an account's privileges, they do not take effect until the account is logged on. If the account is currently logged on, it must first log off and then log on again.

This script accepts two additional command-line switches, described earlier in Table 2.3.

If neither domain nor machine names are specified, the script defaults to the domain of the user running the script.

After you run this script in which privilege modifications are made, you should perform a domain synchronization. Refer to the "Synchronizing Domain Controllers" section in this chapter.

Example 2.9 *Managing User Privileges*

```
01. use Win32::API;
02. use Win32::AdminMisc;
03. use Win32::Lanman;
04.
05. @PRIVILEGES = qw(
06.   SE_CREATE_TOKEN_NAME
07.   SE_ASSIGNPRIMARYTOKEN_NAME
08.   SE_LOCK_MEMORY_NAME
09.   SE_INCREASE_QUOTA_NAME
10.   SE_UNSOLICITED_INPUT_NAME
11.   SE_MACHINE_ACCOUNT_NAME
12.   SE_TCB_NAME
13.   SE_SECURITY_NAME
14.   SE_TAKE_OWNERSHIP_NAME
15.   SE_LOAD_DRIVER_NAME
16.   SE_SYSTEM_PROFILE_NAME
17.   SE_SYSTEMTIME_NAME
18.   SE_PROF_SINGLE_PROCESS_NAME
19.   SE_INC_BASE_PRIORITY_NAME
20.   SE_CREATE_PAGEFILE_NAME
21.   SE_CREATE_PERMANENT_NAME
22.   SE_BACKUP_NAME
```

continues ▶

Example 2.9   *continued*

```
23.   SE_RESTORE_NAME
24.   SE_SHUTDOWN_NAME
25.   SE_DEBUG_NAME
26.   SE_AUDIT_NAME
27.   SE_SYSTEM_ENVIRONMENT_NAME
28.   SE_CHANGE_NOTIFY_NAME
29.   SE_REMOTE_SHUTDOWN_NAME
30.   SE_INTERACTIVE_LOGON_NAME
31.   SE_NETWORK_LOGON_NAME
32.   SE_BATCH_LOGON_NAME
33.   SE_SERVICE_LOGON_NAME
34. );
35.
36. $LPDN = new Win32::API( 'advapi32.dll',
37.                         'LookupPrivilegeDisplayName',
38.                         [P,P,P,P,P], I )
39.      || die "Unable to locate the LookupPrivilegeDisplayName().\n";
40. foreach my $Privilege ( @PRIVILEGES )
41. {
42.   my $Size = 256;
43.   my $szDisplayName = "\x00" x $Size;
44.   my $dwSize = pack( "L", $Size );
45.   my $dwLangId = pack( "L", 0 );
46.   my $PrivString = eval "$Privilege";
47.   $LPDN->Call( $Config{machine}, $PrivString,
48.                $szDisplayName, $dwSize, $dwLangId );
49.   $szDisplayName =~ s/\x00//g;
50.   $PRIVILEGES{$Privilege} = {
51.     comment => $szDisplayName,
52.     display => $PrivString,
53.     name    => $Privilege,
54.   };
55.   $PRIVILEGE_VALUES{uc $PrivString} = $Privilege;
56. }
57.
58. Configure( \%Config, @ARGV );
59. if( $Config{help} )
60. {
61.   Syntax();
62.   exit( 0 );
63. }
64.
65. if( "" ne $Config{domain} )
66. {
67.   Win32::Lanman::NetGetDCName( '',
68.                               $Config{domain},
69.                               \$Config{machine} );
70. }
71. elsif( "" eq $Config{machine} )
72. {
73.   Win32::Lanman::NetGetDCName( '',
74.                               Win32::DomainName(),
```

```
75.                               \$Config{machine} );
76. }
77.
78. if( $Config{display_privileges} )
79. {
80.   my @PrivList;
81.
82.   # Display all privileges
83.   if( scalar @{$Config{items}} )
84.   {
85.     foreach my $Priv ( @{$Config{items}} )
86.     {
87.       $Priv = MatchPrivilege( $Priv ) || next;
88.       push( @PrivList, $Priv );
89.     }
90.   }
91.   else
92.   {
93.     push( @PrivList, sort( keys( %PRIVILEGES ) ) );
94.   }
95.   foreach $Key ( @PrivList )
96.   {
97.     print "$Key:\n";
98.     print "\tDisplay name: $PRIVILEGES{$Key}->{display}\n";
99.     print "\tComment: $PRIVILEGES{$Key}->{comment}\n"
100.         if( "" ne $PRIVILEGES{$Key}->{comment} );
101.     print "\n";
102.   }
103. }
104. elsif( $Config{user_rights} )
105. {
106.   # Display who has been enabled for a specific privilege
107.   foreach $Privilege ( @{$Config{items}} )
108.   {
109.     my @SidList;
110.     my $PrivKey = uc MatchPrivilege( $Privilege ) || next;
111.
112.     print "$PrivKey ($PRIVILEGES{$PrivKey}->{display}):\n";
113.     if( Win32::Lanman::LsaEnumerateAccountsWithUserRight(
114.                         $Config{machine},
115.                         $PRIVILEGES{$PrivKey}->{display},
116.                         \@SidList ) )
117.     {
118.       my @SidData;
119.       Win32::Lanman::LsaLookupSids( $Config{machine},
120.                         \@SidList,
121.                         \@SidData );
122.       foreach my $Data ( @SidData )
123.       {
124.         print "\t", (("" ne $Data->{domain})? "$Data->{domain}\\":"" );
125.         print "$Data->{name}\n";
126.       }
127.     }
```

continues ▶

Example 2.9   *continued*

```
128.    print "\n";
129.    }
130. }
131. else
132. {
133.    # Display what privilege has been enabled for specific accounts
134.    my @AccountList;
135.    my @AccountInfo;
136.    my %TempAccountList;
137.
138.    # Expand any wildcards in the user groups...
139.    foreach my $Account ( @{$Config{items}} )
140.    {
141.      if( $Account =~ /\*$/ )
142.      {
143.        my( $Prefix ) = ( $Account =~ /^(.*)\*$/ );
144.        my @Accounts;
145.        Win32::AdminMisc::GetUsers( $Config{machine},
146.                                    $Prefix,
147.                                    \@Accounts );
148.        map
149.        {
150.          $TempAccountList{lc $_} = $_;
151.        } @Accounts;
152.      }
153.      else
154.      {
155.        $TempAccountList{uc $Account} = $Account;
156.      }
157.    }
158.    # Create a non-duplicate list of user accounts from the temp hash
159.    foreach my $Key ( sort( keys( %TempAccountList ) ) )
160.    {
161.        push( @AccountList, $TempAccountList{$Key} );
162.    }
163.
164.    if( scalar @{$Config{add_privileges}}
165.        || scalar @{$Config{remove_privileges}} )
166.    {
167.      my @SidList;
168.      Win32::Lanman::LsaLookupNames( $Config{machine},
169.                                      \@AccountList,
170.                                      \@SidList );
171.      foreach my $Sid ( @SidList )
172.      {
173.        if( scalar @{Config{add_privileges}} )
174.        {
175.          Win32::Lanman::LsaAddAccountRights( $Config{machine},
176.                                               $Sid->{sid},
177.                                               $Config{add_privileges} );
178.        }
```

```
179.        if( scalar @{Config{remove_privileges}} )
180.        {
181.           Win32::Lanman::LsaRemoveAccountRights( $Config{machine},
182.                                                  $Sid->{sid},
183.                                                  $Config{remove_privileges},
184.                                                  $Config{remove_all} );
185.        }
186.      }
187.    }
188.    ReportAccountPrivileges( @AccountList );
189. }
190.
191. sub ReportAccountPrivileges
192. {
193.   my( @AccountList ) = @_;
194.
195.   $~ = PrivilegeDump;
196.   Win32::Lanman::LsaLookupNames( $Config{machine},
197.                                  \@AccountList,
198.                                  \@AccountInfo );
199.   for( $Index = 0; $Index < scalar @AccountInfo; $Index++ )
200.   {
201.     my @Rights;
202.     my $Account = $AccountInfo[$Index];
203.     $Account->{name} = $AccountList[$Index];
204.     print "$Account->{domain}\\" if( "" ne $Account->{domain} );
205.     print "$Account->{name}";
206.
207.     # Check that the account exists
208.     if( 8 > $Account->{use} )
209.     {
210.       print ":\n";
211.       if( Win32::Lanman::LsaEnumerateAccountRights( $Config{machine},
212.                                                     $Account->{sid},
213.                                                     \@Rights ) )
214.       {
215.         map
216.         {
217.           $Priv{name} = $PRIVILEGE_VALUES{uc $_};
218.           $Priv{display} = $_;
219.           $Priv{comment} = $PRIVILEGES{$Priv{name}}->{comment};
220.           write;
221.         } @Rights;
222.       }
223.     }
224.     else
225.     {
226.         print " ... account does not exist.\n";
227.     }
228.     print "\n";
229.   }
230.   return;
231. }
```

continues ▶

Example 2.9   *continued*

```
232.
233. sub MatchPrivilege
234. {
235.   my( $PrivRoot ) = uc shift @_;
236.   my $PrivKey = $PrivRoot;
237.   # Is the privilege a valid display name privilege?
238.   if( ! defined ( $PrivKey = $PRIVILEGE_VALUES{$PrivKey} ) )
239.   {
240.     # Is the privilege a normal privilege?
241.     $PrivKey = $PrivRoot;
242.     if( ! defined ( $PrivKey = $PRIVILEGES{$PrivKey}->{name} ) )
243.     {
244.       # In case the user entered only the base name of the privilege
245.       $PrivKey = "SE_" . $PrivRoot . "_NAME";
246.       if( ! defined ( $PrivKey = $PRIVILEGES{uc $PrivKey}->{name} ) )
247.       {
248.         # In case the user entered only the base of the display name
249.         $PrivKey = "Se" . $PrivRoot . "Privilege";
250.         if( ! defined ( $PrivKey = $PRIVILEGE_VALUES{uc $PrivKey} ) )
251.         {
252.           # One last chance...
253.           $PrivKey = "SE" . $PrivRoot . "Right";
254.           $PrivKey = $PRIVILEGE_VALUES{uc $PrivKey};
255.         }
256.       }
257.     }
258.   }
259.   return( $PrivKey );
260. }
261.
262. sub Configure
263. {
264.     my( $Config, @Args ) = @_;
265.     while( my $Arg = shift @Args )
266.     {
267.       my( $Prefix ) = ( $Arg =~ /^([+-\/])/ );
268.       if( "" ne $Prefix )
269.       {
270.         $Arg =~ s#^[+-/]##;
271.         if( "+" eq $Prefix )
272.         {
273.           # Adding a privilege
274.           my $Priv = MatchPrivilege( $Arg ) || next;
275.           push( @{$Config->{add_privileges}},
276.                 $PRIVILEGES{$Priv}->{display} );
277.         }
278.         elsif( $Arg =~ /^p$/i )
279.         {
280.           # Request to display all rights
281.           $Config->{display_privileges} = 1;
282.         }
```

```
283.        elsif( $Arg =~ /^s$/i )
284.        {
285.          # Specified displaying user rights
286.          $Config->{user_rights} = 1;
287.        }
288.        elsif( $Arg =~ /^d$/i )
289.        {
290.          # Specify a domain to create the account
291.          $Config->{domain} = shift @Args;
292.        }
293.        elsif( $Arg =~ /^m$/i )
294.        {
295.          # Specify what machine the account lives on
296.          $Config->{machine} = "\\\\" . shift @Args;
297.          $Config->{machine} =~ s/^(\\\\)+/\\\\/;
298.        }
299.        elsif( $Arg =~ /^(\?|h|help)/i )
300.        {
301.            # Request help
302.            $Config->{help} = 1;
303.        }
304.        else
305.        {
306.          if( "/" eq $Prefix )
307.          {
308.            # An unknown switch
309.            $Config->{help} = 1;
310.          }
311.          else
312.          {
313.            # We get here if the prefix was -
314.            # and no valid flag matched the switch therefore...
315.            # Removing a privilege
316.            if( "*" eq $Arg )
317.            {
318.              $Config->{remove_all} = 1;
319.              # Push * onto the remove array. It will be ignored
320.              # anyway since we will use the "remove all" flag.
321.              # This way the script will see the array is not empty
322.              # and attempt to remove privileges.
323.              push( @{$Config->{remove_privileges}}, $Arg );
324.            }
325.            else
326.            {
327.              my $Priv = MatchPrivilege( $Arg )
328.                            || ($Config->{help} = 1);
329.              push( @{$Config->{remove_privileges}},
330.                    $PRIVILEGES{$Priv}->{display} );
331.            }
332.          }
333.        }
334.      }
335.      else
```

continues ▶

Example 2.9   *continued*

```
336.    {
337.       push( @{$Config->{items}}, $Arg );
338.    }
339.  }
340.  if( 0 == scalar @{$Config->{items}} && ! $Config->{display_privileges} )
341.  {
342.      $Config->{help} = 1;
343.  }
344. }
345.
346. sub Syntax
347. {
348.   my( $Script ) = ( $0 =~ /([^\\\/]*?)$/ );
349.   my( $Line ) = "-" x length( $Script );
350.
351.   print <<EOT;
352.
353. $Script
354. $Line
355. Manages account privileges
356.
357. Syntax:
358.     perl $Script [-m Machine | -d Domain] -p
359.     perl $Script [-m Machine | -d Domain] -s Priv [Priv2 ...]
360.     perl $Script [-m Machine | -d Domain] [-|+Priv] Account [Account2 ...]
361.         -m Machine..All accounts and privileges are resident on the
362.                     specifed machine.
363.         -d Domain...All accounts and privileges are resident in the
364.                     specified domain.
365.         -s Priv.....Show all accounts that have been granted the specified
366.                     privilege. Some accounts may not show if they are
367.                     granted the privilege through a group membership.
368.         -Priv.......Removes the privilege from the specified accounts.
369.                     Specify as many of these switches as necessary.
370.                     Specify * to remove ALL privileges.
371.         +Priv.......Adds the privilege to the specified accounts.
372.                     Specify as many of these switches as necessary.
373.         Account.....Show all privileges granted to this specified account.
374.                     If used in conjunction with the -Priv or +Priv then the
375.                     privileges are assigned or removed first. The resulting
376.                     privilege set is then displayed.
377.                     This account can end with a * char to indicate
378.                     all accounts that begin with the specified string.
379.         If no domain or machine is specified then the current domain
380.         is used.
381. EOT
382. }
383.
```

```
384. format PrivilegeDump =
385.    @<<<<<<<<<<<<<<<<<<<<<<<<<<<< ^<<<<<<<<<<<<<<<<<<<<<<<<<<<<<<<<<<<<<<
386.    $Priv{name},                 $Priv{comment}
387. ~                               ^<<<<<<<<<<<<<<<<<<<<<<<<<<<<<<<<<<<<<<
388.                                 $Priv{comment}
389. ~                               ^<<<<<<<<<<<<<<<<<<<<<<<<<<<<<<<<<<<<<<
390.                                 $Priv{comment}
391. .
```

Synchronizing Domain Controllers

In large networks, having multiple DCs is common. All domains must have only one primary domain controller (PDC) but can have any number of backup domain controllers (BDCs). BDCs are literally *backup* domain controllers; if the PDC goes down, one of the BDCs ~~promotes itself to be a temporary PDC.~~ MUST BE MANUALLY PROMOTED TO REPLACE THE PDC.

The job of a DC is to, among other things, process requests for user logons and authenticate users. Any DC can process such requests, whether it is a PDC or BDC. This capability helps distribute the load across multiple machines, preventing both networking and processing bottlenecks.

One problem with such a distributed topology is that each DC must keep its own copy of the user account database. Each BDC therefore must routinely synchronize itself with the PDC. For example, when a user changes her password, the modification is submitted to the PDC. The PDC must propagate the change to all the BDCs so that the user can make use of the new password if she is logged on by one of the BDCs. Under certain conditions, such propagation could take a considerable amount of time.

Example 2.10 enables you to force a BDC to synchronize with its PDC, or it forces full domain synchronization. This process should be performed after account modifications are made, such as creating, deleting, or renaming, or if an individual account is modified (password changes, disabling, unlocking, and so on).

To force a BDC to synchronize with its PDC, just pass in the BDC names:

```
perl domsync.pl server1 server2 server3
```

To force a PDC to synchronize with all its BDCs, use the following:

```
perl domsync.pl -f MyDomain
```

Example 2.10 *Synchronizing Domain Controllers*

```
01. use Getopt::Long;
02. use Win32::Lanman;
03.
04. Configure( \%Config );
05. if( $Config{help} )
06. {
07.   Syntax();
08.   exit( 0 );
09. }
10.
11. if( $Config{full_sync} )
12. {
13.   my $Pdc;
14.   if( Win32::Lanman::NetGetDCName( $server, $Config{domain}, \$Pdc ) )
15.   {
16.     my %Info;
17.     if( Win32::Lanman::LogonControlPdcReplicate( $Pdc, \%Info ) )
18.     {
19.       print "Successfully initiated a full domain synchronization ";
20.       print "for the $Config{domain} domain.\n";
21.     }
22.     else
23.     {
24.       print "Full domain synchronization for the $Config{domain} "
25.             . "domain failed.\n";
26.       print "Error: " . Win32::Lanman::GetLastError() . "\n";
27.     }
28.   }
29.   else
30.   {
31.     print "Unable to locate the primary domain controller for the "
32.           . "domain $Config{domain}\n";
33.     print "Error: " . Win32::Lanman::GetLastError() . "\n";
34.   }
35. }
36. else
37. {
38.   print "Synchronizing the following domain controllers with its PDC:\n";
39.   foreach my $Server ( @{$Config{servers}} )
40.   {
41.     my %Info;
42.     my $Result = Win32::Lanman::LogonControlSynchronize( $Server,
43.                                              \%Info );
44.     printf( "  %-20s %s\n",
45.             $Server,
46.             ( $Result )? "successful" : "failed" );
47.   }
48. }
49.
```

```
50. sub Configure
51. {
52.   my( $Config ) = @_;
53.
54.   Getopt::Long::Configure( "prefix_pattern=(-|\/)" );
55.   $Result = GetOptions( $Config,
56.                         qw(
57.                            full_sync|f
58.                            help|?
59.                         )
60.                       );
61.   $Config->{help} = 1 if( ! $Result );
62.   if( $Config->{full_sync} )
63.   {
64.     $Config->{domain} = shift @ARGV;
65.     $Config->{domain} = Win32::DomainName()
66.                         if( "" eq $Config->{domain} );
67.   }
68.   else
69.   {
70.     push( @{$Config->{servers}}, @ARGV );
71.   }
72.   if(( ! $Config->{full_sync}) && (! scalar @{$Config->{servers}} ))
73.   {
74.     $Config->{help} = 1;
75.   }
76. }
77.
78. sub Syntax
79. {
80.   my( $Script ) = ( $0 =~ /([^\\\/]*?)$/ );
81.   my( $Line ) = "-" x length( $Script );
82.
83.   print <<EOT;
84.
85. $Script
86. $Line
87. Initiates synchronizations between domain controllers.
88.
89. Syntax:
90.     perl $Script -f [Domain] | Server [ Server2 ...]
91.        -f [Domain] Performs a full domain synchronization.
92.                    This will default to the local user's domain unless
93.                    the optional Domain is specified.
94.         Server......Specifies a BDC to synchronize with its PDC.
95. EOT
96. }
```

Conclusion

The Win32 platform provides a rich GUI environment to manage the various aspects of user and group accounts. However, the sheer number of such accounts found in most networks makes it quite impractical to expect any administrator to use the default tools.

This chapter showed how Win32 Perl can be used to effectively manage these tasks and make them not only easier, but automated and less prone to error.

3
Tools

Every good administrator assembles a collection of tools that she simply cannot do without. These tools perform specific tasks that enable her to quickly perform her job. A perfect example of such a utility is the popular XCACLS.EXE program that comes with the *Windows NT Resource Kit*.

This utility (and its little brother CACLS.EXE) dumps any permissions that are applied to a file or directory. Without such a tool, you are doomed to open an Explorer window, select the object in question, right-click, select the Properties context menu, and then go to the Security tab on the resulting property page. If this procedure doesn't sound like very much work, you have not administered a network of thousands of machines with various security permissions applied to various directories and files.

This chapter covers an assortment of scripts that were created for my own toolkit. To be sure, I wrote each of these scripts to simplify and lessen my workload as an administrator. I included these scripts only for the sake of demonstrating how you can leverage Win32 Perl to solve problems that administrators face every day. When you scrutinize the code, it becomes obvious that there is almost no Win32 task that cannot be managed with a bit of Perl coding.

These scripts were not written to be simple or to be tutorials but instead to get into the nitty-gritty of task solving. I recommend that you use a good Win32 API reference while looking at the code that makes up these scripts; in particular, check out Microsoft's MSDN library (http://msdn.microsoft.com/) and, of course, my other book, *Win32 Perl Programming: The Standard Extensions* (New Riders Publishing).

The File System

The Win32 operating system makes copious use of its file system. As an administrator, you have the burden of managing this important resource. Your job covers the entire range of administrative tasks, ranging from securing files and directories to creating directories and updating outdated files. Many different tools and utilities available from various companies can help you administer your machine's file system. However, you will not be able to easily find some tools.

Many of the existing tools are confusing because they reflect aspects of the file system that are not commonly known, such as alternate data streams. Some tools are not used simply because administrators have no idea that they exist, such as tools used to discover hidden directory shares on remote machines. The following sections focus on file system–related tools that can save you a great deal of work.

Discovering Shared Directories

Ever since Windows for Workgroups was released, sharing directories for others to connect to has been quite simple. From a Windows NT/2000 command line, you can easily share a directory by using the net share command. The following line shares a temporary directory with the name TempDir:

```
net share TempDir=c:\temp
```

Alternatively, you can share directories from the File Manager, the Explorer, and the Service Manager GUI applications.

The Win32 world permits you to *hide* shared directories—that is, share a directory that nobody can see when browsing the network. The only way to access the directory is to know it has been shared and explicitly access the hidden share. You hide directories by appending a dollar sign ($) to the end of the share name. For example, the following command line creates a hidden shared directory called MyHiddenShare$:

```
net share MyHiddenShare$=c:\temp
```

Now, only users who know about this hidden share can access it.

You can see which directories your machine is sharing by using this command line:

```
net share
```

This line displays all the shared directories on the local machine. However, there is no easy way to discover shared directories on a remote machine.

You can always open an Explorer window for a particular machine, but this solution is bulky and displays only nonhidden directories.

Let's say that you need to see what shares are available on some remote machine. Explorer won't help you in this case. You could walk over to the machine, log on, and issue the net share command, but this method is not very convenient, especially if the machine is across town or across the country. And assuming that you don't have some type of Telnet daemon installed, this problem is quite serious.

At this point, you can turn to the DumpShares.pl script (shown in Example 3.1). The actual core of the script revolves around line 11, where a call is made into the Win32::Lanman extension to get a list of shared directory names.

As long as you can physically connect to the remote machine, you can see all its shared directories, regardless of whether or not you are granted administrative privileges on the remote machine. If you lack admin privileges on the remote machine, the shared directory's paths are not visible.

The script takes in any number of remote machine names and tries to resolve each passed-in machine name. If nothing is passed in, the local machine's shared directories are displayed.

Example 3.1 *Displaying All Shared Directories on a Remote Machine*

```
01. use Win32;
02. use Win32::Lanman;
03.
04. push( @ARGV, Win32::NodeName() ) if( ! scalar @ARGV );
05. foreach my $Machine ( @ARGV )
06. {
07.    my @List;
08.    $Machine =~ s#^[\\/]*#\\\\#;
09.
10.    print "\nShare list for '$Machine'\n";
11.    if( Win32::Lanman::NetShareEnum( $Machine, \@List ) )
12.    {
13.      foreach my $Share ( @List )
14.      {
15.        my( $Remark, $Path, $NetName );
16.
17.        $NetName = $Share->{netname};
18.        if( "" ne $Share->{remark} )
19.        {
20.          $Remark = "($Share->{remark})";
21.        }
22.        if( "" ne $Share->{path} )
23.        {
24.          $Path = $Share->{path};
25.        }
26.        else
```

continues ▶

Example 3.1 *continued*

```
27.      {
28.         $Path = "No permission to display";
29.      }
30.      push( @ShareList, { name => $NetName,
31.                          remark => $Remark,
32.                          path => $Path } );
33.   }
34.   $~ = Share_Header;
35.   write;
36.
37.   $~ = Share_Info;
38.   $iCount = 0;
39.
40.   foreach $Share ( sort( {
41.                           lc $a->{name} cmp lc $b->{name}
42.                           } @ShareList ) )
43.   {
44.      $iCount++;
45.      write;
46.   }
47.  }
48.  else
49.  {
50.     print "...not available : ";
51.     print Win32::FormatMessage( Win32::Lanman::GetLastError() );
52.  }
53.
54.  print "\n";
55. }
56.
57. format Share_Info =
58. @>>> @<<<<<<<<<<<<<<<< ^<<<<<<<<<<<<<<<<<<<<<< ^<<<<<<<<<<<<<<<<<<<<<<<
59. $iCount, $Share->{name}, $Share->{remark}, $Share->{path}
60. ~                       ^<<<<<<<<<<<<<<<<<<<<<< ^<<<<<<<<<<<<<<<<<<<<<<<
61.                         $Share->{remark}, $Share->{path}
62. ~                       ^<<<<<<<<<<<<<<<<<<<<<< ^<<<<<<<<<<<<<<<<<<<<<<<
63.                         $Share->{remark}, $Share->{path}
64. .
65.
66. format Share_Header =
67. @||| @<<<<<<<<<<<<<<<< @<<<<<<<<<<<<<<<<<<<<<< @<<<<<<<<<<<<<<<<<<<<<<<
68. "Num", "Share Name", "Comment", "Path"
69. ---- ----------------- ---------------------- -----------------------
70. .
```

Volume Information

For an administrator, discovering details of hard drives on remote machines can be essential. Determining how large the volume is, as well as how much space is available, is an important part of drive management. Example 3.2

retrieves such necessary information and other relevant data, such as the volume name, file system type (NTFS, FAT, FAT32, and so on), serial number, and the volume's flags. The flags indicate what features are available for the drive. The flags and their descriptions are listed in Table 3.1.

Table 3.1   Volume Flags

Flag	Description
FS_CASE_IS_PRESERVED	The file system preserves the case of filenames when it places a name on disk.
FS_CASE_SENSITIVE	The file system supports case-sensitive file names.
FS_UNICODE_STORED_ON_DISK	The file system supports Unicode in filenames as they appear on disk.
FS_PERSISTENT_ACLS	The file system preserves and enforces Access Control Lists (ACLs—also known as permissions). For example, NTFS preserves and enforces ACLs, but FAT does not.
FS_FILE_COMPRESSION	The file system supports file-based compression.
FS_VOL_IS_COMPRESSED	The specified volume is a compressed volume—for example, a DoubleSpace volume.
FILE_NAMED_STREAMS	The file system supports named streams.
FILE_SUPPORTS_ENCRYPTION	The file system supports the Encrypted File System (EFS).
FILE_SUPPORTS_OBJECT_IDS	The file system supports object identifiers.
FILE_SUPPORTS_REPARSE_POINTS	The file system supports reparse points. This capability allows for features such as using NTFS links and moving infrequently accessed data to long-term storage such as tape backup.
FILE_SUPPORTS_SPARSE_FILES	The file system supports sparse files. Sparse files have disk storage allocated only for the parts of the file that contain data. Therefore, large blocks of 0s are not stored to disk to conserve drive storage space.
FILE_VOLUME_QUOTAS	The file system supports space allocation limits on a per user basis.

The script accepts a list of drive letters or UNCs like this:

```
perl volume.pl c:\ \\server\share
```

In this case, the script displays volume information for both the local machine's c:\ drive as well as for the volume that is shared by the UNC \\server\share. Figure 3.1 illustrates the output from this code. If no parameter is passed in, information regarding the volume for the current directory is displayed.

The code uses a Win32 API function that was introduced with Windows NT 4.0 and Windows 95 OEM Service Release 2 (OSR2). It will most likely fail on platforms earlier than this.

```
C:\>perl volume.pl c:\ \\server\share\

c:\:
FS    Serial    Volume Name                   Flags
.....  .........  ............................  ...........................
NTFS  DCF6-AF23 This is my test volume         FS_CASE_SENSITIVE
Total Size: 4,301,788,672                      FS_CASE_IS_PRESERVED
Avail Size: 726,140,928                        FS_UNICODE_STORED_ON_DISK
                                               FILE_VOLUME_QUOTAS
                                               FS_FILE_COMPRESSION
                                               FS_PERSISTENT_ACLS
                                               FILE_SUPPORTS_OBJECT_IDS
                                               FILE_SUPPORTS_SPARSE_FILES
                                               FILE_SUPPORTS_REPARSE_POINTS
                                               FILE_SUPPORTS_ENCRYPTION


\\server\share\:
FS    Serial    Volume Name                   Flags
.....  .........  ............................  ...........................
NTFS  8063-FA56 New Volume                     FS_CASE_SENSITIVE
Total Size: 18,202,226,688                     FS_CASE_IS_PRESERVED
Avail Size: 12,755,464,192                     FS_UNICODE_STORED_ON_DISK
                                               FILE_VOLUME_QUOTAS
                                               FS_FILE_COMPRESSION
                                               FS_PERSISTENT_ACLS
                                               FILE_SUPPORTS_OBJECT_IDS
                                               FILE_SUPPORTS_SPARSE_FILES
                                               FILE_SUPPORTS_REPARSE_POINTS
                                               FILE_SUPPORTS_ENCRYPTION
```

Figure 3.1   *Displaying volume information.*

Example 3.2   *Retrieving Volume Information*

```
01. use Win32::API::Prototype;
02.
03. ApiLink( 'kernel32.dll', 'BOOL GetVolumeInformation(
04.                      LPCTSTR lpRootPathName,
05.                      LPTSTR lpVolumeNameBuffer,
06.                      DWORD nVolumeNameSize,
07.                      LPDWORD lpVolumeSerialNumber,
08.                      LPDWORD lpMaximumComponentLength,
09.                      LPDWORD lpFileSystemFlags,
10.                      LPTSTR lpFileSystemNameBuffer,
11.                      DWORD nFileSystemNameSize )' )
```

```
12.      || die "Can not link to GetVolumeInformation()";
13. ApiLink( 'kernel32.dll', 'BOOL GetDiskFreeSpaceEx(
14.                                    LPCTSTR lpDirectoryName,
15.                                    PVOID lpFreeBytesAvailable,
16.                                    PVOID lpTotalNumberOfBytes,
17.                                    PVOID lpTotalNumberOfFreeBytes )' )
18.      || die "Wrong version of NT";
19.
20. %FLAGS = (
21.    0x00000001  =>  'FS_CASE_SENSITIVE',
22.    0x00000002  =>  'FS_CASE_IS_PRESERVED',
23.    0x00000004  =>  'FS_UNICODE_STORED_ON_DISK',
24.    0x00000008  =>  'FS_PERSISTENT_ACLS',
25.    0x00000010  =>  'FS_FILE_COMPRESSION',
26.    0x00000020  =>  'FILE_VOLUME_QUOTAS',
27.    0x00000040  =>  'FILE_SUPPORTS_SPARSE_FILES',
28.    0x00000080  =>  'FILE_SUPPORTS_REPARSE_POINTS',
29.    0x00008000  =>  'FS_VOL_IS_COMPRESSED',
30.    0x00000000  =>  'FILE_NAMED_STREAMS',
31.    0x00020000  =>  'FILE_SUPPORTS_ENCRYPTION',
32.    0x00010000  =>  'FILE_SUPPORTS_OBJECT_IDS',
33. );
34.
35. push( @ARGV, "\\" ) if( 0 == scalar @ARGV );
36.
37. foreach my $Path ( @ARGV )
38. {
39.    my $dwVolSize = 256;
40.    my $szVolName = NewString( $dwVolSize );
41.    my $pdwSerialNum = pack( "L", 0 );
42.    my $pdwMaxLength = pack( "L", 0 );
43.    my $pdwFlags = pack( "L", 0 );
44.    my $dwFSNameSize = 256;
45.    my $szFSName = NewString( $dwFSNameSize );
46.
47.    $Path .= "\\" unless( $Path =~ /\\$/ );
48.    next unless( -d $Path );
49.    $Path = NewString( $Path );
50.
51.    print "\n$Path:\n";
52.    $~ = DumpVol;
53.    if( GetVolumeInformation( $Path, $szVolName,
54.                              $dwVolSize, $pdwSerialNum,
55.                              $pdwMaxLength, $pdwFlags,
56.                              $szFSName, $dwFSNameSize ) )
57.    {
58.      local %Vol = (
59.        path         => $Path,
60.        volume_name => CleanString( $szVolName ),
61.        serial_num  => sprintf( "\U%04x-%04x",
62.                                reverse( unpack( "S2",
```

continues ▶

Example 3.2 *continued*

```
63.                                              $pdwSerialNum ) ) ),
64.        max_length  =>  unpack( "L", $pdwMaxLength ),
65.        flags       =>  DecodeFlags( unpack( "L", $pdwFlags ) ),
66.        fs_name     =>  CleanString( $szFSName )
67.      );
68.      my $pFree  = pack( "L2", 0, 0 );
69.      my $pTotal = pack( "L2", 0, 0 );
70.      my $pTotalFree = pack( "L2", 0, 0 );
71.      if( GetDiskFreeSpaceEx( $Path, $pFree, $pTotal, $pTotalFree ) )
72.      {
73.        $Vol{free} = FormatNumber( MakeLargeInt( unpack( "L2",
74.                                              $pTotalFree ) ) );
75.        $Vol{total} = FormatNumber( MakeLargeInt( unpack( "L2",
76.                                              $pTotal ) ) );
77.      }
78.      write;
79.    }
80. }
81.
82. sub MakeLargeInt
83. {
84.    my( $Low, $High ) = @_;
85.    return( $High * ( 1 + 0xFFFFFFFF ) + $Low );
86. }
87.
88. sub DecodeFlags
89. {
90.    my( $Flags ) = @_;
91.    my $String = "";
92.    foreach my $Key ( keys( %FLAGS ) )
93.    {
94.      if( $Flags & $Key )
95.      {
96.        $String .= sprintf( "%- 30s\n", $FLAGS{$Key} );
97.      }
98.    }
99.    return( $String );
100. }
101.
102. sub FormatNumber
103. {
104.    my( $Num ) = @_;
105.    {} while( $Num =~ s/^(-?\d+)(\d{3})/$1,$2/ );
106.    return( $Num );
107. }
108.
109. format DumpVol =
110. FS    Serial    Volume Name                       Flags
111. ----- --------- -------------------------------- ----------------------------
112. @<<<< @<<<<<<<< @<<<<<<<<<<<<<<<<<<<<<<<<<<<<<<< ^<<<<<<<<<<<<<<<<<<<<<<<<<<<<<
113. $Vol{fs_name}, $Vol{serial_num}, $Vol{volume_name}, $Vol{flags}
```

```
114. Total Size: @<<<<<<<<<<<<<<<<<<<<<<<<<<<<< ^<<<<<<<<<<<<<<<<<<<<<<<<<<<<
115. $Vol{total}                               $Vol{flags}
116. Avail Size: @<<<<<<<<<<<<<<<<<<<<<<<<<<<<< ^<<<<<<<<<<<<<<<<<<<<<<<<<<<<
117. $Vol{free}                                $Vol{flags}
118. ~                                         ^<<<<<<<<<<<<<<<<<<<<<<<<<<<<
119.                                            $Vol{flags}
120. ~                                         ^<<<<<<<<<<<<<<<<<<<<<<<<<<<<
121.                                            $Vol{flags}
122. ~                                         ^<<<<<<<<<<<<<<<<<<<<<<<<<<<<
123.                                            $Vol{flags}
124. ~                                         ^<<<<<<<<<<<<<<<<<<<<<<<<<<<<
125.                                            $Vol{flags}
126. ~                                         ^<<<<<<<<<<<<<<<<<<<<<<<<<<<<
127.                                            $Vol{flags}
128. ~                                         ^<<<<<<<<<<<<<<<<<<<<<<<<<<<<
129.                                            $Vol{flags}
130. ~                                         ^<<<<<<<<<<<<<<<<<<<<<<<<<<<<
131.                                            $Vol{flags}
132. ~                                         ^<<<<<<<<<<<<<<<<<<<<<<<<<<<<
133.                                            $Vol{flags}
134. ~                                         ^<<<<<<<<<<<<<<<<<<<<<<<<<<<<
135.                                            $Vol{flags}
136. .
```

Creating Hard File Links

UNIX users could always create hard links between files, and starting with
Windows 2000, so can users of the Win32 platform. Previous versions of
Windows NT were able to create links by utilizing a POSIX subsystem;
however, with Windows 2000 the link functionality is built directly into the
Win32 API. Unfortunately, these links are not as rich as their UNIX
brethren. You can create links only for files but not directories. And like
UNIX's hard links, they must be located on the same volume. This means
that a link must reside on the same hard drive as the file it is linked to.
Win32, however, does not have the capability to symbolically link across
volumes. The closest equivalent is a shortcut, but that is interpreted by an
application, not the operating system (therefore, you cannot rely on all
programs to understand how to use them).

This hard-linking capability is supported only on NTFS volumes.
Example 3.3 creates such hard links. The script takes in two parameters
like this:

```
perl ln.pl c:\temp\MyExistingFile.txt c:\MyNewLink.txt
```

The first parameter is the existing file, and the second parameter is the path
to where the new linked file will be created. This new link file will be (for
all practical purposes) the same file as specified in the first parameter.

Editing either of these files results in both files being modified. This makes sense because you really have only one file, just two separate file system entries for it.

After a hard link has been created on an NTFS volume, it is literally linked to the original file. Even if you move the original or linked file, they both still point to the same data. Additionally, you can modify the content of either file, and it updates the same data. This can cause concurrency problems if you are accessing multiple files all linked together. Because the file is only a *link* to the original file, it can be deleted without affecting the original file.

Example 3.3   *Creating Hard Links*

```
01. use Win32::API::Prototype;
02.
03. if( 2 != scalar @ARGV )
04. {
05.     print "Syntax:\n  $0 <File to link to> <New Link File>\n";
06.     exit();
07. }
08.
09. my( $NewLink, $File ) = @ARGV;
10. ApiLink( 'kernel32.dll',
11.            'BOOL CreateHardLink( LPCTSTR lpFileName,
12.                                  LPCTSTR lpExistingFileName,
13.                                  LPSECURITY_ATTRIBUTES lpSa )' )
14.    || die "This version of Windows does not support CreateHardLink()";
15. if( CreateHardLink( $File, $NewLink, 0 ) )
16. {
17.     print "Link successfully created.\n";
18. }
19. else
20. {
21.     print "Failed to create link.\nError: ";
22.     print Win32::FormatMessage( Win32::GetLastError() ), "\n";
23. }
```

Creating Directories

Creating directories is not a new concept. All disk-based operating systems such as UNIX, Win32, DOS, and Macintosh have the concept of some file-based container (for example, a directory or folder). You must create a container so that you can move objects such as files and other directories into it. You usually do so by using a command such as md or mkdir. Win32 exposes this functionality through its Win32 API CreateDirectory() and CreateDirectoryEx() functions. It is also available from a DOS box when you use the `mkdir` or `md` command. These techniques, however, fail to create intermediary directories. For example, if you run

```
md Dir1\Dir2
```

and `Dir1` does not already exist, then `Dir2` will not be created.

Tip

On the Windows NT and 2000 platforms, if command extensions are enabled, the DOS box `md` and `mkdir` commands create any intermediary directories. For more information, run `cmd.exe /h`. ◆

Even Win32 Perl fails to create any intermediary directories—most likely because it simply calls into the `c:` library's `mkdir()` function, which, in turn, calls the Win32 API's `CreateDirectory()` function.

Example 3.4 creates as many directories as it needs in order to create the passed-in directory. There is nothing Win32–specific about this particular script; therefore, it could run on any platform that runs Perl. This script accepts only one parameter, which must be either a full path (for example, `C:\temp\Dir1\Dir2`), a relative path (for example, `..\Dir1\Dir2`), or a UNC (for example, `\\server\share\Dir1\Dir2`).

To use this script, just pass in the name of the path to create—for example,

```
perl makedir.pl \\server\share\dir1\dir2
```

Example 3.4   *Creating Intermediary Directories*

```
01. $Dir = shift @ARGV || die "Syntax: $0 <Dir>";
02. $Result = 1;
03. ( $Root, $Path ) = ( $Dir =~ /^(\w:\\?|\\\\.+?\\.+?\\|\\)?(.*)$/ );
04. print "Creating directory '$Dir'...\n";
05.
06. if( -d $Dir )
07. {
08.     print "Directory already exists.\n";
09.     exit;
10. }
11.
12. @DirList = split( /\\/, $Path );
13. $Path = $Root;
14.
15. while( $Result && scalar @DirList )
16. {
17.     $Path .= ( shift @DirList ) . "\\";
18.
19.     next if( -d $Path );
20.     $Result = mkdir( $Path, 0777 );
21. }
22.
23. print ( ( $Result )? "Success" : "Failure (Error: $!)" ), "\n";
```

NTFS Streams

One of the greatest joys of using the NTFS file system is the ability to create multiple streams in a file. However, most administrators, let alone users, are not even aware of this capability.

Just like any file system, an NTFS file contains data. However, unlike other file systems, in this one the data is stored in what is called an NTFS *stream*. This stream is simple data that is associated with the file by means of a name. This is very similar to the way a Perl hash works. A stream name is much like a hash key. Data is associated with a hash key, just as data can be associated with a file stream name. By default, all NTFS files have only one stream, the default stream, which is the place data is stored. However, NTFS allows additional streams to be created in a file. Because each stream has a name (with the exception of the default stream), you access the stream by name.

Thinking of multiple data segments for a single file may be mind-bending—but only because it is not common. Think of multiple streams as you would a *tar file*, which is basically an archive of multiple data files. You could create one file with multiple streams, each stream consisting of data from different files. This would enable you to create a log file for, say, a Web server that consists of only one file. But each day the Web server creates a new log, it creates a new stream in the log file. The end result is that you could have an entire year's worth of Web server log entries consolidated into one convenient file. Then you can easily copy all the logged data from one place to another because you are copying only one file.

A Windows NT/2000 machine can store Macintosh files on its NTFS drives this way. By using alternate data streams, the operating system can store both the Macintosh data and resource forks in one file.

To access an NTFS stream you must refer to the NTFS file as you normally would, but you use a colon followed by the stream name. The format is

```
path\file_name:stream_name
```

Here's an example:

```
C:\temp\MyTestFile.txt:MyFirstStream
```

Perl can read and write to such NTFS streams using the normal file functions. You can test this capability by running Example 3.5 and Example 3.6 on an NTFS drive. Example 3.5 creates a text file with two streams: the main data stream and an alternative stream.

Example 3.6 reads back the data from both streams in the text file. If you examine the resulting text file, you will notice that the file size reflects only the data in the default data stream. If you were unaware that the file contained multiple streams, there would normally be no way to discover this fact. As you will see, Win32 Perl can be used to discover such alternate data streams.

Example 3.5   *Creating a Test File with Multiple Streams*

```
01. $File = "StreamTest.txt";
02. $Stream = "AltDataStream";
03. if( open( STREAM1, "> $File" ) )
04. {
05.   print "Writing to the main data stream.\n";
06.   print STREAM1 "\tWelcome to the main data stream.\n";
07.   close( STREAM1 );
08.
09.   if( open( STREAM2, "> $File:$Stream" ) )
10.   {
11.     print "Writing to alternative stream '$Stream'.\n";
12.     print STREAM2 "\tWelcome to the alternative data stream '$Stream'\n";
13.     close( STREAM2 );
14.   }
15.   else
16.   {
17.     print "Error: $!\n";
18.   }
19. }
20. else
21. {
22.   print "Error: $!\n";
23. }
```

Example 3.6   *Reading Multiple Streams from a Test File*

```
01. $File = "StreamTest.txt";
02. $Stream = "AltDataStream";
03. if( open( STREAM1, "< $File" ) )
04. {
05.   print "This is the main data stream for $File.\n";
06.   while( my $Line = <STREAM1> )
07.   {
08.     print $Line;
09.   }
10.   close( STREAM1 );
11.
12.   if( open( STREAM2, "< $File:$Stream" ) )
13.   {
14.     print "\n\nThis is the data stream $File:$Stream:\n";
15.     while( my $Line = <STREAM2> )
16.     {
```

continues ▶

Example 3.6 *continued*

```
17.     print $Line;
18.   }
19.   close( STREAM2 );
20. }
21. else
22. {
23.   print "Error: $!\n";
24. }
25. }
26. else
27. {
28.   print "Error: $!\n";
29. }
```

On Windows NT/2000, the more command can be coaxed into displaying alternate data streams. You do so by redirecting the input into the more command from a data stream like this:

```
more < test.txt:MyStream
```

Tip

For some reason, most programs do not permit you to enter valid NTFS path-names that include alternate streams. For example, an attempt to load test.txt:MyStream *into Notepad, Microsoft Word, or various other programs will fail. ◆*

Example 3.7 is a replacement for the DOS type command. This script functions the same way, except that it can display NTFS data streams—something that type cannot do.

The script accepts any number of paths to display. This includes paths with wildcards. For example,

```
perl streamdump.pl myfile.txt:altStream1 c:\temp\*.txt
```

Example 3.7 *Displaying NTFS Alternate Data Stream Content*

```
01. foreach my $Mask ( @ARGV )
02. {
03.   my @List;
04.
05.   # Must be careful since glob() does not support
06.   # paths with embedded spaces.
07.   if( @List = glob( $Mask ) )
08.   {
09.     push( @FileList, @List );
10.   }
11.   else
12.   {
13.     push( @FileList, $Mask );
```

```
14.   }
15. }
16. foreach my $Path ( @FileList )
17. {
18.   print $Path, "\n";
19.   print "-" x length( $Path ), "\n";
20.   if( open( FILE, "< $Path" ) )
21.   {
22.     my $Buffer;
23.
24.     binmode( FILE );
25.     while( read( FILE, $Buffer, 1024 ) )
26.     {
27.       print $Buffer;
28.     }
29.     close( FILE );
30.   }
31.   else
32.   {
33.     print "\tError: $!\n";
34.   }
35.   print "\n";
36. }
```

NTFS, Alternative Data Streams, and File Sizes

Interestingly enough, the reported size of a file does not reflect the contents of alternative data streams. For example, if you create a 32-byte file and add an alternative data stream that is 500,000 bytes in size, the file still reports only 32 bytes. This makes it even more impractical for an administrator to determine exactly how much space a file truly takes up.

Just to help complicate NTFS size reporting issues, due to the nature of NTFS, a directory listing may report unexpected available disk space values. For example, if you create this text file

```
C:\>echo Big Old Test > test.txt
```

a directory listing shows how large the file is and how much space is available on the disk:

```
C:\>dir test.txt
 Volume in drive C is unnamed
 Volume Serial Number is DCF6-AF23

 Directory of C:\

06/01/2000  09:14a                    15 test.txt
               1 File(s)              15 bytes
               0 Dir(s)     592,346,112 bytes free
```

If you rewrite the file to a different file size,

```
C:\>echo This is really a test > test.txt
```

a directory listing yields

```
C:\>dir test.txt
 Volume in drive C is unnamed
 Volume Serial Number is DCF6-AF23

 Directory of C:\

06/01/2000  09:14a                   24 test.txt
              1 File(s)              17 bytes
              0 Dir(s)      592,346,112 bytes free
```

Notice that even though the file size changes, the amount of available drive space does not because NTFS calculates two different size values for each file: how large the file is and how much disk space the file takes up. In this case, the file size is either 15 or 24 bytes. However, the file takes up (at least) one sector of disk space. And each sector (on this particular volume) is made up of 1 kilobyte (1024 bytes) of space. Therefore, it takes 1024 bytes of disk space to store only 15 bytes of data. When NTFS computes the available disk space, that amount is based on the amount of unallocated disk space. Because disk space is taken up in 1KB blocks, the available free space is always rounded down to a multiple of 1024.

Enumerating NTFS Streams
The one problem with NTFS streams is that there is no way to enumerate the streams in a file. This problem is rather tragic, considering how powerful NTFS streams can be. Basically, this means that if you forget which streams you have added to a file, there is no way to discover them. This situation is akin to removing the `dir` command from the DOS box: How would you possibly discover which files are in a directory? Yes, bizarre as it sounds, this is the reality of Win32's lack of proper support for NTFS streams.

The good news is that you can use a hack to enumerate streams. This solution involves reading the file as backup software does, using the Win32 API's `BackupRead()` function.

The Streams.pl script (see Example 3.8) displays the names and sizes of all streams in an NTFS file. The script accepts any number of parameters from the command line. Each parameter is a path to a file that is to be examined for alternate streams. The file path can contain wildcards.

Example 3.8   *Enumerating Streams in an NTFS File*

```
01. use Win32::API::Prototype;
02.
03. $OPEN_EXISTING = 3;
04. $GENERIC_READ  = 0x80000000;
```

```
05. $BACKUP_DATA       = 0x00000001;
06. $BACKUP_ALTERNATE_DATA = 0x00000004;
07. $FILE_SHARE_READ = 0x00 00 0001;  $FILE_FLAG_BACKUP_SEMANTICS
08. ApiLink( 'kernel32.dll',                                 = 0x02 000000;
09.          'HANDLE CreateFile( LPCTSTR pszPath,
10.                              DWORD dwAccess,
11.                              DWORD dwShareMode,
12.                              PVOID SecurityAttributes,
13.                              DWORD dwCreationDist,
14.                              DWORD dwFlags,
15.                              HANDLE hTemplate )' )
16.    || die "Can not locate CreateFile()";
17. ApiLink( 'kernel32.dll',
18.          'BOOL CloseHandle( HANDLE hFile )' )
19.    || die "Can not locate CloseHandle()";
20. ApiLink( 'kernel32.dll',
21.          'BOOL BackupRead( HANDLE hFile,
22.                            LPBYTE pBuffer,
23.                            DWORD dwBytesToRead,
24.                            LPDWORD pdwBytesRead,
25.                            BOOL bAbort,
26.                            BOOL bProcessSecurity,
27.                            LPVOID *ppContext)' )
28.    || die "Can not locate BackupRead()";
29. ApiLink( 'kernel32.dll',
30.          'BOOL BackupSeek( HANDLE hFile,
31.                            DWORD dwLowBytesToSeek,
32.                            DWORD dwHighBytesToSeek,
33.                            LPDWORD pdwLowByteSeeked,
34.                            LPDWORD pdwHighByteSeeked,
35.                            LPVOID *pContext )' )
36.    || die "Can not create BackupSeek()";
37.
38. # Generate a list of all files to process
39. # therefore we have to expand any wildcards
40. foreach my $Mask ( @ARGV )
41. {
42.    foreach my $Path ( glob( $Mask ) )
43.    {
44.        push( @Files, $Path ) if( -f $Path );
45.    }
46. }
47.
48. foreach my $File ( @Files )
49. {
50.   print "$File\n";
51.
52.   $hFile = CreateFile( $File,
53.                        $GENERIC_READ,
54.                        undef,
55.                        $OPEN_EXISTING,
56.                        0 ) || die "Can not open the file '$File'\n";
57.
58.
```

Handwritten annotations:
- Line 43: `|| -d $PATH  ← NOTE: DIRECTORIES CAN ALSO HAVE ADS.`
- Line 54: `-0,  $FILE_SHARE_READ`
- Line 57: `-0,  $FILE_FLAG_BACKUP_SEMANTICS`

continues ▶

Example 3.8 *continued*

```
59.
60.    # If CreateFile() failed $hFile is a negative value
61.    if( 0 < $hFile )
62.    {
63.      my $iStreamCount = 0;
64.      my $iTotalSize = 0;
65.      my $pBytesRead = pack( "L", 0 );
66.      my $pContext = pack( "L", 0 );
67.      my $pStreamIDStruct = pack( "L5", 0,0,0,0,0 );
68.
69.      while( BackupRead( $hFile,
70.                         $pStreamIDStruct,
71.                         length( $pStreamIDStruct ),
72.                         $pBytesRead,
73.                         0,
74.                         0,
75.                         $pContext ) )
76.      {
77.        my $BytesRead = unpack( "L", $pBytesRead );
78.        my $Context = unpack( "L", $pContext );
79.        my %Stream;
80.        my( $pSeekBytesLow, $pSeekBytesHigh ) = ( pack( "L", 0 ),
81.                                                  pack( "L", 0 ) );
82.        my $StreamName = "";
83.        my $StreamSize;
84.
85.        # No more data to read
86.        last if( 0 == $BytesRead );
87.
88.        @Stream{ id, attributes,
89.                 size_low, size_high,
90.                 name_size } = unpack( "L5", $pStreamIDStruct );
91.
92.        if( $BACKUP_ALTERNATE_DATA == $Stream{id} )
93.        {
94.          $StreamName = NewString( $Stream{name_size} );
95.          if( BackupRead( $hFile,
96.                          $StreamName,
97.                          $Stream{name_size},
98.                          $pBytesRead,
99.                          0,
100.                          0,
101.                          $pContext ) )
102.        {
103.            my $String = CleanString( $StreamName, 1 );
104.            $String =~ s/^:(.*?):.*$/$1/;
105.            $StreamName = $String;
106.          }
107.        }
108.        elsif( $BACKUP_DATA == $Stream{id} )
109.        {
```

```
110.              $StreamName = "<Main Data Stream>";
111.          }
112.          $StreamSize = MakeLargeInt( $Stream{size_low}, $Stream{size_high} );
113.          $iTotalSize += $StreamSize;
114.
115.          printf( "  % 3d) %s (%s bytes)\n",
116.                      ++$iStreamCount,
117.                      $StreamName,
118.                      FormatNumber( $StreamSize )  ) if( "" ne $StreamName );
119.
120.          # Move to next stream...
121.          if( ! BackupSeek( $hFile,
122.                              $Stream{size_low},
123.                              $Stream{size_high},
124.                              $pSeekBytesLow,
125.                              $pSeekBytesHigh,
126.                              $pContext ) )
127.          {
128.            last;
129.          }
130.          $pBytesRead = pack( "L2", 0 );
131.          $pStreamIDStruct = pack( "L5", 0,0,0,0,0 );
132.      }
133.      printf( "        Total file size: %s bytes\n",
134.              FormatNumber( $iTotalSize ) );
135.      # Abort the backup reading. Win32 API claims we MUST do this.
136.      BackupRead( $hFile, undef, 0, 0, 1, 0, $pContext );
137.      CloseHandle( $hFile );
138.  }
139.  print "\n";
140. }
141.
142. sub FormatNumber
143. {
144.    my( $Num ) = @_;
145.    {} while( $Num =~ s/^(-?\d+)(\d{3})/$1,$2/ );
146.    return( $Num );
147. }
148.
149. sub MakeLargeInt
150. {
151.    my( $Low, $High ) = @_;
152.    return( $High * ( 1 + 0xFFFFFFFF ) + $Low );
153. }
```

Discovering File Versions

Many binary files, such as programs and DLLs, can have version information branded into them. Such branding is not required but is incredibly
helpful. When you install software that has updated binary files, it usually
checks the version information on files to make sure it is not overwriting a
file with an older version.

Figure 3.2 shows all the version information on a given binary file. This particular display is useful in determining not only what version the file is, but also what platform the file was created for (NT, Win32, Win16, DOS).

```
C:\>perl filever.pl c:\winnt\system32\AUTPRX32.DLL
1) c:\winnt\system32\AUTPRX32.DLL
        Comments...........January 15, 1997
        CompanyName........Microsoft Corporation
        FileDescription.....Microsoft Remote Automation Proxy for Windows
                           NT(TM) Operating System
        FileVersion........5.00.3715
        InternalName.......AUTPRX32.DLL
        LangID.............0x0409
        Language...........English (United States)
        LegalCopyright......Copyright ¬ Microsoft Corp. 1995.
        LegalTrademarks.....Microsoft« is a registered trademark of
                           Microsoft Corporation. Windows(TM) is a
                           trademark of Microsoft Corporation
        ProductName........Microsoft Remote Automation
        ProductVersion......5.00.3715
        Internal Info:
            DateStamp.......0
            Debug..........0
            FileType.......dll
            FileVersion.....5.0.37.15
            OS.............nt
            Patched........0
            PreRelease......0
            ProductVersion..5.0.37.15
            SpecialBuild....0
```

Figure 3.2 *Displaying version information on a DLL file.*

Example 3.9 accepts any number of parameters, each representing a path to a binary file. The paths can include wildcards and can be UNCs to access version information residing on remote machines.

Example 3.9 *Displaying File Version Information*

```
01. use Win32::AdminMisc;
02.
03. my $iCount = 0;
04. if( 0 == scalar @ARGV )
05. {
06.   Syntax();
07.   exit;
08. }
09.
10. foreach my $File ( @ARGV )
11. {
12.   my %Info;
```

```
13.
14.    $iCount++;
15.    print "$iCount) $File   ";
16.    if( -f $File )
17.    {
18.      if( Win32::AdminMisc::GetFileInfo( $File, \%Info ) )
19.      {
20.        print "\n";
21.        foreach my $Attr ( sort( keys( %Info ) ) )
22.        {
23.          next if( ref $Info{$Attr} );
24.          Display( $Attr, $Info{$Attr} );
25.        }
26.
27.        if( $Info{FileInfo} )
28.        {
29.          Display( "Internal Info:" );
30.          foreach my $Attr ( sort( keys( %{$Info{FileInfo}} ) ) )
31.          {
32.            next if( ref $Info{FileInfo}->{$Attr} );
33.            Display( "  $Attr", $Info{FileInfo}->{$Attr} );
34.          }
35.        }
36.      }
37.      else
38.      {
39.        print "unable to get version.\n";
40.      }
41.    }
42.    else
43.    {
44.      print "unable to locate file.\n";
45.    }
46.
47. }
48.
49. sub Display
50. {
51.    my( $Attr, $Data ) = @_;
52.
53.    print "\t$Attr";
54.    if( "" ne $Data )
55.    {
56.      print "." x ( 20 - length( $Attr ) ), "$Data";
57.    }
58.    print "\n";
59. }
60.
61. sub Syntax
62. {
63.    my( $Line ) = "-" x length( $0 );
64.
65.    print <<EOT;
```

continues ▶

Example 3.9   *continued*

```
66.
67. $0
68. $Line
69. Display version information on a particular file.
70.
71. Syntax:
72.   perl $0 File[, File2[, ... ]]]
73.
74. EOT
75. }
```

Permissions

Win32 security is, in part, based on permissions. Permissions, which are placed on securable objects (such as files, directories, Registry keys, and network shares), designate which users have access to perform actions. The topic of permissions is quite involved and can easily take up an entire book by itself, so I won't go into detail on how they work. For this type of information, you can consult any number of different resources, including http://www.roth.net/perl/perms/security/.

Displaying Permissions

UNIX machines have always been capable of listing who has permissions on files and directories. You get this listing by using the ls command. Win32's equivalent to ls is dir, but it does not display any permission information.

Example 3.10 displays permission information on any path passed in on the command line. This script accepts a number of parameters representing paths to securable objects, as in this example:

```
perl perm.pl c:\temp\*.txt \\server\HKLM\Software\ActiveState \\server2\Temp$
```

This example displays the permissions for all text files in the c:\temp directory as well as the HKEY_LOCAL_MACHINE\Software\ActiveState Registry key on the machine \\server and the Temp$ share on the machine \\server2.

Example 3.10 displays the permissions in the form of an array of letters. Each letter indicates the type of permission that the specified user has been granted. Table 3.2 describes these letters.

Table 3.2   Permissions by Letter

Letter	Permission
R	User is allowed to open the object for reading.
r	User is *not* allowed to open the object for reading.
W	User is allowed to open the file for writing.

Letter	Permission
w	User is *not* allowed to open the file for writing.
D	User is allowed to delete the object.
d	User is *not* allowed to delete the object.
X	User is allowed to execute the object. When this permission is applied to a directory or Registry key, the user is allowed to access its contents.
x	User is *not* allowed to execute the object. When this permission is applied to a directory or Registry key, the user is *not* allowed to access its contents.
P	User is allowed to change the object's permissions.
p	User is *not* allowed to change the object's permissions.
O	User is allowed to take ownership of the object.
o	User is *not* allowed to take ownership of the object.
A	User has been granted *all* permissions. This permission may be set in addition to other flags.
a	User has been denied *all* permissions. This permission may be set in addition to other flags.

Figure 3.3 shows the permissions on a specific directory (c:\temp). The script first prints the name of the owner and group of the object (in this case, a directory). Next, it prints each user and group account that has been granted or denied access to the object. The type of object that the permission relates to follows the account name. In this example, the Administrator account is granted directory permissions, and the Perltest7 account has been granted both directory and file permissions.

The permissions are then displayed. This seven-letter string indicates which permissions are granted, denied, or not addressed. A capital letter indicates that the related permission has been explicitly granted, and a lowercase letter indicates that the permission has been explicitly denied. You can see that Perltest7 has been granted read and execute but denied write permissions on files in the c:\temp directory. Additionally, the account has been denied permission to take ownership of the directory. On the other hand, the Administrator account has been granted all permissions. The letter A means that the account has been granted *all* permissions. This means that there was no need to explicitly grant the read, write, execute, and delete permissions. Notice that the Joel account has been granted all access (just like the Administrator); however, the delete permission has been explicitly denied. Because explicitly denied access always overrides allowed access, the user has full control over the directory, except that he cannot delete it.

```
C:\>perl perm.pl c:\temp

Permissions for 'c:\temp':
  Owner: BUILTIN\Administrators
  Group: BUILTIN\Domain Admins
          Administrator (Directory)   RWXD--A
                   Joel (Directory)   RWXd--A
              Perltest7 (Directory)   -----o-
              Perltest7 (File)        RwX----
```

Figure 3.3   *Displaying permissions on a directory.*

Notes on Files and Directories

For files and directory paths, wildcards are acceptable; however, for Registry keys, they are not.

You can specify files and directories on remote machines by using a UNC. However, if you're specifying a UNC's root directory, make sure that you terminate the path with a backslash like this:

```
\\server\share\
```

If you do not append the backslash, the permissions of the network share itself are referenced.

Notes on Shared Directories and Printers

Shared directory and printer pathnames must *not* end with a backslash. If you specify a shared directory path with an ending backslash, the permissions for the shared directory's root directory are displayed, not the permissions for the network share itself. An attempt to reference a printer with an ending backslash simply fails.

Also, note that shared directories have neither an owner nor a group.

Notes on Registry Keys

You specify Registry keys with a full Registry key path like this:

```
HKEY_LOCAL_MACHINE\Software
```

You can abbreviate the Registry root by shortening it like this:

```
HKLM\Software
```

You also can specify Registry keys on remote machines by prepending the machine name like this:

```
\\server\HKEY_LOCAL_MACHINE\Software
```

or

```
\\server\HKLM\Software
```

> ### Note
>
> *When accessing remote registries, only the* HKEY_USERS *and* HKEY_LOCAL_MACHINE
> *hives are accessible.* ◆

Example 3.10   *Displaying Permission Information*

```
01. use Win32::Perms;
02.
03. # The %PERM hash maps a permission type to its position in the
04. # permission string array. Notice that there is no 0 position
05. # since that is reserved for unhandled permission types (and
06. # we won't print it).
07. %PERM = (
08.   R   =>  1,
09.   W   =>  2,
10.   X   =>  3,
11.   D   =>  4,
12.   P   =>  5,
13.   O   =>  6,
14.   A   =>  7,
15. );
16.
17. %MAP = (
18.   'FILE_READ_DATA'    => 'R',
19.   'GENERIC_READ'      => 'R',
20.   'KEY_READ'          => 'R',
21.   'DIR_READ'          => 'R',
22.
23.   'FILE_WRITE_DATA'   => 'W',
24.   'KEY_WRITE'         => 'W',
25.   'GENERIC_WRITE'     => 'W',
26.   'FILE_APPEND_DATA'  => 'W',
27.   'DIR_ADD_SUBDIR'    => 'W',
28.   'DIR_ADD_FILE'      => 'W',
29.
30.   'DELETE'            => 'D',
31.   'FILE_DELETE_CHILD' => 'D',
32.
33.   'FILE_EXECUTE'      => 'X',
34.   'FILE_TRAVERSE'     => 'X',
35.   'GENERIC_EXECUTE'   => 'X',
36.   'DIR_TRAVERSE'      => 'X',
37.   'DIR_EXECUTE'       => 'X',
38.
39.   'CHANGE_PERMISSION' => 'P',
40.
41.   'TAKE_OWNERSHIP'    => 'O',
42.
43.   'FILE_ALL_ACCESS'   => 'A',
44.   'GENERIC_ALL'       => 'A',
45.   'DIR_ALL_ACCESS'    => 'A',
```

continues ▶

Example 3.10 *continued*

```
46.    'STANDARD_RIGHTS_ALL' => 'A',
47. );
48.
49. push( @ARGV, "*.*" ) unless( scalar @ARGV );
50. foreach my $Mask ( @ARGV )
51. {
52.    my( @List ) = glob( $Mask );
53.    if( ! scalar @List )
54.    {
55.      push( @List, $Mask );
56.    }
57.    foreach my $Path ( @List )
58.    {
59.      print "\nPermissions for '$Path':\n";
60.      ReportPerms( $Path );
61.      print "\n\n";
62.    }
63. }
64.
65. sub ReportPerms
66. {
67.    my( $Path ) = @_;
68.    my( $Acct, @List );
69.    my( $Perm ) = new Win32::Perms( $Path );
70.    my( %PermList ) = ();
71.    my( $MaxAcctLength ) = 1;
72.
73.    if( ! $Perm )
74.    {
75.        print "Can not obtain permissions for '$Path'\n";
76.        return;
77.    };
78.
79.    printf( "  Owner: %s\n  Group: %s\n",
80.            $Perm->Owner(),
81.            $Perm->Group() );
82.    $Perm->Dump( \@List );
83.    foreach $Acct ( @List )
84.    {
85.      my( $PermMask );
86.      my( $Mask, @M, @F );
87.      my( $DaclType );
88.      my $bAllowAccess = ( "Deny" ne $Acct->{Access} );
89.      my $String;
90.      my $Account;
91.
92.      next if( $Acct->{Entry} ne "DACL" );
93.
94.      if( "" eq $Acct->{Account} )
95.      {
96.        $Account = $Acct->{SID};
97.      }
98.      else
99.      {
```

```
100.        $Account = "$Acct->{Domain}\\" if( "" ne $Acct->{Domain} );
101.        $Account .= $Acct->{Account};
102.      }
103.      if( length( $Account ) > $MaxAcctLength )
104.      {
105.        $MaxAcctLength = length( $Account )
106.      }
107.      $iTotal++;
108.      DecodeMask( $Acct, \@M, \@F );
109.      foreach $Mask ( @M )
110.      {
111.        $PermMask |= 2**$PERM{ $MAP{$Mask} };
112.      }
113.      $DaclType = $Acct->{ObjectName};
114.      if( 2 == $Acct->{ObjectType} )
115.      {
116.        # We have either a file or directory. Therefore we need to
117.        # figure out if this DACL represents an object (file) or
118.        # a container (dir)...
119.        if( $Acct->{Flag} & DIR )
120.        {
121.          $DaclType = "Directory";
122.        }
123.        else
124.        {
125.          $DaclType = "File";
126.        }
127.      }
128.      if( ! defined $PermList{$Account}->{$DaclType} )
129.      {
130.        # Create the permission string array. The first element in the
131.        # array must be blank since all unhandled permissions will default
132.        # to that position (and we won't print it).
133.        my $TempHash = [
134.                         " ",
135.                         split( //, "-" x scalar( keys( %PERM ) ) )
136.                       ];
137.        $PermList{$Account}->{$DaclType} = $TempHash;
138.
139.      }
140.      foreach $Mask ( keys( %PERM ) )
141.      {
142.        if( $PermMask & 2**$PERM{$Mask} )
143.        {
144.          $String = $PermList{$Account}->{$DaclType};
145.          # If we already have a denied permission then skip this step
146.          # since denied access overrides any explicitly allowed access
147.          if( $String->[$PERM{$Mask}] !~ /[a-z]/ )
148.          {
149.            my $TempMask = $Mask;
150.            $TempMask = lc $Mask if( 0 == $bAllowAccess );
151.            $String->[$PERM{$Mask}] = $TempMask ;
152.          }
153.        }
```

continues ▶

Example 3.10 *continued*

```
154.    }
155.  }
156.
157.  if( ! $iTotal )
158.  {
159.    # There are no DACL entries therefore...
160.    print "\t Everyone has full permissions.\n";
161.  }
162.  else
163.  {
164.    foreach my $Permission ( sort( keys( %PermList ) ) )
165.    {
166.      foreach my $DaclType ( sort( keys( %{$PermList{$Permission}} ) ) )
167.      {
168.        my $String = $PermList{$Permission}->{$DaclType};
169.        printf( "  % " . $MaxAcctLength . "s % -11s %s\n",
170.                $Permission,
171.                "($DaclType)",
172.                join( '', @$String ) );
173.      }
174.    }
175.  }
176. }
```

Displaying Verbose Permissions

Example 3.10 in the "Displaying Permissions" section displays the permissions for various securable objects, such as files and directories. That particular script distills the complex world of permissions into a few very basic and simple permission sets. Using that script, you can easily get an idea of which users have which permissions. However, to display the permissions in a simple way, many assumptions and interpretations must be made, which can leave out details that may be critical for administrators to successfully maintain true security.

Example 3.11 displays the full set of permissions that an object has. No interpretations are made, and all permissions, flags, and types are displayed in their full, confusing glory. If you're not familiar with the different permissions that can be set on an object, the display may be more than just confusing.

Figure 3.4 shows the output this script produces. To be sure, it is not for the faint at heart. This particular example is a permission dump for the same c:\temp directory shown in Figure 3.3. Unlike Example 3.10, this script displays *all* the permission information. Some of these permissions may not make much sense, but they are documented in the Win32 API SDK (http://msdn.microsoft.com/).

```
C:\>perl vperm.pl c:\temp

Permissions for 'c:\temp':
  Owner: BUILTIN\Administrators
  Group: BUILTIN\Domain Admins
            Account              Permissions              Flags
  .............................  ......................  .......................

  CREATOR OWNER                  DELETE                  INHERIT_ONLY_ACE
  Deny Access                                            OBJECT_INHERIT_ACE
  (Directory)                                            CONTAINER_INHERIT_ACE


  ROTH.NET\Perltest7             FILE_WRITE_DATA         INHERIT_ONLY_ACE
  Deny Access                    FILE_APPEND_DATA        OBJECT_INHERIT_ACE
  (File)                         FILE_WRITE_EA
                                 FILE_WRITE_ATTRIBUTES

  ROTH.NET\Perltest7             DIR_ADD_SUBDIR          OBJECT_INHERIT_ACE
  Deny Access                    TAKE_OWNERSHIP          CONTAINER_INHERIT_ACE
  (Directory)                    CHANGE_PERMISSION


  CREATOR OWNER                  DIR_READ                INHERIT_ONLY_ACE
  Allow Access                   DIR_ADD_FILE            OBJECT_INHERIT_ACE
  (Directory)                    DIR_ADD_SUBDIR          CONTAINER_INHERIT_ACE
                                 DIR_READ_EATTRIB
                                 DIR_WRITE_EATTRIB
                                 DIR_EXECUTE
                                 DIR_DEL_SUBDIR
                                 DIR_READ_ATTRIB
                                 DIR_WRITE_ATTRIB
                                 READ_CONTROL
                                 TAKE_OWNERSHIP

  ROTH.NET\Administrator         DIR_READ                OBJECT_INHERIT_ACE
  Allow Access                   DIR_ADD_FILE            CONTAINER_INHERIT_ACE
  (Directory)                    DIR_ADD_SUBDIR
                                 DIR_READ_EATTRIB
                                 DIR_WRITE_EATTRIB
                                 DIR_EXECUTE
                                 DIR_DEL_SUBDIR
                                 DIR_READ_ATTRIB
                                 DIR_WRITE_ATTRIB
                                 STANDARD_RIGHTS_ALL

  ROTH.NET\Perltest7             FILE_READ_DATA          INHERIT_ONLY_ACE
  Allow Access                   FILE_READ_EA            OBJECT_INHERIT_ACE
  (File)                         FILE_EXECUTE
                                 FILE_READ_ATTRIBUTES
                                 READ_CONTROL
                                 SYNCHRONIZE
```

Figure 3.4   *The true permissions placed on a file.*

Example 3.11 accepts any number of paths on the command line. Each path can contain wildcards. Additionally, an optional /F switch is accepted; it reports the so-called *friendly* permissions. Most administrators are familiar with these permissions, such as FULL_CONTROL, CHANGE, and READ. Such friendly permissions are, however, far from complete and do not necessarily explain the true nature of the permissions. For example, no friendly permission describes that a file has both READ and DELETE access.

Refer to the "Displaying Permissions" section to learn how to address different paths.

Example 3.11 *Displaying the Full Details of an Object's Permissions*

```
01. use Getopt::Long;
02. use Win32::Perms;
03.
04. # Turn off aggressive domain controller lookups
05. Win32::Perms::LookupDC( 0 );
06. Configure( \%Config );
07. if( $Config{help} )
08. {
09.     Syntax();
10.     exit();
11. }
12.
13. foreach my $Mask ( @{$Config{masks}} )
14. {
15.     my( @List ) = glob( $Mask );
16.     if( ! scalar @List )
17.     {
18.         push( @List, $Mask );
19.     }
20.     foreach $Path ( @List )
21.     {
22.         print "\nPermissions for '$Path':\n";
23.         ReportPerms( $Path );
24.         print "\n\n";
25.     }
26. }
27.
28. sub ReportPerms
29. {
30.   my( $Path ) = @_;
31.   my( $Acct, @List );
32.   my( $Perm ) = new Win32::Perms( $Path );
33.
34.   if( ! $Perm )
35.   {
36.     print "Can not obtain permissions for '$Path'\n";
37.     return;
38.   };
39.
```

```
40.   printf( "  Owner: %s\n  Group: %s\n", $Perm->Owner(), $Perm->Group() );
41.   $Perm->Dump( \@List );
42.   $~ = PermissionHeader;
43.   write;
44.   foreach $Acct ( @List )
45.   {
46.     my( $PermMask );
47.     my( @String ) = split( //, "-" x scalar( keys( %PERM ) ) );
48.     my( $Mask, @Permissions, @Friendly );
49.     local $DaclType;
50.     local $Access = $Acct->{Access};
51.     local $Account;
52.
53.     $~ = Permission;
54.
55.     next if( $Acct->{Entry} ne "DACL" );
56.     $iTotal++;
57.
58.     DecodeMask( $Acct, \@Permissions, \@Friendly );
59.     DecodeFlag( $Acct, \@Flag );
60.     # Pad each flag and permission with spaces so that they correctly
61.     # break into one permission/flag per line when printed. This is a
62.     # trick when working with write/formats
63.     $Flags = join( " " x 10 . "\n", @Flag );
64.     $Perms = join( " " x 10 . "\n",
65.                     ( $Config{friendly} )? @Friendly : @Permissions );
66.     if( "" eq $Acct->{Account} )
67.     {
68.       $Account = $Acct->{SID};
69.     }
70.     else
71.     {
72.       $Account = "$Acct->{Domain}\\" if( "" ne $Acct->{Domain} );
73.       $Account .= $Acct->{Account};
74.     }
75.     $DaclType = $Acct->{ObjectName};
76.     if( 2 == $Acct->{ObjectType} )
77.     {
78.       # We have either a file or directory. Therefore we need to
79.       # figure out if this DACL represents an object (file) or
80.       # a container (dir)...
81.       if( $Acct->{Flag} & DIR )
82.       {
83.         $DaclType = "Directory";
84.       }
85.       else
86.       {
87.         $DaclType = "File";
88.       }
89.     }
90.     write;
91.     print "\n";
92.   }
```

continues ▶

Example 3.11 *continued*

```
93.
94.   if( ! $iTotal )
95.   {
96.     print "\t Everyone has full permissions.\n";
97.   }
98. }
99.
100. sub Configure
101. {
102.   my( $Config ) = @_;
103.   my $Result;
104.
105.   Getopt::Long::Configure( "prefix_pattern=(-|\/)" );
106.   $Result = GetOptions( $Config,
107.                         qw(
108.                            friendly|f
109.                            help|?|h
110.                         )
111.   );
112.   push( @{$Config->{masks}}, @ARGV );
113.   $Config->{help} = 1 unless( $Result &&  scalar @{$Config->{masks}} );
114. }
115.
116. sub Syntax
117. {
118.   my( $Script ) = ( $0 =~ /([^\\\/]*?)$/ );
119.   my( $Line ) = "-" x length( $Script );
120.
121.   print <<EOT;
122.
123. $Script
124. $Line
125. Displays verbose permissions set on securable objects.
126.
127. Syntax:
128.    perl $Script [-f] Path [ Path2 ... ]
129.         -f..........Show "friendly" permissions.
130.         Path........The path to a securable object.
131.                     This path can consist of ? and * wildcards.
132.
133. EOT
134. }
135.
136. format PermissionHeader =
137. @||||||||||||||||||||||||||| @||||||||||||||||||||| @|||||||||||||||||||||||
138. "Account",               "Permissions",       "Flags"
139. ----------------------   ---------------------   ---------------------
140. .
141.
142. format Permission =
143. ^<<<<<<<<<<<<<<<<<<<<<<<<< ^<<<<<<<<<<<<<<<<<<<<<< ^<<<<<<<<<<<<<<<<<<<<<<<
```

```
144. $Account,                       $Perms,                    $Flags
145. ^<<<<<<<<<<<<<<<<<<<<<<<< ^<<<<<<<<<<<<<<<<<<<<<< ^<<<<<<<<<<<<<<<<<<<<<<<
146. $Account,                       $Perms,                    $Flags
147. @<<<<<<<<<<<<<<           ^<<<<<<<<<<<<<<<<<<<<<< ^<<<<<<<<<<<<<<<<<<<<<<<
148. "$Access Access",               $Perms,                    $Flags
149. @<<<<<<<<<<<<<<           ^<<<<<<<<<<<<<<<<<<<<<< ^<<<<<<<<<<<<<<<<<<<<<<<
150. "($DaclType)",                  $Perms,                    $Flags
151. ~                        ^<<<<<<<<<<<<<<<<<<<<<< ^<<<<<<<<<<<<<<<<<<<<<<<
152.                                 $Perms,                    $Flags
153. ~                        ^<<<<<<<<<<<<<<<<<<<<<< ^<<<<<<<<<<<<<<<<<<<<<<<
154.                                 $Perms,                    $Flags
155. ~                        ^<<<<<<<<<<<<<<<<<<<<<< ^<<<<<<<<<<<<<<<<<<<<<<<
156.                                 $Perms,                    $Flags
157. ~                        ^<<<<<<<<<<<<<<<<<<<<<< ^<<<<<<<<<<<<<<<<<<<<<<<
158.                                 $Perms,                    $Flags
159. ~                        ^<<<<<<<<<<<<<<<<<<<<<< ^<<<<<<<<<<<<<<<<<<<<<<<
160.                                 $Perms,                    $Flags
161. ~                        ^<<<<<<<<<<<<<<<<<<<<<< ^<<<<<<<<<<<<<<<<<<<<<<<
162.                                 $Perms,                    $Flags
163. ~                        ^<<<<<<<<<<<<<<<<<<<<<< ^<<<<<<<<<<<<<<<<<<<<<<<
164.                                 $Perms,                    $Flags
165. ~                        ^<<<<<<<<<<<<<<<<<<<<<< ^<<<<<<<<<<<<<<<<<<<<<<<
166.                                 $Perms,                    $Flags
167. .
```

Ownership

Almost all securable objects have an *owner*. The owner is an account (either a user or group account) that has ultimate access over the file. The owner of an object can never be denied access to it. He can read, write, delete, and modify permissions, as well as do anything else that is possible.

To discover who is the owner of a particular object (file, directory, or Registry key), you need to locate the security information for the object. For files and directories, you typically use the Explorer program to select the object's properties and then select the Security tab on the displayed property page. For a Registry key, you display the key's permission information from within the REGEDT32.EXE program.

Ownership of an object was designed such that it could only be taken, not given. For example, an administrator could become the owner of a file (take ownership) so that she could usurp permissions placed on the file. However, because she could not assign ownership to another user (give ownership), it would be obvious as to who had bypassed security because the administrator would remain the owner until someone else took owner-ship. Because an administrator must grant a user account with the privilege to take ownership (the SE_TAKE_OWNERSHIP_NAME privilege to be precise), this paradigm was deemed safe.

It did not take long, however, for programmers to discover that backup software somehow had to be able to restore a file with its original owner intact. That meant that there was a way to *give* ownership! The technique for doing so lies in the ability for a process to act like backup software. This, of course, requires that the user has a special privilege (SE_RESTORE_NAME).

All this leads to Example 3.12, which enables you not only to discover who is the owner for a given object but also to change the object's owner (provided that you have permission to do so). Any user can use this script to view who is the owner, but a user requires the SE_RESTORE_NAME privilege to change the ownership of a secured object.

This script accepts a number of parameters representing paths to securable objects. To set the owner on the specified objects, you pass in an -s switch followed by the account name of the new owner. Consider these two examples:

```
perl owner.pl c:\temp\*.txt \\server\HKLM\Software\ActiveState
```

```
perl owner.pl -s JOEL c:\temp\*.txt \\server\HKLM\Software\ActiveState
```

The first example displays the owner for all text files in the c:\temp directory as well as the HKEY_LOCAL_MACHINE\Software\ActiveState Registry key on the machine \\server.

The second example is essentially the same as the first example, except that it first sets all the objects' owners to Joel and then displays who is the owner. If the user running the script has the appropriate privileges, Joel is displayed as the new owner for each object.

Tip

When referring to an account name, you can pass in the name of an account and have Win32 decide if the account is a domain or local machine account. Alternatively, you can explicitly specify what domain or machine the account belongs to.

To specify a domain account, refer to it by specifying the domain followed by a backslash and account name as in

```
MyDomain\joel
"Some Domain\Domain Admins"
```

To specify a particular machine account, pass in the server name beginning with double backslashes. Then append a backslash and account name as in

```
\\Server1\joel
"\\Server1\Domain Admins"  ◆
```

Refer to the notes in the "Displaying Permissions" section for information regarding how to address different paths.

Example 3.12   *Retrieving and Setting the Owner of a Securable Object*

```perl
01. use Getopt::Long;
02. use Win32::Perms;
03.
04. # Turn off intense domain lookups
05. Win32::Perms::LookupDC( 0 );
06.
07. Configure( \%Config );
08. if( $Config{help} )
09. {
10.   Syntax();
11.   exit();
12. }
13.
14. $~ = OwnerHeader;
15. write;
16. $~ = Owner;
17. foreach $Mask ( @{$Config{masks}} )
18. {
19.   my( @List ) = glob( $Mask );
20.   if( ! scalar @List )
21.   {
22.     push( @List, $Mask );
23.   }
24.   foreach $Path ( @List )
25.   {
26.     my $Perm;
27.
28.     if( ! ( $Perm = new Win32::Perms( $Path ) ) )
29.     {
30.       $Owner = "Can't get permissions.\n";
31.     }
32.     else
33.     {
34.       if( "" ne $Config{owner} )
35.       {
36.         $Perm->Owner( $Config{owner} );
37.         $Perm->Set();
38.       }
39.       $Owner = $Perm->Owner();
40.     }
41.     write;
42.   }
43. }
44.
45. sub Configure
46. {
47.   my( $Config ) = @_;
48.   my $Result;
```

continues ▶

Example 3.12   *continued*

```
49.
50.    Getopt::Long::Configure( "prefix_pattern=(-|\/)" );
51.    $Result = GetOptions( $Config,
52.                          qw(
53.                             owner|o|s=s
54.                             help|?|h
55.                             )
56.    );
57.    push( @{$Config->{masks}}, @ARGV );
58.    $Config->{help} = 1 unless( $Result &&  scalar @{$Config->{masks}} );
59. }
60.
61. sub Syntax
62. {
63.    my( $Script ) = ( $0 =~ /([^\\\/]*?)$/ );
64.    my( $Line ) = "-" x length( $Script );
65.
66.    print <<EOT;
67.
68. $Script
69. $Line
70. Displays (and sets) the owner of securable objects.
71.
72. Syntax:
73.     perl $Script [-s Account] Path [ Path2 ... ]
74.         -s Account..Set the owner to the specified account.
75.         Path........The path to a securable object.
76.                     This path can consist of ? and * wildcards.
77.
78. EOT
79. }
80.
81. format OwnerHeader =
82. @<<<<<<<<<<<<<<<<<<<<<<<<<<<<<<<<< @<<<<<<<<<<<<<<<<<<<<<<<<<<<<<
83. "Path", "Owner"
84. --------------------------------- -----------------------------
85. .
86.
87. format Owner =
88. @<<<<<<<<<<<<<<<<<<<<<<<<<<<<<<<<< @<<<<<<<<<<<<<<<<<<<<<<<<<<<<<
89. $Path, $Owner
90. .
```

DCOM Configurations

Most users never know that their programs communicate with each other using COM. They paste spreadsheets inside their word processing documents without ever knowing that this capability is made possible by *object linking and embedding* (OLE) technology, which is based on COM.

However, you need to be vigilant regarding security because recent versions of Windows have enabled Distributed COM (DCOM). This technology enables one computer to communicate with a program running on another machine. This capability is ideal for administration purposes but potentially dangerous if renegade hackers break into a machine.

Windows provides the DCOMCNFG.EXE utility, which is used to configure DCOM security. This tool enables you to select who has access to a computer via DCOM. It has two problems, though: it is GUI-based, and it runs only on a local machine.

Because the program is GUI-based, getting a quick overview of how a machine's DCOM is configured is difficult. Instead, you must move from tab to tab clicking on buttons. Doing so is not only annoying but a time burden as well.

Because the utility reports only the DCOM configuration for the machine it is running on, its use is quite limited. This limitation requires that you walk to each server, log on, and then run the utility if you want to check your server farm.

Example 3.13 displays a machine's DCOM configuration quickly and without any GUI. You can also check a remote machine's DCOM configuration by passing in the machine's name when running the script.

Note

Every machine that is a member of a domain has a machine account (similar to user account) in the domain. When the machine is booted up and comes online, it logs into the domain using the machine account and a password. When examining a machine's DCOM configuration, you might find references to user, group, and machine accounts. ◆

Figure 3.5 shows the output of Example 3.13. Notice that the Guest account has been explicitly denied in all the security-related configurations. The script shows whether access was granted or denied.

```
C:\>perl dcom.pl \\server1

DCOM settings for \\Server1:
  DCOM is enabled.
  COM Internet Services are enabled.

  The following accounts are allowed to launch COM applications:
    Allow  NT AUTHORITY\SYSTEM
    Allow  NT AUTHORITY\INTERACTIVE
    Deny   SERVER1\Guest
    Allow  BUILTIN\Administrators
```

continues ▶

```
        Allow  SERVER1\IUSR_SERVER1
        Allow  SERVER1\IWAM_SERVER1

    Accounts with access to this machine via DCOM:
        Allow  NT AUTHORITY\SYSTEM
        Allow  NT AUTHORITY\INTERACTIVE
        Deny   SERVER1\Guest
        Allow  BUILTIN\Administrators
        Allow  SERVER1\IUSR_SERVER1
        Allow  SERVER1\IWAM_SERVER1
        Allow  BUILTIN\Administrators

    Accounts with access to COM/OLE configuration:
        Allow  BUILTIN\Administrators
        Allow  CREATOR OWNER
        Deny   SERVER1\Guest
        Allow  Everyone
        Allow  BUILTIN\Power Users
        Allow  NT AUTHORITY\SYSTEM
        Allow  BUILTIN\Users

    The following protocols are permitted for use with DCOM:
        ncacn_ip_tcp
        ncacn_spx
        ncacn_nb_nb
        ncacn_nb_ipx
```

Figure 3.5   *Examining a DCOM configuration.*

Example 3.13   *Displaying DCOM Configurations*

```perl
01. use Win32::Registry;
02. use Win32::Perms;
03.
04. # Prevent aggressive domain controller lookups
05. Win32::Perms::LookupDC( 0 );
06. %PATH = (
07.     ole      => 'SOFTWARE\Microsoft\Ole',
08.     rpc      => 'SOFTWARE\Microsoft\RPC',
09. );
10.
11. $Perm = new Win32::Perms() || die "Cannot create Permissions object";
12. if( scalar @ARGV )
13. {
14.     $Machine = "\\\\" . shift @ARGV;
15. }
16. else
17. {
18.     $Machine = "\\\\" . Win32::NodeName();
19. }
20. $Machine =~ s/^\\+/\\\\/;
21. $HKEY_LOCAL_MACHINE->Connect( $Machine, $Root )
```

```
22.     || die "Can not connect";
23. print "\nDCOM settings for $Machine:\n";
24. if( $Root->Open( $PATH{ole}, $Key ) )
25. {
26.   my( $Flag, $Type, $Value, $Sd );
27.
28.   undef $Value;
29.   $Key->QueryValueEx( "EnableDCOM", $Type, $Value );
30.   print "  DCOM is ", ( "y" eq lc $Value )? "":"not ", "enabled.\n";
31.
32.   $Key->QueryValueEx( "EnableDCOMHTTP", $Type, $Value );
33.   print "  COM Internet Services are ",
34.         ( "y" eq lc $Value )? "":"not ", "enabled.\n";
35.
36.   print "\n  The following accounts are allowed to "
37.         . "launch COM applications:\n";
38.   if( $Key->QueryValueEx( "DefaultLaunchPermission", $Type, $Sd ) )
39.   {
40.     DisplayPerms( $Sd ) if( REG_BINARY == $Type );
41.   }
42.
43.   print "\n  Accounts with access to this machine via DCOM:\n";
44.   if( $Key->QueryValueEx( "DefaultAccessPermission", $Type, $Sd ) )
45.   {
46.     DisplayPerms( $Sd ) if( REG_BINARY == $Type );
47.   }
48.
49.   print "\n  Accounts with access to COM/OLE configuration:\n";
50.   DisplayPerms( "$Machine\\HKEY_CLASSES_ROOT" );
51.
52.   print "\n  The following protocols are permitted "
53.         . "for use with DCOM:\n";
54.   if( $Root->Open( $PATH{rpc}, $Key2 ) )
55.   {
56.     my $MString;
57.     if( $Key2->QueryValueEx( "DCOM Protocols", $Type, $MString ) )
58.     {
59.       foreach my $Protocol ( split( "\x00", $MString ) )
60.       {
61.         print "    $Protocol\n";
62.       }
63.     }
64.     $Key2->Close();
65.   }
66.   $Key->Close();
67. }
68. $Root->Close();
69.
70. sub DisplayPerms
71. {
72.   my( $Sd ) = @_;
73.   my @List;
74.
```

continues ▶

Example 3.13   *continued*

```
75.   $Perm->Import( $Sd );
76.   $Perm->Dump( \@List );
77.
78.   foreach my $Ace ( @List )
79.   {
80.     my $Account;
81.     if( "" ne $Ace->{Account} )
82.     {
83.       $Account = "$Ace->{Domain}\\" if( "" ne $Ace->{Domain} );
84.       $Account .= $Ace->{Account};
85.     }
86.     else
87.     {
88.       $Account = $Ace->{SID};
89.     }
90.
91.     # Object Type of 1 represents a DACL
92.     next if( 1 != $Ace->{ObjectType} );
93.
94.     printf( "    %-6s %-30s\n", $Ace->{Access}, $Account );
95.   }
96.   return;
97. }
```

Registry

Win32 platforms make use of the Registry to store configuration information. Programs and system services alike populate Registry keys with values that represent various settings of some sort. Information on services and system drivers are stored along with details on how they are loaded and where their files are located. The Registry is where you can find COM component configurations, TCP settings, and auto logon settings, just to name a few.

Regfind

The Registry is a vast wasteland of configuration information. It's so vast, in fact, that locating anything held therein can be quite daunting. Because the Registry is a database of configuration data, you would hope that you could search it and efficiently locate necessary tidbits of information. However, you would be disappointed to learn that this is not possible. The Win32 API does not have any mechanism that enables such searching. Considering that this database, even on a notebook, can grow several tens of megabytes in size, locating data is comparable to finding a needle in a haystack.

The lack of such search functionality is probably due, in part, to the lack of any real need. After all, the repository of information was designed for processes to hold configuration data—what used to be held in .INI files. The presumption here is that software would know where it stored data in the Registry, so it would never need to look for it. This presumption, however, is based on the notion that software behaves itself.

All too often when you uninstall software, it leaves, intact, traces of itself, such as COM registration information. Under these circumstances, searching the Registry for a given GUID or string can be quite valuable. To give another, but altogether pertinent, example, often, for some odd reason, some software moves a window to a location just off of the screen. Such repositioning of a window may occur if you are using dual monitors but have to temporarily resort to using only one. This could also occur if, from time to time, you use a higher resolution display. Either way, every time the application is run, the window the user interacts with is located where it cannot be seen. Because most users do not know where, say, Notepad may locate its configuration store in the Registry, a search becomes quite important.

Example 3.14 performs such searches. When you pass in Registry paths and search strings, the script scans the Registry and displays its findings as it proceeds. You can pass in multiple paths and multiple search strings. All you need to do is specify each path with a -p switch—as many of them as necessary. Then pass in as many strings as required.

You can locate each path on a remote machine by prepending the machine name to the path. You can also abbreviate the Registry root keys as in Table 3.3.

Table 3.3   Registry Roots and Their Abbreviations

Registry Root	Abbreviation
HKEY_LOCAL_MACHINE	HKLM
HKEY_CURRENT_USER	HKCR
HKEY_CLASSES_ROOT	HKCU
HKEY_USERS	HKU
HKEY_CURRENT_CONFIG	HKCC

Consider this example:

```
perl regfind.pl -p HKEY_LOCAL_MACHINE\Software
-p \\server1\HKLM\Software winamp "windows media"
```

This particular instance searches the HKEY_LOCAL_MACHINE\Software Registry paths on the current machine as well as on \\Server1. The Registry is searched for the string winamp or "windows media". The search is not case sensitive, so WinAmp also triggers a match. The search traverses the entire specified Registry paths. Therefore, it could take some time to complete.

Output is printed to STDOUT, but information about how the search is proceeding is printed to STDERR. This way, you can redirect output to a file while still observing the findings of the search.

Example 3.14   *Locating Strings in the Registry*

```
01. use Getopt::Long;
02. use Win32::Registry;
03.
04. %HIVE_LIST = (
05.   HKEY_LOCAL_MACHINE  =>  $HKEY_LOCAL_MACHINE,
06.   HKEY_CURRENT_USER   =>  $HKEY_CURRENT_USER,
07.   HKEY_CLASSES_ROOT   =>  $HKEY_CLASSES_ROOT,
08.   HKEY_USERS          =>  $HKEY_USERS,
09.   HKEY_CURRENT_CONFIG =>  $HKEY_CURRENT_CONFIG,
10. );
11. %HIVE_LIST_ABBR = (
12.   HKLM       =>  $HKEY_LOCAL_MACHINE,
13.   HKCU       =>  $HKEY_CURRENT_USER,
14.   HKCR       =>  $HKEY_CLASSES_ROOT,
15.   HKU        =>  $HKEY_USERS,
16.   HKCC       =>  $HKEY_CURRENT_CONFIG,
17. );
18. foreach my $Key ( keys( %HIVE_LIST ) )
19. {
20.   $HIVE_LIST_REVERSE{$HIVE_LIST{$Key}} = $Key;
21. }
22. $iTotalKeys = $iTotalMatch = 0;
23. Configure( \%Config );
24. if( $Config{help} )
25. {
26.   Syntax();
27.   exit();
28. }
29.
30. while( my $Path = shift @{$Config{paths}} )
31. {
32.   my( $Temp, $Machine, $Hive ) = ( $Path =~ /^((\\\\.*?)\\)?(.*)/ );
33.   my( $Hive, $Temp2, $Path ) = ( $Hive =~ /^([^\\]*)(\\(.*))?/ );
34.   my $Root = OpenHive( $Hive, $Machine );
35.   if( 0 != $Root )
36.   {
37.     my @Keys;
38.     my @List;
39.
40.     if( "" ne $Machine )
41.     {
42.       $Hive = "$Machine\\$Hive";
```

```
43.      }
44.
45.      if( $Root->Open( $Path, $Key ) )
46.      {
47.        $Path = "\\$Path" if( "" ne $Path );
48.        print "Scanning $Hive$Path\n";
49.        ProcessKey( $Key, "$Hive$Path", $KeyName );
50.      }
51.      else
52.      {
53.        print "Unable to open $Hive\\$Path\n";
54.      }
55.      $Root->Close();
56.    }
57.    else
58.    {
59.        # Can not connect.
60.    }
61. }
62.
63. print STDERR "\n------------------\n";
64. print STDERR "Total values checked: $iTotalKeys\n";
65. print STDERR "Total values matching criteria: $iTotalMatch\n";
66.
67. sub OpenHive
68. {
69.    my( $Hive, $Machine ) = @_;
70.    my $Root;
71.    my $HiveKey = $HIVE_LIST_ABBR{uc $Hive};
72.
73.    if( "Win32::Registry" ne ref $HiveKey )
74.    {
75.      $HiveKey = $HIVE_LIST{uc $Hive}
76.    }
77.
78.    if( "" ne $Machine )
79.    {
80.      if( ! $HiveKey->Connect( $Machine, $Root ) )
81.      {
82.        print STDERR "Could not connect to '$Machine'\n";
83.        $Root = 0;
84.      }
85.    }
86.    else
87.    {
88.      $Root = $HiveKey;
89.    }
90.    return( $Root );
91. }
92.
93. sub ProcessKey
94. {
95.    my( $Key, $Path, $KeyName ) = @_;
```

continues ▶

Example 3.14 *continued*

```
96.    my $TempKey;
97.
98.    if( $Key->Open( $KeyName, $TempKey ) )
99.    {
100.      my( $SubKey, $Value, @Keys, %Values, $iCount );
101.      my $ThisPath = $Path;
102.      $ThisPath .= "\\$KeyName" if( "" ne $KeyName );
103.      if( $TempKey->GetValues( \%Values ) )
104.      {
105.        foreach my $Value ( sort( keys( %Values ) ) )
106.        {
107.          my( $Name, $Type, $Data ) = @{$Values{$Value}};
108.          $iTotalKeys++;
109.          printf( STDERR "% 10s keys checked; %s matched.\r",
110.                         FormatNumber( $iTotalKeys ),
111.                         FormatNumber( $iTotalMatch ) );
112.          foreach my $Target ( @{$Config{target}} )
113.          {
114.            if( "$Name\x00$Data" =~ /$Target->{find}/i )
115.            {
116.              if( REG_BINARY == $Type )
117.              {
118.                $Data = "<Binary Data>";
119.              }
120.              print STDERR " " x 60, "\r";
121.              printf( STDOUT "% d) %s\\%s: (%s) '%s'\n",
122.                             ++$iTotalMatch,
123.                             $ThisPath,
124.                             $Value,
125.                             ValueType( $Type ),
126.                             $Data );
127.            }
128.          }
129.        }
130.      }
131.      $TempKey->GetKeys( \@Keys );
132.
133.      foreach $SubKey ( sort( @Keys ) )
134.      {
135.          ProcessKey( $TempKey, $ThisPath, $SubKey );
136.      }
137.      $TempKey->Close();
138.    }
139. }
140.
141. sub ValueType
142. {
143.    my( $Type ) = @_;
144.    my( $ValueType );
145.
146.    if( REG_SZ == $Type )
```

```
147.   {
148.     $ValueType = "REG_SZ";
149.   }
150.   elsif( REG_EXPAND_SZ == $Type )
151.   {
152.     $ValueType = "REG_EXPAND_SZ";
153.   }
154.   elsif( REG_MULTI_SZ == $Type )
155.   {
156.     $ValueType = "REG_MULTI_SZ";
157.   }
158.   elsif( REG_DWORD == $Type )
159.   {
160.     $ValueType = "REG_DWORD";
161.   }
162.   elsif( REG_BINARY == $Type)
163.   {
164.     $ValueType = "REG_BINARY";
165.   }
166.   else
167.   {
168.     $ValueType = "Unknown Type";
169.   }
170.   return( $ValueType );
171. }
172.
173. sub FormatNumber
174. {
175.   my( $Number ) = @_;
176.   while( $Number =~ s/^(-?\d+)(\d{3})/$1,$2/ ){};
177.   return( $Number );
178. }
179.
180. sub Configure
181. {
182.   my( $Config ) = @_;
183.   my $Result;
184.
185.   Getopt::Long::Configure( "prefix_pattern=(-|\/)" );
186.   $Result = GetOptions( $Config,
187.                         qw(
188.                           paths|p=s@
189.                           help|?|h
190.                         )
191.   );
192.   foreach my $Target ( @ARGV )
193.   {
194.     push( @{$Config->{target}}, { find => $Target } );
195.   }
196.   if( ! scalar @{$Config->{paths}} )
197.   {
198.     push( @{$Config->{paths}}, 'HKLM' );
199.   }
```

continues ▶

Example 3.14   *continued*

```
200.    $Config->{help} = 1 unless( scalar @{$Config->{target}} );
201.    $Config->{help} = 1 unless( $Result );
202.    return;
203. }
204.
205. sub Syntax
206. {
207.    my( $Script ) = ( $0 =~ m#([^\\/]+)$# );
208.    my $Line = "-" x length( $Script );
209.    print << "EOT";
210.
211.    $Script
212.    $Line
213.    Locates specified strings in the registry.
214.    Syntax: $Script [-p <path>]<find> [<find2> ...]
215.       Path.........Registry path to look into such as
216.                    HKEY_LOCAL_MACHINE or HKEY_CURRENT_USER
217.                    Abbreviations are allowed (eg. HKLM).
218.                    Default: HKEY_LOCAL_MACHINE
219.       Find.........String to search for.
220.
221.    Remote registries are allowed by prepending a machine name
222.    such as: \\\\server1\\hklm\\software
223.
224. EOT
225. }
```

Setting Autologon

There is a little-known ability to configure a Windows NT/2000 machine to autologon. This means that when a machine boots up, it automatically logs on as a specific user. You can set this autologon by manipulating some settings in the Registry. Using such a configuration is a terrific way to autoconfigure a machine.

Say that you need to configure 100 brand new machines. You could create an administrator-like account with a special logon script (covered in Chapter 6, "Logon Scripts"). The logon script would perform any functions that it needs to properly configure the machine—creating proper directories, copying files from a master file server, installing ODBC drivers and other software packages, and so on. Often, however, many programs need to reboot the computer before they can finish installing. Autologon handles this task. Before the logon script finishes, it sets the necessary information in the Registry and reboots the computer. The computer reboots and logs on automatically using the specified user ID. That user ID causes a logon script to run; the script recognizes the state of the machine and finishes whatever it needs to do. Finally, the logon script removes the autologon settings and either logs off or reboots again.

Using this particular example, all you need to do is walk over to each machine and log on with the special account. You do so 100 times, and you're finished. Consider this to be a poor man's version of Microsoft's Systems Management Server (SMS).

The dark side of autologon is that a username and password are added into the Registry, and they can be discovered with relative ease. The information is not encoded, so anyone with permission to view the Registry key can see both the username and password. You can remedy this by applying permissions so that only administrators and the System accounts have read access on the key and can both change permissions and take ownership.

Example 3.15 turns on or off the autologon feature, depending on what you pass into the script. The syntax is

```
perl setlogon.pl [-m Machine] [-clear] [<Domain\User | User> <Password>]
```

The switches are described in Table 3.4. If a username is specified, a password must be specified as well. The user account's domain should be specified but does not need to be. However, a logon problem may occur if another user account in the local machine's user database has the same name as one in the default domain.

Table 3.4   Autologon Switches

Switch	Description
-m Machine	This switch specifies for which machine to configure autologon. If this switch is not specified, the default is the local machine.
clear	This switch clears the autologon configuration. The username, domain, and password are cleared, and autologon is turned off.
User	The username of the account to log on automatically.
Domain	The domain of the account to log on automatically. This switch is optional.
Password	The password of the account to log on automatically.

Example 3.15   *Setting the Autologon User Account*

```
01. use Getopt::Long;
02. use Win32::Registry;
03.
04. $PATH = "Software\\Microsoft\\Windows NT\\CurrentVersion\\Winlogon";
05. Configure( \%Config );
06. if( $Config{help} )
07. {
08.   Syntax();
09.   exit();
```

continues ▶

Example 3.15   *continued*

```perl
10. }
11.
12. my $Root = $HKEY_LOCAL_MACHINE;
13. my $Key;
14.
15. if( "" ne $Config{machine} )
16. {
17.   print "Connecting to $Config{machine}...\n";
18.   if( ! $Root->Connect( $Config{machine}, $Root ) )
19.   {
20.     print "Can not connect to $Machine\n";
21.     exit();
22.   }
23. }
24.
25. if( $Root->Create( $PATH, $Key ) )
26. {
27.   foreach my $Param ( keys( %{$Config{params}} ) )
28.   {
29.     my $Result = $Key->SetValueEx( $Param,
30.                                    0,
31.                                    REG_SZ,
32.                                    $Config{params}->{$Param} );
33.     print "Setting $Param to '$Config{params}->{$Param}': ",
34.           ( $Result )? "success":"failure", "\n";
35.   }
36.   $Key->Close();
37. }
38. else
39. {
40.   print "Unable to open the $PATH key.\n";
41. }
42.
43. if( "" ne $Config{machine} )
44. {
45.   $Root->Close();
46. }
47.
48. sub Configure
49. {
50.   my( $Config ) = @_;
51.   my $Result;
52.   my $Params = {
53.     DefaultDomainName => "",
54.     DefaultUserName => "",
55.     DefaultPassword => "",
56.     AutoAdminLogon => 0,
57.   };
58.
59.   Getopt::Long::Configure( "prefix_pattern=(-|\/)" );
60.   $Result = GetOptions( $Config,
61.                         qw(
62.                         machine|m=s
63.                         clear|c
```

```
64.                         help|?|h
65.                      )
66.   );
67.   $Config->{help} = 1 unless( $Result );
68.
69.   if( ! $Config->{clear} )
70.   {
71.     $Params->{DefaultDomainName} = shift @ARGV;
72.     if( "" ne $Params->{DefaultDomainName} )
73.     {
74.       ( $Params->{DefaultDomainName},
75.         $Params->{DefaultUserName} ) = ( $Params->{DefaultDomainName}
76.                                   =~ /((.*)\\)?(.*)$/ )[1..3];
77.     }
78.     $Params->{DefaultPassword} = shift @ARGV;
79.     $Params->{AutoAdminLogon} = 1;
80.   }
81.   else
82.   {
83.     $Params->{AutoAdminLogon} = 0;
84.   }
85.   if( ( "" eq $Params->{DefaultUserName} )
86.       && ( ! $Config->{clear} ) )
87.   {
88.     $Config->{help} = 1;
89.   }
90.   $Config->{params} = $Params;
91.   return;
92. }
93.
94. sub Syntax
95. {
96.   my( $Script ) = ( $0 =~ m#([^\\/]+)$# );
97.   my $Line = "-" x length( $Script );
98.   my $WhiteSpace = " " x length( $Script );
99.   print << "EOT";
100.
101.   $Script
102.   $Line
103.   This utility will set the default logon information such as
104.   Userid, Domain, Password and whether or not the computer
105.   automatically logs on the default user.
106.
107.   Syntax: $Script [-m Machine] <Domain\\User|User> <Password>
108.           $WhiteSpace -clear [-m Machine]
109.
110.   User...........The userid to autologon as
111.   Domain.........The domain of the autologon userid
112.   Password.......The autologon userid's password
113.   -m Machine.....Specifies what machine to set/unset.
114.   -clear.........Remove the domain, username and password
115.
116. EOT
117. }
```

TCP/IP Configuration

You can configure multiple network cards on Windows machines. You also can bind multiple TCP/IP addresses to a given network card, which can make it difficult to track which computer has what IP address. All this information is held in the Registry on each computer. Being able to track this information, however, can be quite tedious.

Example 3.16 displays a machine's TCP/IP configuration, including addresses procured by means of DHCP. All addresses for all network cards are displayed. The information from other, remote machines can be displayed in addition to the local machine.

The script takes a single parameter that represents which machine to query. If no machine name is passed in, the local machine is assumed. For example,

```
perl tcpinfo.pl \\server1
```

In this case, the TCP configuration information is obtained for the machine \\server1.

Example 3.16 *Displaying a Machine's TCP/IP Configuration*

```
01. use Win32::Registry;
02.
03. %KeyName = (
04.    serviceroot          => 'System\CurrentControlSet\Services',
05.    tcplink              => 'Tcpip\Linkage',
06.    tcplink_disabled     => 'Tcpip\Linkage\Disabled',
07.    win2k_tcplink        => 'Tcpip\Parameters\Interfaces',
08.    deviceparam_tcp      => 'Parameters\Tcpip',
09. );
10.
11. $Root = $HKEY_LOCAL_MACHINE;
12.
13. if( $Machine = $ARGV[0] )
14. {
15.    $HKEY_LOCAL_MACHINE->Connect( $Machine, $Root )
16.        || die "Could not connect to the registry on '$Machine'\n";
17. }
18.
19. if( $Root->Open( $KeyName{serviceroot}, $ServiceRoot ) )
20. {
21.    # First check if this is Win2k...
22.    if( $ServiceRoot->Open( $KeyName{win2k_tcplink}, $Links ) )
23.    {
24.      my @Interfaces;
25.      if( $Links->GetKeys( \@Interfaces ) )
26.      {
27.        foreach my $DeviceName ( @Interfaces )
28.        {
29.          push( @Devices, [
```

```
30.                              "$KeyName{win2k_tcplink}\\$DeviceName",
31.                              $DeviceName
32.                         ] );
33.       }
34.     }
35.     $Links->Close();
36.   }
37.   # Get the device names of the cards tcp is bound to...
38.   else
39.   {
40.     if( $ServiceRoot->Open( $KeyName{tcplink}, $Links ) )
41.     {
42.       my( $Data );
43.       if( $Links->QueryValueEx( "Bind", $DataType, $Data ) )
44.       {
45.         $Data =~ s/\n/ /gs;
46.         $Data =~ s/\\Device\\//gis;
47.         $Data =~ s/^\s+(.*)\s+$/$1/gs;
48.         foreach my $DeviceName ( split( /\c@+/, $Data ) )
49.         {
50.           push( @Devices,
51.                   [
52.                     "$DeviceName\\$KeyName{deviceparam_tcp}",
53.                     $DeviceName
54.                   ] );
55.         }
56.       }
57.       $Links->Close();
58.     }
59.     # Get the device names of cards that tcp is bound to but disabled...
60.     if( $ServiceRoot->Open( $KeyName{tcplink_disabled}, $Links ) )
61.     {
62.       my( $Data );
63.
64.       if( $Links->QueryValueEx( "Bind", $DataType, $Data ) )
65.       {
66.         $Data =~ s/\s+//gs;
67.         $Data =~ s/\\Device\\//gis;
68.         foreach my $DeviceName ( split( /\c@+/, $Data ) )
69.         {
70.           push( @Devices,
71.                   [
72.                     "$DeviceName\\$KeyName{deviceparam_tcp}",
73.                     $DeviceName
74.                   ] );
75.         }
76.       }
77.       $Links->Close();
78.     }
79.   }
80.
81.   foreach my $Device ( @Devices )
82.   {
```

continues ▶

Example 3.16   *continued*

```
83.     my( $DeviceTCPKey );
84.     my( $Path ) = $Device->[0];
85.     my( $DeviceName ) = $Device->[1];
86.
87.     if( $ServiceRoot->Open( $Path, $DeviceTCPKey ) )
88.     {
89.       my %Hash;
90.       my( @IP, @Subnet, @Gateway, @DHCP, @DNS );
91.       my( $Data, $DataType, $Domain );
92.
93.       # Get the domain...
94.       $DeviceTCPKey->QueryValueEx( "Domain", $DataType, $Domain );
95.
96.       # Get the IP addresses...
97.       if( $DeviceTCPKey->QueryValueEx( "IPAddress",
98.                                        $DataType,
99.                                        $Data ) )
100.      {
101.        $Data =~ s/\s+//g;
102.        $Data =~ s/0\.0\.0\.0//g;
103.        $Data =~ s/\c@+/\c@/g;
104.        push( @IP, split( /\c@/, $Data ) );
105.        push( @DHCP, ( "no" ) x scalar split( /\c@/, $Data ) );
106.      }
107.
108.      # Get the Subnet masks...
109.      if( $DeviceTCPKey->QueryValueEx( "SubnetMask",
110.                                       $DataType,
111.                                       $Data ) )
112.      {
113.        $Data =~ s/\s+//g;
114.        $Data =~ s/0\.0\.0\.0//g;
115.        $Data =~ s/\c@+/\c@/g;
116.        push( @Subnet, split( /\c@/, $Data ) );
117.      }
118.                      # Get the default gateways...
119.                      if( $DeviceTCPKey->QueryValueEx( "DefaultGateway",
120.                                       $DataType,
121.                                       $Data ) )
122.                          {
123.                          $Data =~ s/\s+//g;
124.                          $Data =~ s/0\.0\.0\.0//g;
125.                          $Data =~ s/\c@+/\c@/g;
126.                          push( @Gateway, split( /\c@/, $Data ) );
127.                          }
128.      # Get the name servers...
129.      if( $DeviceTCPKey->QueryValueEx( "NameServer",
130.                                       $DataType,
131.                                       $Data ) )
132.      {
133.        $Data =~ s/0\.0\.0\.0//g;
```

```
134.          push( @DNS, split( /\s+/, $Data ) );
135.      }
136.
137.      # Query DHCP stats
138.      if( $DeviceTCPKey->QueryValueEx( "EnableDHCP",
139.                                       $DataType,
140.                                       $Data ) )
141.      {
142.        $Hash{dhcp} = (( $Data )? "yes":"no" );
143.
144.         # Get the DHCP domain...
145.        $DeviceTCPKey->QueryValueEx( "DhcpDomain",
146.                                     $DataType,
147.                                     $Domain );
148.
149.        # Get the DHCP IP Addresses...
150.        if( $DeviceTCPKey->QueryValueEx( "DHCPIPAddress",
151.                                         $DataType,
152.                                         $Data ) )
153.        {
154.          $Data =~ s/\s+//g;
155.          $Data =~ s/0\.0\.0\.0//g;
156.          $Data =~ s/\c@+/\c@/g;
157.          push( @IP, split( /\c@/, $Data ) );
158.          push( @DHCP, ( "yes" ) x scalar split( /\c@/, $Data ) );
159.        }
160.
161.        # Get the DHCP subnet masks...
162.        if( $DeviceTCPKey->QueryValueEx( "DHCPSubnetMask",
163.                                         $DataType,
164.                                         $Data ) )
165.        {
166.          $Data =~ s/\s+//g;
167.          $Data =~ s/0\.0\.0\.0//g;
168.          $Data =~ s/\c@+/\c@/g;
169.          push( @Subnet, split( /\c@/, $Data ) );
170.        }
171.
172.        # Get the DHCP gateways...
173.        if( $DeviceTCPKey->QueryValueEx( "DHCPDefaultGateway",
174.                                         $DataType,
175.                                         $Data ) )
176.        {
177.          $Data =~ s/\s+//g;
178.          $Data =~ s/0\.0\.0\.0//g;
179.          $Data =~ s/\c@+/\c@/g;
180.          push( @Gateway, split( /\c@/, $Data ) );
181.        }
182.
183.        # Get the DHCP name servers...
184.        if( $DeviceTCPKey->QueryValueEx( "DHCPNameServer",
185.                                         $DataType,
186.                                         $Data ) )
```

continues ▶

Example 3.16 *continued*

```
187.        {
188.            $Data =~ s/0\.0\.0\.0//g;
189.            push( @DNS, split( /\s+/, $Data ) );
190.        }
191.       }
192.      next if( 0 == scalar @IP );
193.      $Hash{name} = $DeviceName;
194.      $Hash{ip} = join( " " x 8, @IP );
195.      $Hash{subnet} = join( " " x 8, @Subnet );
196.      $Hash{gateway} = join( " " x 8, @Gateway );
197.      $Hash{dhcp} = join( " " x 8, @DHCP );
198.      $Hash{dns} = join( " " x 8, @DNS );
199.      $Hash{domain} = $Domain;
200.
201.      # Push our newfound data onto the stack...
202.      push( @TCPConfig, \%Hash );
203.
204.      $DeviceTCPKey->Close();
205.    }
206.  }
207.  print "The machine $Machine has the following IP addresses:\n";
208.  foreach $IP ( @TCPConfig )
209.  {
210.    print "\nInterface: $IP->{name}\n";
211.    print "Domain: $IP->{domain}\n";
212.
213.    $~ = TCPHeader;
214.    write;
215.    $~ = TCPDump;
216.    write;
217.  }
218.  $ServiceRoot->Close();
219. }
220.
221. format TCPHeader =
222.   @<<< @<<<<<<<<<<<<<< @<<<<<<<<<<<<<< @<<<<<<<<<<<<<< @<<<<<<<<<<<<<<
223.   "DHCP", "IP Address", "Subnet Mask", "Gateway", "DNS"
224.   ---- --------------- --------------- --------------- ---------------
225. .
226.
227. format TCPDump =
228.   ^<<< ^<<<<<<<<<<<<<< ^<<<<<<<<<<<<<< ^<<<<<<<<<<<<<< ^<<<<<<<<<<<<<<
229.   $IP->{dhcp}, $IP->{ip}, $IP->{subnet}, $IP->{gateway}, $IP->{dns}
230. ~ ^<<< ^<<<<<<<<<<<<<< ^<<<<<<<<<<<<<< ^<<<<<<<<<<<<<< ^<<<<<<<<<<<<<<
231.   $IP->{dhcp}, $IP->{ip}, $IP->{subnet}, $IP->{gateway}, $IP->{dns}
232. ~ ^<<< ^<<<<<<<<<<<<<< ^<<<<<<<<<<<<<< ^<<<<<<<<<<<<<< ^<<<<<<<<<<<<<<
233.   $IP->{dhcp}, $IP->{ip}, $IP->{subnet}, $IP->{gateway}, $IP->{dns}
234. ~ ^<<< ^<<<<<<<<<<<<<< ^<<<<<<<<<<<<<< ^<<<<<<<<<<<<<< ^<<<<<<<<<<<<<<
235.   $IP->{dhcp}, $IP->{ip}, $IP->{subnet}, $IP->{gateway}, $IP->{dns}
236. ~ ^<<< ^<<<<<<<<<<<<<< ^<<<<<<<<<<<<<< ^<<<<<<<<<<<<<< ^<<<<<<<<<<<<<<
237.   $IP->{dhcp}, $IP->{ip}, $IP->{subnet}, $IP->{gateway}, $IP->{dns}
238. ~ ^<<< ^<<<<<<<<<<<<<< ^<<<<<<<<<<<<<< ^<<<<<<<<<<<<<< ^<<<<<<<<<<<<<<
```

```
239.    $IP->{dhcp}, $IP->{ip}, $IP->{subnet}, $IP->{gateway}, $IP->{dns}
240.  ~ ^<<< ^<<<<<<<<<<<<<< ^<<<<<<<<<<<<<< ^<<<<<<<<<<<<<< ^<<<<<<<<<<<<<<
241.    $IP->{dhcp}, $IP->{ip}, $IP->{subnet}, $IP->{gateway}, $IP->{dns}
242.  ~ ^<<< ^<<<<<<<<<<<<<< ^<<<<<<<<<<<<<< ^<<<<<<<<<<<<<< ^<<<<<<<<<<<<<<
243.    $IP->{dhcp}, $IP->{ip}, $IP->{subnet}, $IP->{gateway}, $IP->{dns}
244.  .
```

Conclusion

There are dozens of different tools that an administrator can use to make her job easier. Tools ranging from open source code to commercial shrink-wrapped packages provide the necessary utilities to accomplish an administrative goal.

This chapter demonstrates Perl's remarkable capability to exercise the Win32 API to accomplish tasks. We have uncovered ways to use Perl to manage the Win32 file system, permissions, and the Registry. The tools discussed are useful and help define techniques that can be modified to target other tasks.

4

Crisis Management

Sooner or later some crisis will rear its head, and your team will have to jump to action. This group of people will either be heralded as heroes or be walking toward the unemployment line, depending on their swift resolution of the situation at hand. Of course, a simple solution to this problem is to institute routine preventive maintenance, such as cycling a server every seven days or backing up data to tape every evening. This routine maintenance can go a long way toward preventing serious problems and providing solutions if they do arise. However, regardless of how well prepared your team is, some situations will invariably leave you wishing you had thought about them earlier.

It has been my observation that the biggest problems are not those of magnitude but of details. For example, you can easily explain to a director or CIO that a file server crashed and is being rebuilt; *that* he can understand. However, having to explain that the file server is healthy but data cannot be accessed because a NULL DACL is preventing files from being accessed can prove to be considerably more difficult.

Many shrink-wrapped, off-the-shelf solutions can manage such crises. As an example, the typical backup software is designed to quickly restore backed-up files from tape to disk. However, some situations do not require such drastic measures—for example, if an administrator accidentally revoked permissions on all files in a shared directory. If each file and sub-directory has different permissions, re-creating the permissions correctly can be a daunting task, especially if you have hundreds of objects to touch. Restoring from tape could result in the overwriting of megabytes of data collected since a previous backup. If, however, permissions were previously backed up, all it takes is a short Perl script to reapply the permissions appropriately without losing any data.

Backing Up and Restoring Network Shares

For file servers, it is not uncommon to have many shared directories. Some may be public for everyone to access, and others may be secured so that only certain users are granted particular permissions. Likewise, some shares may be hidden from browsing, whereas others are visible to all.

Having many shared directories can be quite unwieldy to manage. Just ask any administrator who has had to reinstall an operating system on a file server. However, this does not have to be so difficult. As a matter of fact, it can be quite easy to manage with the proper tools.

Example 4.1 provides a simple script that connects to a machine and attempts to discover its various shared directory configurations. This approach to backing up shared directories is ideal because it generates configuration data in a simple text-based format. This format makes it quite easy for you to modify the configuration by using a text editor.

Example 4.1   *Dumping Shared Directory Configurations*

```
01. use Win32::Lanman;
02. use Win32::Perms;
03.
04. $DELIMITER = ";";
05.
06. # Create a hash to get the name of the share type based on the type value
07. %SHARE_TYPE = (
08.    eval( STYPE_DEVICE )   =>  'STYPE_DEVICE',
09.    eval( STYPE_PRINTQ )   =>  'STYPE_PRINTQ',
10.    eval( STYPE_DISKTREE )=>  'STYPE_DISKTREE',
11.    eval( STYPE_IPC )      =>  'STYPE_IPC',
12.    eval( STYPE_SPECIAL ) =>  'STYPE_SPECIAL',
13. );
14.
15. %PERM_SHARE_TYPE = (
16.    eval( STYPE_PRINTQ )   =>  5,  # Shared Printers
17.    eval( STYPE_DISKTREE )=>  4,  # Shared Directories
18. );
19.
20. # Default to the local machine
21. $Machine = Win32::NodeName() unless( $Machine = shift @ARGV );
22. # Fix any double backslashes on the machine name
23. ( $Machine = "\\\\$Machine" ) =~ s/^\\{2,}/\\\\/;
24. # We don't want to use rigorous domain controller lookups
25. Win32::Perms::LookupDC( 0 );
26. $Perm = new Win32::Perms()
27.        || die "Can not create an empty Perm object\n";
28.
29. if( Win32::Lanman::NetShareEnum( $Machine, \@ShareList ) )
30. {
31.    foreach my $Share ( @ShareList )
32.    {
```

```
33.     my( @Acl );
34.     my $ObjectType = $PERM_SHARE_TYPE{$Share->{type}};
35.     print "[$Share->{netname}]\n";
36.     $Share->{type} = ComputeType( $Share->{type} );
37.     foreach my $Attribute ( sort( keys( %$Share ) ) )
38.     {
39.       if( "security_descriptor" eq $Attribute )
40.       {
41.         DumpSD( $Share->{$Attribute}, $ObjectType );
42.       }
43.       else
44.       {
45.         print "$Attribute=$Share->{$Attribute}\n";
46.       }
47.     }
48.   print "\n";
49.   }
50. }
51.
52. sub ComputeType
53. {
54.   my( $Type ) = @_;
55.   my( @List );
56.
57.   push( @List, $SHARE_TYPE{&STYPE_SPECIAL} ) if( $Type & &STYPE_SPECIAL );
58.   $Type &= ~ &STYPE_SPECIAL;
59.   push( @List, $SHARE_TYPE{$Type} );
60.   return( join( "|", @List ) );
61. }
62.
63. sub DumpSD
64. {
65.   my( $SD, $ObjectType ) = @_;
66.   $Perm->Remove( -1 );
67.   $Perm->Import( $SD );
68.   $Perm->Dump( \@Acl );
69.   foreach my $Ace ( @Acl )
70.   {
71.     my $Account = $Ace->{Account};
72.     my( @MaskPerms, @FriendlyPerms, @Flags, @Types );
73.
74.     $Account = $Ace->{Domain} . "\\" . $Account if( "" ne $Ace->{Domain} );
75.
76.     # Neither Owner nor Group are applicable on shares
77.     next if( "Owner" eq $Ace->{Entry} || "Group" eq $Ace->{Entry} );
78.
79.     # Set the Ace to be of type "Share". Since we imported the
80.     # security descriptor there is no way for Win32::Perms to know that
81.     # it was for a share.
82.     $Ace->{ObjectType} = $ObjectType;
83.     Win32::Perms::DecodeMask( $Ace, \@MaskPerms, \@FriendlyPerms );
84.     Win32::Perms::DecodeType( $Ace->{Type}, \@Types );
85.     Win32::Perms::DecodeFlag( $Ace->{Flag}, \@Flags );
```

continues ▶

Example 4.1 *continued*

```
86.    print "Perm=$Account", $DELIMITER;
87.    print join( "|", @Types ), $DELIMITER;
88.    print join( "|", @Flags ), $DELIMITER;
89.    print join( "|", @MaskPerms ), "\n";
90.  }
91. }
92.
93. # For some reason Win32::Lanman forgot to export this constant
94. sub STYPE_SPECIAL
95. {
96.   return( 0x80000000 );
96. }
```

You can pass in the name of a machine on your network as the only parameter into the script, which causes the script to discover the configuration of all shared directories on that machine, provided that your script has administrative privileges on that machine. If no machine name is specified, the local machine is used.

The script dumps the configuration to STDOUT, so if you want to save the configuration, you can redirect it to a file as follows:

```
perl DumpShares.pl \\server > server_shares.ini
```

The outputted data appears in the standard Windows .INI file format.

Because the file can be executed remotely, you could designate one machine on your network to run this script for each file server you administer. Such a library of shared directory configuration files could be used to re-create a server's shared directories if the need arises. Because the configuration files are text-based .INI files, you could modify the files, enabling them to modify directories by removing them and then re-creating them using the modified configuration script.

To create shared directories from the configuration files, run the script in Example 4.2 and pass in the name of the configuration file. To re-create the directories backed up in the previous example, you could use the following:

```
perl MakeShares.pl server_shares.ini
```

Example 4.2 *Creating Shared Directories*

```
01. use Win32::Lanman;
02. use Win32::Perms;
03. use Win32::API;
04.
05. $DELIMITER = ";";
06. $File = shift( @ARGV ) || die "No config file specified\n";
07. $Machine = Win32::NodeName() unless( $Machine = shift( @ARGV ) );
08. ( $Machine = "\\\\$Machine" ) =~ s/^\\{2,}/\\\\/;
```

```
09.
10. %PERM_TYPE = (
11.   Allow => ALLOW,
12.   Deny  => DENY,
13. );
14. # We don't want to use rigorous domain controller lookups
15. Win32::Perms::LookupDC( 0 );
16.
17. if( ProcessFile( $File, \%Config ) )
18. {
19.   foreach my $Share ( keys( %Config ) )
20.   {
21.     print "Creating $Machine\\$Config{$Share}->{netname}...";
22.     if( CreateShare( $Machine, $Config{$Share} ) )
23.     {
24.       print "Success";
25.     }
26.     else
27.     {
28.       print "failure: ";
29.       print Win32::FormatMessage( Win32::Lanman::GetLastError() );
30.     }
31.     print "\n";
32.   }
33. }
34.
35. sub CreateShare
36. {
37.   my( $Machine, $Share ) = @_;
38.   my $Result = 0;
39.
40.   if( $Share->{type} & &STYPE_SPECIAL )
41.   {
42.     print "  SPECIAL SHARE! Ignore this.\n";
43.     return( 0 );
44.   }
45.   if( scalar @{$Share->{perm}} )
46.   {
47.     $Perm = new Win32::Perms();
48.     foreach my $PermLine ( @{$Share->{perm}} )
49.     {
50.       my( $Account, $Type, $Flag, $Mask ) = split( $DELIMITER,
51.                                                     $PermLine );
52.       $Perm->Add( $Account,
53.                           eval( $Mask ),
54.                           eval( $Type ),
55.                           eval( $Flag ) );
56.     }
57.     $Share->{security_descriptor}
58.                 = $Perm->GetSD( SD_RELATIVE );
59.   }
60.   if( STYPE_DISKTREE == $Share->{type} )
61.   {
```

continues ▶

Example 4.2   *continued*

```
62.    $Result = Win32::Lanman::NetShareAdd( $Machine, $Share );
63.    }
64.    elsif( STYPE_PRINTQ == $Share->{type} )
65.    {
66.      print "can't share a printer!\n";
67.    }
68.
69.    return( $Result );
70. }
71.
72. sub ProcessFile
73. {
74.    my( $File, $ShareList ) = @_;
75.    my $iResult = 0;
76.
77.    if( open( SHAREDATA, "<$File" ) )
78.    {
79.      $iResult = ParseShares( *SHAREDATA, $ShareList );
80.      close( SHAREDATA );
81.    }
82.    else
83.    {
84.      print "Unable to open '$File': $!\n";
85.    }
86.    return( $iResult );
87. }
88.
89. sub ParseShares
90. {
91.    my( $FileHandle, $ShareList ) = @_;
92.    my $ShareName = "";
93.    my $iTotal = 0;
94.
95.    while( $Line = <$FileHandle> )
96.    {
97.      my( $Name, $Value );
98.
99.      next if( $Line =~ /^\s*[#;]/ );
100.      next if( $Line =~ /^\s*$/ );
101.      if( ( $Name ) = ( $Line =~ /^\s*\[\s*(.*?)\s*\]/ ) )
102.      {
103.        $ShareName = lc $Name;
104.        $iTotal++;
105.        next;
106.      }
107.      next if( "" eq $ShareName );
108.
109.      ( $Name, $Value ) = ( $Line =~ /^\s*(.*?)=(.*)\s*$/ );
110.      if( "" ne $Name )
111.      {
112.        $Name = lc $Name;
```

```
113.      if( "perm" eq $Name )
114.      {
115.        push( @{$ShareList->{$ShareName}->{$Name}}, $Value );
116.      }
117.      else
118.      {
119.        $Value = eval( $Value ) if( "type" eq $Name );
120.        $ShareList->{$ShareName}->{$Name} = $Value;
121.      }
122.    }
123.  }
124.  return( $iTotal );
125. }
126.
127. # For some reason Win32::Lanman forgot to export this constant
128. sub STYPE_SPECIAL
129. {
130.   return( 0x80000000 );
131. }
```

Backing Up and Restoring User and Machine Accounts

Account creation is relatively simple (refer to Chapter 2, "Account Maintenance"), but if your primary domain controller (PDC) goes kaput on a network with only one DC and you have no backups, you may as well go home early—and look for another job. This scenario may be more common than you think. Many administrators configure Web sites to be in an extremely small domain consisting of just a Web server. Having a single domain controller reside on a mini-network with a Web server itself can speed up access to account information. Such a configuration is terrific for e-commerce sites but can be quite costly if the DC crashes.

You can back up the accounts database in several ways. Some involve costly software that makes a physical backup of the SAM database to a device such as a tape backup unit. If you have the equipment and the cash to afford such utilities, this solution can be quite efficient. Not everyone can afford such solutions, and these types of packages have their own problems. For example, if you want to re-create your workstation or domain from scratch, you might not want to re-create an identical copy of the database. Or if you need to create local service accounts on hundreds of workstations, a physical copy of the SAM database will do you no good.

So, this is where Perl comes to the rescue again. An administrator can query a machine for its list of user accounts, thus enabling a Perl script to fetch the account name and its attributes. A script could store this information away in a text file that could later be used to re-create the accounts.

Example 4.3 retrieves user account information from either a machine or a domain. It dumps all account information to STDOUT, so you can redirect it into a file as follows:

```
perl DumpAccounts.pl -d MyDomain > users.ini
```

The script can accept a few different command-line switches that expand its capabilities. These switches are listed in Table 4.1.

Table 4.1   Switch Options for Example 4.3

Option	Description
-m Machine	Identifies which specific machine performs the query. Use this option if you want to obtain a specific machine's user accounts or if you want a specific machine (such as a DC) to generate the list.
-d Domain	Specifies a domain you want the account list to come from. This option overrides the -m switch. The PDC for the specified domain generates the account list.
-p Prefix	Lists only accounts that begin with the Prefix string. Because some domains and machines have thousands of accounts, you might want to break them into more manageable sized groups.
-t user | machine	Determines the type of account to list. By default, user accounts are listed. However, machine accounts for a specified domain can be listed instead.

To generate a list of all user accounts on the machine \\WEBSERVER and store the account configuration in a WEBSERVER.INI file, you can use the following command:

```
perl DumpAccounts.pl -m \\WEBSERVER > webserver.ini
```

Backing Up Machine Accounts

Every computer that participates in a domain has a machine account. It is almost identical to a user account except that it has a different flag set. Additionally, a machine account name must end with a dollar sign ($). To generate a list of machine names in a domain, use this command:

```
perl DumpAccounts.pl -d MyDomain -t machine > machines.ini
```

Restoring Accounts

After you have successfully generated a list of accounts (machine or user), you can restore them by using the script in Example 4.4. This script reads the contents of a configuration file previously created (using Example 4.3) and re-creates its accounts. If the account already exists, it is not modified.

You can invoke the script as follows:

```
perl MakeAccounts.pl webserver.ini \\webserver
```

The first parameter passed in is the configuration file's path, and the optional second parameter specifies what machine is to create the accounts. If no machine name is specified, the local machine is assumed. If you are re-creating a domain's user or machine accounts, you need to specify the domain's PDC as the second parameter.

Example 4.3 *Retrieving User or Machine Account Information*

```
01. use Win32::Lanman;
02. use Getopt::Long;
03.
04. %Config = (
05.   level  => 1
06. );
07. Configure( \%Config, @ARGV );
08. if( $Config{help} )
09. {
10.   Syntax();
11.   exit 0;
12. }
13. if( defined $Config{domain} )
14. {
15.   Win32::Lanman::NetGetDCName( $Config{machine},
16.                                $Config{domain},
17.                                \$Config{machine} );
18. }
19. if( Win32::Lanman::NetGetDisplayInformationIndex( $Config{machine},
20.                       $Config{level},
21.                       $Config{prefix},
22.                       \$Index ) )
23. {
24.   do
25.   {
26.     Win32::Lanman::NetQueryDisplayInformation( $Config{machine},
27.                                $Config{level},
28.                                $Index,
29.                                10,
30.                                \@Accounts );
31.     foreach my $Account ( @Accounts )
32.     {
33.       print "[$Account->{name}]\n";
34.       print STDERR "$Account->{name}\n";
35.       $Index = $Account->{next_index};
36.       if( Win32::Lanman::NetUserGetInfo( $Config{machine},
37.                               $Account->{name},
38.                               \%Info ) )
39.       {
40.         foreach my $Attribute ( sort( keys( %Info ) ) )
```

continues ▶

Example 4.3   *continued*

```
41.         {
42.            my $Value = $Info{$Attribute};
43.            $Value =~ s/([^\w_+-])/sprintf( "\\x%02x", unpack( "C", $1 ) )/eg;
44.            print "$Attribute=$Value\n";
45.         }
46.      }
47.      print "\n";
48.    }
49.  }while( scalar @Accounts );
50. }
51.
52. sub Configure
53. {
54.    my( $Config ) = @_;
55.    my $Result = 0;
56.    Getopt::Long::Configure( "prefix_pattern=(-|\/)" );
57.    $Result = GetOptions( $Config,
58.        qw(
59.           domain|d=s
60.           machine|m=s
61.           prefix|p=s
62.           type|t=s
63.           help|?|h
64.        )
65.    );
66.
67.    if( lc $Config->{type} eq "user" )
68.    {
69.        $Config->{level} = 1;
70.    }
71.    elsif( lc $Config->{type} eq "machine" )
72.    {
73.        $Config->{level} = 2;
74.    }
75.    $Config->{help} = 1 if( ! $Result );
76. }
77.
78. sub Syntax
79. {
80.   my( $Script ) = ( $0 =~ /([^\\\/]*?)$/ );
81.   my( $Line ) = "-" x length( $Script );
82.
83.   print <<EOT;
84.
85. $Script
86. $Line
87. Dumps user account information into a file.
88.
89. Syntax:
90.   perl $Script [-t user | machine][-m Machine][-p Prefix][-d Domain]
```

```
91.    -m..............Machine whose user accounts will be dumped.
92.            Defaults to the local machine.
93.    -t..............Specifies what type of accounts to dump.
94.            user: user accounts (Default)
95.            machine: machine accounts
96.    -p Prefix.......Specifies an account prefix to use. Only
97.            accounts beginning with this string are
98.            queried.
99.    -d Domain.......Specifies a domain to use.
100. EOT
101. }
```

Example 4.4 *Restoring User or Machine Accounts*

```
01. use Win32::Lanman;
02.
03. $File = shift( @ARGV ) || die "No config file specified\n";
04. $Machine = Win32::NodeName() unless( $Machine = shift( @ARGV ) );
05. ( $Machine = "\\\\$Machine" ) =~ s/^\\{2,}/\\\\/;
06.
07. if( ProcessFile( $File, \%Config ) )
08. {
09.   foreach my $Account ( keys( %Config ) )
10.   {
11.     print "Creating $Machine\\$Config{$Account}->{netname}...";
12.     if( CreateAccount( $Machine, $Config{$Account} ) )
13.     {
14.       print "Success";
15.     }
16.     else
17.     {
18.       print "failure: ";
19.       print Win32::FormatMessage( Win32::Lanman::GetLastError() );
20.     }
21.     print "\n";
22.   }
23. }
24.
25. sub CreateAccount
26. {
27.   my( $Machine, $Account ) = @_;
28.   my $Result = 0;
29.
30.   # Is this a machine account?
31.   if( $Account->{name} =~ /\$$/ )
32.   {
33.     # Follow the rules to create a machine account...
34.     $Account->{name} = uc $Account->{name};
35.     ($Account->{password}) = ( lc $Account->{name} =~ /^(.{0,14})/ );
36.     $Account->{password} =~ s/\$$//;
37.   }
38.
```

continues ▶

Example 4.4 *continued*

```perl
39.    $Result = Win32::Lanman::NetUserAdd( $Machine, $Account );
40.
41.    return( $Result );
42. }
43.
44. sub ProcessFile
45. {
46.    my( $File, $AccountList ) = @_;
47.    my $iResult = 0;
48.
49.    if( open( ACCOUNTDATA, "<$File" ) )
50.    {
51.      $iResult = ParseAccounts( *ACCOUNTDATA, $AccountList );
52.      close( ACCOUNTDATA );
53.    }
54.    else
55.    {
56.      print "Unable to open '$File': $!\n";
57.    }
58.    return( $iResult );
59. }
60.
61. sub ParseAccounts
62. {
63.    my( $FileHandle, $AccountList ) = @_;
64.    my $AccountName = "";
65.    my $iTotal = 0;
66.
67.    while( $Line = <$FileHandle> )
68.    {
69.      my( $Name, $Value );
70.
71.      next if( $Line =~ /^\s*[#;]/ );
72.      next if( $Line =~ /^\s*$/ );
73.      if( ( $Name ) = ( $Line =~ /^\s*\[\s*(.*?)\s*\]/ ) )
74.      {
75.        $AccountName = lc $Name;
76.        $iTotal++;
77.        next;
78.      }
79.      next if( "" eq $AccountName );
80.
81.      ( $Name, $Value ) = ( $Line =~ /^\s*(.*?)=(.*)\s*$/ );
82.      if( "" ne $Name )
83.      {
84.        $Name = lc $Name;
85.        $Value =~ s/\\x(\w{2})/pack("c",hex($1))/ge;
86.        $AccountList->{$ShareAccountName}->{$Name} = $Value;
87.      }
88.    }
89.    return( $iTotal );
```

```
90. }
91.
92. # For some reason Win32::Lanman forgot to export this constant
93. sub STYPE_SPECIAL
94. {
95.   return( 0x80000000 );
96. }
```

Backing Up and Restoring Permissions

Backing up files can be as easy as copying them to another drive or as complex as installing, configuring, and executing a backup software package. However, backing up the owner, auditing, and security information on the directory tree is another issue. You can employ a simple Perl script to make backups of directory tree and Registry tree permissions.

Most backup programs can back up NT File System (NTFS) object information, such as owner, security, and auditing information. Finding one that can restore only that information and not the entire file, however, is more difficult. Likewise, finding such a backup program that can also save security information for files, directories, Registry keys, network shares, and shared printers is quite difficult.

Imagine that some administrator accidentally reset permissions on all users' home directories. Depending on the number of users, this situation could be quite a mess. Assuming that each user directory had specific permissions, such as for the employee, the employee's manager, and secretary, programmatically applying permissions would be difficult unless they had been backed up earlier.

Another example to consider is a Web server that had various permission sets placed on various directories. Such permissions could represent who can access what Web data. Accidentally resetting these directories could lead to the entire Web gaining access to your Web site.

The obvious solution to these problems is to periodically back up permissions and auditing information. The script in Example 4.5 dumps security information for a securable object, such as files, directories, Registry keys, and so on. The information is gathered and dumped to STDOUT. This allows the output to be redirected to a file.

The script accepts any number of paths as input parameters. These paths can be of any of the types defined in Table 4.2. File and directory paths can contain wildcards and can be relative paths; all other types must specify absolute paths. Also, any mix of paths can be passed into the script.

For example, to back up all permissions of files in a user's networked home directory and Registry's Software key, you can use the following:

```
perl DumpPerms.pl \\server\home$\JOEL\*.*
    HKEY_CURRENT_USER\Software "HKEY_CURRENT_USER\Control Panel" > Joel.ini
```

Table 4.2   Path Types That Can Be Used with Example 4.5

Path Type	Example
File	C:\boot.ini ..\myfile.doc \\server\share\myotherfile.txt
Directory	C:\temp \\server\share\
Registry key	HKEY_LOCAL_MACHINE\Software \\server\HKEY_LOCAL_MACHINE\Software
Network share	\\server\share
Printer share	\\server\printer

After you back up the security information, you can quickly reapply it by using the code in Example 4.6. This script simply accepts a configuration file created with Example 4.5. Pass in the path to the backup configuration file as in:

```
perl MakePerms.pl Joel.ini
```

Note

Because you can create the configuration script with relative file and directory paths as well as Registry paths that pertain to a specific machine, running the restoration script from the same location it was generated is very important. ◆

Example 4.5   *Dumping Security Information for a Securable Object*

```
01. use Win32::Perms;
02.
03. $DELIMITER = ";";
04. push( @ARGV, "*.*" ) if( 0 == scalar @ARGV );
05. foreach my $Mask ( @ARGV )
06. {
07.   if( $Mask =~ /[*?]/ )
08.   {
09.     push( @Paths, glob( $Mask ) );
10.   }
```

```
11.   else
12.   {
13.     push( @Paths, $Mask );
14.   }
15. }
16.
17. foreach my $Path ( @Paths )
18. {
19.   print STDERR "$Path ";
20.   if( ! ProcessPath( $Path ) )
21.   {
22.     print STDERR "...FAILED!\n";
23.   }
24.   print STDERR "\n";
25. }
26.
27. sub ProcessPath
28. {
29.   my( $Path ) = @_;
30.   my @Acl;
31.   my $Perm;
32.   return( 0 ) unless( $Perm = new Win32::Perms( $Path ) );
33.   print "[$Path]\n";
34.   $Perm->Dump( \@Acl );
35.   foreach my $Ace ( @Acl )
36.   {
37.     my $Account = $Ace->{Account};
38.     $Account = $Ace->{Domain} . "\\" . $Account if( "" ne $Ace->{Domain} );
39.     if( "Group" eq $Ace->{Entry} || "Owner" eq $Ace->{Entry} )
40.     {
41.       print "$Ace->{Entry}=$Account\n";
42.     }
43.     else
44.     {
45.       my( @MaskPerms, @FriendlyPerms, @Flags );
46.       print "$Ace->{Entry}=";
47.       Win32::Perms::DecodeMask( $Ace, \@MaskPerms, \@FriendlyPerms );
48.       Win32::Perms::DecodeFlag( $Ace->{Flag}, \@Flags );
49.
50.       print join( $DELIMITER, ( $Account, $Ace->{Access},
51.             join( "|", @Flags ),
52.             join( "|", @MaskPerms ) ) );
53.       print "\n";
54.     }
55.   }
56.   print "\n";
57.   return( 1 );
58. }
```

Example 4.6   *Reapplying Security Permissions*

```
01. use Win32::Perms;
02. $DELIMITER = ";";
03. Win32::Perms::LookupDC( 0 );
04. $File = shift( @ARGV ) || die "No config file specified\n";
05. $Machine = Win32::NodeName() unless( $Machine = shift( @ARGV ) );
06. ( $Machine = "\\\\$Machine" ) =~ s/^\\{2,}/\\\\/;
07.
08. if( ProcessFile( $File, \%Config ) )
09. {
10.   foreach my $Object ( keys( %Config ) )
11.   {
12.     print "Creating $Machine\\$Object...";
13.     if( ApplyPerms( $Machine, $Config{$Object} ) )
14.     {
15.       print "Success";
16.     }
17.     else
18.     {
19.       print "failure: ";
20.       print Win32::FormatMessage( Win32::Lanman::GetLastError() );
21.     }
22.     print "\n";
23.   }
24. }
25.
26. sub ApplyPerms
27. {
28.   my( $Machine, $PermObject ) = @_;
29.   my $Perm;
30.   my @Acl;
31.
32.   return( 0 )
33.         unless( $Perm = new Win32::Perms( $PermObject->{path} ) );
34.   $Perm->Remove( -1 );
35.   $Perm->Owner( $PermObject->{owner} )
36.                 if( defined $PermObject->{owner} );
37.   $Perm->Group( $PermObject->{group} )
38.                 if( defined $PermObject->{group} );
39.   foreach my $Ace ( @{$PermObject->{dacl}}, @{$PermObject->{sacl}} )
40.   {
41.     my( $Account, $Access, $Flags, $Mask ) = split( $DELIMITER, $Ace );
42.     $Perm->Add( $Account,
43.                 eval( uc $Mask ),
44.                 eval( uc $Access ),
45.                 eval( uc $Flags ) );
46.   }
47.   $Perm->Set();
48.   print "\n";
49. }
50.
51. sub ProcessFile
```

```perl
52. {
53.   my( $File, $PermList ) = @_;
54.   my $iResult = 0;
55.
56.   if( open( PERMSDATA, "<$File" ) )
57.   {
58.     $iResult = ParsePerms( *PERMSDATA, $PermList );
59.     close( PERMSDATA );
60.   }
61.   else
62.   {
63.     print "Unable to open '$File': $!\n";
64.   }
65.   return( $iResult );
66. }
67.
68. sub ParsePerms
69. {
70.   my( $FileHandle, $PermList ) = @_;
71.   my $ObjectName = "";
72.   my $iTotal = 0;
73.
74.   while( $Line = <$FileHandle> )
75.   {
76.     my( $Name, $Value );
77.
78.     next if( $Line =~ /^\s*[#;]/ );
79.     next if( $Line =~ /^\s*$/ );
80.     if( ( $Name ) = ( $Line =~ /^\s*\[\s*(.*?)\s*\]/ ) )
81.     {
82.       $ObjectName = lc $Name;
83.       $iTotal++;
84.       $PermList->{$ObjectName}->{path} = $ObjectName;
85.       next;
86.     }
87.     next if( "" eq $ObjectName );
88.
89.     ( $Name, $Value ) = ( $Line =~ /^\s*(.*?)=(.*)\s*$/ );
90.     if( "" ne $Name )
91.     {
92.       $Name = lc $Name;
93.       if( ( "dacl" eq $Name ) || ( "sacl" eq $Name ) )
94.       {
95.         push( @{$PermList->{$ObjectName}->{$Name}}, $Value );
96.       }
97.       else
98.       {
99.         $PermList->{$ObjectName}->{$Name} = $Value;
100.      }
101.    }
102.  }
103.  return( $iTotal );
104. }
```

Discovering Open Files

Each machine that shares files and directories maintains a list of what is currently in use by each user. When you need to track which resources a particular user has opened, this list can be more than invaluable. Example 4.7 connects to a specified machine (the local machine if one is not specified) and procures the list of opened resources.

You can easily imagine how useful this particular script can be. Consider that you are tracking which files a user has open. If someone has breached network security by logging on as some user, you can quickly discover which files that person has opened on which file servers. Figure 4.1 demonstrates this particular situation.

```
C:\ >perl openfiles -m * -m dev -u Joel


Open files on \\DATA:
ID      Locks  User              Path
.....   ....   .................  ............................................
  9959     0   Joel              \PIPE\spoolss
 31339     0   Joel              \PIPE\winreg
 35419     0   Joel              e:\CDROM\MSDN Disk 2.cdi
 36506     0   Joel              e:\Data\rothd\template\mcpglobl.dot
 36784     0   Joel              e:\Data\rothd\docume ... andbook\~WRL0002.tmp
 36793     0   Joel              e:\Data\rothd\docume ... ndbook\Chapter 4.doc
 41968     0   Joel              \PIPE\srvsvc


Open files on \\PROXY:
ID      Locks  User              Path
.....   ....   .................  ............................................


Open files on \\dev:
ID      Locks  User              Path
.....   ....   .................  ............................................
    25     0   Joel              C:\temp
    26     0   Joel              \PIPE\srvsvc
```

Figure 4.1 *Dumping the list of open files.*

This example shows that all domain servers (-m *) in addition to one other server (-m dev) are queried for any connections made by the user Joel (-u Joel). The result shows that the user has several open resources on the server (\\DATA), including a connection open to both the printer spooler (\PIPE\spoolss) and the Registry (\PIPE\winreg). As an administrator, you should become suspicious at the Registry connection.

The user has connected to the file sharing service (\PIPE\srvsvc) on \\dev, which is normal when a user connects to a shared resource. A connection is also open to the c:\temp directory, probably in the Explorer program; however, the user has no connections open to the machine \\PROXY.

Example 4.7   *Listing Files Opened Remotely*

```
01. use vars qw( %Data $PATH $USERS );
02. use Getopt::Long;
03. use Win32;
04. use Win32::Lanman;
05.
06. %PATH = (
07.     max    => 45,
08.     filler => ' ... ',
09. );
10.
11. Configure( \%Config );
12. if( $Config{help} )
13. {
14.     Syntax();
15.     exit();
16. }
17.
18. $USERS = ";" . join( ";", @{$Config{users}} ) . ";";
19.
20. if( ! scalar @{$Config{servers}} )
21. {
22.     push( @{$Config{servers}}, Win32::NodeName() );
23. }
24.
25. foreach my $Server ( sort( @{$Config{servers}} ) )
26. {
27.     my @FileInfo;
28.     next if( lc $Server eq $PrevServer );
29.     $PrevServer = lc $Server;
30.
31.     print "Open files on \\\\$Server:\n";
32.     $~ = OUTPUT_HEADER;
33.     write;
34.     $~ = OUTPUT;
35.     $: = "\\-_+";
36.
37.     foreach my $Path ( @$Config{paths} )
38.     {
39.         my( @Info, $User );
40.         if( Win32::Lanman::NetFileEnum( $Server,
41.                                         $Path,
42.                                         $User,
43.                                         \@Info ) )
44.         {
45.             push( @FileInfo, @Info );
```

continues ▶

Example 4.7   *continued*

```
46.          }
47.      }
48.
49.      foreach my $File ( @FileInfo )
50.      {
51.          undef %Data;
52.          $Data{path}  = $File->{pathname};
53.          $Data{user}  = $File->{username};
54.          $Data{locks} = $File->{num_locks};
55.          $Data{id}    = $File->{id};
56.
57.          if( scalar @{$Config{users}} )
58.          {
59.              next unless( $USERS =~ /;$Data{user};/i );
60.          }
61.
62.          if( ! $Config{full} )
63.          {
64.              if( $PATH{max} < length( $Data{path} ) )
65.              {
66.                  my $PathLength = int( ( $PATH{max}
67.                                      - length( $PATH{filler} ) ) ) / 2 );
68.                  my $FillerLength = length( $PATH{filler} );
69.                  $Data{path} = $File->{pathname}
70.                  $Data{path} =~
71.          s/^(.{$PathLength})(.*?)(.{$PathLength})$/$1$PATH{filler}$3/;
72.              }
73.          }
74.          write;
75.      }
76.      print "\n";
77.  }
78.
79.  sub Configure
80.  {
81.      my( $Config ) = @_;
82.      my $Result = 0;
83.      Getopt::Long::Configure( "prefix_pattern=(-|\/)" );
84.      $Result = GetOptions( $Config,
85.                  qw(
86.                      users|u=s@
87.                      full|f
88.                      machine|m=s@
89.                      help|?|h
90.                  ) );
91.      push( @{$Config->{paths}}, @ARGV );
92.      foreach my $Machine ( @{$Config->{machine}} )
93.      {
94.          if( "*" eq $Machine )
95.          {
96.              my $Domain = Win32::DomainName();
97.              my @List;
```

```
98.                if( Win32::Lanman::NetServerEnum( '',
99.                                        $Domain,
100.                                       TYPE_SERVER,
101.                                       \@List ) )
102.            {
103.              map
104.              {
105.                push( @{$Config->{servers}}, $_->{name} );
106.              } @List;
107.            }
108.        }
109.        else
110.        {
111.            push( @{$Config->{servers}}, $Machine );
112.        }
113.    }
114.    $Config->{help} = 1 unless( $Result );
115. }
116.
117. sub Syntax
118. {
119.    my( $Script ) = ( $0 =~ /([^\\\/]*?)$/ );
120.    my( $Line ) = "-" x length( $Script );
121.
122.    print <<EOT;
123.
124. $Script
125. $Line
126. Display what files are open on a server.
127.
128. Syntax:
129.    perl $Script [-f] [-u User] [-m Machine] [Path [$Path2 [...]]]
130.        -u..........Display only files opened by this user.
131.                    Use as many -u switches as needed.
132.        -f..........Display full path of each open file.
133.        -m..........Examine this machine.
134.                    Specify * for all machines sharing files.
135.                    Default is the local machine.
136.        Path........The path to examine local to the specified server.
137.                    This can be either a file or a directory path.
138.                    Default will be ALL files on the server.
139.
140. EOT
141.
142. }
143.
144. format OUTPUT_HEADER=
145.  @<<<<<< @<<<<< @<<<<<<<<<<<<<<< @<<<<<<<<<<<<<<<<<<<<<<<<<<<<<<<<<<<<<<<<<<<<<
146. 'ID', 'Locks', 'User', 'Path'
147. ------- ------ ---------------- ---------------------------------------------
148. .
149.
150. format OUTPUT =
```

continues ▶

Example 4.7   *continued*

```
151. @>>>>>> @>>>>> @<<<<<<<<<<<<<<<< ^<<<<<<<<<<<<<<<<<<<<<<<<<<<<<<<<<<<<<<<<<
152. $Data{id}, $Data{locks}, $Data{user}, $Data{path}
153. ~                                 ^<<<<<<<<<<<<<<<<<<<<<<<<<<<<<<<<<<<<<<<<<
154.                                    $Data{path}
155. ~                                 ^<<<<<<<<<<<<<<<<<<<<<<<<<<<<<<<<<<<<<<<<<
156.                                    $Data{path}
157. ~                                 ^<<<<<<<<<<<<<<<<<<<<<<<<<<<<<<<<<<<<<<<<<
158.                                    $Data{path}
159..
```

Closing Open Connections

In Figure 4.1, shown in the preceding section, notice that the user has a connection to the Registry on machine \\DATA. Assuming that the user is not an administrator, that user should have no reason to be examining the Registry of a file server. From a security perspective, this situation could be quite dangerous; therefore, it is important to disconnect the user from the service.

The script in Example 4.8 closes a file or other resource that has been opened remotely. Only remotely accessed files can be closed using this script. Figure 4.2 shows the use of this script to close the user's connection to the Registry.

```
C:\>perl closefile.pl -m data 31339

The following files were forced closed:
ID      Locks  User             Path
------- ------ ---------------- ----------------------------------------
  31339      0 Joel             \PIPE\winreg
```

Figure 4.2   *Closing a remote connection to a shared resource.*

The script can accept a machine name (the local machine is assumed if none is specified) and any number of open file IDs. You can obtain the list of ID numbers by using Example 4.7.(See the earlier section, "Discovering Open Files," for more details.)

Example 4.8   *Closing Files Opened Remotely*

```
01. use vars qw( $PATH );
02. use Getopt::Long;
03. use Win32::Lanman;
04.
05. %PATH = (
06.   max    => 45,
07.   filler => ' ... ',
08. );
```

```
09.
10. Configure( \%Config );
11. if( $Config{help} )
12. {
13.   Syntax();
14.   exit();
15. }
16.
17. foreach my $FileID ( @{$Config{ids}} )
18. {
19.   my( %File );
20.   if( Win32::Lanman::NetFileGetInfo( $Config{machine},
21.                                      $FileID,
22.                                      \%File ) )
23.   {
24.     undef %Data;
25.     $Data{path}  = $File{pathname};
26.     $Data{user}  = $File{username};
27.     $Data{locks} = $File{num_locks};
28.     $Data{id}    = $File{id};
29.
30.     if( $PATH{max} < length( $Data{path} ) )
31.     {
32.       my $PathLength = int( ( $PATH{max}
33.                            - length( $PATH{filler} ) ) / 2 );
34.       my $FillerLength = length( $PATH{filler} );
35.       $Data{path} =~
36.       s/^(.{$PathLength})(.*?)(.{$PathLength})$/$1$PATH{filler}$3/;
37.     }
38.
39.     if( ! Win32::Lanman::NetFileClose( $Config{machine},
40.                                        $FileID ) )
41.     {
42.       my( %Temp ) = %Data;
43.       push( @Failed, \%Temp );
44.     }
45.     else
46.     {
47.       my( %Temp ) = %Data;
48.       push( @Succeeded, \%Temp );
49.     }
50.   }
51.   else
52.   {
53.     my %Temp = (
54.       id       => $FileID,
55.       pathname => 'File ID is not in use on this server.',
56.     );
57.     push( @Failed, \%Temp );
58.   }
59. }
60.
61. if( scalar @Succeeded )
```

continues ▶

Example 4.8 *continued*

```
62. {
63.   print "\nThe following files were forced closed:\n";
64.   $~ = OUTPUT_HEADER;
65.   write;
66.   $~ = OUTPUT;
67.
68.   foreach my $File ( @Succeeded )
69.   {
70.     %Data = %$File;
71.     write;
72.   }
73. }
74.
75. if( scalar @Failed )
76. {
77.   print "\nThe following attempts to close files failed:\n";
78.   $~ = OUTPUT_HEADER;
79.   write;
80.   $~ = OUTPUT;
81.
82.   foreach my $File ( @Failed )
83.   {
84.     %Data = %$File;
85.     write;
86.   }
87. }
88.
89.
90. format OUTPUT_HEADER=
91. @<<<<<< @<<<<< @<<<<<<<<<<<<<<< @<<<<<<<<<<<<<<<<<<<<<<<<<<<<<<<<<<<
92. 'ID', 'Locks', 'User', 'Path'
93. ------- ------ ----------------- ------------------------------------
94. .
95.
96. format OUTPUT=
97. @>>>>>> @>>>>> @<<<<<<<<<<<<<<< @<<<<<<<<<<<<<<<<<<<<<<<<<<<<<<<<<<<
98. $Data{id}, $Data{locks}, $Data{user}, $Data{path}
99. .
100.
101. sub Configure
102. {
103.   my( $Config ) = @_;
104.   my $Result = 0;
105.   Getopt::Long::Configure( "prefix_pattern=(-|\/)" );
106.   $Result = GetOptions( $Config,
107.         qw(
108.           machine|m=s
109.           help|?|h
110.         ) );
111.
112.   if( 0 == scalar @ARGV )
```

```
113.  {
114.    $Config->{help} = 1;
115.  }
116.  else
117.  {
118.    push( @{$Config->{ids}}, @ARGV );
119.  }
120.
121. }
122.
123. sub Syntax
124. {
125.   my( $Script ) = ( $0 =~ /([^\\\/]*?)$/ );
126.   my( $Line ) = "-" x length( $0 );
127.
128.   print <<EOT;
129.
130. $0
131. $Line
132. Force an open file on a server to close.
133.
134. Syntax:
135.   perl $0 [-m Machine] FileID [ FileID2 [ ... ] ]
136.     -m.........Close files on the specified machine.
137.     FileID......The file ID of the open file.
138.
139. EOT
140. }
```

Recovering Documents

The Windows operating system has always used file extensions to map a particular file to the application that created it. For example, Microsoft Word documents have a .doc file extension, and Adobe Photoshop files have a .psd extension. If a file is inadvertently renamed with a different extension, determining what type of document the file represents can be quite difficult.

A perfect example is if a hard drive's directory structure is corrupted. When this problem occurs, you would run the CHKDSK.EXE utility or something comparable. All too often, running this utility results in a series of fragmented files with some ambiguous names. Even though some of these files may be fully intact, you have no clue as to what types of files they are. And if you have hundreds of files, you could be spending long nights trying to recover these files.

Fortunately, Win32 employs a few nifty techniques for discovering a document's type. When a script attempts to create a COM object based on the file, Win32 uses different mechanisms to determine the file type, including checking the file's extension and examining the document's class ID, to name just a couple.

Example 4.9 takes advantage of this functionality by attempting to load the document as a COM object. If the document successfully loads, the script attempts to rename the document based on the file's title, subject, and file type. You can pass in any number of file paths, including wildcards, as shown here:

```
perl Documents.pl *.* c:\found\*.* c:\recovered\File001
```

The script is a bit heavy on the Microsoft Office applications but can easily be modified to work with other applications as well.

You need to be aware of a caveat regarding the types of documents that can be resolved: The software for a particular application must be installed on the machine running the script even if the file in question is located on another machine. For example, if you have installed MS Office 98, an MS Word 2000 document may not resolve correctly.

Example 4.9   *Recovering Renamed Documents*

```
01. use Win32::OLE;
02.
03. my %Total = (
04.    tested   => 0,
05.    files    => 0,
06.    recovered => 0,
07. );
08. foreach my $Mask ( @ARGV )
09. {
10.    if( $Mask =~ /[*?]/ )
11.    {
12.      push( @FileList, glob( $Mask ) );
13.    }
14.    else
15.    {
16.      push( @FileList, $Mask );
17.    }
18. }
19.
20. foreach my $File ( @FileList )
21. {
22.    my $Obj;
23.    next if( $File eq "." || $File eq ".." );
24.
25.    $Total{files}++;
26.    print "$Total{files}) '$File' ";
27.
```

```perl
28.    if( $Obj = Win32::OLE->GetObject( $File ) )
29.    {
30.      my( $Type, $Ext, $Subject, $Title );
31.      my $NewFileName = "";
32.
33.      $Total{recovered}++;
34.
35.      $Type = join( "", Win32::OLE->QueryObjectType( $Obj ) );
36.      $App  = $Obj->{Application}->{Name};
37.      if( $App =~ /word/i )
38.      {
39.        $Ext = ".doc";
40.        $Total{type}->{word}++;
41.      }
42.      elsif( $App =~ /excel/i )
43.      {
44.        $Ext = ".xls";
45.        $Total{type}->{excel}++;
46.      }
47.      elsif( $App =~ /project/i )
48.      {
49.        $Ext = ".mpp";
50.        $Total{type}->{project}++;
51.      }
52.      elsif( $App =~ /powerpoint/i )
53.      {
54.        $Ext = ".ppt";
55.        $Total{type}->{powerpoint}++;
56.      }
57.      else
58.      {
59.        $Ext = ".$Type";
60.        $Total{type}->{lc $Type}++;
61.      }
62.
63.      $Title = $Obj->BuiltinDocumentProperties( "Title" )->{Value};
64.      $Subject = $Obj->BuiltinDocumentProperties( "Subject" )->{Value};
65.
66.      my ( $Path, $FileName, $FileExt )
67.         = ( $File =~ /(.*?[\\\/]?)([^\\\/]*?)(\..*)$/ );
68.      if( ( "" ne $Title ) || ( "" ne $Subject ) )
69.      {
70.        $FileName = ( "" ne $Title )? $Title : $Subject;
71.
72.        # Replace any bad chars
73.        $FileName =~ s/[\\\/.?*]/-/g;
74.        $FilePath = "$FileName$Ext";
75.      }
76.      print " $App document\n";
77.
78.      if( ( $Ext ne $FileExt ) && ( $File ne $FilePath ) )
79.      {
```

continues ▶

Example 4.9 *continued*

```perl
80.       my $iCount = 1;
81.       while( ( -e "$Path$FilePath" )
82.             || ( defined $UsedFileNames{lc $FilePath} ) )
83.       {
84.         $iCount++;
85.         $FilePath = "$FileName$iCount$Ext";
86.       }
87.       $UsedFileNames{lc $FilePath} = 1;
88.       push( @RenameFiles, [$File, $FilePath] );
89.     }
90.     else
91.     {
92.       print " No need to rename.";
93.       print " The file is correctly named already.\n";
94.     }
95.
96.     # Try to properly close the application
97.     if( ! $Obj->Close( 0 ) )
98.     {
99.       if( ! $Obj->Quit( 0 ) )
100.      {
101.        $Obj->Exit( 0 );
102.      }
103.    }
104.  }
105.  print "\n";
106. }
107.
108. print "Renaming files:\n" if( scalar @RenameFiles );
109. foreach $File ( @RenameFiles )
110. {
111.   my $Result = 0;
112.   print "  '$File->[0]' -> '$File->[1]' ";
113.   $Result = rename( $File->[0], $File->[1] );
114.   print (($Result)? "Success" : "Failed" );
115.   push( @FailedToRename, $File->[0] ) if( ! $Result );
116.   print "\n";
117. }
118.
119. print "\n\nTotals:\n";
120. foreach my $Type ( sort( keys( %{$Total{type}} ) ) )
121. {
122.   print "\t\u$Type files: $Total{type}->{$Type}\n";
123. }
124. print "\t--------------------------------\n";
125. print "\tTotal tested: $Total{files}\n";
126. print "\tTotal recovered: $Total{recovered}\n\n";
127.
128. if( scalar @FailedToRename )
129. {
130.   print "\tThe following files are good but failed to rename:\n";
131.   map { print "\t\t$_\n"; } @FailedToRename;
132. }
```

Conclusion

It is reasonable to presume that crises will occur on your network. Whether a workstation's drive becomes corrupt or a file server crashes, it is not a matter of "if" but more a matter of "when." When such a crisis arises, it is best to be ready so that you can take action for a swift resolution. Perl is the perfect language to prepare for such crises, as well as react to them.

The interesting thing about leveraging Perl in this regard is that it is simply a tool. The administrator is required to design a Perl-based solution that is specific for his network. But when the language is married to such a solution, you can rest assured that you will be ready for any problem.

5

Monitoring and Reporting

Most network administrators' job descriptions explain that the position entails maintenance and planning. However, any administrator who has been at the job more than a week can tell you that this is only one-third of the work. Extinguishing fires typically ends up being the bulk of the job. With a bit of foresight and planning, however, many of these fires can be prevented.

Reporting is a way of monitoring events that are taking place and being able to address them when they occur. For example, a smoke alarm monitors the air quality and begins to beep if too many smoke particles or intense heat is detected. Reporting typically is performed in two discrete phases: detection and alerting.

Detection

The first phase of reporting is the detection phase. This particular phase is concerned with monitoring events. An event may be a service stopping or a machine going offline. Typically, detection is performed by polling; that is, a script continuously requests an update on the state of some device or process.

Polling techniques can present problems because there could be several points of failure between the querying process and the device to be queried. For example, if one machine is monitoring another, it may attempt to contact the monitored box every minute. If the monitored machine fails to respond, an assumption is made that the machine has gone down. However, this assumption may or may not be correct. A router between the monitoring machine and the supposedly downed server may have been overwhelmed by a burst of network activity. Therefore, the monitoring script must take this situation into consideration, possibly by waiting until the connection test fails repeatedly over a span of time to account for a few dropped network packets.

There is no one simple technique to monitoring an event. Each task requires its own unique method. For example, you might test a server to see whether it is alive by pinging its IP address. You can do so by using the Net::Ping module or shelling out to the PING.EXE program. In this case, both approaches would work; however, each technique would require different processing. One technique examines the results of a function call, and the other parses the text output of an external program.

Alerting

When a monitored event occurs, the second phase of reporting begins. This is the process of alerting.

The results of some monitoring action can be reported in several ways. The first should be the Win32 Event Log. Using this log is the standard way of journaling system events that take place on an NT or Windows 2000 machine. This log is always available, it can be remotely accessed, any account can write to it, and it logs the time and date of each entry, among other things.

Event Logs

Windows NT/2000 provides journaling capability so that informational as well as critical events can be logged. This feature is known as the Event Log.

The Event Log's function is similar to that of UNIX's syslog daemon. An application (or device driver, service, component, or any executable piece of code) can register an *event* on any machine for which it has permissions. You can review these events by running the EVENTVWR.EXE application.

Typically, a server has three Event Logs: Application, System, and Security. Windows 2000 Server also adds Directory Service, DNS Server, and File Replication Service logs. Normally, an application reports events only under the appropriate log. So, security-related events are reported to the Security log, and system events (driver failures, network cards binding to DHCP addresses, and so on) are reported under the System log.

Two Win32 Perl extensions expose the Event Log API functions: Win32::EventLog and Win32::Lanman. Either one would suffice for logging events. A third extension, called Win32::EventLog::Message, works in conjunction with either of them.

Event Logs and Message Tables

The `Win32::EventLog::Message` extension provides a *message table* that permits formatting of your Event Log message. A message table is simply a list of formats that can be used to display information. Typically, a message table has precomposed text strings in a particular format. These text strings have placeholders that are swapped with variable information for display onscreen or in the Event Log. For example, say that you write code that displays a dialog box indicating the time of day. You may create this entry in a message table: `The current time is: %1!s!`. When you display the dialog box, the `%1!s!` is swapped with some string that the program decides on at runtime. This extension works similarly to `printf()`.

The beauty of message tables is that if you need to change languages, you can simply replace the resource .DLL file that contains the message table. Say that you "internationalize" your program in both English and Turkish. Let's also say that the English version of the message table results in a message box that looks like Figure 5.1. However, when you swap the English message table with a Turkish version, the dialog box magically appears like the one in Figure 5.2. This change occurs without having to recompile your program; all you need to do is create the new message table .DLL file.

Figure 5.1   *A simple message table.*

Figure 5.2   *The same dialog box as in Figure 5.1, using a Turkish message table.*

In an Event Log, message tables are referred to as *sources*. A source is associated with a particular log. For example, a user may want to create a source for some Perl script that runs as a service. She would probably want to associate the source under the System log (where most services go). A program must *register* an Event Log source by specifying the source name and path to a resource library (typically a .DLL, .EXE, or .SYS file that contains a message table. After a source is properly registered, Event Log entries that are associated with the particular source link to the source's message table.

Each log entry can be associated with an *event ID*, which indicates which entry in the message table to use. The message table entry is typically some text message that has modifiable fields. For example, Figure 5.3 contains this message:

```
A request to suspend power was denied by WINWORD.EXE.
```

This message comes from the Win32k event source, which is mapped to `%SystemRoot%\System32\win32k.sys`. The event ID is 240, so when the Event Log displays this particular entry, it opens the `%SystemRoot%\System32\win32k.sys` file and looks up the message from row 240 of the file's message table. That particular table entry consists of this string:

```
A request to suspend power was denied by %1!s!.
```

When the Event Log entry was made, a number of strings were provided. The `%1!s!` is simply replaced by the contents of the first string and interpreted as a text string. If `%2!d!` appeared in the message, it would have been replaced with the contents of the second string (interpreted as a numeric value).

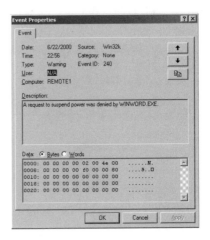

Figure 5.3   *An Event Log entry.*

When Perl reports an Event Log entry (using `Win32::EventLog` or `Win32::Lanman`), it can specify a source, event ID, and strings (at least these are the three most important things). However, most users want to report an event on behalf of their Perl script. Because a Perl script does not, by default, have a source associated with a message table, the Perl script's log entry ends up looking like Figure 5.4. Notice that the strings passed in are displayed, but not in an elegant fashion.

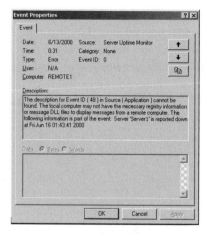

Figure 5.4   *An Event Log entry without a message table.*

This is where The `Win32::EventLog::Message` extension comes in. It provides a simple message table with one entry, which contains

    %1!s!

This table entry simply expands to whatever you passed in. Therefore, your Perl script can pass in any formatted text (with carriage returns, multiple spaces, tabs, and so on). Figure 5.5 illustrates how the same string in Figure 5.4 looks when using this extension's message table.

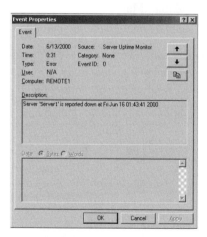

Figure 5.5   *An Event Log entry using `Win32::EventLog::Message`.*

Because the message table that `Win32::EventLog::Message` uses is very simple and contains no text itself, it does not allow for internationalization. After all, how do you internationalize the `%1!s!` string? The extension does, however, allow a script to register and unregister other message tables as sources. Therefore, a coder could create a message table using some message table compiler (such as MC.EXE, Microsoft's message table compiler) and a C compiler and then use this extension to register the resulting .DLL file as an Event Log source. This provides a mechanism to customize and internationalize the Event Log display.

Event Log Sources

Each Event Log can have several different sources, and typically, it does. It usually has an Event Log source for every program that may need to report an event. Often multiple programs share the same source (message file).

You can discover what sources are registered by using `Win32::EventLog::Message`'s `GetSourceList()` function. Example 5.1 shows how to use this function. The script accepts the Event Log as the first parameter, which can be any of the Event Logs, such as System, Application, Security, or any other Event Log that has been registered. The script displays all event sources registered under the specified Event Log.

If the script is passed any additional parameters, they are interpreted as source names. The message table paths for only the specified source names are then displayed.

For example, the command line

```
perl DumpEventSources.pl System
```

may result in the display illustrated in Figure 5.6. Notice that the last source listed (line 22) points to the `Win32::EventLog::Message` Perl extension .DLL file. This is the result of registering the `Win32::EventLog::Message` extension as the "My Perl Log" System Event Log source.

```
C:\>perl DumpEventSources.pl system
System Event Log:
  Count Source Log Name            Path To Message Table
  ----- ------------------------   ------------------------------------------
      1 Alerter                    %SystemRoot%\System32\netmsg.dll
      2 Application Popup          %SystemRoot%\System32\ntdll.dll
      3 AsyncMac                   %SystemRoot%\System32\mprmsg.dll
      4 AtmElan                    %SystemRoot%\System32\netevent.dll
      5 Atmarpc                    %SystemRoot%\System32\netevent.dll
      6 AviatorPro                 %SystemRoot%\System32\netevent.dll
                                   %SystemRoot%\System32\drivers\webdrv2.sys
      7 Browser                    %SystemRoot%\System32\netevent.dll
```

```
 8 DCOM                            %SystemRoot%\System32\netevent.dll
 9 DfsDriver                       %SystemRoot%\System32\netevent.dll
10 DfsSvc                          %SystemRoot%\System32\netevent.dll
11 Dhcp                            %SystemRoot%\System32\dhcpcsvc.dll
12 Distributed Link Tracking C     %SystemRoot%\System32\netevent.dll
13 Dnsapi                          %SystemRoot%\System32\netevent.dll
14 Dnscache                        %SystemRoot%\System32\netevent.dll
15 IISCTLS                         C:\WINNT\System32\inetsrv\iisrstas.exe
16 IISLOG                          C:\WINNT\System32\inetsrv\iscomlog.dll
17 IISMAP                          C:\WINNT\System32\iismap.dll
18 IPBOOTP                         %SystemRoot%\System32\ipbootp.dll
19 IPNATHLP                        %SystemRoot%\System32\ipnathlp.dll
20 IPRIP2                          %SystemRoot%\System32\iprip2.dll
21 IPRouterManager                 %SystemRoot%\System32\mprmsg.dll
22 My Perl Log                     C:\Perl\site\lib\auto\Win32\EventLog\
                                   Message\Message.dll
```

Figure 5.6   *Output from Example 5.1.*

The script calls the GetSource() function from Win32::EventLog::Message to discover properties for each Event Log source. The path is one of the properties that the function retrieves.

Example 5.1   *Displaying an Event Log's Various Sources and Event Table Files*

```
01. use Win32::EventLog::Message;
02.
03. $LogName = lc shift @ARGV
04.     || die "Syntax: $0 <Event Log Name> [source [source2 [...]]]";
05. print "\u$LogName Event Log:\n";
06.
07. $~ = MessageLogHeader;
08. write;
09.
10. $~ = MessageLogPath;
11.
12. if( scalar @ARGV )
13. {
14.     push( @List, @ARGV );
15. }
16. else
17. {
18.     GetSourceList( $LogName, \@List );
19. }
20.
21. $Num = 0;
22. foreach $Name ( sort( @List ) )
23. {
24.     if( GetSource( $LogName, $Name, \%Config ) )
25.     {
26.         $Num++;
```

continues ▶

Example 5.1   *continued*

```
27.         $Path = join( " " x 30, split( /[,;]/, $Config{path} ) );
28.         write;
29.    }
30. }
31.
32. format MessageLogHeader =
33.    @>>>> @<<<<<<<<<<<<<<<<<<<<<<< @<<<<<<<<<<<<<<<<<<<<<<<<<<<<<<<<<
34.    "Count", "Source Log Name",             "Path To Message Table"
35.    ..... ........................  ...................................
36. .
37.
38. format MessageLogPath =
39.    @>>>> @<<<<<<<<<<<<<<<<<<<<<<< ^<<<<<<<<<<<<<<<<<<<<<<<<<<<<<<<<<
40.    $Num, $Name,                   $Path
41. ~                                 ^<<<<<<<<<<<<<<<<<<<<<<<<<<<<<<<<<
42.                                   $Path
43. ~                                 ^<<<<<<<<<<<<<<<<<<<<<<<<<<<<<<<<<
44.                                   $Path
45. ~                                 ^<<<<<<<<<<<<<<<<<<<<<<<<<<<<<<<<<
46.                                   $Path
47. ~                                 ^<<<<<<<<<<<<<<<<<<<<<<<<<<<<<<<<<
48.                                   $Path
49. ~                                 ^<<<<<<<<<<<<<<<<<<<<<<<<<<<<<<<<<
50.                                   $Path
51. .
```

Monitoring

Monitoring implies that you are waiting for some event to occur and will perform some action when it does. Such events include change of state (such as a service transitioning from the running to the stopped state), a configuration change (such as a registry key value being modified), and a structural change (such as the deletion or creation of files and directories). For example, if someone copies a file to a directory, a monitoring script can detect the change and perform a virus scan. Or, maybe the script could update a database with details of the new file.

A monitoring script can be implemented in many different ways. It can be designed to run either as a standalone script or as a daemon. Standalone scripts are run by an administrator only when she needs to begin monitoring some process. A daemon starts when the computer boots and continues monitoring until either the machine is shut down or the administrator stops it (refer to Chapter 8, "Win32 Services," to learn more details about daemons and services).

Monitoring Internal Processes

Say that you have a Web server that runs a series of CGI scripts. These CGI scripts must shell out to separate processes from time to time. These processes could be anything from NBTSTAT.EXE (to display NetBEUI statistics) to NETSTAT.EXE (to display network connections). As requests to the Web server increase, the server, of course, slows down. The impact on performance can cause scripts to run events more slowly, taking longer for a process to finish. As this occurs, more Web requests may come in, creating new CGI scripts and processes and further compounding the problem.

Many Web servers can specify a script timeout value. If a script does not finish in the specified amount of time, the Web server terminates it. This, however, does not allow you to discriminate between one script that requires a long time to process and another process that should not take a long time at all. A workable solution would be to design a service that terminates only selected processes after a specified duration.

Such a solution could also be used for other reasons, such as preventing a user from running programs longer than an allotted time. This could be for the sake of billing a customer in an Internet café or guaranteeing that a process does not enter a deadlock condition.

Example 5.2 monitors all processes and terminates any that have been alive for longer than the permitted time. In this particular script, only two processes are monitored: Telnet and FTP. These processes, and their timeout values, are configured in lines 17 through 20. The Telnet process is allowed to run for no more than 120 seconds. The FTP program is granted 0 seconds of runtime. This is effectively the same as saying that the FTP process is prevented from running (actually, the process can run, but it is terminated almost instantly).

Most of the code is based on the typical Win32::Daemon framework (refer to Chapter 8). The real engine is on line 89 and lines 132 through 156. Line 89 procures a WMI COM object that is used for the duration of the service (refer to Chapter 9, "ADSI and WMI," for more details on WMI). Lines 132 through 156 use the WMI COM object to walk through each process (via the collection of Win32_Process WMI objects), checking for a monitored process. If the process is monitored, the number of seconds it has been running is calculated and is compared to the permitted time threshold for the particular process. If the running time equals or exceeds the allotted time, the process is terminated.

This script uses WMI to walk through the list of all processes on a machine. The process list can be procured from any machine on a network, thus enabling the script to monitor processes on remote machines. Lines 52 and 53 create the WMI moniker. Notice that the $Config{machine} hash key is referenced on line 53. This is where another machine name can be specified. By default, this value equates to the period (".") character, indicating that the local machine is to be monitored. You can specify a remote machine by passing in the -m Machine_Name parameter when installing the service.

The script can monitor remote machines just as well as a local machine. This is done by passing in the -m switch followed by a machine name when installing the service. When the service is installed to monitor remote machines, it must be configured to log on as a user account (and not the default Local System account). This is required because the Local System account has administrative rights, but only on the local machine. The Local System does not have rights to access remote resources. Therefore, the service must log on using an account that has administrative privileges on the remote machine. For example,

```
perl procmon.pl -install -m Server1 -u MonitorDaemon -p AdminPassword
```

assumes that the MonitorDaemon account has administrative privileges on the machine \\Server1.

If you are installing this to run on a local machine, there is no need to specify an account name and password. Notice that in lines 264 and 265, the specified username and password are assigned to the service configuration hash. If no user account and password are specified, these will be empty, which Win32::Daemon interprets as the Local System account.

WMI must be installed on both the machine running the service and the machine that is being monitored. Windows 2000 comes with WMI installed, but NT 4.0 and Windows 95/98 must have WMI installed. The technology can be downloaded from Microsoft's Web site. See Chapter 9 for more details on WMI.

Example 5.2 *Monitoring for Prohibited Processes*

```
01. use Time::Local;
02. use Getopt::Long;
03. use Win32::Daemon;
04. use Win32::OLE qw( in );
05. use Win32::EventLog;
06. use Win32::EventLog::Message;
07.
08. $SUCCESS = 0;
09.
10. # How much time do we sleep between polling the service state?
11. $SERVICE_SLEEP_TIME = 1;
12.
13. # The list of process names and seconds they are allowed to run
14. # Keys are the full names (must be lowercase) and values are the
15. # number of seconds permitted to run.  A zero value indicates the
```

```
16. # process must be terminated as soon as possible.
17. %PROC_LIST = (
18.   "telnet.exe"  => 120,
19.   "ftp.exe"     => 0,
20. );
21.
22. $SERVICE_ALIAS = "ProcMon";
23. $SERVICE_NAME = "Process Monitor";
24.
25. $LOG_FILE_PATH = ( Win32::GetFullPathName( $0 ) =~ /^(.*)?\.[^.]*$/ )[0];
26. $LOG_FILE_PATH .= ".log";
27.
28. %Config = (
29.   machine => ".",
30.   logfile => $LOG_FILE_PATH,
31. );
32.
33. Configure( \%Config, @ARGV );
34. if( $Config{install} )
35. {
36.   InstallService();
37.   exit;
38. }
39. elsif( $Config{remove} )
40. {
41.   RemoveService();
42.   exit;
43. }
44. elsif( $Config{help} )
45. {
46.   Syntax();
47.   exit;
48. }
49.
50. # This is the WMI moniker that will connect to a machine's
51. # CIM (Common Information Model) repository
52. $CLASS = "winmgmts:{impersonationLevel=impersonate}!"
53.       . "//$Config{machine}/root/cimv2";
54.
55.
56. # Register our simple Event Log message table resource DLL with
57. # the System Event Log's $SERVICE_NAME source
58. Win32::EventLog::Message::RegisterSource( 'System', $SERVICE_NAME );
59.
60. # Try to open a log file. We report what the service is doing and
61. # what process are terminated.
62. if( open( LOG, ">$Config{logfile}" ) )
63. {
64.   # Select the LOG filehandle...
65.   my $BackupHandle = select( LOG );
66.   # ...then turn on autoflush (no buffering)...
67.   $| = 1;
68.   # ...then restore the previous selected I/O handle
```

continues ▶

Example 5.2   *continued*

```
69.    select( $BackupHandle );
70.  }
71.
72.  # Start the service...
73.  if( ! Win32::Daemon::StartService() )
74.  {
75.    ReportError( "Could not start the $0 service" );
76.    exit();
77.  }
78.
79.  $PrevState = SERVICE_STARTING;
80.  Write( "$SERVICE_NAME service is starting...\n" );
81.  while( SERVICE_STOPPED != ( $State = Win32::Daemon::State() ) )
82.  {
83.    if( SERVICE_START_PENDING == $State )
84.    {
85.      ReportInfo( "Starting $SERVICE_NAME service. "
86.                      . "Monitoring $Config{machine}" );
87.      # Initialization code:
88.      # Get the WMI (Microsoft's implementation of WBEM) interface
89.      if( $WMI = Win32::OLE->GetObject( $CLASS ) )
90.      {
91.        Win32::Daemon::State( SERVICE_RUNNING );
92.        ReportInfo( "$SERVICE_NAME service has started: "
93.                        . "Monitoring $Config{machine}" );
94.        $PrevState = SERVICE_RUNNING;
95.      }
96.      else
97.      {
98.        Win32::Daemon::State( SERVICE_STOPPED );
99.        ReportError( "$SERVICE_NAME service could not access "
100.                        . "WMI: Aborting." );
101.      }
102.    }
103.    elsif( SERVICE_PAUSE_PENDING == $State )
104.    {
105.      # "Pausing...";
106.      Win32::Daemon::State( SERVICE_PAUSED );
107.      ReportWarn( "$SERVICE_NAME service has paused." );
108.      $PrevState = SERVICE_PAUSED;
109.      next;
110.    }
111.    elsif( SERVICE_CONTINUE_PENDING == $State )
112.    {
113.      # "Resuming...";
114.      Win32::Daemon::State( SERVICE_RUNNING );
115.      ReportInfo( "$SERVICE_NAME service has resumed." );
116.      $PrevState = SERVICE_RUNNING;
117.      next;
118.    }
119.    elsif( SERVICE_STOP_PENDING == $State )
```

```
120.    {
121.      # "Stopping...";
122.      undef $WMI;
123.      Win32::Daemon::State( SERVICE_STOPPED );
124.      ReportWarn( "$SERVICE_NAME service is stopping." );
125.      $PrevState = SERVICE_STOPPED;
126.      next;
127.    }
128.    elsif( SERVICE_RUNNING == $State )
129.    {
130.      # The service is running as normal...
131.      # Get the collection of Win32_Process objects
132.      foreach my $Proc ( in( $WMI->InstancesOf( "Win32_Process" ) ) )
133.      {
134.        my $ProcName = $Proc->{Name};
135.        my $lcProcName = lc $ProcName;
136.        my $ProcCreation = $Proc->{CreationDate};
137.
138.        if( ( defined $PROC_LIST{$lcProcName} )
139.          && ( defined $Proc->{CreationDate} ) )
140.        {
141.          my $ProcSeconds = DateInSeconds( $ProcCreation );
142.          if( $PROC_LIST{$lcProcName} <= ( time() - $ProcSeconds ) )
143.          {
144.            if( $SUCCESS == $Proc->Terminate( 0 ) )
145.            {
146.              ReportWarn( "Killed $ProcName created on "
147.                    . localtime( $ProcSeconds ) );
148.            }
149.            else
150.            {
151.              ReportError( "Failed to Kill $ProcName created on "
152.                    . localtime( $ProcSeconds ) );
153.            }
154.          }
155.        }
156.      }
157.    }
158.    else
159.    {
160.      # Got an unhandled control message. Set the state to
161.      # whatever the previous state was.
162.      Write( "Got odd state $State. Setting state to '$PrevState'" );
163.      Win32::Daemon::State( $PrevState );
164.    }
165.    sleep( $SERVICE_SLEEP_TIME );
166.  }
167.
168.  sub DateInSeconds
169.  {
170.    my( $Date ) = @_;
171.    my( @List ) = ($Date =~ /(\d{4})(\d{2})(\d{2})(\d{2})(\d{2})(\d{2})/);
172.    my( $Seconds ) = timelocal( $List[5], $List[4], $List[3],
```

continues ▶

Example 5.2   *continued*

```
173.                    $List[2], $List[1] - 1, $List[0] - 1900 );
174.   return( $Seconds );
175. }
176.
177. sub ReportError
178. {
179.   my( $Message) = @_;
180.   return( Report( $Message,
181.           $SERVICE_NAME,
182.           EVENTLOG_ERROR_TYPE ) );
183. }
184.
185. sub ReportWarn
186. {
187.   my( $Message ) = @_;
188.   return( Report( $Message,
189.           $SERVICE_NAME,
190.           EVENTLOG_WARNING_TYPE ) );
191. }
192.
193. sub ReportInfo
194. {
195.   my( $Message) = @_;
196.   return( Report( $Message,
197.           $SERVICE_NAME,
198.           EVENTLOG_INFORMATION_TYPE ) );
199. }
200.
201. sub Report
202. {
203.   my( $Message, $LogSource, $Type ) = @_;
204.
205.   Write( "$Message\n" );
206.   if( my $EventLog = new Win32::EventLog( $LogSource ) )
207.   {
208.     $EventLog->Report(
209.       {
210.         Strings => $Message,
211.         EventID => 0,
212.         EventType => $Type,
213.         Category  => undef,
214.       }
215.     );
216.     $EventLog->Close();
217.   }
218. }
219.
220. sub InstallService
221. {
222.   my $Service = GetService();
223.
224.   if( "." ne $Config{machine} )
```

```
225.    {
226.       # Remove any slashes
227.       $Config{machine} =~ s#[\\/]##;
228.       $Service->{parameters} .= " -m \"$Config{machine}\""
229.    }
230.    $Service->{parameters} .= " -l \"$Config{logfile}\"";
231.    if( Win32::Daemon::CreateService( $Service ) )
232.    {
233.      print "The $Service->{display} was successfully installed.\n";
234.    }
235.    else
236.    {
237.      print "Failed to add the $Service->{display} service.\n";
238.      print "Error: " . GetError() . "\n";
239.    }
240. }
241.
242. sub RemoveService
243. {
244.    my $Service = GetService();
245.
246.    if( Win32::Daemon::DeleteService( $Service->{name} ) )
247.    {
248.      print "The $Service->{display} was successfully removed.\n";
249.    }
250.    else
251.    {
252.      print "Failed to remove the $Service->{display} service.\n";
253.      print "Error: " . GetError() . "\n";
254.    }
255. }
256.
257. sub GetService
258. {
259.    my $ScriptPath = join( "", Win32::GetFullPathName( $0 ) );
260.    my %Hash = (
261.      name  => $SERVICE_ALIAS,
262.      display => $SERVICE_NAME,
263.      path  => $^X,
264.      user  => $Config{user},
265.      password   => $Config{password},
266.      description => "Monitors processes.",
267.      parameters => "\"$ScriptPath\"",
268.    );
269.    return( \%Hash );
270. }
271.
272. sub GetError
273. {
274.    return( Win32::FormatMessage( Win32::Daemon::GetLastError() ) );
275. }
276.
277. sub Write
```

continues ▶

Example 5.2   *continued*

```
278. {
279.   my( $Message ) = @_;
280.   $Message = "[" . scalar( localtime() ) . "] $Message";
281.   if( fileno( LOG ) )
282.   {
283.     print LOG $Message;
284.   }
285. }
286.
287. sub Configure
288. {
289.   my( $Config, @Args ) = @_;
290.   my $Result;
291.
292.   Getopt::Long::Configure( "prefix_pattern=(-|\/)" );
293.   $Result = GetOptions( $Config,
294.                 qw(
295.                   install|i
296.                   remove|r
297.                   machine|m=s
298.                   logfile|l=s
299.                   user|u|a|account=s
300.                   password=s
301.                   help
302.                 )
303.               );
304.   $Config->{help} = 1 if( ! $Result );
305. }
306.
307. sub Syntax
308. {
309.   my( $Script ) = ( $0 =~ /([^\\]*?)$/ );
310.   my $Whitespace = " " x length( $Script );
311.   print << "EOT";
312.
313. Syntax:
314.     $Script -install [-a Account][-p Password][-m Machine][-l Path]
315.     $Whitespace -remove
316.     $Whitespace -help
317.
318.         -install...........Installs the service.
319.             -a.............Specifies what account the service runs under.
320.                            Default: Local System
321.             -p.............Specifies the password the service uses.
322.             -m.............Specifies what machine to monitor.
323.                            Default: Local machine
324.             -l.............Specifies a log file path.
325.                            Default: $LOG_FILE_PATH
326.         -remove...........Removes the service.
327. EOT
328. }
```

Monitoring Network Server States

A perfect example of a monitoring daemon is a service that monitors machines for network uptime. The service occasionally pings a host and reports when the host does not respond. Example 5.3 does exactly this.

The service runs and monitors the machines in the @HOSTS array defined in lines 18 through 22. In this case, the IP addresses 127.0.0.1, 192.168.3.22, and www.mydomain.com are monitored. You can replace these addresses with a list of IP addresses or computer names to monitor.

Lines 18 and 22 decide which path to use to store a log file. You can easily modify these lines to specify the path of a named pipe so that you can monitor the service in real-time by using Example 8.13 in Chapter 8.

Notice that line 51 registers an Event Log source, which guarantees that any reports made to the Event Log will be, at least, formatted nicely. This is significant because if you're reading the logged events, you might overlook any event that is not properly formatted (thinking that the event was either a mistake or not something to take seriously).

The script reports an event to the Event Log when significant issues arise, such as the starting and stopping of the service as well as a server being unreachable.

Lines 292 through 297 define the Alert() function. You can customize this monitoring script by adding code to this function to send out an alert. Such alerts could alert you of the downed machine by sending email, paging you, dialing a telephone, activating an X10 module, or whatever other clever technique you can think of.

To install this service, simply run it and pass in an install parameter as follows:

```
perl monitor.pl -install
```

To remove a service that has already been installed, run the following:

```
perl monitor.pl -remove
```

Example 5.3 *A Machine Monitoring Service*

```
01. use Net::Ping;
02. use Getopt::Long;
03. use Win32::Daemon;
04. use Win32::EventLog;
05. use Win32::EventLog::Message;
06.
07. # How long to wait for a ping ($PING_TIMEOUT), how long to wait between
08. # ping attempts ($PING_INTERVAL) and how many pings to try before
09. # concluding that a server is down ($PING_MAX_COUNT)
10. $PING_TIMEOUT = 5;
11. $PING_INTERVAL = 10;
```

continues ▶

Example 5.3 *continued*

```perl
12. $PING_MAX_COUNT = 5;
13.
14. # How much time do we sleep between polling the service state?
15. $SERVICE_SLEEP_TIME = 5;
16.
17. # The list of machines to monitor
18. @HOSTS = qw(
19.        127.0.0.1
20.        192.168.3.22
21.        www.mydomain.com
22. );
23.
24. $SERVICE_ALIAS = "UpMon";
25. $SERVICE_NAME = "Server Uptime Monitor";
26. $LOG_FILE_PATH = ( Win32::GetFullPathName( $0 ) =~ /^(.*)?\.[^.]*$/ )[0];
27. $LOG_FILE_PATH .= ".log";
28.
29. %Config = (
30.    logfile => $LOG_FILE_PATH,
31. );
32. Configure( \%Config, @ARGV );
33. if( $Config{install} )
34. {
35.    InstallService();
36.    exit;
37. }
38. elsif( $Config{remove} )
39. {
40.    RemoveService();
41.    exit;
42. }
43. elsif( $Config{help} )
44. {
45.    Syntax();
46.    exit;
47. }
48.
49. # Register our simple Event Log message table resource DLL with
50. # the System Event Log's $SERVICE_NAME source
51. Win32::EventLog::Message::RegisterSource( 'System', $SERVICE_NAME );
52.
53. # Try to open the log file
54. if( open( LOG, ">$Config{logfile}" ) )
55. {
56.    # Select the LOG filehandle...
57.    my $BackupHandle = select( LOG );
58.    # ...then turn on autoflush (no buffering)...
59.    $| = 1;
60.    # ...then restore the previous selected I/O handle
61.    select( $BackupHandle );
62. }
```

```
63.
64. # Initialize servers...
65. foreach my $Host ( @HOSTS )
66. {
67.   $Servers->{lc $Host}->{count} = $PING_MAX_COUNT;
68. }
69.
70. # Start the service...
71. if( ! Win32::Daemon::StartService() )
72. {
73.   ReportError( "Could not start the $0 service" );
74.   exit();
75. }
76.
77. $PrevState = SERVICE_STARTING;
78. Write( "$SERVICE_NAME service is starting...\n" );
79. while( SERVICE_STOPPED != ( $State = Win32::Daemon::State() ) )
80. {
81.   if( SERVICE_START_PENDING == $State )
82.   {
83.     # Initialization code
84.     if( $PingObject = Net::Ping->new( "icmp", $PING_TIMEOUT ) )
85.     {
86.       ReportInfo( "Monitoring hosts:\n   "
87.             . join( ", ", @HOSTS ) );
88.       Win32::Daemon::State( SERVICE_RUNNING );
89.       ReportInfo( "$SERVICE_NAME service has started." );
90.       $PrevState = SERVICE_RUNNING;
91.     }
92.     else
93.     {
94.       Win32::Daemon::State( SERVICE_STOPPED );
95.       ReportError( "$SERVICE_NAME service could not create "
96.             . "a Ping object: Aborting." );
97.     }
98.   }
99.   elsif( SERVICE_PAUSE_PENDING == $State )
100.  {
101.    # "Pausing...";
102.    Win32::Daemon::State( SERVICE_PAUSED );
103.    ReportWarn( "$SERVICE_NAME service has paused." );
104.    $PrevState = SERVICE_PAUSED;
105.    next;
106.  }
107.  elsif( SERVICE_CONTINUE_PENDING == $State )
108.  {
109.    # "Resuming...";
110.    Win32::Daemon::State( SERVICE_RUNNING );
111.    ReportInfo( "$SERVICE_NAME service has resumed." );
112.    $PrevState = SERVICE_RUNNING;
113.    next;
114.  }
115.  elsif( SERVICE_STOP_PENDING == $State )
```

continues ▶

Example 5.3   *continued*

```
116.   {
117.     # "Stopping...";
118.     $PingObject->close();
119.     undef $PingObject;
120.     Win32::Daemon::State( SERVICE_STOPPED );
121.     ReportWarn( "$SERVICE_NAME service is stopping." );
122.     $PrevState = SERVICE_STOPPED;
123.     next;
124.   }
125.   elsif( SERVICE_RUNNING == $State )
126.   {
127.     # The service is running as normal...
128.     if( time() > $NextPingTime )
129.     {
130.       PingServers( $PingObject, \%Servers, @HOSTS );
131.       $NextPingTime = time() + $PING_INTERVAL;
132.     }
133.   }
134.   else
135.   {
136.     # Got an unhandled control message. Set the state to
137.     # whatever the previous state was.
138.     Write( "Got odd state $State. Setting state to '$PrevState'" );
139.     Win32::Daemon::State( $PrevState );
140.   }
141.   CheckServers( \%Servers );
142.   sleep( $SERVICE_SLEEP_TIME );
143. }
144.
145. sub PingServers
146. {
147.   my( $PingObject, $Servers, @Hosts ) = @_;
148.
149.   return unless( defined $PingObject );
150.
151.   foreach my $Host ( @HOSTS )
152.   {
153.     if( ! $PingObject->ping( $Host ) )
154.     {
155.       $Servers->{lc $Host}->{count}--;
156.     }
157.     else
158.     {
159.       $Servers->{lc $Host}->{count} = $PING_MAX_COUNT;
160.     }
161.   }
162.   return;
163. }
164.
165. sub CheckServers
166. {
```

```
167.    my( $Servers ) = @_;
168.
169.    foreach $Host ( keys %$Servers )
170.    {
171.      if( 0 >= $Servers->{lc $Host}->{count} )
172.      {
173.        ReportServerDown( $Host );
174.        $Servers->{lc $Host}->{count} = $PING_MAX_COUNT;
175.      }
176.    }
177. }
178.
179. sub ReportServerDown
180. {
181.    my( $Host ) = @_;
182.    my $Error = "Server '$Host' is reported down at " . localtime();
183.
184.    ReportError( $Error );
185.    Alert( $Host );
186. }
187.
188. sub ReportError
189. {
190.    my( $Message) = @_;
191.    return( Report( $Message,
192.            $SERVICE_NAME,
193.            EVENTLOG_ERROR_TYPE ) );
194. }
195.
196. sub ReportWarn
197. {
198.    my( $Message ) = @_;
199.    return( Report( $Message,
200.            $SERVICE_NAME,
201.            EVENTLOG_WARNING_TYPE ) );
202. }
203.
204. sub ReportInfo
205. {
206.    my( $Message) = @_;
207.    return( Report( $Message,
208.            $SERVICE_NAME,
209.            EVENTLOG_INFORMATION_TYPE ) );
210. }
211.
212. sub Report
213. {
214.    my( $Message, $Log, $Type ) = @_;
215.
216.    Write( "$Message\n" );
217.    if( my $EventLog = new Win32::EventLog( $Log ) )
218.    {
219.      $EventLog->Report(
```

continues ▶

Example 5.3 *continued*

```
220.      {
221.         Strings => $Message,
222.         EventID => 0,
223.         EventType => $Type,
224.         Category  => undef,
225.      }
226.    );
227.    $EventLog->Close();
228.  }
229. }
230.
231. sub InstallService
232. {
233.   my $Service = GetService();
234.
235.   $Service->{parameters} .= " -l \"$Config{logfile}\"";
236.   if( Win32::Daemon::CreateService( $Service ) )
237.   {
238.     print "The $Service->{display} was successfully installed.\n";
239.   }
240.   else
241.   {
242.     print "Failed to add the $Service->{display} service.\n";
243.     print "Error: " . GetError() . "\n";
244.   }
245. }
246.
247. sub RemoveService
248. {
249.   my $Service = GetService();
250.
251.   if( Win32::Daemon::DeleteService( $Service->{name} ) )
252.   {
253.     print "The $Service->{display} was successfully removed.\n";
254.   }
255.   else
256.   {
257.     print "Failed to remove the $Service->{display} service.\n";
258.     print "Error: " . GetError() . "\n";
259.   }
260. }
261.
262. sub GetService
263. {
264.   my $ScriptPath = join( "", Win32::GetFullPathName( $0 ) );
265.   my %Hash = (
266.     name  => $SERVICE_ALIAS,
267.     display => $SERVICE_NAME,
268.     path  => $^X,
269.     user  => $Config{user},
270.     password   => $Config{password},
271.     description => "Monitors remote machine's uptime.",
```

```
272.      parameters => "\"$ScriptPath\"",
273.    );
274.    return( \%Hash );
275. }
276.
277. sub GetError
278. {
279.    return( Win32::FormatMessage( Win32::Daemon::GetLastError() ) );
280. }
281.
282. sub Write
283. {
284.    my( $Message ) = @_;
285.    $Message = "[" . scalar( localtime() ) . "] $Message";
286.    if( fileno( LOG ) )
287.    {
288.      print LOG $Message;
289.    }
290. }
291.
292. sub Alert
293. {
294.    my( $Host ) = @_;
295.    # You could add code here to alert administrators via email,
296.    # pager, network message or some other means.
297. }
298.
299. sub Configure
300. {
301.    my( $Config, @Args ) = @_;
302.    my $Result;
303.
304.    Getopt::Long::Configure( "prefix_pattern=(-|\/)" );
305.    $Result = GetOptions( $Config,
306.                  qw(
307.                    install|i
308.                    remove|r
309.                    logfile|l=s
310.                    user|u|a|account=s
311.                    password=s
312.                    help
313.                  )
314.                );
315.    $Config->{help} = 1 if( ! $Result );
316. }
317.
318. sub Syntax
319. {
320.    my( $Script ) = ( $0 =~ /([^\\]*?)$/ );
321.    my $Whitespace = " " x length( $Script );
322.    print << "EOT";
323.
324. Syntax:
```

continues ▶

Example 5.3 *continued*

```
325.  $Script -install [-account Account][-password Password][-l Logfile]
326.  $Whitespace -remove
327.  $Whitespace -help
328.
329.      -install........Installs the service.
330.        -account.......Specifies what account the service runs under.
331.                       Default: Local System
332.        -password......Specifies the password the service uses.
333.        -l.............Specifies a log file path.
334.                       Default: $LOG_FILE_PATH
335.
336.      -remove.........Removes the service.
337. EOT
338. }
```

Scanning Event Logs for Errors

Many computer problems can be traced back to Event Log entries. These events typically describe what happened just before problems occurred. The ability to scan Event Log files on demand is of great importance to you as an administrator.

Two different Win32 Perl extensions provide access into the Event Log: Win32::EventLog and Win32::Lanman. Either one performs the function of Event Log entry retrieval. However, Win32::Lanman requires that a script fetch all entries at one time. The script specifies a range of entry numbers, and the extension retrieves all of them, creating an anonymous hash for each entry and populating an array. I find this to be a bit awkward because it forces the memory use to bloat. Even if a script requests a small number of records in each request, Win32::Lanman must create a new connection to the Event Log and request the information. This seems to be unnecessary overhead.

Win32::EventLog, on the other hand, is an object-oriented extension. Creating a Win32::EventLog object makes the connection to the Event Log itself. Therefore, as long as the object is not undef'ed, the connection to the Event Log is valid. This capability is useful if you expect to walk sequentially through log entries.

Example 5.4 connects to an Event Log and displays all events that were requested. This script accepts a variety of parameters, as described in Table 5.1.

Table 5.1   Parameter Options for Example 5.4

Parameter	Function
-m Machine	Specifies that the Event Log on the specified machine should be examined.
	You can specify as many of these switches as you need.
-l Log	Specifies what Event Log to examine. Typically, it is one of the following: Application Security System
	However, it could be another Event Log, such as Directory Service DNS Server File Replication Service
-s Source	Specifies which event source to examine. By default, all sources are considered.
	The specified sources are used in a regex, so they will be any valid regular expression—for example: IISLOG ^MS.*SVC$ Service Control
-t EventType	Specifies what event type to display. Valid types are as follows: ERROR INFORMATION WARNING AUDIT_SUCCESS AUDIT_FAILURE
	You can specify as many of these switches as you need.
-h Hours	Shows only the specified number of hours' worth of entries. If a value of 2 is passed in, only events generated in the previous two hours are displayed.
	This switch can be used in conjunction with the -d switch.
-d Days	Shows only the specified number of days' worth of entries. If a value of 2 is passed in, only events generated in the previous two days are displayed.
	This switch can be used in conjunction with the -h switch.
-date Date	Displays only events generated between the current and specified dates. This parameter must be in international time format, such as 2000.07.19.

The actual engine of the script is quite simple. Line 69 creates a
Win32::EventLog object for a specific machine. Lines 76 through 97 read an
event entry from the Event Log. If the entry was successfully read and its

timestamp is within the user's specified time range, the event is processed. Line 96 writes to screen only if the event's type matches one of the user's specified event types.

Notice that the actual Read() method in lines 76-79 pass in the flag EVENTLOG_BACKWARDS_READ | EVENTLOG_SEQUENTIAL_READ. This flag indicates that each call into Read() expects to fetch the next record sequentially, so there is no need to specify a record number. Additionally, the flag specifies to read the records backward, starting with the most recent entry.

For example, to use this script, you can enter the following:

```
perl GetEvents.pl -m server1 -m server2 -l system -t error -t warning -d 7
```

This command displays all error and warning events over the past seven days for the system Event Log on both \\server1 and \\server2.

Another example:

```
perl GetEvents.pl -m server1 -l system -t error -t warning -s MSFTPSVC -s "Service
Control"
```

This will display all system errors and warnings on the server \\Server1 that were generated by the Microsoft FTP service or the service control manager.

Example 5.4 *Examining an Event Log*

```
01. use Getopt::Long;
02. use Time::Local;
03. use Win32::EventLog;
04.
05. $SEC = 1;
06. $MIN = 60 * $SEC;
07. $HOUR = 60 * $MIN;
08. $DAY = 24 * $HOUR;
09.
10. %EVENT_TYPE = (
11.   eval EVENTLOG_AUDIT_FAILURE   =>  'AUDIT_FAILURE',
12.   eval EVENTLOG_AUDIT_SUCCESS   =>  'AUDIT_SUCCESS',
13.   eval EVENTLOG_ERROR_TYPE      =>  'ERROR',
14.   eval EVENTLOG_WARNING_TYPE    =>  'WARNING',
15.   eval EVENTLOG_INFORMATION_TYPE =>  'INFORMATION',
16. );
17.
18. %Config = (
19.   log   =>  'System',
20. );
21. Configure( \%Config );
22. if( $Config{help} )
23. {
24.   Syntax();
25.   exit;
26. }
27. if( defined $Config{date} )
```

```
28. {
29.    my( $Year, $Month, $Day )
30.      = ( $Config{date} =~ /^(\d{4}).(\d{2}).(\d{2})/ );
31.    $TIME_LIMIT = timelocal( 0, 0, 0, $Day, $Month - 1, $Year - 1900 );
32. }
33. elsif( $Config{hour} || $Config{day} )
34. {
35.    $TIME_LIMIT = time() - ( $DAY * $Config{day} )
36.              - ( $HOUR * $Config{hour} );
37. }
38.
39. if( ! scalar @{$Config{machine}} )
40. {
41.    push( @{$Config{machine}}, Win32::NodeName );
42. }
43.
44. if( defined( $Config{type} ) )
45. {
46.    foreach my $Mask ( @{$Config{type}} )
47.    {
48.      # Try referencing the EVENTLOG_xxxx_TYPE and EVENTLOG_xxxxx
49.      # constants. One of them is bound to work.
50.      $EVENT_MASK |= eval( "EVENTLOG_" . uc( $Mask ) . "_TYPE" );
51.      $EVENT_MASK |= eval( "EVENTLOG_" . uc( $Mask ) );
52.    }
53. }
54. else
55. {
56.    map
57.    {
58.      $EVENT_MASK |= 0 + $_;
59.    }( keys( %EVENT_TYPE ) );
60. }
61.
62. # Tell the extension to always attempt to fetch the
63. # event log message table text
64. $Win32::EventLog::GetMessageText = 1;
65. $~ = EventLogFormat;
66. foreach my $Machine ( @{$Config{machine}} )
67. {
68.    my $EventLog;
69.    if( $EventLog = Win32::EventLog->new( $Config{log}, $Machine ) )
70.    {
71.      my %Records;
72.      # Next line is a local variables instead
73.      # of a lexically scoped variable (using 'my') since it
74.      # needs to print out in the format
75.      local %Event;
76.      while( ( $EventLog->Read( EVENTLOG_BACKWARDS_READ
77.                | EVENTLOG_SEQUENTIAL_READ,
78.                  0,
79.                  \%Event ) )
80.          && ( $Event{TimeGenerated} > $TIME_LIMIT ) )
```

continues ▶

Example 5.4   *continued*

```
81.    {
82.      # Display the event if it is one of our requested
83.      # event types
84.      if( scalar @{$Config{sources}} )
85.      {
86.        my $fDisplayEvent = 0;
87.        map
88.        {
89.         if( $Event{Source} =~ /$_/i )
90.         {
91.          $fDisplayEvent = 1;
92.         }
93.        } @{$Config{sources}};
94.        next unless( $fDisplayEvent );
95.      }
96.      write if( $Event{EventType} & $EVENT_MASK );
97.    }
98.  }
99.  else
100.  {
101.    print "Can not connect to the $Config{log} ";
102.    print "Event Log on $Machine.\n";
103.  }
104. }
105.
106. sub Configure
107. {
108.   my( $Config ) = @_;
109.
110.   Getopt::Long::Configure( "prefix_pattern=(-|\/)" );
111.   $Result = GetOptions( $Config,
112.             qw(
113.                machine|m=s@
114.                log|l=s
115.                type|t=s@
116.                hour|h=i
117.                day|d=i
118.                date=s
119.                sources|s=s@
120.                help|?
121.             )
122.          );
123.   $Config->{help} = 1 if( ! $Result );
124.   push( @{$Config->{machine}}, Win32::NodeName() ) unless
              ( scalar @{$Config->{machine}} );
125. }
126.
127. sub Syntax
128. {
129.   my( $Script ) = ( $0 =~ /([^\\]*?)$/ );
130.   my $Whitespace = " " x length( $Script );
131.   print << "EOT";
132.
```

```
133. Syntax:
134.    $Script [-m Machine] [-t EventType] [-l Log] [-s Source]
135.    $Whitespace [-h Hours] [-d Days] [-date Date]
136.    $Whitespace [-help]
137.       -m Machine......Name of machine whose Event Log is to be examined.
138.                       This switch can be specified multiple times.
139.       -t EventType....Type of event to display:
140.                          ERROR
141.                          WARNING
142.                          INFORMATION
143.                          AUDIT_SUCCESS
144.                          AUDIT_FAILURE
145.                       This switch can be specified multiple times.
146.       -l Log.........Name of Event Log to examine.
147.                       Common examples:
148.                          Application
149.                          Security
150.                          System
151.                       This switch can be specified multiple times.
152.       -s Source.......Name of a particular event source.
153.                       This switch can be specifed multiple times.
154.       -h Hours.......Will consider events between now and the specified
155.                       number of hours previous.
156.       -d Days........Will consider events between now and the specified
157.                       number of days previous.
158.       -date Date......Will consider events between now and the specified
159.                       date.  Date is in international time format
160.                       (eg. 2000.07.18)
161. EOT
162. }
163.
164. format EventLogFormat =
165. -----------------------------
166. @>>>>> @<<<<<<<<<<<<<<<<<<<<<<<<   ^<<<<<<<<<<<<<<<<<<<<<<<<<<<<<<<<<<
167. $Event{RecordNumber}, "\\\\" . $Event{Computer},    $Event{Message}
168.        @<<<<<<<<<<<<<<<<<<<<<<<<   ^<<<<<<<<<<<<<<<<<<<<<<<<<<<<<<<<<<
169. scalar localtime( $Event{TimeGenerated} ), $Event{Message}
170.        Type: @<<<<<<<<<<<<<<<<<<   ^<<<<<<<<<<<<<<<<<<<<<<<<<<<<<<<<<<
171. $EVENT_TYPE{$Event{EventType}}, $Event{Message}
172.        Source: @<<<<<<<<<<<<<<<<   ^<<<<<<<<<<<<<<<<<<<<<<<<<<<<<<<<<<
173. $Event{Source},                    $Event{Message}
174. ~                                  ^<<<<<<<<<<<<<<<<<<<<<<<<<<<<<<<<<<
175.                                    $Event{Message}
176. ~                                  ^<<<<<<<<<<<<<<<<<<<<<<<<<<<<<<<<<<
177.                                    $Event{Message}
178. ~                                  ^<<<<<<<<<<<<<<<<<<<<<<<<<<<<<<<<<<
179.                                    $Event{Message}
180. ~                                  ^<<<<<<<<<<<<<<<<<<<<<<<<<<<<<<<<<<
181.                                    $Event{Message}
182. ~                                  ^<<<<<<<<<<<<<<<<<<<<<<<<<<<<<<<<<<
183.                                    $Event{Message}
184.
185. .
```

Creating an Alert

In many cases, monitoring scripts can manage events programmatically. If a service stops, for example, a monitoring script can restart it. Or if a hard drive fills up, a script that detects this state can delete old files to free up space. However, when a program cannot relieve a problem, some type of alert must be triggered. Such an alert can be created by sending a network message, sending email, or even paging a system administrator.

Network Messages

Win32 machines can send network messages to other Win32 machines. These messages can be sent to a user, a machine, or a domain (or workgroup). These network messages can be viewed by any NT or Windows 2000 machine running the Messenger service or a Windows 95/98/ME machine running the WINPOPUP.EXE program.

Sending network messages is incredibly easy. One method is to shell out and run the net send command. However, this method works only on Windows NT/2000. Another method is to use the Win32::Message extension, as in Example 5.5. This script sends a message to any number of specified users. The specified recipients can be usernames, computer names, or NT domain names.

When you use the Win32::Message's Send() function, the recipient can be a machine or domain name appended with an asterisk (*), which indicates to send the message to every user on the machine or in the domain. The result is that all users currently interactively logged on to the machine or domain will receive the message.

A monitoring script that needs to send out an alert to a list of recipients can use the same SendAlert() function defined in Example 5.5, lines 5 through 22.

A downside to sending network messages is that there is no guarantee that the user will receive the message. If the receiver's messenger service (or WINPOPUP.EXE) is paused or stopped, the message is not received. Additionally, if a user logs on to multiple computers at once, the alert finds only the machine that the user last logged on.

Example 5.5 *Sending Network Messages*

```
01. use Win32::Message;
02. $Message = shift @ARGV;
03. SendAlert( $Message, @ARGV );
04.
05. sub SendAlert
06. {
07.   my( $Message, @List ) = @_;
```

```
08.
09.    foreach my $Recipient ( @List )
10.    {
11.      print "Sending message to $Recipient...";
12.      if( Win32::Message::Send( "", $Recipient, "", $Message ) )
13.      {
14.        print "successful";
15.      }
16.      else
17.      {
18.        print "failed";
19.      }
20.      print "\n";
21.    }
22. }
```

Paging

Perl can send out pages using various techniques. Ideally, you could use the Net::SNPP module to send messages to pagers and cell phones using the Simple Network Paging Protocol (SNPP). However, not many paging companies have SNPP servers online for public use. Most do have, however, a Web page that can be used to submit paging requests.

You can write a script to submit HTML forms to a paging service Web server or use a module called Net::Pager. The module interfaces with a paging back-end server hosted by www.simplewire.com that does the work for your script. The Net::Pager Perl module is available on CPAN or from http://www.simplewire.com/.

Example 5.6 sends out alerts to pagers and cell phones by using the Net::Pager module. Here, as in Example 5.5, a monitoring program can use the SendAlert() function to send in various pager and cell phone numbers.

To use Example 5.6, just pass in the message to send out, followed by a list of pager PIN numbers or cell phone numbers. This assumes, of course, that the recipients are using the service defined on line 12 (in this case AT&T). For example,

```
perl SendPage.pl "This is my test message" 8005551212 1234567890
```

will send the message to the cell phone or pager that has the PIN number 8005551212 and 1234567890.

Example 5.6 *Sending Paging Alerts*

```
01. use Net::Pager;
02. $Message = shift @ARGV;
03. SendAlert( $Message, @ARGV );
04.
05. sub SendAlert
06. {
```

continues ▶

Example 5.6   *continued*

```
07.     my( $Message, @List ) = @_;
08.     my $Pager = new Net::Pager || return( 0 );
09.     # AT&T PCS services has a service number of 7. Check with the
10.     # Net::Pager documentation to discover other paging service
11.     # values.
12.     my $SERVICE = 7;
13.     my $FROM = "Perl Pager";
14.
15.     foreach my $Recipient ( @List )
16.     {
17.         print "Sending message to $Recipient...";
18.         if( $Pager->sendPage( $SERVICE, $Recipient,
19.                               $FROM, $Message, undef ) )
20.         {
21.             print "successful";
22.         }
23.         else
24.         {
25.             print "failed";
26.         }
27.         print "\n";
28.     }
29. }
```

Email

Alerts usually must be fast. Otherwise, by the time you receive the alert, it may be too late to correct a problem. Network messaging and paging generally are good mechanisms to deliver alert information because they are fast; however, both can fail. A message may be sent successfully, but you might be out of range when the page is sent. For these reasons, a message sent as email will most likely find its way to the recipient and provide a good historical trail.

Example 5.7 demonstrates sending an alert via email. You can add the SendAlert() function to any monitoring script to provide email alert support. The Net::SMTP module comes as part of the libnet archive, available on CPAN.

To use Example 5.7, just pass in the message email out followed by the email addresses of the recipients—for example:

```
perl SendEMail.pl "This is my test message" joel@mydomain.com betty@mydomain.com
```

In this script, we are using the Net::SMTP module, but you could use a variety of other email transport mechanisms. This could be as low-level as opening up your own socket to an email server to as high-level as using COM to create a MAPI session via CDO. Alternatively, you could just shell out to some third-party application, such as SENDMAIL.EXE or BLAT.EXE. The decision to implement Net::SMTP was made due to simplicity and ubiquity.

Example 5.7 *Sending Email Alerts*

```
01. use Net::SMTP;
02. $Message = shift @ARGV;
03. SendAlert( $Message, @ARGV );
04.
05. sub SendAlert
06. {
07.   my( $Message, @List ) = @_;
08.
09.   foreach my $Recipient ( @List )
10.   {
11.     my $Smtp;
12.     my( $Host ) = ( $Recipient =~ /\@(.*)/ );
13.
14.     print "Sending message to $Recipient...";
15.     if( $Smtp = new Net::SMTP( $Host ) )
16.     {
17.       $Smtp->mail( "Perl Pager" );
18.       $Smtp->to( $Recipient );
19.       $Smtp->data();
20.       $Smtp->datasend( "To: $Recipient\n" );
21.       $Smtp->datasend( "Subject: ALERT\n" );
22.       $Smtp->datasend( "\n" );
23.       $Smtp->datasend( "$Message\n" );
24.       $Smtp->dataend();
25.       $Smtp->quit();
26.       print "successful";
27.     }
28.     else
29.     {
30.       print "failed";
31.     }
32.     print "\n";
33.   }
34. }
```

Conclusion

The ability to both monitor and report events that take place on your machine and network are crucial to successfully managing your domain. This chapter demonstrated that services and standalone scripts can be employed to lead an administrator's team to solving issues before they become problems. This proactive approach to administration not only can save time, but save money as well.

6

Logon Scripts

When a user logs on to an NT machine, a *logon script* can be executed. This script enables you, as the network administrator, to dynamically customize the user's environment. Such flexibility has been a part of computer systems since the beginning. UNIX shell scripts have, for example, always provided facilities to customize the user's environment during the logon process.

The name *logon script* is a bit of a misnomer because it does not really have to be a script per se. It can be any executable program, such as an application, a batch file, a Java application, a Visual Basic script, or even a Perl script. Traditionally, logon scripts have been batch files.

Because Windows NT enables different users to log on to different machines, setting up a computer for only one user is difficult. Logon scripts provide the mechanism required to guarantee that drives can be mapped to appropriate network servers, printers can be reconnected to local printing devices, environment variables can be updated, and so on.

How Logon Scripts Work

When a user attempts to log on to a Win32 domain, her machine contacts a *domain controller (DC)*. The DC holds a copy of the domain's user database. This database contains each user account's configuration information. The DC authenticates the user and (if her password is correct), she is be permitted to log on to the domain.

A DC that services a logon request is known as the logon session's *logon server*. If a network has several DCs, a request to log on may be serviced by different DCs at different times. Which machine services your logon request is based, in part, on which controller is least busy.

Note

Logon scripts run only when a user interactively logs in to a domain (such as when logging on using the keyboard or via a terminal server client). If the user logs in over a network (as in mapping a drive letter to a server) or if the user's account is impersonated (such as when a Web server authenticates a user account), the logon script is not executed. ◆

After a user successfully logs in to a domain, the machine attempts to run the user's logon script. The logon script is always run from the logon server's NetLogon shared directory. For example, if a user account is authenticated by the DC called LogonServer, and the user's logon script is MyLogonScript.exe, Win32 attempts to run the following:

```
\\LogonServer\NetLogon\MyLogonScript.exe
```

This means that all user account logon scripts must be a path relative to a DC's NetLogon shared directory. If the file does not exist or is inaccessible (maybe because of security permissions), the attempt to execute the logon script simply fails, but no error message is displayed to the user.

Tip

If you have many DCs on your network, maintaining up-to-date copies of any logon scripts on each controller is important. This is what the Replication Service was designed for. It enables you to designate one controller, typically the primary domain controller (PDC), as the logon script repository.

Any script updates are made to scripts in the repository. Scripts that have been modified are then replicated to all the other DCs. ◆

A logon script does not really have to be a script at all. It can be an executable program, a batch file, or a script such as Perl, Java, Python, or Visual Basic. For example, a logon script can be configured to be a Perl script like this:

```
UserScripts\MyPerlLogonScript.pl
```

This example assumes, of course, that the machine the user logs on to has the .pl extension associated with Perl (refer to Chapter 1, "Perl and the Admin," for details).

In a user account, the logon script attribute is really just an arbitrary string. This means that an account can be configured to be more than just a path to a logon script. It can contain parameters to be passed in as well. For example, an account can be configured to pass in the name of the user as well as the local computer name (using environment variables):

```
UserScripts\MyLogonScriptProgram.exe %USERNAME% %COMPUTERNAME%
```

Because logon script attributes are arbitrary strings, you can use them to run Perl from the logon server and pass in the name of the logon script. For example, say that you have installed Perl in a Perl directory under the NetLogon share on all your DCs. You can configure your user accounts to have this logon script:

```
perl\bin\perl.exe %LOGONSERVER%\NetLogon\UserScripts\MyLogonScript.pl
```

Of course, when this script is run, the logon server and NetLogon share are prepended, so Win32 actually executes the following:

```
\\MyLogonServer\NetLogon\perl\bin\perl.exe
\\MyLogonServer\NetLogon\UserScripts\MyLogonScript.pl
```

In this case, the %LOGONSERVER% environment variable is replaced with the name of the DC (\\MyLogonServer) that is authenticating the user. By doing this, you don't need to install Perl on individual user machines but instead only on the DCs. Accessing Perl across the network in this manner does present some pitfalls, however. Refer to Chapter 1 for more information.

Configuring Logon Scripts

Logon scripts are configured as a part of a user account, enabling one user to have a logon script, while another user is configured with a different script. This is an ideal way to provide each user with a personalized experience. You can modify what logon script a user account is configured to use by using the User Manager program (on Windows NT) or the Computer Management MMC (on Windows 2000). Additionally, you can configure user accounts by using a scripting language such as Perl.

Example 6.1 illustrates how you can use Perl to discover what logon script is used by a user. Run the script, passing in any number of user account names. The script will display each user's logon script.

Example 6.1 *Displaying a User's Logon Script*

```
01. use Win32;
02. use Win32::AdminMisc;
03.
04. if( ! scalar @ARGV )
05. {
06.   my( $Script ) = ( $0 =~ /([^\\]*?)$/ );
07.   print << "EOT";
08.   Syntax
09.     perl $Script <User Account> [ <User Account 2> [ ... ] ]
10.
11.   Example:
12.     perl $Script administrator
```

continues ▶

Example 6.1 *continued*

```
13.     perl $Script somedomain\\administrator accounting\\joel
14. EOT
15.
16.  exit();
17. }
18.
19. foreach my $Account ( @ARGV )
20. {
21.   my %Info;
22.
23.   print "$Account logon script: ";
24.   if( Win32::AdminMisc::UserGetMiscAttributes( '', $Account, \%Info ) )
25.   {
26.     if( "" eq $Info{USER_SCRIPT_PATH} )
27.     {
28.       $Info{USER_SCRIPT_PATH} = "No logon script configured";
29.     }
30.     print "$Info{USER_SCRIPT_PATH}\n";
31.   }
32.   else
33.   {
34.     print Win32::FormatMessage( Win32::AdminMisc::GetError() );
35.   }
36. }
```

Displaying a user account's logon script is certainly useful, but so is being able to modify the account. Example 6.2 accepts the name of a user account and a logon script path. This code modifies the user account's logon script path.

Example 6.2 *Setting a User's Logon Script*

```
01. use Win32;
02. use Win32::AdminMisc;
03.
04. if( ! scalar @ARGV )
05. {
06.   my( $Script ) = ( $0 =~ /([^\\]*?)$/ );
07.   print << "EOT";
08.   Syntax:
09.     perl $Script <User Account> <Logon Script Path>
10.
11.   Example:
12.     perl $Script administrator scripts\\administrator.bat
13.     perl $Script accounting\\joel "genericlogon.pl"
14.
15.   To remove a logon script set the path to "" as in:
16.     perl $Script accounting\\joel ""
17. EOT
18.   exit();
```

```
19. }
20.
21. my( $Account, $Path ) = @ARGV;
22. if( "" eq $Path )
23. {
24.   print "Removing the logon script for the $Account account.\n";
25. }
26. else
27. {
28.   print "Configuring the $Account account with a logon script of:\n";
29.   print "$Path\n";
30. }
31. if( Win32::AdminMisc::UserSetMiscAttributes( '',
32.                                     $Account,
33.                                     USER_SCRIPT_PATH => $Path ) )
34. {
35.   print "Successful\n";
36. }
37. else
38. {
39.   print "An error occurred: ";
40.   print Win32::FormatMessage( Win32::AdminMisc::GetError() );
41. }
```

Modifying the User Environment

A logon script can be programmed to perform such a variety of activities that it is futile to consider discussing all of them. However, one of the more common activities—querying and modifying environment variables—is well worth covering.

Environment Variables

Windows NT was designed as a multiuser operating system. Therefore, it makes distinctions between user and system resources. One such resource is the list of environment variables.

A user's profile can contain environment variables that are defined by the user himself. For example, if the user JOEL adds an environment variable called INCLUDE, it will be there whenever the user logs on. If another user logs on to the same machine, she will see her own set of variables that may be different.

Additionally, if the users are configured to use roaming profiles, this set of environment variables follows each user from machine to machine. No matter what computer the user logs on to, the INCLUDE environment variable appears as he configured it.

User environment variables are separate from system environment variables. The system has its own set of variables that it uses from boot time until shutdown. This set includes such important variables as PATH and is set by either the system itself or a user with administrator privileges.

Typically, user variables override system variables. For example, if a system environment variable INCLUDEPATH is set to c:\SystemInclude, and a user who has a user environment variable INCLUDEPATH set to c:\MyInclude logs on, then any application that uses the INCLUDEPATH variable will see only the user version: c:\MyInclude. This can be a problem because it means that a user can use either the system variable value or the user variable value, but not both at the same time.

The workaround is to embed the system variable within the user variable. To continue the preceding example, if the user variable INCLUDEPATH is set to %INCLUDEPATH%;c:\SystemInclude, an application that uses this environment variable sees INCLUDEPATH as c:\MyInclude;c:\SystemInclude. Notice how the %INCLUDEPATH% expands as the system version of the variable. When you place a reference to the environment variable within the user variable, it inherits the system variable's value. This trick works only in that direction. A system variable cannot inherit from a user variable. If it did, this could result in redundant loops of variable inheritance. The moral here is that if a user variable refers to itself, it is really referring to the system environment variable by the same name.

As you already learned, a user variable will override a system variable by the same name. This is true for all but one—the PATH variable. This variable is special because it is required by the system. In this case, any user-defined PATH variable is appended to the system's version. Thus, if a user defines PATH to be c:\temp and the system's PATH is set to c:\winnt;c:\winnt\system32, the resulting PATH is c:\winnt;c:\winnt\system32;c:\temp. This allows such configurations as a user defining his personal PATH to point back to his home directory—for example, \\server\home\joel\bin. This enables the user to place tools and applications he uses often in one place so that he can seamlessly access them from anywhere on the LAN.

Perl and Environment Variables

Because a user variable can override a system variable, it is difficult for a Perl script to discover the version of the variable that the system administrator intended an application to use. Perl accesses environment variables by using the %ENV hash. It accesses only the set of variables exposed by the current environment. This environment, just like a DOS box, does not have a way to distinguish system versus user variables. Therefore, Perl is unable to see system variables if a user variable exists with the same name.

In Windows, each application has access to an *environment*, which is a block of memory allocated for a process that contains such information as the list of environment variables and their values. Each running process can have its very own copy of the environment. When a change to an environmental variable takes place (such as when a user uses the Control Panel to change a variable's value), all running programs are notified, and they can choose to reload the updated values into their environment. Therefore, a running Windows program should see such changes immediately. (Whether the program sees changes depends on how the application was designed. Some Windows programs may not see these changes immediately.) Console applications, on the other hand, typically do not listen for such messages. Therefore, legacy DOS applications, Perl, the DOS window, and other console-based applications do not see these changes until the console environment is terminated and re-created. This means that a Perl script must be stopped, the console window it runs in closed, a new console window opened, and the Perl script run again before the variable change is seen.

Console applications can update their environment when changes are detected, but most usually do not do so. Perl is one example of an application that does not listen for environment changes. Changes to this environment are performed only by a Perl script using the %ENV hash.

Querying Variables

Even though Perl cannot directly discern the difference between system and user environment variables using the %ENV hash, it can query system and user variables by relying on alternative methods. Example 6.3 shows how user and system environment variables can be queried independently using the Win32::AdminMisc extension. The script fetches the list of system and user environment variables into a hash (lines 5 and 14) and then displays them. When the script is run, the output shows which environment variables are embedded in other environment variables.

Example 6.4 is another script that makes use of a little-known function called Win32::ExpandEnvironmentStrings() that expands any references to environment variables in the string passed in. Any environment variables embedded within other variables are expanded. Comparing the output between these two examples is interesting.

Example 6.3   *Displaying System and User Environment Variables*

```
01. use Win32;
02. use Win32::AdminMisc;
03. $~ = VariableFormat;
04. print "System Variables:\n";
05. if( Win32::AdminMisc::GetEnvVar( \%System, ENV_SYSTEM ) )
```

continues ▶

Example 6.3   *continued*

```
06. {
07.    foreach $VarName ( sort( keys( %System ) ) )
08.    {
09.        $VarValue = $System{$VarName};
10.        write;
11.    }
12. }
13. print "\nUser Variables:\n";
14. if( Win32::AdminMisc::GetEnvVar( \%User, ENV_USER ) )
15. {
16.    foreach $VarName ( sort( keys( %User ) ) )
17.    {
18.        $VarValue = $User{$VarName};
19.        write;
20.    }
21. }
22.
23. format VariableFormat =
24.    @<<<<<<<<<<<<<<<<<<<<< ^<<<<<<<<<<<<<<<<<<<<<<<<<<<<<<<<<<
25.    $VarName,             $VarValue
26. ~                       ^<<<<<<<<<<<<<<<<<<<<<<<<<<<<<<<<<<
27.                         $VarValue
28. ~                       ^<<<<<<<<<<<<<<<<<<<<<<<<<<<<<<<<<<
29.                         $VarValue
30. ~                       ^<<<<<<<<<<<<<<<<<<<<<<<<<<<<<<<<<<
31.                         $VarValue
32. ~                       ^<<<<<<<<<<<<<<<<<<<<<<<<<<<<<<<<<<
33.                         $VarValue
34. ~                       ^<<<<<<<<<<<<<<<<<<<<<<<<<<<<<<<<<<
35.                         $VarValue
36. ~                       ^<<<<<<<<<<<<<<<<<<<<<<<<<<<<<<<<<<
37.                         $VarValue
38. .
```

Example 6.4   *Displaying Expanded System and User Environment Variables*

```
01. use Win32;
02. use Win32::AdminMisc;
03. $~ = VariableFormat;
04. print "System Variables:\n";
05. if( Win32::AdminMisc::GetEnvVar( \%System, ENV_SYSTEM ) )
06. {
07.    foreach $VarName ( sort( keys( %System ) ) )
08.    {
09.        $VarValue = Win32::ExpandEnvironmentStrings( $System{$VarName} );
10.        write;
11.    }
12. }
13. print "\nUser Variables:\n";
14. if( Win32::AdminMisc::GetEnvVar( \%User, ENV_USER ) )
15. {
```

```
16.    foreach $VarName ( sort( keys( %User ) ) )
17.    {
18.      $VarValue = Win32::ExpandEnvironmentStrings( $User{$VarName} );
19.      write;
20.    }
21. }
22.
23. format VariableFormat =
24.    @<<<<<<<<<<<<<<<<<<<<< ^<<<<<<<<<<<<<<<<<<<<<<<<<<<<<<<<<<<<<<
25.    $VarName,             $VarValue
26. ~                       ^<<<<<<<<<<<<<<<<<<<<<<<<<<<<<<<<<<<<<<
27.                         $VarValue
28. ~                       ^<<<<<<<<<<<<<<<<<<<<<<<<<<<<<<<<<<<<<<
29.                         $VarValue
30. ~                       ^<<<<<<<<<<<<<<<<<<<<<<<<<<<<<<<<<<<<<<
31.                         $VarValue
32. ~                       ^<<<<<<<<<<<<<<<<<<<<<<<<<<<<<<<<<<<<<<
33.                         $VarValue
34. ~                       ^<<<<<<<<<<<<<<<<<<<<<<<<<<<<<<<<<<<<<<
35.                         $VarValue
36. ~                       ^<<<<<<<<<<<<<<<<<<<<<<<<<<<<<<<<<<<<<<
37.                         $VarValue
38. .
```

Earlier you learned that console applications can update their environment with the latest environment variable values. Example 6.5 illustrates this point perfectly. The code defines an UpdateEnv() subroutine, which can be called at any time to update the Perl process' environment variable values.

The UpdateEnv() function works by procuring the latest list of system environment variables and setting Perl's %ENV hash to reflect the updated variables. Notice that the first system variables are set, followed by user variables. This order is important because user variables take precedence over system variables. Also, note that the variables are not expanded before being set.

Example 6.5 *Updating Perl's Copy of Environment Variables*

```
01. use Win32::AdminMisc;
02.
03. UpdateEnv();
04.
05. sub UpdateEnv
06. {
07.   my %VarList;
08.   if( Win32::AdminMisc::GetEnvVar( \%VarList, ENV_SYSTEM ) )
09.   {
10.     print "Updating system environment variables:\n";
11.     foreach my $Var ( keys( %VarList ) )
12.     {
13.       print " $Var\n";
```

continues ▶

Example 6.5 *continued*

```
14.        $ENV{$Var} = $VarList{$Var};
15.      }
16.    }
17.    if( Win32::AdminMisc::GetEnvVar( \%VarList, ENV_USER ) )
18.    {
19.      print "Updating user environment variables:\n";
20.      foreach my $Var ( keys( %VarList ) )
21.      {
22.        print " $Var\n";
23.        $ENV{$Var} = $VarList{$Var};
24.      }
25.    }
26. }
```

Modifying Variables

Generally speaking, a logon script does not need to modify environment variables. Typically, a script queries such a variable so that it can make logical decisions. For example, a logon script may query the Temp variable to determine the path of the temporary file directory, possibly to clean it out. Such querying is common, but setting environment variables from a logon script is not common. There are, however, exceptions to this rule, such as when a logon script wants to record the time and date when the user logged in.

A nonadministrative user's logon script has permissions to modify only the user set of environment variables, not the system set (unless administrative privileges have been granted). Consider a machine with a system environment variable called INCLUDE that consists of a list of semicolon-separated paths pointing to where C++ header files are located. This is a system variable, so it cannot accidentally be modified by a user. When a developer needs to point to her own set of include directories, she could create a user environment variable named INCLUDE that would override the system version, thus losing whatever values the system administrator had set. If the INCLUDE system variable contained a reference to %INCLUDE%, then the user variable would expand the reference into the system variable. This would allow the user to modify the INCLUDE variable's value without modifying the value directly.

You can implement another strategy to ensure that the system variable is always first in a path. For example, if the user adds his own version of the INCLUDE variable

```
C:\MyInclude;%INCLUDE%
```

the system INCLUDE variable is positioned after the user's version. In cases where this use is unacceptable, you can add a reference to the user variable by a different name. So, if the system variable INCLUDE consists of

```
C:\dev\include;\\server\share\include;%_INCLUDE%
```

the user _INCLUDE variable expands at the end of the system variable. The only problem here is that a user can create his own INCLUDE variable, overriding the system one. Example 6.6 comes in at this point.

This script shows how environment variables can be modified by a logon (or any other) script. This particular script searches for any user variable that has the same name as a system variable. If the system variable references the variable name prepended with an underscore, the user's version of the variable is deleted, and a new one is created prepended by an underscore.

As you learned earlier, Perl's %ENV hash reflects only the Perl script's personal copy of the environment. Therefore, changes made to this hash may affect how the Perl script functions but may not be seen by any other application. For this reason, modifications to the environment that must persist across applications should be made using Win32::AdminMisc's SetEnvVar() or DelEnvVar() functions.

Lines 4 and 5 retrieve the list of user and system variables. Notice that the script does not rely on the %ENV hash because it does not discern between user and system environment variables. Lines 9 through 18 simply iterate through the list looking for any user variable that has the same name as a system variable, *and* the system variable references an "underscored" version of the user variable.

Lines 24 and 32 contain the real meat of the script. Line 24 sets the new "underscored" user variable name, and line 32 deletes the original user variable. Note that lines 28 and 34 set the new variable and remove the original variable, respectively, from the %ENV hash. This is important if the script continues to process environment variables using %ENV. If these lines did not exist, the %ENV hash would have no idea that these changes were made.

Example 6.6   *Modifying Environment Variables*

```
01. use Win32;
02. use Win32::AdminMisc;
03.
04. Win32::AdminMisc::GetEnvVar( \%System, ENV_SYSTEM );
05. Win32::AdminMisc::GetEnvVar( \%User, ENV_USER );
06.
07. @NewUserVar = ();
08.
09. foreach $VarName ( keys( %System ) )
```

continues ▶

Example 6.6 *continued*

```
10. {
11.   if( defined $User{$VarName} )
12.   {
13.     if( $System{$VarName} =~ /_$VarName/ )
14.     {
15.       push( @NewUserVar, $VarName );
16.     }
17.   }
18. }
19.
20. # Modify the user env var space
21. foreach $VarName ( @NewUserVar )
22. {
23.   print "Setting new user var: _$VarName\n";
24.   if( Win32::AdminMisc::SetEnvVar( "_$VarName",
25.                                    $User{$VarName},
26.                                    ENV_USER ) )
27.   {
28.     $ENV{"_$VarName"} = $User{$VarName};
29.
30.     # Remove conflicting user env vars
31.     print "Deleting user var: $VarName\n";
32.     if( Win32::AdminMisc::DelEnvVar( $VarName, ENV_USER ) )
33.     {
34.       delete $ENV{$VarName};
35.     }
36.   }
37. }
```

Effectively Processing Logon Scripts

Many administrators provide users with their own, unique logon scripts. This is very useful for fine-tuning each user's experience; however, it can become an absolute nightmare to manage as the number of users increases. Say that all user scripts map a drive letter to a file server. If the name of the file server changes, all user scripts must be modified. In a network of thousands of users, modifying so many scripts is both time-consuming and tedious. One way around this problem is to leverage user groups.

Most users are members of groups that pertain to their position in an organization. For example, all accountants may be in the Accounting group and all administrators in the Administrators group. Because most of these users require resources that correspond to the groups they are in, it makes sense to create one script for each group. The accountants' script may map a drive to the accounting file server or a printer to some particular print server. The administrators' script, on the other hand, may start a Web browser that loads an administrative page indicating the current status of all the network servers.

Such an infrastructure would be ideal if it were not for having to modify each user's account to point to the correct script. An administrator's logon script may be

```
scripts\administrators.pl
```

and an accountant's logon script may be

```
scripts\accountants.pl
```

However, this solution breaks down if the organization has accountant administrators—that is, members of both the Administrators and Accountants groups. Likewise, this solution does not scale well as the number of users increases. Constantly making modifications every time someone moves from one position to another in the organization becomes quite unmanageable.

A much more effective method to manage such scalability issues is to use the same logon script for all users—a sort of unified logon script.

Unified Logon Scripts

An efficient method to manage user logon scripts is to use a *unified logon script*. Such a script enables you to configure every user to use the same logon script. When you create a new user account, you simply configure it to execute the same logon script as all the other users. This efficient technique allows the logon script itself to implement the logic to figure out what it should do for the user during the logon sequence.

Unified logon scripts can be beneficial because they are shared by all users. Consider such a script that collects the current date, time, IP address, computer name, and username and then submits that information to a centralized database. This information provides you with quick access to efficiently find what machine a user is on. In a large environment, this information can be quite advantageous for pinpointing the location of a particular user at a particular time. This is especially true if a user may have logged on to multiple machines, making it difficult to find him based on his network-registered username (because network-based usernames are unique and can be registered on only one machine at a time).

Processing User Groups

As you learned earlier in the section "Effectively Processing Logon Scripts," breaking out logon scripts based on user group membership can greatly enhance effectiveness of the logon scripts. The problem is that if a network implements a unified logon script, you cannot easily decide which groups a given user belongs to. If the unified logon script could discover which groups the user belongs to, it could execute each related group script.

Example 6.7 contains a simple example of discovering group membership using the Win32::Lanman extension. Lines 9-12 call NetUserGetLocalGroups() with the LG_INCLUDE_INDIRECT flag. This call discovers any local group the user is a member of in addition to any local group that the user is indirectly a member of (if the local group contains a global group the user is a member of). Lines 13-15 discover what global groups the user is a member of. The script accepts a username as the first parameter but uses the current logged-on user if nothing is passed in.

You can easily adopt this script to a logon script, as shown later in Example 6.9.

Example 6.7   *Discovering Group Membership Using* Win32::Lanman

```
01. use Win32;
02. use Win32::NetAdmin;
03. use Win32::Lanman;
04.
05. $Name = Win32::LoginName() unless( $Name = shift @ARGV );
06. $Domain = Win32::DomainName();
07. Win32::NetAdmin::GetAnyDomainController( '', $Domain, $Dc );
08.
09. Win32::Lanman::NetUserGetLocalGroups( $Dc,
10.                                       $Name,
11.                                       LG_INCLUDE_INDIRECT,
12.                                       \@LocalGroups );
13. Win32::Lanman::NetUserGetGroups( $Dc,
14.                                  $Name,
15.                                  \@GlobalGroups );
16.
17. foreach my $Hash ( sort( { $a->{name} cmp $b->{name} }
18.                    ( @LocalGroups, @GlobalGroups ) ) )
19. {
20.     print "\t";
21.     print "$Hash->{name}\n";
22. }
```

Machine Setup Script

One of the more mundane aspects of system administration is configuring new machines. This process can be quite slow and tedious. Each machine requires that you install the operating system, configure it, install appropriate software, and configure that as well. An easy way to automate this process is to leverage logon scripts.

By creating a special administrative account that has a special logon script, you can simply walk over to a new machine, log on, and then walk away. The logon script runs and begins the work of reconfiguring the computer. When it is finished, the logon script can reboot the computer so that it is ready for use by a user. And all it took was someone simply logging on with the special account.

You could rewrite the logon script so that it creates the appropriate directories, copies files, sets permissions, creates local accounts and groups, registers particular services, and even sets up scheduled tasks to execute on a routine schedule.

Example 6.8 is an example of such a setup script. It was designed with the expectation that an administrative user account would call it as its logon script. Of course, an administrator would have to modify this script to reflect her own requirements, server names, paths, and so on.

Currently, the script adds the Domain Admins group into the local machine's Administrators group. This gives any domain administrator access over the machine.

Next, the drive that holds the Perl tree is converted to NTFS so that the Perl directory tree can be secured from modification by users. After the conversion is complete and the Perl tree has been secured, Perl is copied from a network file server, and the system's PATH environment variable is modified to include the perl\bin directory.

Finally, the current user is removed from the Registry so that the next user to log on will not see what account was used to run this script. A log entry is made to a log file on a remote file server, and the machine is rebooted.

Example 6.8   *An Automated Machine Setup Logon Script*

```
01. use Win32;
02. use Win32::Perms;
03. use Win32::NetAdmin;
04. use Win32::Registry;
05. use Win32::AdminMisc;
06.
07. $Machine = Win32::NodeName();
08. $Domain = Win32::DomainName();
09.
10. $PerlDrive = 'c:';
11. $PerlPath = '\perl';
12.
13. $REMOTE_PERL_PATH = '\\\\server\perlshare$\perl';
14. $NTFS_CONVERSION_APP = "convert.exe";
15. $NTFS_CONVERSION_PARAM = "/FS:NTFS /V";
16.
17. ConfigGroup( $Domain );
18. if( ConfigDrive( $PerlDrive ) )
19. {
20.    SecureDir( "$PerlDrive$PerlPath" );
21.    CopyDir( $REMOTE_PERL_PATH, "$PerlDrive$PerlPath" );
22.    ConfigPath( "$Dir\\bin" );
23. }
24.
25. ConfigLastUser( "" );
```

continues ▶

Example 6.8   *continued*

```
26. Log( $LogFile );
27. RebootMachine();
28. print "Finished.\n";
29.
30. sub Log
31. {
32.  my( $LogFile ) = @_;
33.
34.  if( open( LOG, ">> $LogFile" ) )
35.  {
36.   flock( LOG, 2 );
37.   seek( LOG, 0, 2 );
38.   print LOG Win32::NodeName(), "\t", scalar( localtime() ), "\n";
39.   flock( LOG, 8 );
40.   close( LOG );
41.  }
42. }
43.
44. # Reboot the machine
45. sub RebootMachine
46. {
47.   Win32::AdminMisc::ExitWindows( EWX_REBOOT | EWX_FORCE );
48. }
49.
50. # Remove the "Last Logged On User" so nobody knows
51. sub ConfigLastUser
52. {
53.   my( $User ) = @_;
54.   my $Key;
55.   my $Path = 'SOFTWARE\Microsoft\Windows NT\CurrentVersion\Winlogon';
56.   if( $HKEY_LOCAL_MACHINE->Create( $Path, $Key ) )
57.   {
58.     $Key->SetValueEx( $Key, 0, REG_SZ, $User );
59.     $Key->Close();
60.   }
61. }
62.
63. sub ConfigGroup
64. {
65.   my( $Domain ) = @_;
66.
67.   $Domain .= "\\" if( '' ne $Domain );
68.
69.   # Add the Domain Admins group to the Administrators group
70.   Win32::NetAdmin::LocalGroupAddUsers( "",
71.                                        "Administrators",
72.                                        "$Domain" . "Domain Admins" );
73.
74. }
75.
76. sub ConfigPath
77. {
78.   my( $Dir ) = @_;
79.   my $RegexDir = "$Dir";
```

```perl
80.    my $Path;
81.
82.    # First check to see if the $Dir is already in the path...
83.    $Path = Win32::AdminMisc::GetEnvVar( 'PATH' );
84.
85.    # Prepare $Dir for a regex...
86.    $RegexDir =~ s/([.\\\$])/\\$1/g;
87.    if( $Path !~ /$Dir/i )
88.    {
89.      # Add $Dir to the system (not user) PATH
90.      Win32::AdminMisc::SetEnvVar( 'PATH', "$Path;$Dir" );
91.    }
92.    return( 1 );
93.  }
94.
95.  sub CopyDir
96.  {
97.    my( $RemoteDir, $DestDir ) = @_;
98.
99.    print "Copying files from '$RemoteDir' to '$DestDir' ...\n";
100.
101.    # XCOPY.EXE will autocreate the destination dir
102.    `xcopy "$RemoteDir\\*.*" "$DestDir\\*.*" /s`;
103.  }
104.
105.  sub SecureDir
106.  {
107.    my( $Dir ) = @_;
108.    my( $Perm, $Result );
109.
110.    print "Securing the $Dir directory...\n";
111.
112.    `md "$Dir"`;
113.
114.    if( $Perm = new Win32::Perms( $Dir ) )
115.    {
116.      # Remove *all* entries...
117.      $Perm->Remove( -1 );
118.
119.      $Perm->Allow( 'Administrators', FULL_CONTROL_FILE, FILE );
120.      $Perm->Allow( 'Administrators', FULL_CONTROL_DIR, DIR );
121.
122.      $Perm->Allow( 'Everyone', READ_FILE, FILE );
123.      $Perm->Allow( 'Everyone', LIST_DIR, DIR );
124.
125.      $Perm->Owner( 'Administrators' );
126.
127.      $Result = $Perm->Set();
128.    }
129.    else
130.    {
131.      print " Unable to create security descriptor. ";
132.      print "Directory is not secured.\n";
133.    }
```

continues ▶

Example 6.8 *continued*

```
134.
135.  return( 0 != $Result );
136. }
137.
138. sub ConfigDrive
139. {
140.   my( $Drive ) = @_;
141.   my %Info;
142.
143.   print "Configuring the $Drive drive ...\n";
144.
145.   # Make sure that the drive exists
146.   if( ! -e $Drive )
147.   {
148.     print " The $Drive drive does not exist.\n";
149.     return( 0 );
150.   }
151.
152.   # Do we have a fixed hard drive?
153.   if( DRIVE_FIXED != Win32::AdminMisc::GetDriveType( $Drive ) )
154.   {
155.     print " The $Drive drive is not a local fixed hard drive. ";
156.     print "Skipping drive formatting.\n";
157.     return( 0 );
158.   }
159.
160.   # If the drive is not NTFS then convert it into NTFS
161.   %Info = Win32::AdminMisc::GetVolumeInfo( $Drive );
162.   if( 'NTFS' ne $Info{FileSystemName} )
163.   {
164.     my $Cmd = "$NTFS_CONVERSION_APP $Drive $NTFS_CONVERSION_PARAMS";
165.     print " The $Drive drive is not an NTFS drive.\n";
166.     print " Converting from the $Info{FileSystemName} format...\n";
167.     @{$Log{ntfs_conversion}} = `$Cmd`;
168.   }
169.
170.   return( 1 );
171. }
```

CASE STUDY **Implementing a Unified Logon Script**

A new network administrator was hired into a medium-sized company. One of her first tasks was to revamp the logon process for her users. She was in charge of several thousand users, each of whom ran one of several different logon scripts. These scripts were quite elaborate and designed to perform specific tasks, making it difficult to adapt them to groups of users.

The administrator decided to utilize a unified logon script for all her users. Because each user was a member of one of several NT groups, she decided to make the main logon script call out and run separate group-based logon scripts. This way, she could manage large groups of users by simply changing their NT group memberships.

Her network had many subnets, some of which were located across slow frame relay links. Therefore, she decided that it would be best to replicate all the logon scripts across all the DCs on each subnet. She set up the controllers so that they replicated from the PDC at a regular interval. As a result, updating scripts was as easy as changing them in only one location. In the NetLogon network share, she created a subdirectory called Scripts where she placed all the group-based scripts.

She wrote a script for most of her domain's groups, such as Accounting.pl, Marketing.pl, Developers.pl, and, of course, Administrators.pl.

She also created a subdirectory called Users. In this directory, she could place logon scripts for every user who required one. For certain network administrators and upper management users who had specialized needs that required their own personal logon script, the Users directory contained Perl scripts named after the specific user account it belonged to. The unified logon script made use of the infrastructure illustrated in Example 6.9.

Lines 9 through 14 create a hash that contains logon-related information. Notice that the domain controller key (dc) hash has been assigned the undef value. This is done because Win32::NetAdmin's GetAnyDomainController() function (lines 24 and 25) requires that *something* is assigned to the variable before it is passed into the function.

Line 28 fetches a list of all the DCs. The script then walks through this list, one machine at a time, looking for the particular shared directory. For each machine that is sharing the logon scripts, a ping test is performed to find the closest server (lines 36 through 42). (This process may not be as effective on larger networks that have many DCs and subnets because it might take awhile to ping all machines. It also increases network traffic.). Line 46 then sets the user environment variable ScriptServer with the server name so that scripts that run later during the logon session can discover what machine was used to run the logon scripts.

At this point, an attempt is made to connect to an ODBC database (line 50). This is done before any additional scripts are loaded so that they can take advantage of the database connection. In this particular script, the connection to the ODBC database is made using a Data

continues ▶

Source Name (DSN). It may be easier to rely instead on a DSN connection string hard-coded into the script. This would prevent any problems that would arise if the computer's DSN is removed or altered.

Next, the script discovers which groups the user belongs to by using the Win32::Lanman extension (lines 53 through 61) discussed earlier in the section "Processing User Groups." Lines 65 through 71 actually perform the work of loading each group logon script. Notice that it uses the require function. Therefore, each logon script *must* return a TRUE value (any nonzero return value is fine). Lines 75 through 78 simply load the user's personal logon script, if one exists.

Lines 81 through 114 modify the user's environment variables so they do not collide with system variables of the same name. This was discussed in detail in the earlier section "Modifying Variables."

The code from lines 118 through 130 removes all the files in the temporary directory that are older than two weeks. Notice that it actually does this for both the user's temporary directory as well as the system-defined temporary directory. Finally, lines 132 through 143 submit an update to the logging database with the time and date, username, user's domain, and machine name. This information allows administrators to quickly discover what machine a given user has logged on to.

After all accounts were changed to use the unified logon script, the administrator found that she was spending less time having to make changes to dozens of scripts just because a file server was taken offline or a user switched groups, and she was spending more time tending to other important network administration tasks.

Example 6.9   *Case Study of a Unified Logon Script*

```
01. use Win32;
02. use Win32::Lanman;
03. use Win32::NetAdmin;
04. use Win32::AdminMisc;
05. use Win32::ODBC;
06.
07. my $TempFileGracePeriod = 2 * $WEEK;
08. my $DSN = "LogonDatabase";
09. my %Logon = (
10.     account => Win32::LoginName(),
11.     machine => Win32::NodeName(),
12.     domain  => Win32::DomainName(),
13.     dc      => undef,
14. );
```

```perl
15. my %LogonPath = (
16.     share   => 'NetLogon',
17.     rootdir => 'Scripts',
18.     userdir => 'Users',
19. );
20. my $SERVER_TYPE = SV_TYPE_DOMAIN_CTRL | SV_TYPE_DOMAIN_BAKCTRL;
21. my $ScriptsUnc = "";
22. my @GroupList = ();
23.
24. Win32::NetAdmin::GetAnyDomainController( '', $Logon{domain},
25.                                          $Logon{dc} );
26.
27. # Discover the local Perl server...
28. if( Win32::NetAdmin::GetServers( '', '', $SERVER_TYPE, \@List ) )
29. {
30.   my $Time = 0xFFFF;
31.   foreach my $Machine ( @List )
32.   {
33.     my $Unc = "\\\\$Machine\\$LogonPath{share}\\$LogonPath{rootdir}";
34.     if( -d $Unc )
35.     {
36.       my $Output = join( " ", `ping -n 1 $Machine` );
37.       my( $NewTime ) =~ /Reply from.*?\s+time[=<>](\d+)ms/is );
38.       if( ( "" ne $NewTime ) && ( $NewTime < $Time ) )
39.       {
40.         $Time = $NewTime;
41.         $ScriptsUnc = $Unc;
42.       }
43.     }
44.   }
45. }
46. Win32::AdminMisc::SetEnvVar( 'ScriptServer', $ScriptsUnc, ENV_USER, 10 );
47.
48. # Before we call any other scripts first open the database
49. # so that each script can use it.
50. $db = new Win32::ODBC( $DSN );
51.
52. # Discover what local groups the user is a member of...
53. Win32::Lanman::NetUserGetLocalGroups( $Logon{dc},
54.                                       $Logon{account},
55.                                       LG_INCLUDE_INDIRECT,
56.                                       \@LGroups );
57.
58. # Discover what global groups the user is a member of...
59. Win32::Lanman::NetUserGetGroups( $Logon{dc},
60.                                  $Logon{account},
61.                                  \@GGroups );
62.
63. print "Starting the unified logon process...\n";
64.
65. foreach my $Group ( @LGroups, @GGroups )
66. {
```

Handwritten annotation near line 35: = (join (" ", @ OUTPUT)

continues ▶

Example 6.9 *continued*

```perl
67.    my $GroupName = $Group->{name};
68.    my $Script = "$ScriptsUnc\\$GroupName.pl";
69.    print " Calling $Script\n";
70.    require $Script if( -f $Script );
71. }
72.
73.
74. # If the user has his own logon script run it...
75. if( -f "$ScriptsUnc\\$LogonPath{userdir}\\$Logon{account}.pl" )
76. {
77.   require "$ScriptsUnc\\$LogonPath{userdir}\\$Logon{account}.pl";
78. }
79.
80. # Fix any user overriding of system variables
81. if( ( Win32::AdminMisc::GetEnvVar( \%System, ENV_SYSTEM ) )
82.     && ( Win32::AdminMisc::GetEnvVar( \%User, ENV_USER ) ) )
83. {
84.   my @NewUserVar = ();
85.   foreach $VarName ( keys( %System ) )
86.   {
87.     if( defined $User{$VarName} )
88.     {
89.       if( $System{$VarName} =~ /_$VarName/ )
90.       {
91.         push( @NewUserVar, $VarName );
92.       }
93.     }
94.   }
95.
96.   # Modify the user env var space
97.   foreach $VarName ( @NewUserVar )
98.   {
99.     print "Setting new user var: _$VarName\n";
100.    if( Win32::AdminMisc::SetEnvVar( "_$VarName",
101.                                     $User{$VarName},
102.                                     ENV_USER ) )
103.    {
104.      $ENV{"_$VarName"} = $User{$VarName};
105.
106.      # Remove conflicting user env vars
107.      print "Deleting user var: $VarName\n";
108.      if( Win32::AdminMisc::DelEnvVar( $VarName, ENV_USER ) )
109.      {
110.        delete $ENV{$VarName};
111.      }
112.    }
113.  }
114. }
115.
116. # Clean up the temp directory...
117. # First start with the system temp directory...
118. push( @TempDirs, Win32::AdminMisc::GetEnvVar( 'Temp', ENV_SYSTEM ) );
```

```
119.  push( @TempDirs, Win32::AdminMisc::GetEnvVar( 'Temp', ENV_USER ) );
120.  foreach my $TempDir ( @TempDirs )
121.  {
122.    foreach my $Path ( glob( "$TempDir\\*.*" ) )
123.    {
124.      next if( ! -f $Path );
125.      if( $TempFileGracePeriod < time() - (stat( $Path ))[10] )
126.      {
127.        unlink( $Path);
128.      }
129.    }
130.  }
131.
132.  # Update the logon database...
133.  if( $db )
134.  {
135.    my $Query = "INSERT INTO UserLogon
136.                  (Domain, Account, Machine, Date)
137.                  VALUES ('$Logon{domain}',
138.                          '$Logon{account}',
139.                          '$Logon{machine}',
140.                          {fn Now()})";
141.    $db->Sql( $Query );
142.    $db->Close() if( $db );
143.  }
144.
145.  BEGIN
146.  {
147.    $SECOND = 1;
148.    $MINUTE = 60 * $SECOND;
149.    $HOUR = 60 * $MINUTE;
150.    $DAY = 24 * $HOUR;
151.    $WEEK = 7 * $DAY;
152.  }
```

Conclusion

Seeing a radical increase in productivity is not uncommon when you simply revamp the way logon scripts are implemented. Implementing them differently can free up a system administrator's time and provide the user with a personalized logon anywhere on the network. Such scripts are powerful indeed whether they are used to log on a user or act as a launching point to automate the configuration of a machine. And Perl is, of course, a powerful ally in working with logon scripts.

7

Processes

One fundamental purpose of modern day computers is to run applications. These applications can be in such forms as services and daemons, programs, automated batch jobs, or Visual Basic, Java, or even Perl scripts. Because this capability is common among almost all computers, it stands to reason that they share similarities. For the most part, that is true.

The Win32 world, however, has several idiosyncrasies that coders from the UNIX discipline find laughable. To be sure, from a UNIX background, these issues are considered limitations and are indeed mockable. However, they are not necessarily a bad thing; actually, they can be quite useful and empowering. The real issue is that UNIX coders are not familiar with Win32 process creation. If Win32 had come before UNIX, you can be assured that Win32 folks would be mocking UNIX process techniques.

This chapter discusses various methods for creating and managing processes. Different techniques for process creation are discussed. Common traps and pitfalls are also described.

Win32 Processes

Whenever a user double-clicks a program icon or runs an application (such as Perl) from a command line, she is instructing Win32 to create a new process. Normally, users don't think twice about this procedure; they simply run Excel, Photoshop, or maybe a new session of Quake. Regardless of what program is started, Win32 allocates a block of memory, loads the program and any library files it requires into this block of memory, and then creates a primary thread to execute the loaded code. After all this is done and the program is running, it is referred to as a *process*. A process can access any of the memory that it has been given by the operating system, but only that memory. You can think of each process as having its own little sandbox in which it can do what it likes but cannot step out of. This sandbox is known as a *process space*. If you prevent a process from accessing resources outside its process space, you can maintain system security.

Many words represent processes. *Daemons, services, applications,* and *programs* are just a few that simply refer to processes. Each may have different purposes for running, but they all share the same physical manifestations in the computer: They are processes.

Several processes typically run at the same time. Normally, one running process enables you to share printers and directories (the server service); another enables you to connect to other machines (the workstation service); one manages logon security (the winlogon service); and some, like the TCP echo service, do simple things. As administrator, you can add additional services or processes, such as email services or word processing applications.

Such process creation isn't new; it's been around since computers have been able to dynamically load program code into memory. However, Win32 departs from the traditional paradigm that UNIX coders have come to depend on. Capabilities such as splitting a running program into two identical copies of itself (*forking*) have long been a staple of UNIX daemon coding. However, this particularly useful functionality has not been implemented into the Win32 family of operating systems—much to the mortification of programmers porting over UNIX code.

The good news is that Microsoft opted out of forking for a more efficient approach: *threading.* Just as UNIX or Win32 can multitask many applications at once, so can an application multithread many subtasks within an application. Multithreading is efficient because all the threads live within the same process, so they all share the same memory and security attributes. This means costly interprocess communication calls (IPC) such as shared memory, pipes, and sockets are not necessary.

Contrary to the forking method, the threads can access each other's data structures directly. A forked process results in two processes with identical copies of memory. Because both processes are running in different memory spaces, there is no inherent way for one process to access the memory of the other process. IPC can be used to access the other process, but that takes both processes working in concert to make such access possible.

So, Win32 has its threading model, and UNIX has its forking model. Win32's model, however, is not too unique because UNIX has had variations of threads for years. What is unique, however, is the lack of a forking mechanism, which is where this story on processes begins.

Following in the fine tradition of UNIX coding, Perl hacks have used forking in their scripts for many reasons. Even though Perl is a cross-platform language, any script that was based on forking broke when run on a Win32 machine. There are no exceptions to this rule because Win32 itself does not support forking.

Masses of Perl coders were forced to rewrite their scripts, moving from forking to threading. They began the process with good intentions and high hopes, only to fall victim to the cruelest of jokes—Win32 did not have thread support for Perl. Oh, the humanity!

Okay, so coders could neither fork nor thread. This was quickly becoming a situation in which Java or Visual Basic was looking more and more attractive. Then Perl 5.005 was released, hinting at the promise of Win32 threading. It was still experimental, but it looked like this release could be the panacea that everyone had been seeking.

Then Perl 5.6 was introduced and brought with it not only threading (still experimental) but forking as well. This forking (at least on Win32 platforms) was emulated. This means that Perl made it look as though the process had been forked, even though it really had not. Perl would create a copy of the Perl interpreter object and give it its own thread to run on.

This emulated forking works for the most part, but other issues can easily crop up. For example, if a Perl extension is not designed to be *multithread safe*, running a script in a new thread (as fork emulation does) may lead to inaccurate results because one thread may overwrite global variables and data structures used by another thread.

Even with these new threading and forking capabilities, Win32 Perl still can create (or *spawn*) new processes. Even though spawning new processes can be slower, more cumbersome, and rife with limitations, a bit of creative thinking can allow clever coders to achieve the results they desire.

Creating Processes

You can find a good reference on creating processes using Win32 Perl in my book *Win32 Perl Programming: The Standard Extensions* (New Riders Publishing). It covers the various methods for spawning new processes and explains the flags and other parameters that the process-creation functions accept. However, this chapter covers the most common process-creation methods from piping, the system command, spawning, Win32::Process and Win32::AdminMisc, and forking.

The first, and easiest, way to create a new process is to use backticks.

Backticks

Using backticks is probably one of the quickest and least complicated ways to spawn new processes. When you simply specify a command line between backticks, the command is executed by Win32, and each line of output the new process sends to STDOUT is captured and returned as an element in an array. This is exactly what Example 7.1 does.

Example 7.1 *Using Backticks to Create a New Process*

```
01. my @Output = `dir c:\\temp`;
02. print @Output;
```

As you can see, using backticks is very simple. Before you go out and start backticking everything in sight, though, you must be aware of the Win32 pitfalls; so, read on.

File Extension Problems

If you have associated some file extension (such as .pl) with PERL.EXE, Perl scripts execute when only their names are referenced. (Refer to Chapter 1, "Perl and the Admin," for details on associating file extensions with Perl.) Example 7.2 demonstrates this use. Notice that you don't need to indicate the PERL.EXE executable, just the Perl script path.

> **Note**
>
> *Sometimes you need to pass in Perl switches, such as* -w *and* -d, *when a file extension has been mapped to PERL.EXE. In this case, you can reference the entire command line, including* perl.exe, *as in*
>
> ```
> perl.exe -d -w c:\temp\test.pl
> ```
>
> *or add the flags to the "sha-bang" line. Refer to Chapter 1 for details.* ◆

Example 7.2 *Backticks and File Associations*

```
01. my @Output = `c:\\temp\\perltest.pl`;
02. print @Output;
```

This point makes sense. After all, you can enter the same path on a command line, and it magically works as well. On Windows 2000 machines, you can modify the PATHEXT environment variable to include the .pl extension (refer to Chapter 1). This way, Windows considers .pl to be an executable extension just as it does with the .exe, .bat, and .cmd extensions. You can simply type the name of a Perl script without its extension, such as "perltest". This assumes that the perltest.pl script is either in your current directory or somewhere in the path.

Long Filenames

The Win32 family of operating systems has always supported long filenames. Much like a UNIX filename, a Win32 filename can be rather long—up to 255 characters to be exact. You can use much of the normal character set for a filename, including embedded spaces (limitations include the backslash (\), double quotation mark ("), forward slash (/), and colon (:), to name a few). Unlike UNIX, however, Win32 filenames are not case-sensitive.

At this point, you may be seriously wondering about this slight departure into file system theory. Actually, processes and filenames are related but not necessarily in a good way. Files can have long pathnames with embedded whitespace. That indeed is nice, but after you get used to it, the novelty quickly dies. When this excitement leaves, you will begin to notice how Perl does not really seem to like these long filenames.

When you use backticks to create a process, long filenames can cause you hours of debugging fun. The problem comes not from long filenames in general, but from long filenames that have spaces in them. Example 7.3 illustrates that a long filename can indeed work when executed with backticks.

Example 7.3   *Backticks and Long Filenames*

```
01. my $Name = "MyLongPerlScriptName.pl";
02. my @Output = `$Name`;
03. print @Output;
```

Example 7.4 shows the same script, except that the Perl script to be executed has embedded spaces in its name. These spaces cause the execution of the script to fail, even if you specify the full path, such as

```
`c:\perl\bin\perl.exe c:\temp\My Long Perl Script Name.pl`;
```

Example 7.4   *Backticks and Long Filenames with Spaces*

```
01. my $Name = "My Long Perl Script Name.pl";
02. # Next line will fail since the long file name has spaces
03. my @Output = `$Name`;
04. print @Output;
```

You can choose from two fixes for this dilemma. The first one is quite simple: Surround the long filename with double quotation marks (not single quotation marks):

```
`c:\\perl\\bin\\perl.exe "c:\\temp\\My Long Perl Script Name.pl"`;
```

This fix, however, does not always work. Depending on the command that is to be executed, some paths simply do not fair well even when surrounded by quotation marks. For example, the following line does not work:

```
`"c:\\Program Files\\My Long Perl Script Name.pl"`;
```

In this case, even though the .pl extension is correctly associated with the PERL.EXE program, the following error message occurs:

```
'c:\program' is not recognized as an internal or external command,
operable program or batch file.
```

The reason for such a failure has to do with how the .pl extension was associated with the PERL.EXE program. Many administrators incorrectly associate the .pl extension with the command line

```
ftype PerlFile=c:\perl\bin\perl.exe %1 %*
```

This is a mistake because when the filename has embedded spaces (such as `"c:\Program Files\My Long Perl Script Name.pl"`), this command expands to be

```
c:\perl\bin\perl.exe c:\Program Files\My Long Perl Script Name.pl
```

This will cause Perl to attempt to load a script called `c:\Program` and pass in parameters: `Files\My`, `Long`, `Perl`, `Script`, and `Name.pl`. The way to correct this is to rerun the `ftype` command surrounding the `%1` parameter with quote marks (refer to Chapter 1 for more details), as in

```
ftype PerlFile=c:\perl\bin\perl.exe "%1" %*
```

Because a script cannot depend that the .pl extension has been correctly associated, it can use a second, and more effective, fix (I have yet to see this technique fail). Simply convert the long filename to a short name.

For the sake of backward compatibility with DOS and Win16 applications (those old Windows 3.1x programs), Win32 allows each file to have a long and a short name. For example, for this long filename

```
My list of files.txt
```

the short name version of that file might be

```
MYLIST~1.TXT
```

The only reliable way a program can discover the short pathname of a file is by calling the Win32 API's `GetShortPathName()` function. It just so happens that the Perl Win32 extension exposes this function. Example 7.5 demonstrates both fixes.

Example 7.5   *Resolving the Problem of Having Backticks with Long Filenames with Spaces*

```
01. use Win32;
02. my $Name = "My Long Perl Script Name.pl";
03.
04. # Fix 1: Surround the long file name with quotes...
05. my @Output = `"$Name"`;
06. print @Output;
07.
08. # Fix 2:
09. $Name = Win32::GetShortPathName( $Name );
10. @Output = `$Name`;
11. print @Output;
```

Redirecting Input and Output Handles

In Win32, a script can redirect the standard input and outputs (STDIN, STDOUT, and STDERR). By using Win32 command redirect tokens, you can effectively redirect these streams.

Win32 command lines recognize the < and > redirection characters, which tell the command interpreter to redirect input (<) into or output (>) from a process. Consider this example:

```
dir *.* > directory.txt
```

This command line redirects the output from the dir *.* command into a file called directory.txt. However, NT provides a bit more power by enabling you to specify which output stream to be redirected. By default, the STDOUT output stream (which is always file handle 1) is redirected. Therefore, the preceding command is equivalent to this:

```
dir *.* 1> directory.txt
```

If you want to redirect the STDERR of a command, simply specify the STDERR file handle number (which happens to be 2):

```
rd MyDir 2> error.txt
```

In this case, if the directory, MyDir, does not exist, an error message is saved into a file called error.txt.

Now the cool part is that you can also specify a stream to redirect into by specifying an ampersand (&) character and the stream's file handle number:

```
rd MyDir 2>&1
```

This command line redirects the STDERR output into the STDOUT. If you were to combine this with the backtick execution, you would successfully get all STDOUT and STDERR returned. Example 7.6 does exactly this. The array @Output in line 3 is assigned each line of both outputs. The first part of the array is STDOUT, followed by STDERR. Example 7.7 is called by Example 7.6 and provides output for the sake of demonstration.

Example 7.6   *Redirecting STDERR to STDOUT Using Backticks*

```
01. my $Name = "MyScript.pl";
02.
03. my @Output = `$Name 2>&1`;
04. print @Output;
```

Example 7.7   *The MyScript.pl Script for Example 7.6*

```
01. print STDERR "This is STDERR line #1\n";
02. print STDOUT "This is STDOUT line #1\n";
03. print STDERR "This is STDERR line #2\n";
04. print STDOUT "This is STDOUT line #2\n";
```

Piping (with *open()*)

Many system administrators have used the open() function to create processes. The Perl script can redirect the process' STDIN or STDOUT to a Perl file handle.

When a script opens a new child process using the piped open() function, it can continue processing asynchronously from the new process. That is, both processes run at the same time. The output of the child process is buffered in the file handle specified in the call to open(). The parent process therefore can continue doing whatever it needs to do and read from the file handle if and when it needs to. Because reading from a file handle can cause a blocking state (if no data is waiting to be read), the parent process effectively stops processing until either the child task sends a line of data or the child side of the pipe closes (as when the child process terminates).

The semantics surrounding the execution of the processes are consistent with backticks. Example 7.8 is identical to Example 7.6, except that instead of using backticks, the process is created using a piped open() function. Line 2 opens the process and redirects the STDERR into the STDOUT, which is all piped into the file handle.

This script illustrates that backticks and piped opens are very similar. They even share the same long filename problems. If $Name were assigned a value with embedded spaces, then line 2 would have to look like this:

```
if( open( FILE, "\"$Name\" 2>&1 |" ) )
```

Notice that $Name is delimited by double quotation marks. For more details, refer to the discussion of issues surrounding backticks in the "Backticks" section in this chapter.

Example 7.8   *Redirecting STDERR to STDOUT Using a Piped* open()

```
01. my $Name = "MyScript.pl";
02. if( open( FILE, "$Name 2>&1 |" ) )
03. {
04.   while( my $Line = <FILE> )
05.   {
06.     print $Line;
07.   }
08.   close( FILE );
09. }
```

The *system()* function

Most Perl coders coming from UNIX backgrounds are familiar with the system() command, which launches an application passed into the function. This command really serves the same function as using backticks or open() with a pipe. For example, if you were to use the line

```
system( 'test.pl' );
```

in a Perl script, the test.pl script would successfully execute, assuming that .pl is associated with perl.exe.

Just as with the other process-creation functions already discussed, on a Windows 2000 machine, you can pass in the name of the executable without an extension, as in

```
system( 'test' );
```

provided that the extension has been properly associated with an executable (for example, .pl associated with perl.exe; again, see Chapter 1 for details) *and* the extension has been added to the PATHEXT environment variable.

Like the other process-creation functions, a process path with embedded spaces must be surrounded by quotation marks, as shown here:

```
system( '"my long file name.exe"' );
```

The major difference between the system() function and the others is that it does not capture the STDOUT from the new process. Even though a script does not have to wait to capture the output of the system() function, the script enters a blocking state and waits until the new process has terminated.

Win32::Spawn()

So far, you have examined several process creating functions, all of which have their own unique qualities. They all do, however, share one discouraging commonality: They all block while the new process runs (with the exception of fork(), which is available only in Perl version 5.6 and higher, and piped opens when not reading from the pipe). You need a way to spawn a process that runs independently from the calling script. The Win32::Spawn() function does just that.

Win32::Spawn() is unique to Perl because it exists only on Win32 machines. This function is quite simple:

```
Win32::Spawn( $App, $Args, $Pid );
```

The first parameter you pass in is the path to the program to be executed. The second parameter is the arguments to pass into the application. The third parameter *must* be a scalar variable (such as $Pid); it cannot be a constant (such as 1 or "hello").

You really should know about a couple of things before using this function, so be sure to read the next few paragraphs; otherwise, you may be pulling out your hair in frustration. If the path has embedded spaces, you *do not* have to surround the path with double quotation marks. Because the first parameter represents only the path, you don't need to delimit the path from anything else.

The application that you specify must be either a full path to the executable (such as c:\winnt\notepad.exe) or a relative path (such as notepad.exe or ..\notepad.exe). If you specify a relative path, the current drive and directory are automatically prepended to the application name. Therefore, don't pass in NOTEPAD.EXE expecting it to run just because the application can be located by the PATH environment variable.

The $Args parameter is pretty simple to understand. If you're running the Notepad program and want it to open a particular file, pass in the path to the file as the second parameter. Simple enough, right? Well, almost. What is not so obvious is that the $Args parameter *must* start with the name of the executable. Yes, you read correctly: You need to specify the executable twice (once in the first parameter and again in the second). To be more accurate, you need to specify something (actually anything) in the beginning of the $Args parameter that represents the executable. It can be anything, such as

```
Win32::Spawn( 'c:\winnt\notepad.exe', "blah c:\\temp\\test.txt", $Pid );
```

When Win32 creates the new process, it passes in the $Args parameter as the command line to the new process. This entire string is parsed and presented to a C program as its argv. Therefore, in this example, a C program's argv[0] value would be "blah". The third parameter, $Pid, must be a scalar variable because after the new process is created, the scalar passed in as the third parameter is set to the value of the new process identifier. The silly thing is that if you pass in a constant, the function fails, but only after the process has been created.

As an aside, you can pass in a reference as the third parameter, like this:

```
Win32::Spawn( $App, $Args, \$Pid );
```

This reference works; however, who knows what will happen to \$Pid? I mention this point because no checking is done to make sure that the third parameter is a reference. If you do pass in a scalar reference, the scalar itself is not set correctly.

The truly unfortunate aspect of this function is that you cannot specify any environment variables in the parameters. If $App is "%SystemRoot%\\notepad.exe", the function fails because the path contains environment strings. You can call into Win32::ExpandEnvironmentStrings(), and the function returns the passed-in string with all environment variables expanded. This is truly a convenience. Example 7.9 shows an example.

Example 7.9   *Expanding Environment Variables for Win32::Spawn()*

```
01. use Win32;
02. my $App = "%SystemRoot%\\notepad.exe";
03. my $Args = "notepad %temp%\\test.txt";
04. $App = Win32::ExpandEnvironmentStrings( $App );
05. $Args = Win32::ExpandEnvironmentStrings( $Args );
```

```
06. if( Win32::Spawn( $App, $Args, $Pid ) )
07. {
08.    print "$App was successfully created with PID $Pid\n";
09.}
```

Another way to expand the variables is to use Perl's %ENV hash to specify environment variables. Consider Example 7.10 as an example.

Example 7.10 *Expand Environment Variables Using the %ENV Hash*

```
01. use Win32;
02. my $App = "%SystemRoot%\\notepad.exe";
03. my $Args = "notepad %temp%\\test.txt";
04. $App =~ s/%(.*?)%/$ENV{$1}/g;
05. $Args =~ s/%(.*?)%/$ENV{$1}/g;
06. if( Win32::Spawn( $App, $Args, $Pid ) )
07. {
08.      print "$App was successfully created with PID $Pid\n";
09. }
```

Win32::Process

By now, it should be clear that there are more ways to create a process using Win32 Perl than you can shake a stick at, but you're not quite done yet. Two more exciting functions are awaiting you. The first is from the Win32::Process extension. This particular extension is quite useful for managing a process. The Win32::Process::Create() function creates a new Win32 process. If it is successful, it returns a Win32::Process object that can later be used to pause, kill, or wait for the process to die.

Frankly, almost everything you can do with Win32::Process you can accomplish with other functions. You can create and kill a process in other ways as well. However, this extension outshines the others in its capability to manage a process.

You create a Win32::Process by using the Create() method:

```
Win32::Process::Create( $Process $App, $Args, $Inherit, $Flag, $Dir )
```

The first parameter *must* be a scalar variable. If the creation is successful, this variable is set with a reference to a Win32::Process object.

The second and third parameters, $App and $Args, are identical to the first and second parameters in the Win32::Spawn() function. Refer to the section "Win32::Spawn()" for more details.

The fourth parameter, $Inherit indicates whether the new process will inherit any open file handles and sockets. Keep in mind, however, that they are Win32, not Perl, file handles and sockets. Therefore, setting this parameter to 1 (indicating inheritance will occur) may not really benefit a script much.

The fifth parameter, $Flag, allows a script to specify various creation flags. These flags determine just how the process is created. The following three flags are worth noting:

- CREATE_NO_WINDOW creates the process with no window if it is a console application (such as a Perl script). The process runs, but no console window (DOS-like box) is created for it. Therefore, STDOUT and STDERR are not displayed.

- CREATE_NEW_CONSOLE creates the process with a new console window. If the created process is a regular Windows application (with a graphic window), this flag doesn't do anything. STDOUT and STDERR from the process are displayed in the new window.

- CREATE_SUSPENDED is a useful flag if you need to perform benchmarking or synchronize the new process. The process is created but is automatically suspended in a paused state. You can resume the process with a call to the Resume() method. This method works for any process, console- or window-based. When the process is created, it does not show its window until it resumes. If you specify the CREATE_NO_WINDOW flag as well, a console-based application's window never appears, even after resuming.

Typically, scripts specify CREATE_NEW_CONSOLE when creating new Perl script processes. This way, the user can see the output of the process. However, if you have some service or daemon that creates processes quite often, always having a window pop up to take the focus may be distracting and annoying. In that case, you should specify the CREATE_NO_WINDOW flag.

If you specify neither the CREATE_NO_WINDOW nor CREATE_NEW_CONSOLE flags, all output from a new console process is dumped into the same window as the original Perl script. Seeing outputs from different processes intermixed on the same window can become quite chaotic.

Finally, the last parameter is the default directory that will be set for the new process.

Example 7.11 uses NOTEPAD.EXE to display a text file for a specified amount of time. After the timeout value is exceeded, the process is killed. Even though this approach is not an elegant way of displaying a message of the day, it could be useful in something like a logon script. The nature of this particular script is to demonstrate the usefulness of the Win32::Process extension.

Note that using the CREATE_SUSPENDED flag (line 8) is not necessary; it is here only to demonstrate how to create a suspended process. Likewise, calling the Resume() method (line 20) is necessary only because the process is created in a suspended state.

While looking over the script, you may question what line 20 is for. It is not very intuitive, but it serves a very good purpose. When a process is suspended (either by calling the process object's Suspend() method or by creating the process in a suspended state), Win32 increases an internal counter. This counter indicates how many times the process has been suspended. Because a process can be suspended multiple times, this counter keeps track of the level of suspension. A call to the object's Resume() method causes the counter to decrease.

The Resume() method returns the suspension level that the process was under *before* the call to Resume(). This means that when Resume() returns a value of 1, the process is no longer suspended. Considering that a process can be suspended multiple times (even by other processes), line 20 continuously calls Resume() until the process is no longer suspended.

Line 23 calls the Wait() method, causing the script to block until either the process is terminated or the timeout value expires. The timeout value, in milliseconds, is passed into the Wait() method. When a call to Wait() returns, if its return value is 0, the timeout value expired; otherwise, the process was terminated.

Line 27 shows how you can kill the process. The value passed into the Kill() method is the process' exit code. All processes can return a numeric value when they exit (or are killed).

Example 7.11   *Creating a Suspended Process*

```
01. use Win32::Process;
02. $Timeout = 5;
03. $File = $0;
04. $App = "$ENV{SystemRoot}\\notepad.exe";
05. $Cmd = "notepad $File";
06. $bInherit = 0;
07. $Dir = ".";
08. $Flag = CREATE_SUSPENDED | CREATE_NEW_CONSOLE;
09. if( Win32::Process::Create( $Process,
10.                             $App,
11.                             $Cmd,
12.                             $bInherit,
13.                             $Flag,
14.                             $Dir ) )
15. {
16.   $Pid = $Process->GetProcessID();
17.   print "The process was created in a suspended state ";
18.   print "with an ID of $Pid.\n";
19.   print "Now resuming the process...\n";
20.   while( 1 < $Process->Resume() ){};
21.   print "Now we will wait for $Timeout seconds for the process to\n";
22.   print "terminate...\n";
23.   $Result = $Process->Wait( $Timeout * 1000 );
24.   if( ! $Result )
25.   {
```

continues ▶

Example 7.11 *continued*

```
26.    print "The process did not terminate so we will now kill it...\n";
27.    $Process->Kill( 0 );
28.    }
29.    else
30.    {
31.      print "The process was terminated by the user.\n";
32.    }
33. }
34. else
35. {
36.   print "Unable to create new process.\n";
37.   print "Error: " . Win32::FormatMessage( Win32::GetLastError() );
38. }
```

Win32::AdminMisc

The last two process-creation functions worth noting come from the
Win32::AdminMisc extension: CreateProcess() and CreateProcessAsUser(). The
latter is discussed in the "Running Processes as Another User" section.

Fundamentally, they are both identical; they take the same parameters.
These functions can be as simple as Win32::Spawn() and can be more complex than Win32::Process::Create(). They are called with this syntax:

```
Win32::AdminMisc::CreateProcess( $Cmd [, %Config ] )
```

With this function, unlike Win32::Spawn() and Win32::Process::Create(),
you need to specify only a command line with parameters—something like
perl c:\temp\myscript.pl or winword.exe file1.doc.

The optional second parameter is actually a list of attributes and their
values. You don't need to specify any of the attributes, but if you do, they
are used instead of a default value. These attributes can specify the X and Y
coordinates where the window should be located as well as how the process
should initially appear (hidden, maximized, minimized, and so on). Check
with the Win32::AdminMisc documentation for more details. And refer to
Example 7.14 later in this chapter for an example of using these functions.

Forking

Note

This section applies only to Win32 Perl version 5.6 and higher. ◆

With the introduction of Perl 5.6, Win32 can now fork. Traditionally, forking has always resulted in the operating system creating an identical copy of
the running process space. This way, a Perl script can literally clone itself.
Because the forked process is an identical copy of its parent process, it has

the same open file handles and sockets as its parent. This makes for a good way to process incoming socket requests, for example. The parent simply accepts an incoming socket request, forks, and then closes the socket. The forked child process inherits the open socket, so it then reads and writes to the socket as it needs to. The fact that the parent process closes the socket does not affect the child's copy of the socket at all.

Because Win32 does not have any concept of forking, Perl has to emulate the fork. That is, Perl creates a copy of its internal objects (such as global variables, open files and sockets, and so on) and creates a new thread to access this copy. For the most part, this approach is an inventive way to achieve forking, even though it is still quite limited.

However, forking (and threading, for that matter) is still experimental in Perl 5.6 (as of this writing), so you can expect bugs to creep up until future versions perfect the function.

Note

The use of threads is not covered because they are very experimental, and the Thread.pm interface is expected to change in future versions. This is documented in the Thread.pm file:

WARNING: Threading is an experimental feature. Both the interface and implementation are subject to change drastically. In fact, this documentation describes the flavor of threads that was in version 5.005. Perl 5.6.0 and later have the beginnings of support for interpreter threads, which (when finished) is expected to be significantly different from what is described here. The information contained here may therefore soon be obsolete. Use at your own risk! ◆

Because the fork() method is well documented in various other Perl resources (including online documentation that comes with Perl), this chapter provides only a cursory overview.

When a script executes the fork() function, an identical copy of the script is created. This new copy is called the *child* process, and the original is called the *parent* process.

The fork() command returns one of three different values, as shown in Table 7.1.

Table 7.1   Return Values from the fork() Function

Return Value	Description
undef	If the fork() failed, it returns an undefined value.
0	The child process always returns a 0 value.
Nonzero value	The parent process always returns a nonzero value. This value is the process identifier (PID) of the newly created child process.

Simple forking can be achieved in a script, such as in Example 7.12. In this script, a fork takes place, and both the parent and child processes count from 100 to 0, printing each number along the way. The purpose here is to demonstrate how a fork works.

Line 2 is very important, although the reason may not be so obvious. This line enables autoflush mode, which means that when the script prints something, it is automatically flushed, and the printed text is forced to the screen. Without this line, all output to the screen would be buffered, resulting in delayed printing. That would make it look as though one process ran and finished, and then the other process ran and finished with no concurrency in their executions.

Line 5 performs the actual forking. Notice that the script checks whether the command returned undef. If it does, the fork fails and the script dies. Otherwise, two running processes call the Count() subroutine.

Example 7.12   *Example of Forking*

```
01. # Turn off output buffering (turn on auto flush)
02. $| = 1;
03.
04. # Fork the process
05. defined( $Pid = fork() ) || die "Could not fork: $!\n";
06. if( 0 == $Pid )
07. {
08.    # We get here if we are the child process
09.    Count( "Child: " );
10. }
11. else
12. {
13.    # We get here if we are the parent process
14.    Count( "Parent: " );
15. }
16.
17. # Both parent and child will get here
18. $String = ( ( $Pid )? "Parent" : "Child" ) . " process has finished.\n";
19. print $String;
20.
21. sub Count
22. {
23.    my( $String ) = @_;
24.    my $iCount = 100;
25.
26.    while( $iCount-- )
27.    {
28.      print "$String $iCount\n";
29.    }
30. }
```

Forking is really quite simple. Just make sure that the script can determine whether it is a child or parent process and execute code accordingly. A better example of how to use fork is Example 7.24.

> **Caution**
>
> *Win32 Perl's fork emulation appears to solve many problems that this chapter has so far addressed. However, this emulation is still relatively young and has many bugs to be worked out. In my test lab, most processes that loop creating forked children almost always eventually crash. Therefore, use caution before implementing Win32 Perl's* `fork()` *if you plan on deploying such scripts in a production environment.* ◆

Running Processes as Another User

Since Windows NT was developed, administrators have been lamenting over the lack of a UNIX-like *super user* (SU) utility. In UNIX, anyone could run the SU utility, provide the correct password, and be treated as if he were the super user. The Win32 world does not have a super user account; instead, it has the Administrator account. But the only way to be treated as the administrator is to log on as the administrator. Doing so requires anyone currently logged on to close all applications and log off first. This approach is not very user friendly.

Several years ago I got around this problem by writing a script called RunAs.pl (see Example 7.14). When calling the script, you provide a user-name (and optionally a domain), a password, and an application to run. If you are logged in with the correct privileges on your account, the application runs, impersonating the specified username. This capability has come in quite handy. Typically, I do something like this:

```
perl runas.pl mydomain\administrator myadminpwd cmd.exe
```

The result is a DOS box that runs under the Administrator account. I can then perform administrative tasks such as deleting secured files. If you were to run a simple WhoAmI.pl script (see Example 7.13), it would print the following:

```
Currently logged on as:
. . . . . . . . . . . . . . . . . . . . . .
Domain:   mydomain
Computer: TEST_PC
Userid:   Administrator
```

This output shows that the new process (CMD.EXE) is running as the administrator and not the current user—unless, of course, the current user *is* the administrator.

Example 7.13   *A Simple WhoAmI Script*

```
01.    use Win32;
02.    print "\n\nCurrently logged on as:\n";
03.    print "--------------------\n";
04.    print "Domain:  ";
05.    print Win32::DomainName(), "\n";
06.    print "Computer: ";
07.    print Win32::NodeName(),  "\n";
08.    print "Userid:  ";
09.    print Win32::LoginName(), "\n\n";
```

Windows 2000 comes with a utility called RunAs.exe, which performs much the same function as Example 7.14. The much more powerful Windows 2000 version can load the specified user's profile, Registry hive, and environment. Adding the code to enable the same functionality for Example 7.14 would not take much work, however. Until everyone upgrades to Windows 2000, though, Example 7.14 provides a working substitute on Windows 3.5, 3.51, and 4.0.

The magic this script uses is a combination of two Win32::AdminMisc functions: LogonAsUser() and CreateProcessAsUser(). The LogonAsUser() function is pretty simple: You pass in the domain, name, and password of the user you want to impersonate, along with a logon type flag. If the function is successful, the script continues running under the impersonated credentials of the specified user. It continues until the script terminates or a call to Win32::AdminMisc::LogoffAsUser() is made. At this point, the CreateProcessAsUser() function comes in.

Say that you run a Perl script that successfully impersonates another user by using LogonAsUser(). Only that script can run as the impersonated user. Therefore, if you spawn another program (a DOS box, Microsoft Word, a Web browser, or whatever), it does *not* run as the impersonated user. The script would have to create the new process using CreateProcessAsUser() instead.

The trick with using the Win32::AdminMisc::LogonAsUser() function (as in Example 7.14) is that the logged-on user (the account running the script) must be granted the following privileges:

- SeTcbPrivilege to act as part of the operating system
- SeAssignPrimary to replace a process level
- SeIncreaseQuota to increase quotas
- SeChangeNotify to bypass traverse checking

Because these privileges are local, a user must have these privileges on each computer that she intends to run scripts that call the LogonAsUser() function. In Chapter 2, "Account Maintenance," Example 2.9 contains a tool that enables a administrator to manage these privileges from the command line.

Additionally, the user account that will be impersonated requires the correct logon right. Typically, the LOGON32_LOGON_INTERACTIVE flag is used (it is the default if one is not specified). This particular account right allows the user to log on to the machine by using the keyboard (interactively). Other rights allow the account to log on as a batch job, a service, or through the network.

> **Note**
>
> *If the* LOGON32_LOGON_NETWORK *flag is specified during a call to* Win32::AdminMisc: :LogonAsUser(), *an attempt to call* Win32::AdminMisc::CreateProcessAsUser() *may fail on versions of NT before 4.0 because a primary process token cannot be generated through a network logon. Windows NT 4.0 allows an impersonation token to be duplicated as a primary token. This simply means that if you can avoid* LOGON32_LOGON_NETWORK, *do not use* it. ◆

If the script is successful at impersonating a user through LogonAsUser(), a new process created using CreateProcessAsUser() inherits the impersonated user's credentials. Therefore, even though the script terminates—or if the script explicitly stops impersonating with a call to Win32::AdminMisc: :LogoffAsUser()—the new process continues impersonating.

Example 7.14   *Running a Process as Another User*

```
01. use Win32::AdminMisc;
02. my( $Domain, $User ) = ( ( shift @ARGV ) =~ /((.*)\\)?(.*?)$/ )[1..2];
03. $Password = shift @ARGV;
04. $Process = join( " ", @ARGV );
05. print "\nStarting \"$Process\" as $User in ";
```

continues ▶

Example 7.14 *continued*

```
06. print "the \U$Domain\E domain...\n\n";
07. $Result = Win32::AdminMisc::LogonAsUser( $Domain,
08.                                           $User,
09.                                           $Password,
10.                                           LOGON32_LOGON_INTERACTIVE );
11. if( $Result )
12. {
13.    $LogonUser = Win32::AdminMisc::GetLogonName();
14.    print "Successfully logged on as $LogonUser.\n";
15.    $Result = Win32::AdminMisc::CreateProcessAsUser(
16.                 $Process,
17.                 "Flags" => CREATE_NEW_CONSOLE,
18.                 "XSize" => 640,
19.                 "YSize" => 400,
20.                 "X"     => 200,
21.                 "Y"     => 175,
22.                 "XBuffer"=> 80,
23.                 "YBuffer"=> 175,
24.                 "Show" => SW_MAXIMIZE,
25.                 "Title" => "\u$User\'s $Process program",
26.                 "Fill" => BACKGROUND_BLUE   |
27.                           FOREGROUND_RED    |
28.                           FOREGROUND_BLUE   |
29.                           FOREGROUND_GREEN  |
30.                           FOREGROUND_INTENSITY );
31.    if( $Result )
32.    {
33.      print "Successful! The new process' PID is $Result.\n";
34.    }
35.    else
36.    {
37.      print "Failed.\n\tError: ", Error(), "\n";
38.    }
39. }
40. else
41. {
42.    print "Failed to logon.\n\tError: ", Error(), "\n";
43. }
44.
45. sub Error
46. {
47.    return( Win32::FormatMessage( Win32::AdminMisc::GetError() ) );
48. }
```

Enumerating Processes

Getting a list of currently running processes can be quite tricky. By far, the easiest way to obtain such a list is to run the Task Manager (see Figure 7.1). You can run this program by pressing Ctrl+Shift+Esc. You can also run this program by right-clicking the taskbar and then selecting Task Manager.

Unfortunately, these methods kick up a GUI application that users must interact with. For most users, this is probably fine, but Perl coders need to achieve the same results programmatically.

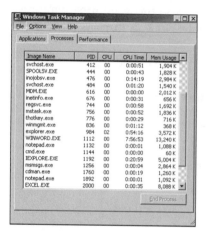

Figure 7.1   *The Task Manager window.*

You can obtain the process list, but doing so is not easy. You need to extract information from the Registry. To be more precise, you take the information from the Registry's performance root key (HKEY_PERFORMANCE_ DATA). You could write a Perl script to do so, but writing such a script is very slow and extremely messy.

Jutta Klebe authored a Perl extension called Win32::PerfLib. It provides a simple and fast way to extract the necessary performance data from the Registry. Even though this extension manages much of the work, it is still messy—just not as messy as it would be if you had to use the Win32::Registry extension.

By using Jutta's extension, you can not only get a list of PIDs, but you can also obtain interesting information regarding each process—data such as how much memory is currently allocated (the *working set*) and the largest amount of memory the process has used (the *peak working set*). Other information such as how many threads and handles each process has opened, timing, and process priority can also be procured.

Example 7.15 uses the Win32::PerfLib to dump the process list with some details about each process. When you run this code, it dumps various properties of each process running on the machine. When the script runs, it displays process statistics running on the local computer. You can obtain process information for a remote machine by passing in its name (Win32 computer name, DNS name, or IP address) as a parameter from the command line.

An example of the output generated by Example 7.15 is listed in Figure 7.2. It was generated using the following command line:

```
perl.exe ps.pl \\SERVER1
```

Notice that the script lists process information for a remote machine. If you don't pass in a machine name, it displays process information for the local machine.

```
Collecting process info for \\SERVER1...
PID   Parent   Process Name   Threads    Memory     Memory Peak   Handles
----  ------   ------------   -------   ----------   -----------   -------
   0      0    _Total            264    52,156 K     88,380 K       4323
1024    984    perl                1      2,596 K      2,660 K         25
 140      8    smss                6         32 K      2,004 K         33
 168    140    csrss              11      2,144 K      2,996 K        339
 188    140    winlogon           17      2,308 K     10,952 K        383
 216    188    services           46      4,336 K      5,420 K        795
 228    188    lsass              17      1,000 K      4,340 K        309
 364    216    svchost             8      1,408 K      2,720 K        258
 444    216    svchost            37      3,904 K      6,472 K        473
 492    216    spoolsv            11      1,200 K      2,660 K        122
 560    216    inojobsv           21      2,216 K      5,416 K        110
 600    216    regsvc              5      3,292 K      3,428 K        187
 624    216    mstask              7      1,480 K      2,936 K        102
 704    984    ntvdm               4        304 K      2,092 K         46
 708    188    taskmgr             3      1,836 K      1,836 K         41
 768     96    WINWORD             4     13,560 K     14,212 K        188
   8      0    System             35         28 K        636 K        271
 912     96    mobsync             6      3,984 K      4,300 K        172
 920     96    thotkey             2        520 K        988 K         19
 928     96    TPWRSAVE            1        184 K        916 K         26
 936     96    TFUNCKEY            1        252 K      1,152 K         23
 956     96    realmon             2        580 K      2,076 K         49
  96    544    explorer           16      3,672 K      5,732 K        294
 984     96    cmd                 2      1,304 K      2,420 K         58
```

Figure 7.2 *Output generated from Example 7.15.*

Note

Example 7.15 works on any NT or Windows 2000 machine. However, if the script collects process information from a Windows NT machine, the Parent field (refer to Figure 7.2) is left blank. ◆

Whereas the Win32::PerfLib extension makes extracting the process list considerably easier, it still requires a bit of processing. You can find information on how to process the data that Win32::PerfLib provides on Jutta's Web site (http://www.bybyte.de/jmk) and Microsoft's Developer Network (http://msdn.microsoft.com).

Example 7.15 *Fetching the Process List on NT Using* `Win32::PerfLib`

```perl
01. use Win32::PerfLib;
02. my $Server;
03. my $ProcessIndex;
04. my $ProcessObject;
05.
06. $Server = Win32::NodeName unless( $Server = $ARGV[0] );
07. print "Collecting process info for $Server...\n";
08. Win32::PerfLib::GetCounterNames( $Server, \%StringIndex );
09. map { $String{$StringIndex{$_}} = $_; } ( keys( %StringIndex ) );
10. $ProcessIndex = $String{Process};
11.
12. # Connect to the server's performance data
13. $Perf = new Win32::PerfLib( $Server );
14. if( ! $Perf )
15. {
16.     print "Could not obtain the process list.\n";
17.     exit();
18. }
19. $ProcessList = {};
20.
21. # get the performance data for the process object
22. $Perf->GetObjectList( $ProcessObject, $ProcessList );
23. $Perf->Close();
24. $InstanceHash = $ProcessList->{Objects}->{$ProcessIndex}->{Instances};
25. foreach my $ProcessObject ( sort( keys( %{$InstanceHash} ) ) )
26. {
27.   my $ProcessCounter = $InstanceHash->{$ProcessObject}->{Counters};
28.   my %ThisProcess;
29.   $ThisProcess{Name} = $InstanceHash->{$ProcessObject}->{Name};
30.   foreach my $Attrib ( keys( %$ProcessCounter ) )
31.   {
32.     my $AttribName = $StringIndex{$ProcessCounter->{$Attrib}->
33.                         {CounterNameTitleIndex}}|| '';
34.     $ThisProcess{$AttribName} = Format( $ProcessCounter->{$Attrib},
35.                         $ProcessList->{Objects}->{$ProcessIndex} );
36.   }
37.   $ProcessList{$ThisProcess{'ID Process'}} = \%ThisProcess;
38. }
39.
40. $~ = PROCESS_HEADER;
41. write;
42. $~ = PROCESS_INFO;
43. foreach $Process ( sort( keys( %ProcessList ) ) )
44. {
45.   # Don't make $Proc lexically scoped since it is
46.   # used in a formatted
47.   # write.
48.   $Proc = $ProcessList{$Process};
49.   write;
50. }
```

continues ▶

Example 7.15 *continued*

```
51.
52. sub Format
53. {
54.    my( $Proc, $ObjectList ) = @_;
55.    my $Value = $Proc->{Counter};
56.    my $Type = $Proc->{CounterType};
57.    my $TB = $ObjectList->{PerfFreq};
58.    my $Y = $ObjectList->{PerfTime};
59.
60.    if( PERF_100NSEC_TIMER == $Type )
61.    {
62.      $Value = 100 * ( $Value / 1000000 ) ;
63.    }
64.    elsif( PERF_ELAPSED_TIME == $Type )
65.    {
66.      my( $Hour, $Min, $Sec );
67.      # Convert the value into seconds...
68.      $Value = ( $Y - $Value ) / $TB;
69.
70.      $Hour = $Value / ( 60 * 60 );
71.      $Min = ( $Hour - int( $Hour ) ) * 60;
72.      $Sec = ( $Min - int( $Min ) ) * 60;
73.      $Value = sprintf( "%d:%02d:%02d", int( $Hour ), int( $Min ), int( $Sec ) );
74.    }
75.    return( $Value );
76. }
77.
78. sub FormatNumber
79. {
80.    my( $Number ) = @_;
81.    my( $Suffix ) = "";
82.    my $K = 1024;
83.    if( $K <= $Number )
84.    {
85.      $Suffix = " K";
86.      $Number /= $K;
87.    }
88.    $Number =~ s/(\.\d{0,2})\d*$/$1/;
89.    while ($Number =~ s/^(-?\d+)(\d{3})/$1,$2/){};
90.    return( $Number . $Suffix );
91. }
92.
93. format PROCESS_HEADER =
94. @||| @||||| @|||||||||||||| @|||||| @||||||||||| @||||||||||||| @|||||
95. PID, Parent, "Process Name", "Threads", "Memory", "Memory Peak", "Handles"
96. ---- ------ -------------------- ------- ------------- ------------- -------
97. .
98.
99. format PROCESS_INFO =
100. @||| @||||| @<<<<<<<<<<<<<<< @>>>>>> @>>>>>>>>>>> @>>>>>>>>>>>> @>>>>>>
```

```
101. $Proc->{'ID Process'}, $Proc->{'Creating Process ID'} || "---",
        $Proc->{Name}, $Proc->{'Thread Count'},
        FormatNumber( $Proc->{'Working Set'} ),
        FormatNumber( $Proc->{'Working Set Peak'} ),
        $Proc->{'Handle Count'}
102. .
```

As an exercise to demonstrate how much work the Win32::PerfLib saves, compare the two scripts in Example 7.15 and Example 7.16. The former uses Win32::PerfLib, and the latter uses the Registry (by using the Win32API::Registry extension).

Example 7.16   *Fetching the Process List on NT Using the Registry*

```
01. use Getopt::Long;
02. use Win32API::Registry qw( :ALL );
03.
04. %FLAG = (
05.   friendly  => 'f',  # Show memory sizes in M or K
06. );
07.
08. Configure( \%Config, @ARGV );
09. if( $Config->{help} )
10. {
11.   Syntax();
12.   exit();
13. }
14.
15. $STRINGS_KEY = 'SOFTWARE\Microsoft\Windows NT\CurrentVersion\Perflib\009';
16. $hRootKey = HKEY_LOCAL_MACHINE;
17. %STRUCT = (
18.   process          => "L2pLplL4",
19.   counter          => "L2LLLlL4",
20.   counter_block    => "L",
21.   instance         => "L3lL2",
22.   perf_object      => "a8L6lL10A10",
23.   perf_object_type => "L4PLPL2l2LL8",
24. );
25.
26. if( "" ne $Config{machine} )
27. {
28.   if( ! RegConnectRegistry( $Config{machine}, $hRootKey, $hRootKey ) )
29.   {
30.     print "Unable to connect to $Config{machine}.\n";
31.     exit();
32.   }
33. }
34.
35. if( RegOpenKeyEx( $hRootKey, $STRINGS_KEY, 0, KEY_READ, $hKey ) )
36. {
37.   $Data = GetKeyValue( $hKey, 'Counters' );
38.   RegCloseKey( $hKey );
39. }
```

continues ▶

Example 7.16   *continued*

```
40.
41. @Data = split( "\c@", $Data );
42. for( $iIndex = 0; $iIndex < $#Data; $iIndex += 2 )
43. {
44.   $STRINGS{lc $Data[$iIndex + 1]} = $Data[$iIndex];
45.   $STRINGS_INDEX{$Data[$iIndex]} = $Data[$iIndex + 1];
46. }
47. $hRootKey = HKEY_PERFORMANCE_DATA;
48. if( "" ne $Config{machine} )
49. {
50.   if( ! RegConnectRegistry( $Config{machine}, $hRootKey, $hRootKey ) )
51.   {
52.     print "Unable to connect to $Config{machine}.\n";
53.     exit();
54.   }
55. }
56.
57. $Data = GetKeyValue( $hRootKey, $STRINGS{process} );
58.
59. # We did not open the key since it is a performance data key (no need to
60. # open it). However we must close it so the system knows we are no
61. # longer monitoring.
62. RegCloseKey( $hRootKey );
63.
64. # Okay we have the data now let's walk through it...
65. # First get the PerfObject structure...
66. UnpackPerfObject( $Data, \%Object );
67. $Data = Offset( $Data, $Object{HeaderLength} );
68.
69. # Now that we have the PerfObject walk through each
70. # object until we find the one we want...
71. $iIndex = $Object{NumObjectTypes};
72. while( $iIndex-- )
73. {
74.   # Next we need to get an ObjectType structure so we have to
75.   # move to the ObjectType structure in our $Data...
76.   UnpackObjectType( $Data, \%Type );
77.   if( $STRINGS{process} eq $Type{ObjectNameTitleIndex} )
78.   {
79.     ParseProcesses( $Data, \%Processes );
80.     last;
81.   }
82.   $Data = Offset( $Data, $Type{HeaderLength} );
83. }
84.
85. $~ = PROCESS_HEADER;
86. write;
87.
88. $~ = PROCESS_INFO;
89. foreach $Process ( keys( %Processes ) )
90. {
```

```
91.    # Don't make $Proc lexically scoped since it is
92.    # used in a formatted
93.    # write.
94.    $Proc = $Processes{$Process};
95.    write;
96. }
97.
98. format PROCESS_HEADER =
99. @||| @||||||||| @||||||||||||| @|||||| @|||||||||||| @||||||||||||
100. "PID", "Parent PID", "Process Name", "Threads", "Memory", "Memory Peak"
101. ---- ---------- --------------- ------- ------------- ------------
102. .
103.
104. format PROCESS_INFO =
105. @||| @||||||||| @<<<<<<<<<<<<< @>>>>>> @>>>>>>>>>>>> @>>>>>>>>>>>>
106. $Proc->{'ID Process'}, $Proc->{'Creating Process ID'},
       $Proc->{Title}, $Proc->{'Thread Count'},
       FormatNumber( $Proc->{'Working Set'} ),
       FormatNumber( $Proc->{'Working Set Peak'} )
107. .
108.
109. sub ParseProcesses
110. {
111.   my( $Data, $Processes ) = @_;
112.   my %Type;
113.   my $pTypeData = $Data;
114.   my $iIndex;
115.   my( $pCounterBlock, $pThisProcess );
116.
117.   # Here we walk through each process and collect info about it.
118.   # We already had one but we did not pass it into this sub.
119.   UnpackObjectType( $pTypeData, \%Type );
120.
121.   # Move to the first process instance...
122.   $pThisProcess = Offset( $Data, $Type{DefinitionLength} );
123.
124.   # We have the object type so let's move the $Data to the next structure
125.   # we need...
126.   $Data = Offset( $Data, $Type{DefinitionLength} );
127.
128.   $iIndex = 0;
129.
130.   print "Collecting process data for $Config{machine} ...   0%";
131.
132.   while( $iIndex++ < $Type{NumInstances} )
133.   {
134.     my( %Instance, %CounterBlock );
135.     my $Percent;
136.
137.     UnpackInstance( $pThisProcess, \%Instance );
138.     if( ( 0 < $Instance{NameLength} ) && ( 0 < $Instance{NameOffset} ) )
139.     {
140.       my $TempProcess;
141.       my $Title;
```

continues ▶

Example 7.16 *continued*

```
142.      my $pTempInstance;
143.
144.      $pTempInstance = Offset( $pThisProcess, $Instance{NameOffset} );
145.      $Title = unpack( "a$Instance{NameLength}", $pTempInstance );
146.      $Title =~ s/\x00//g;
147.      CollectCounterValues( $pThisProcess, $pTypeData, \%{$Processes->{lc $Title}} );
148.      $Processes->{lc $Title}->{Title} = $Title;
149.    }
150.    $pCounterBlock = Offset( $pThisProcess, $Instance{ByteLength} );
151.    UnpackCounterBlock( $pCounterBlock, \%CounterBlock );
152.    $pThisProcess = Offset( $pCounterBlock, $CounterBlock{ByteLength} );
153.
154.    print "\ch" x 5;
155.    printf( "% 4d%%", int( $iIndex / $Type{NumInstances} * 100 ) );
156.  }
157.  print "\n";
158. }
159.
160. sub CollectCounterValues
161. {
162.   my( $Data, $ObjectData, $Process ) = @_;
163.   my( %Type, %Instance );
164.   my( $iIndex, $pCounterBlock, $pThisCounterDef );
165.
166.   UnpackInstance( $Data, \%Instance );
167.   UnpackObjectType( $ObjectData, \%Type );
168.
169.   $pThisCounterDef = Offset( $ObjectData, $Type{HeaderLength} );
170.
171.   $pCounterBlock = Offset( $Data, $Instance{ByteLength} );
172.   $iIndex = $Type{NumInstances} - 1;
173.
174.   while( --$iIndex )
175.   {
176.     my( $pThisCounter, %ThisCounterDef, $iIndex, $Property );
177.     my $Value = 0;
178.     my $CounterType = 0;
179.
180.     UnpackCounter( $pThisCounterDef, \%ThisCounterDef );
181.     $pThisCounter = Offset( $pCounterBlock, $ThisCounterDef{CounterOffset} );
182.     # $pThisCounter now points to the counter data
183.
184.     $Property = $STRINGS_INDEX{ $ThisCounterDef{CounterNameTitleIndex} };
185.     # Let's assume that the information we seek is always
186.     # an unsigned long (a DWORD)
187.     $CounterType = 0x300 & $ThisCounterDef{CounterType};
188.     if( 0x300 == $CounterType )
189.     {
190.       # The length of the value is defined in $ThisCounterDef
191.       # We don't do variable length in this version
192.     }
```

```
193.    elsif( 0x200 == $CounterType )
194.    {
195.      # How odd; in this case the counter has a length of 0
196.      $Value = 0;
197.    }
198.    elsif( 0x100 == $CounterType )
199.    {
200.      # We have a 64 bit value
201.      my( $Lo, $Hi) = unpack( "L2", $pThisCounter );
202.      $Value = ( $Hi * 0xFFFFFFFF ) + $Lo;
203.    }
204.    else
205.    {
206.      # The value is a 32 DWORD
207.      $Value = unpack( "L", $pThisCounter );
208.    }
209.    $Process->{$Property} = $Value;
210.    $pThisCounterDef = Offset( $pThisCounterDef,
211.                              $ThisCounterDef{ByteLength} );
212.  }
213. }
214.
215. sub UnpackCounter
216. {
217.    my( $Data, $Counter ) = @_;
218.    my( @Perf ) = unpack( $STRUCT{counter}, $Data );
219.    my $iIndex = 0;
220.    my $CNTI = $Counter->{CounterNameTitleIndex};
221.    $Counter->{ByteLength}            = $Perf[$iIndex++];
222.    $Counter->{CounterNameTitleIndex} = $Perf[$iIndex++];
223.    $Counter->{CounterNameTitle}      = $Perf[$iIndex++];
224.    $Counter->{CounterHelpTitleIndex} = $Perf[$iIndex++];
225.    $Counter->{CounterHelpTitle}      = $Perf[$iIndex++];
226.    $Counter->{DefaultScale}      = $Perf[$iIndex++];
227.    $Counter->{DetailLevel}       = $Perf[$iIndex++];
228.    $Counter->{CounterType}       = $Perf[$iIndex++];
229.    $Counter->{CounterSize}       = $Perf[$iIndex++];
230.    $Counter->{CounterOffset}      = $Perf[$iIndex++];
231.    $Counter->{Title} = $STRINGS_INDEX{$CNTI};
232. }
233.
234. sub UnpackInstance
235. {
236.    my( $Data, $Instance ) = @_;
237.    my( @Perf ) = unpack( $STRUCT{instance}, $Data );
238.    my $iIndex = 0;
239.
240.    $Instance->{ByteLength}        = $Perf[$iIndex++];
241.    $Instance->{ParentObjectTitleIndex} = $Perf[$iIndex++];
242.    $Instance->{ParentObjectInstance} = $Perf[$iIndex++];
243.    $Instance->{UniqueID}         = $Perf[$iIndex++];
244.    $Instance->{NameOffset}       = $Perf[$iIndex++];
245.    $Instance->{NameLength}        = $Perf[$iIndex++];
```

continues ▶

Example 7.16   *continued*

```
246. }
247.
248. sub UnpackPerfObject
249. {
250.   my( $Data, $Object ) = @_;
251.   my( @Perf ) = unpack( $STRUCT{perf_object}, $Data );
252.   # Check the signature of the data structure
253.   if( "P\x00E\x00R\x00F\x00" eq $Perf[0] )
254.   {
255.     my $iIndex = 0;
256.
257.     $Object->{Signature}       = $Perf[$iIndex++];
258.     $Object->{LittleEndian}    = $Perf[$iIndex++];
259.     $Object->{Version}         = $Perf[$iIndex++];
260.     $Object->{Revision}        = $Perf[$iIndex++];
261.     $Object->{TotalByteLength}  = $Perf[$iIndex++];
262.     $Object->{HeaderLength}     = $Perf[$iIndex++];
263.     $Object->{NumObjectTypes}   = $Perf[$iIndex++];
264.     $Object->{DefaultObjectType} = $Perf[$iIndex++];
265.     $Object->{SystemTime} = 0xFFFFFFFF
266.                             * $Perf[$iIndex++]
267.                             + $Perf[$iIndex++];
268.     $Object->{PerfTime} = 0xFFFFFFFF
269.                             * $Perf[$iIndex++]
270.                             + $Perf[$iIndex++];
271.     $Object->{PerfFreq} = 0xFFFFFFFF
272.                             * $Perf[$iIndex++]
273.                             + $Perf[$iIndex++];
274.     $Object->{PerfTime100nSec} = 0xFFFFFFFF
275.                                 * $Perf[$iIndex++]
276.                                 + $Perf[$iIndex++];
277.     $Object->{SystemNameLength}  = $Perf[$iIndex++];
278.     $Object->{SystemNameOffset}  = $Perf[$iIndex++];
279.     $Object->{Name}        = $Perf[$iIndex++];
280.   }
281. }
282.
283. sub UnpackObjectType
284. {
285.   my( $Data, $Type ) = @_;
286.   my( @Perf ) = unpack( $STRUCT{perf_object_type}, $Data );
287.   my $iIndex = 0;
288.
289.   $Type->{TotalByteLength}    = $Perf[$iIndex++];
290.   $Type->{DefinitionLength}   = $Perf[$iIndex++];
291.   $Type->{HeaderLength}       = $Perf[$iIndex++];
292.   $Type->{ObjectNameTitleIndex} = $Perf[$iIndex++];
293.   $Type->{ObjectNameTitle}    = $Perf[$iIndex++];
294.   $Type->{ObjectHelpTitleIndex} = $Perf[$iIndex++];
295.   $Type->{ObjectHelpTitle}    = $Perf[$iIndex++];
296.   $Type->{DetailLevel}        = $Perf[$iIndex++];
```

```
297.  $Type->{NumCounters}     = $Perf[$iIndex++];
298.  $Type->{DefaultCounter}  = $Perf[$iIndex++];
299.  $Type->{NumInstances}    = $Perf[$iIndex++];
300.  $Type->{CodePage}        = $Perf[$iIndex++];
301.  $Type->{PerfTime} = 0xFFFFFFFF
302.                       * $Perf[$iIndex++] + $Perf[$iIndex++];
303.  $Type->{PerfFreq} = 0xFFFFFFFF
304.                       * $Perf[$iIndex++] + $Perf[$iIndex++];
305. }
306.
307. sub UnpackCounterBlock
308. {
309.   my( $Data, $Block ) = @_;
310.   my( @Perf ) = unpack( $STRUCT{counter_block}, $Data );
311.   my $iIndex = 0;
312.
313.   $Block->{ByteLength}    = $Perf[$iIndex++];
314. }
315.
316. sub GetKeyValue
317. {
318.   my( $hKey, $Value ) = @_;
319.   my $Data;
320.   my $BufferSize = 0;
321.   my $CurrentBufferSize = 10240;
322.
323.   # If a call to RegQueryValueEx() is made with too small a buffer it
324.   # will fail but set $BufferSize to the size it should be.
325.   # However it is possible that by the time a call is re-issued the
326.   # buffersize requirements will have changed. Therefore we continue to
327.   # increase the buffer until it works.
328.   do
329.   {
330.     $BufferSize = $CurrentBufferSize += $BufferSize;
331.   }
332.   while( ! RegQueryValueEx( $hKey, $Value, [],
333.                       $Type, $Data, $BufferSize ) );
334.   return( $Data );
335. }
336.
337. sub Offset
338. {
339.   my( $Data, $Offset ) = @_;
340.   my( $Temp );
341.   ($Temp, $Data) = unpack( "a" . $Offset . "a*", $Data );
342.   return( $Data );
343. }
344.
345. sub FormatNumber
346. {
347.   my( $Number ) = @_;
348.   my( $Suffix ) = "";
349.
```

continues ▶

Example 7.16   *continued*

```
350.   if( defined $Config{$FLAG{friendly}} )
351.   {
352.     my( $K, $M ) = ( 1024, ( 1024 * 1024 ) );
353.     if( ( $K <= $Number ) && ( $M > $Number ) )
354.     {
355.       $Suffix = " K";
356.       $Number /= $K;
357.     }
358.     elsif ( $M <= $Number )
359.     {
360.       $Suffix = " M";
361.       $Number /= $M;
362.     }
363.   }
364.   $Number =~ s/(\.\d{0,2})\d*$/$1/;
365.
366.   while($Number =~ s/^(-?\d+)(\d{3})/$1,$2/){};
367.
368.   return( $Number . $Suffix );
369. }
370.
371. sub Configure
372. {
373.   my( $Config, @Args ) = @_;
374.   my $Result;
375.
376.   $Config->{machine} = Win32::NodeName();
377.   Getopt::Long::Configure( "prefix_pattern=(-|\/)" );
378.   $Result = GetOptions( $Config,
379.             qw( f help|?|h ) );
380.
381.   $Config->{machine} = shift @ARGV if( scalar @ARGV );
382.   $Config->{help} = 1 unless( $Result );
383. }
384.
385. sub Syntax
386. {
387.   my( $Script ) = ( $0 =~ /([^\\\/]*?)$/ );
388.   my( $Line ) = "-" x length( $Script );
389.
390.   print <<EOT;
391.
392. $Script
393. $Line
394. Displays the list of running processes.
395.
396. Syntax:
397.     perl $Script [-f] [Machine]
398.         -f.........Display memory values in a "friendly" format of
399.                      Megabytes or Kilobytes.
400.         Machine.....Name of a machine to procure the list
```

```
401.                    of processes.
402.                    Defaults to local machine.
403. EOT
404. }
```

The PSAPI Library

In the preceding section, you learned that the Win32 API does not offer simple API functions that provide quick access to process information. This is quite unfortunate; however, to help rectify this problem Microsoft released a library that does most of the dirty work for you. This library, known as the Process Status API (PSAPI), is a DLL that is available for free download from Microsoft's Web site. It also comes with the Win32 SDK as well as Windows 2000.

The library itself, called psapi.dll, is quite small (just under 30KB in size). When you use this library, a Perl script can enumerate the list of processes quite easily. You need only the psapi.dll library (stored in the path such as the System32 directory) and the Win32::API extension.

The PSAPI supplies functions that not only generate the PID list but also can open each process so that a script can discover the list of modules (such as DLLs, OCXs, and EXEs) that it has loaded. A full discussion about this API is available through MSDN (http://msdn.microsoft.com/library/psdk/winbase/psapi_25ki.htm).

So, you may now feel that all hope is not lost. But there's a catch. The PSAPI works only on Windows NT/2000. For non-NT machines such as Windows 95 and 98, the situation is a bit different, and your scripts have to rely on a library called TOOLHELP32, which is cleverly embedded in the kernel32.dll file. Back in Windows 3.0 and 3.1, this library was located in a file called toolhelp.dll. The library was updated for Win32 and added to the kernel.

Example 7.17 demonstrates how to use the PSAPI. This example accepts a list of PIDs passed in on the command line as follows:

```
perl.exe modules.pl 1472 168 188 216
```

It displays both the current and peak memory usages for each specified process. Additionally, it prints each module that the process has loaded. If no PIDs are specified on the command line, the code uses the PSAPI to procure the list of all process identifiers (refer to the GetPidList() function in Example 7.17).

To get information from a process, the script must open the process, which is conceptually similar to opening a file. Unfortunately, some processes (in particular security and system processes) prevent a user-level application from opening them. For these processes, the script displays only a PID and the name Unknown. You could employ techniques to discover such information; however, a discussion of them is far beyond the scope of this book. Refer to the MSDN for articles on these techniques.

Example 7.17 *Discovering a Process' Module List*

```
01. use Win32::API;
02.
03. # Define some constants
04. $DWORD_SIZE = 4;
05. $PROC_ARRAY_SIZE = 100;
06. $MODULE_LIST_SIZE = 100;
07.
08. # Define some Win32 API constants
09. $PROCESS_QUERY_INFORMATION = 0x0400;
10. $PROCESS_VM_READ = 0x0010;
11.
12. foreach $Param ( @ARGV )
13. {
14.   push( @PidList, $Param ) if( $Param =~ /^\d+$/ );
15. }
16. $OpenProcess = new Win32::API( 'kernel32.dll', 'OpenProcess',
17.                    [N,I,N], N ) || die;
18. $CloseHandle = new Win32::API( 'kernel32.dll', 'CloseHandle',
19.                    [N], I ) || die;
20. $EnumProcesses = new Win32::API( 'psapi.dll', 'EnumProcesses',
21.                    [P,N,P], I ) || die;
22. $EnumProcessModules = new Win32::API( 'psapi.dll',
23.                    'EnumProcessModules',
24.                    [N,P,N,P], I ) || die;
25. $GetModuleBaseName = new Win32::API( 'psapi.dll',
26.                    'GetModuleBaseName',
27.                    [N,N,P,N], N ) || die;
28. $GetModuleFileNameEx = new Win32::API( 'psapi.dll',
29.                    'GetModuleFileNameEx',
30.                    [N,N,P,N], N ) || die;
31. $GetProcessMemoryInfo = new Win32::API( 'psapi.dll',
32.                    'GetProcessMemoryInfo',
33.                    [N,P,N], I ) || die;
34.
35. if( 0 == scalar @PidList )
36. {
37.   @PidList = GetPidList();
38. }
39. if( Win32::IsWinNT() )
40. {
41.   my $iTotal = 0;
```

```
42.
43.    # Create a buffer
44.    $ProcArray = MakeBuffer( $DWORD_SIZE * $PROC_ARRAY_SIZE );
45.    $ProcNum = MakeBuffer( $DWORD_SIZE );
46.
47.    foreach $Pid ( @PidList )
48.    {
49.      my $iModuleCount = 0;
50.      my $ProcInfo = GetProcessInfo( $Pid );
51.      print "\n$ProcInfo->{pid} ($ProcInfo->{name})\n";
52.      if( scalar @{$ProcInfo->{modules}} )
53.      {
54.        printf( " Current memory use: %s\n Peak memory use: %s\n",
55.            FormatNumber( $ProcInfo->{workingset} ),
56.            FormatNumber( $ProcInfo->{workingsetpeak} ) );
57.        print " Module list:\n";
58.        foreach $Module ( @{$ProcInfo->{modules}} )
59.        {
60.          printf( "  %03d) %s\n", ++$iModuleCount, $Module );
61.        }
62.      }
63.      else
64.      {
65.        print " Unable to get process information.\n";
66.      }
67.    }
68. }
69.
70. sub GetPidList()
71. {
72.    my( @PidList );
73.
74.    # Create a buffer
75.    $ProcArray = MakeBuffer( $DWORD_SIZE * $PROC_ARRAY_SIZE );
76.    $ProcNum = MakeBuffer( $DWORD_SIZE );
77.    if( 0 != $EnumProcesses->Call( $ProcArray, $PROC_ARRAY_SIZE, $ProcNum ) )
78.    {
79.      # Get the number of bytes used in the array
80.      # Check this out -- divide by the number of bytes in a DWORD
81.      # and we have the number of processes returned!
82.      $ProcNum = unpack( "L", $ProcNum ) / $DWORD_SIZE;
83.
84.      # Let's play with each PID
85.      # First we must unpack each PID from the returned array
86.      @PidList = unpack( "L$ProcNum", $ProcArray );
87.    }
88.    return( @PidList );
89. }
90.
91. sub GetProcessInfo()
92. {
93.    my( $Pid ) = @_;
94.    my( %ProcInfo );
```

continues ▶

Example 7.17 *continued*

```perl
95.
96.    $ProcInfo{name} = "unknown";
97.    $ProcInfo{pid} = $Pid;
98.    @{$ProcInfo{modules}} = ();
99.
100.   # We can not open the system Idle process so just hack it.
101.   $ProcInfo{name} = "Idle" if( 0 == $Pid );
102.
103.   my( $hProcess ) = $OpenProcess->Call( $PROCESS_QUERY_INFORMATION
104.                                         | $PROCESS_VM_READ,
105.                                         0, $Pid );
106.   if( $hProcess )
107.   {
108.     my( $BufferSize ) = $MODULE_LIST_SIZE * $DWORD_SIZE;
109.     my( $MemStruct ) = MakeBuffer( $BufferSize );
110.     my( $iReturned ) = MakeBuffer( $BufferSize );
111.
112.     if( $EnumProcessModules->Call( $hProcess, $MemStruct,
113.                                    $BufferSize, $iReturned ) )
114.     {
115.       my( $StringSize ) = 255 * ( ( Win32::API::IsUnicode() )? 2 : 1 );
116.       my( $ModuleName ) = MakeBuffer( $StringSize );
117.       my( @ModuleList ) = unpack( "L*", $MemStruct );
118.       my $hModule = $ModuleList[0];
119.       my $TotalChars;
120.
121.       # Like EnumProcesses() divide $Returned by
122.       # the # of bytes in an HMODULE
123.       # (which is the same as a DWORD)
124.       # and that is the number of module handles returned.
125.       # In this case we only want 1; the first returned in the array is
126.       # always the module of the process (typically an executable).
127.       $iReturned = unpack( "L", $iReturned ) / $DWORD_SIZE;
128.
129.       if( $TotalChars = $GetModuleBaseName->Call( $hProcess,
130.                                                   $hModule,
131.                                                   $ModuleName,
132.                                                   $StringSize ) )
133.       {
134.         $ProcInfo{name} = FixString( $ModuleName );
135.       }
136.       else
137.       {
138.         $ProcInfo{name} = "unknown";
139.       }
140.       for( $iIndex = 0; $iIndex < $iReturned; $iIndex++ )
141.       {
142.         $hModule = $ModuleList[$iIndex];
143.         $ModuleName = MakeBuffer( $StringSize );
144.         if( $GetModuleFileNameEx->Call( $hProcess,
145.                         $hModule,
```

```
146.                     $ModuleName,
147.                     $StringSize ) )
148.        {
149.          if( 0 == $iIndex )
150.          {
151.            $ProcInfo{fullname} = FixString( $ModuleName );
152.          }
153.          push( @{$ProcInfo{modules}}, FixString( $ModuleName ) );
154.        }
155.      }
156.    }
157.    $BufSize = 10 * $DWORD_SIZE;
158.    $MemStruct = pack( "L10", ( $BufSize, split( "", 0 x 9 ) ) );
159.    if( $GetProcessMemoryInfo->Call( $hProcess, $MemStruct, $BufSize ) )
160.    {
161.      my( @MemStats ) = unpack( "L10", $MemStruct );
162.      $ProcInfo{workingsetpeak} = $MemStats[2];
163.      $ProcInfo{workingset} = $MemStats[3];
164.      $ProcInfo{pagefileuse} = $MemStats[8];
165.      $ProcInfo{pagefileusepeak} = $MemStats[9];
166.
167.    }
168.    $CloseHandle->Call( $hProcess );
169.  }
170.  return( \%ProcInfo );
171. }
172.
173. sub MakeBuffer
174. {
175.   my( $BufferSize ) = @_;
176.   return( "\x00" x $BufferSize );
177. }
178.
179. sub FixString
180. {
181.   my( $String ) = @_;
182.   $String =~ s/(.)\x00/$1/g if( Win32::API::IsUnicode() );
183.   return( unpack( "A*", $String ) );
184. }
185.
186. sub FormatNumber
187. {
188.   my( $Number ) = @_;
189.   while ($Number =~ s/^(-?\d+)(\d{3})/$1,$2/){};
190.   return( $Number );
191. }
```

To demonstrate the usefulness of Example 7.17, I noticed that the Task Manager showed that my machine was running a process called realmon. I thought that somehow a Real Networks monitor program was installed. I was a bit concerned because I had never installed such a program. To help shed light on this mystery, I ran my process listing script (refer to Example 7.15) to obtain the PID of the rogue process. Figure 7.2 showed the result of running this script. Next, I ran the modules.pl script (refer to Example 7.17), passing in the PID like this:

```
perl.exe modules.pl 956
```

Suddenly, realmon made sense; it was a real-time monitor for Inoculan's antivirus software. Take a look at Figure 7.3. Notice that module numbers 1, 3, 14, 15, and 26 come from the Inoculan directory—proof positive that Perl can ease an administrator's burdened mind!

```
956 (realmon.exe)
  Current memory use: 598,016
  Peak memory use: 2,125,824
  Module list:
    001) C:\Inoculan\realmon.exe
    002) C:\WINNT\System32\ntdll.dll
    003) C:\Inoculan\icommon.dll
    004) C:\WINNT\system32\MPR.dll
    005) C:\WINNT\system32\KERNEL32.DLL
    006) C:\WINNT\system32\ADVAPI32.DLL
    007) C:\WINNT\system32\RPCRT4.DLL
    008) C:\WINNT\system32\USER32.DLL
    009) C:\WINNT\system32\GDI32.DLL
    010) C:\WINNT\System32\WINSPOOL.DRV
    011) C:\WINNT\system32\SHELL32.dll
    012) C:\WINNT\system32\SHLWAPI.DLL
    013) C:\WINNT\system32\COMCTL32.DLL
    014) C:\Inoculan\ICORE.DLL
    015) C:\Inoculan\ALBUILD.dll
    016) C:\WINNT\System32\WSOCK32.dll
    017) C:\WINNT\System32\WS2_32.DLL
    018) C:\WINNT\system32\MSVCRT.DLL
    019) C:\WINNT\System32\WS2HELP.DLL
    020) C:\WINNT\System32\NETAPI32.dll
    021) C:\WINNT\System32\SECUR32.DLL
    022) C:\WINNT\System32\NETRAP.DLL
    023) C:\WINNT\System32\SAMLIB.DLL
    024) C:\WINNT\system32\WLDAP32.DLL
    025) C:\WINNT\System32\DNSAPI.DLL
    026) C:\Inoculan\CSCTRLU.DLL
    027) C:\WINNT\System32\CTL3D32.dll
```

Figure 7.3 *The Output from the modules.pl script.*

Killing a Process

Generally speaking, a process continues to run until it comes to the end of its processing, a user requests that it stop (typically by selecting some Exit command or menu item), or the process crashes. You can, however, force a process to terminate.

All processes have at least one thread. A process begins by starting a thread of execution at the beginning of the program. This first thread is called the *primary thread*. When this primary thread terminates (for whatever reason), all threads come to a halt, and the process is purged from memory.

TerminateProcess()

You can terminate a process by calling the Win32 API's `TerminateProcess()` function, which terminates the primary thread—thus ending the program's life. This is what happens when you terminate a process by using the Task Manager.

When a process terminates, it returns an integer value to its parent process. This *result code* is typically used to determine whether the process was successful or had an error during processing. In Windows, such result codes are not often observed, but batch file writers use them to determine whether XCOPY.EXE or MOVE.EXE functioned correctly.

kill()

Perl's `kill()` function terminates a process that the calling script has permission to terminate. This function does not work on services, however. It works by calling the Win32 API `TerminateProcess()` function to terminate a process without prejudice; therefore, you should not expect the process to save any open documents or graciously unlock files and such. Use of the `kill()` function can have unexpected results because it may leave files in a partially stored state. Additionally, if the process is communicating through COM, DCOM, named pipes, or sockets (to name a few forms of IPC), you could have some problems, such as COM objects that have not been properly shut down or released. In general, don't use `kill()` unless you know what you're doing.

You call the function by passing in at least two parameters:

```
$Total = kill( $ResultCode, $Pid1 [, $Pid2 [, … $Pidn] ] ] )
```

The first parameter is a numeric integer that will be the result code that the process reports as its termination value. Typically, if you need to kill a process, you are not very concerned about its return value. However, if a batch file, for example, checks the return code of the process, you might want to return a particular value so that the script will process normally.

The rest of the parameters ($Pid1, $Pid2, and so on) are the PIDs of each process to be terminated. You can list as many as need termination. The function returns the total number of processes that were killed.

Contrary to what you might assume, the kill() function does not always work. Under certain circumstances, kill() fails, such as when the process is secured (for example, the WinLogon service), if a process is interacting with DCOM, or even sometimes if the process is interacting with the network (for example, when resolving DNS names).

Example 7.18 goes a step beyond Perl's kill() function. This script accepts any number of PIDs passed in on the command line and attempts to kill each one. However, if Perl's kill() function fails to terminate a process, it acts as a debugger so that it can attach to the process. After it is attached, you can kill it from the inside as though the TerminateProcess() were called from within the process, therefore eliminating the security issue.

Even though this script goes through many steps, some processes (in particular the security services) still refuse to die. For those services, you can't do much other than shut down Windows. Even if you could terminate them, they would immediately trigger a system reboot anyhow.

This script assumes that the user running it has the debug processes privilege (SE_DEBUG_NAME) assigned to her. Otherwise, the script's attempt to set this privilege will fail.

Example 7.18   *Killing Processes*

```
01. use Win32::API;
02.
03. # Inform each process to return this value to its parent
04. $PROC_TERMINATION_VALUE = 0;
05.
06. if( 0 == scalar @ARGV )
07. {
08.    Syntax();
09.    exit;
10. }
11. Configure();
12. foreach my $Pid ( @ARGV )
13. {
14.    my $iResult = 0;
15.
16.    # If the user passed in text values skip it.
17.    next unless( $Pid =~ /^\d+$/ );
```

```
18.
19.   if( !( $iResult = kill( $PROC_TERMINATION_VALUE, $Pid ) ) )
20.   {
21.     $iResult = ForceKill( $Pid );
22.   }
23.
24.   if( $iResult )
25.   {
26.     print "Process $Pid was successfully killed.\n";
27.   }
28.   else
29.   {
30.     my $Error = Win32::FormatMessage( Win32::GetLastError() );
31.     $Error =~ s/\r|\n//g;
32.     print "Process $Pid failed to terminate. ($Error)\n";
33.   }
34. }
35.
36. sub ForceKill
37. {
38.   my( $Pid ) = @_;
39.   my $iResult = 0;
40.   my $phToken = pack( "L", 0 );
41.   # Fetch the process's token
42.   if( $OpenProcessToken->Call( $GetCurrentProcess->Call(),
43.                                $TOKEN_ADJUST_PRIVILEGES
44.                                | $TOKEN_QUERY,
45.                                $phToken ) )
46.   {
47.     my $hToken = unpack( "L", $phToken );
48.     # Set the debug privilege on the token
49.     if( SetPrivilege( $hToken, $SE_DEBUG_NAME, 1 ) )
50.     {
51.       # Now that we have debug privileges on the process
52.       # open the process so we can mess with it.
53.       my $hProcess = $OpenProcess->Call( $PROCESS_TERMINATE, 0, $Pid );
54.       if( $hProcess )
55.       {
56.         # We no longer need the debug privilege since we have opened
57.         # the process so remove the privilege.
58.         SetPrivilege( $hToken, $SE_DEBUG_NAME, 0 );
59.         # Let's terminate the process
60.         $iResult = $TerminateProcess->Call( $hProcess, 0 );
61.         $CloseHandle->Call( $hProcess );
62.       }
63.     }
64.     $CloseHandle->Call( $hToken );
65.   }
66.   return( $iResult );
67. }
68.
69. sub SetPrivilege
70. {
```

continues ▶

Example 7.18   *continued*

```perl
71.   my( $hToken, $pszPriv, $bSetFlag ) = @_;
72.   my $pLuid = pack( "Ll", 0, 0 );
73.   # Look up the LUID of the privilege
74.   if( $LookupPrivilegeValue->Call( "\x00\x00", $pszPriv, $pLuid ) )
75.   {
76.      # Unpack the LUID
77.      my $pPrivStruct = pack( "LLlL", 1, unpack( "Ll", $pLuid ), ( ( $bSetFlag )?
            $SE_PRIVILEGE_ENABLED : 0 ) );
78.      # Now modify the process's token to set the required privilege
79.      $iResult = ( 0 != $AdjustTokenPrivileges->Call( $hToken,
80.                                                      0,
81.                                                      $pPrivStruct,
82.                                                      length( $pPrivStruct ),
83.                                                      0, 0 ) );
84.   }
85.   return( $iResult );
86. }
87.
88. sub Configure
89. {
90.   $TOKEN_QUERY            = 0x0008;
91.   $TOKEN_ADJUST_PRIVILEGES  = 0x0020;
92.   $SE_PRIVILEGE_ENABLED    = 0x02;
93.   $PROCESS_TERMINATE       = 0x0001;
94.   $SE_DEBUG_NAME           = "SeDebugPrivilege";
95.
96.   # Prepare to use some specialized Win32 API calls
97.   $GetCurrentProcess = new Win32::API( 'Kernel32.dll',
98.                                        'GetCurrentProcess',
99.                                        [], N ) || die;
100.  $OpenProcessToken = new Win32::API( 'AdvApi32.dll',
101.                                       'OpenProcessToken',
102.                                       [N,N,P], I ) || die;
103.  $LookupPrivilegeValue = new Win32::API( 'AdvApi32.dll',
104.                                           'LookupPrivilegeValue',
105.                                           [P,P,P], I ) || die;
106.  $AdjustTokenPrivileges = new Win32::API( 'AdvApi32.dll',
107.                                            'AdjustTokenPrivileges',
108.                                            [N,I,P,N,P,P], I ) || die;
109.  $OpenProcess = new Win32::API( 'Kernel32.dll',
110.                                  'OpenProcess',
111.                                  [N,I,N], N ) || die;
112.  $TerminateProcess = new Win32::API( 'Kernel32.dll',
113.                                       'TerminateProcess',
114.                                       [N,I], I ) || die;
115.  $CloseHandle = new Win32::API( 'Kernel32.dll',
116.                                  'CloseHandle',
117.                                  [N], I ) || die;
118. }
119.
120. sub Syntax()
```

```
121. {
122.   my( $Script ) = ( $0 =~ /([^\\]*?)$/ );
123.   my $Line = "-" x length( $Script );
124.   print <<EOT;
125.
126. $Script
127. $Line
128.   Syntax:
129.   $Script Pid [ Pid2 [ Pid3 [ ... ] ] ]
130. EOT
131. }
```

The kill command is also useful if you start a process and want to terminate it after a specified amount of time, as shown in Example 7.19.

Example 7.19 *Creating a Process and Then Killing It*

```
01. use Win32;
02. my $Path = "$ENV{SystemRoot}";
03. my $Program = "notepad.exe";
04. my $App = "$Path\\$Program";
05. my $Args = "$Program $ENV{Temp}\\test.txt ";
06. my $Pid = 0;
07. my $Time = 10;
08.
09. print "Creating new process: $Program\n";
10. if( Win32::Spawn( $App, $Args, $Pid ) )
11. {
12.   print "Waiting for $Time seconds...\n";
13.   sleep( $Time );
14.
15.   print "Killing PID $Pid\n";
16.   kill 0, $Pid;
17. }
18. else
19. {
20.   print "Could not create the process.\n";
21.   print "Error: " . Win32::FormatMessage( Win32::GetLastError() ) . "\n";
22. }
```

Inheriting File Handles (Pseudo-Forking)

When Win32 creates a new process, a flag indicates whether to inherit open file handles. They are Win32 file handles, not C runtime or Perl file handles. However, Perl file handles are based on C runtime handles, and C handles are based on Win32 file handles. This means that when Perl spawns a new process, open file and socket handles can be inherited. The problem is that a new Perl process cannot create a file or socket handle from a Win32 handle.

One way around this problem is to redirect a common handle, such as STDOUT, to a socket or file. If a script is to then create a new process inheriting file handles, the new process' STDOUT would already be mapped to the Win32 handle. Confusing? Sure, but it is very important because this is the basis of mimicking a fork() command.

When a script opens a file or a socket, the result is a handle that can be used with a variety of functions. For example, if you open a file, you can print to it by using the print() function, as in Example 7.20.

Example 7.20   *Printing to a File Handle*

```
01. if( open( FILE, "> test.txt" ) )
02. {
03.   print FILE "Hello there!\n";
04.   close( FILE );
05. }
```

Instead of explicitly specifying the file handle to print to (as in Example 7.20), a script can redirect STDOUT to a file handle. This concept is probably old hat to you, but understanding it is very important because it's the basis of redirecting input and output for a child process. Example 7.21 shows how this is done. Notice that line 3 creates a new file handle called STDOUT_BACKUP by reopening the STDOUT file handle. This line essentially makes a backup copy of STDOUT for later use. Next, line 4 performs much the same as line 3, but this time it redirects STDOUT to the file opened in line 1. Line 5 prints "Hello there!". Because no file handle is specified, it is automatically printed to STDOUT, which has been redirected to FILE. Therefore, line 5 is equivalent to the following:

```
print FILE "Hello there!\n";
```

Line 6 puts things back the way they were originally by changing STDOUT to redirect to STDOUT_BACKUP, which is the saved version of the original STDOUT. By the time the script reaches line 9, everything is as it was before any of the code ran: STDOUT prints to the screen and no files are open.

Example 7.21   *Printing to a File Handle by Redirecting STDOUT*

```
01. if( open( FILE, "> test.txt" ) )
02. {
03.   open( STDOUT_BACKUP, ">&STDOUT" );
04.   open( STDOUT, ">&FILE" );
05.   print "Hello there!\n";
06.   open( STDOUT, ">&STDOUT_BACKUP" );
07.   close( STDOUT_BACKUP );
08.   close( FILE );
09. }
```

At this point, you might be asking why any of this information is important. After all, Example 7.20 produces the same results as Example 7.21 using twice as much code. This concept is important because it illustrates how a script can redirect one of the standard I/O handles to a file or socket handle. Say that you did just that—you redirected STDOUT to a socket. If you then create a new Win32 process while specifying that you want to inherit all file handles, the new process also redirects STDOUT to the socket. This means that you can pass file and socket handles across process boundaries. In other words, you have a simple way of emulating a fork().

Keep in mind that this is not the same as a true fork() in that the new process does not have access to a copy of its parent variables; nor does it continue processing where the parent process spawned the new process. It does, however, enable a daemon process to "fork" off a new process, handing it the open file or socket handle.

Now look at Example 7.22, which is a simple socket daemon script. When it runs, it binds to a port and waits for a client to connect. When that occurs, the script redirects STDOUT to the socket, creates a new process, replaces STDOUT with its original value, closes the socket (which does not affect the new process at all), and waits for another connection.

The magic here lies in the MyFork() subroutine in lines 42 through 70. Line 55 saves STDOUT to a backup handle for later use. Line 56 redirects STDOUT to the socket, which is connected to a client that connected to the daemon.

Line 58 performs the actual process creation. Notice that the variable $bInherit is set to TRUE (a value of 1). This is the secret: It forces the new process to inherit the open file handles, which include STDOUT redirected to the socket. The only other process-creation functions that can perform such a feat are Win32::AdminMisc's CreateProcess() and CreateProcessAsUser() functions (unless you want to consider using Win32::API and manually calling the Win32 API CreateProcess() function).

The script creates a new Perl process (line 48) by running the same Perl script (represented as $0 in line 49). A command-line argument is passed in declaring that the new process is a child (the child:$iProcessCount in line 49). When the new process starts, lines 4 through 8 process the script as a child, not as a daemon.

Line 52 is very important to making this emulated fork() work. This line sets the CreateProcess() flag to 0. Normally, when creating a new Perl process, you specify the flag CREATE_NEW_CONSOLE. However, that would cause the STDIN, STDOUT, and STDERR handles to be reset as the new window is created. This means that the remapping of STDOUT to the socket (line 56) would be lost, and the new Perl process would not have any way to access the socket.

Example 7.22   *Socket Daemon*

```
01. use IO::Socket;
02. $iProcessCount = 0;
03. $Port = 8080;
04. if( ( $iChildNum ) = ( $ARGV[0] =~ /child:(\d+)/i ) )
05. {
06.   ProcessAsChild( fileno( STDOUT ) );
07.   exit();
08. }
09. if( $Socket = IO::Socket::INET->new( LocalPort => $Port, Listen => 5 ) )
10. {
11.   while( 1 )
12.   {
13.     print "\nListening for a connection...\n";
14.     last unless ( $Connection = $Socket->accept() );
15.     $iProcessCount++;
16.     print STDERR "Server: Connection $iProcessCount\n";
17.
18.     MyFork( $Connection );
19.     $Connection->close();
20.   }
21. }
22.
23. sub ProcessAsChild
24. {
25.   my( $SocketHandle ) = @_;
26.   my $Socket;
27.
28.   if( $Socket = IO::Socket::INET->new_from_fd( $SocketHandle, "+>" ) )
29.   {
30.     $Socket->send( "Child process $iChildNum has "
31.                    . "started at " . localtime() . "\n" );
32.     while(1)
33.     {
34.       $Socket->recv( $In, 100 );
35.       last if( $In eq "\n" || $In eq "" );
36.       $Socket->send( "You entered: $In" );
37.     }
38.   }
39.   $Socket->close();
40. }
41.
42. sub MyFork
43. {
44.   my( $Socket ) = @_;
45.
46.   use Win32::Process;
47.   my $Process;
48.   my $App = 'c:\perl\bin\perl.exe';
49.   my $Cmd = "perl \"$0\" child:$iProcessCount";
50.   my $bInherit = 1;
51.   my $Dir = ".";
```

```
52.    my $Flags = 0;
53.    my $Child = 0;
54.
55.    open( OLD_STDOUT, ">&STDOUT" ) || die "Can not backup STDOUT: $!\n";
56.    open( STDOUT, ">&" . $Socket->fileno() )
57.         || die "Can not redirect STDOUT: $!\n";
58.    if( ! Win32::Process::Create( $Process,
59.                                  $App,
60.                                  $Cmd,
61.                                  $bInherit,
62.                                  $Flags,
63.                                  $Dir ) )
64.    {
65.      print STDERR "Server: unable to create process.\n";
66.    }
67.    open( STDOUT, ">&OLD_STDOUT" )
68.           || die "Can not redir STDIN to orig value: $!\n";
69.    close( OLD_STDOUT );
70. }
71.
72. END
73. {
74.    if( $iChildNum )
75.    {
76.      print STDERR " Child $iChildNum: Terminating.\n";
77.    }
78.    else
79.    {
80.      print STDERR "Server: Terminating.\n";
81.    }
82. }
```

Example 7.23 is a simple client script that connects to the daemon and allows a user to interact. To test this script, open a few different command-line windows (DOS boxes). In one, run the daemon (refer to Example 7.22), and in a couple of the other windows, run the client. You might want to open yet another command-line window and run the process list script (refer to Example 7.15 or Example 7.16) and see the multiple instances of the daemon code running as child processes. This shows that the fork emulation is hard at work.

A special thank you goes out to Stephen Johnson of Digital Paper. His white paper illustrated the use of the IO::Socket::INET->new_from_fd() method to re-create the socket in the child process. The white paper appeared in the "Script Junkie" column in the March 2000 issue of *Web Techniques* magazine. It can be found online at http://www.webtechniques.com/archives/2000/03/junk/.

This forking emulation can help solve the problem of Win32 Perl's lack of fork() support in versions before 5.6. However, recent versions of Win32 Perl now support forking. To demonstrate how efficient it is to use "real" forking in this same script, refer to Example 7.24. This script is considerably shorter, and it results in more efficient use of the machine's CPU because Perl 5.6's fork emulation results in the creation of a new thread, not a new process.

Example 7.23   *Socket Daemon Client*

```perl
01. use IO::Socket;
02.
03. $Host = "localhost" unless( $Host = $ARGV[0] );
04. $Port = 8080;
05.
06. print "Connecting to $Host:$Port...\n";
07. if( $Socket = IO::Socket::INET->new( "$Host:$Port" ) )
08. {
09.   while( $In = $Socket->getline() )
10.   {
11.     print "Socket client: $In";
12.
13.     my $Data = <STDIN>;
14.     $Socket->print( $Data );
15.   }
16.   $Socket->close();
17. }
18. else
19. {
20.   print "Failed to connect.\n";
21. }
```

Example 7.24   *Socket Daemon (from Example 7.22) Implemented Using Perl 5.6's Forking Capabilities*

```perl
01. # Forking for Win32 starts with version 5.006
02. require 5.006;
03. use IO::Socket;
04.
05. $iProcessCount = 0;
06. $Port = 8080;
07.
08. if( $Socket = IO::Socket::INET->new( LocalPort => $Port, Listen => 5 ) )
09. {
10.   while( 1 )
11.   {
12.     print "\nListening for a connection...\n";
13.     last unless ( $Connection = $Socket->accept() );
14.     $iProcessCount++;
15.     print STDERR "Server: Connection $iProcessCount\n";
```

```
16.
17.     MyFork( $Connection );
18.     $Connection->close();
19.   }
20. }
21.
22. sub ProcessAsChild
23. {
24.   my( $Socket ) = @_;
25.
26.   $Socket->send( "Child process $iProcessCount has started "
27.                     . "at " . localtime() . "\n" );
28.   while(1)
29.   {
30.     $Socket->recv( $In, 100 );
31.     last if( $In eq "\n" || $In eq "" );
32.     $Socket->send( "You entered: $In" );
33.   }
34.   print "\tChild $iProcessCount is closing.\n";
35.   $Socket->close();
36. }
37.
38. sub MyFork
39. {
40.   my( $Socket ) = @_;
41.   my $Pid = fork();
42.
43.   if( 0 == $Pid )
44.   {
45.     # We get here only if we are a child process
46.     $| = 1;
47.     ProcessAsChild( $Socket );
48.     exit();
49.   }
50. }
```

Conclusion

Processes are rather simple beasts to tame, but they can be quite unruly to create. The most straightforward UNIX conventions, such as forking, were left by the wayside in Win32 Perl until just recently.

In this chapter, you learned that a Perl coder needs to contend with many issues just to create a new process. Embedded spaces, blocking process-creation functions, and unkillable processes are just the beginning. However, with a bit of thought and patience, you can accomplish almost anything.

8

Win32 Services

UNIX administrators know them as *daemons,* and Win32 administrators know them as *services:* They are processes that run from bootup to shutdown. These pieces of code usually perform very specific tasks and always need to be running.

The ability to autorun Perl scripts (and other applications) at boot time has always been of great interest to administrators. Such abilities provide a method to begin monitoring and other applications without requiring any user interaction. This chapter discusses the various issues related to just such an endeavor.

What Are Win32 Services?

In the world of operating systems, certain programs often must run continuously. Such programs are designed to perform some type of function that other processes rely on or accomplish some important task. This is what a Win32 *service* is. In a UNIX environment, these types of services are known as *daemons.* For all practical purposes, a Win32 service can be considered the equivalent of a UNIX daemon.

You interact with these services every day. Processes such as Web, email, databases, streaming media, and logon services are all programs that begin to run when the machine boots up. They continue running until they are stopped by an administrator or the machine shuts down.

Win32 employs a Service Manager to oversee all services and device drivers. This manager contains a database of what services are to run at what time. When the computer boots, the Service Manager walks through the list of services and determines which services to start first, second, third, and so on. It also determines which services depend on what other services. For example, a Web service relies on network card drivers and the TCP/IP protocols. Therefore, the Service Manager guarantees that the Web service starts only after the network cards are loaded and TCP/IP is successfully bound to the cards. Likewise, an email service may depend on some user authorization service, so the Service Manager starts the email service only after the authorization service has successfully started.

Some services incorrectly report to the Service Manager that they have successfully started before they have actually finished starting. This can play havoc on another service that must interact with such a service. In this case, the Service Manager starts the dependent service before the original service is fully ready for any interaction. Therefore, if you write a service that depends on other services, you might find it useful to put a slight delay before interacting with any services your service depends on.

A Win32 service is simply a program that knows how to talk to the Service Manager. And talk it does. When a service first starts, it must tell the Service Manager that it is starting and point the Manager to a function called the *event handler*. The event handler's only function is to listen and respond to the Service Manager. For example, if the administrator pauses the service, the Service Manager sends a SERVICE_CONTROL_PAUSE control message to the service informing it that it should be pausing. The service immediately tells the Service Manager that it is preparing to pause by returning a SERVICE_PAUSE_PENDING message. That service then does whatever it needs to do to pause itself before finally sending the Service Manager a SERVICE_PAUSED message. The service then waits for more requests from the manager. This type of conversation with the Service Manager is really the only requirement of a service. It can pretty much process just as any other application does, with a few exceptions, such as not being able to interact with the user.

A service runs in a special environment that is different from what a normal logged-on user experiences. Simply stated, a service does not see a desktop, mouse, or keyboard. There is no simple way for a service to directly communicate with a user, and vice versa. Conceptually there is no need for a service to interact with a user. Most services perform some type of processing that is void of user interaction. For example, a Web server never needs to interact with the logged-on user.

If a service does need to communicate for the sake of debugging or logging events, for example, it can do so by writing to the Win32 Event Log or maybe opening and storing information to a file or named pipe. The latter approach is quite useful because you can run a Perl script that creates a named pipe. The service can connect to the named pipe, dumping log information into it, and the Perl script can simply read from the pipe and display the contents on the screen.

Every Win32 machine has some services running. By default, all Windows 2000 and Windows NT machines run the Local Security Authority Security Service (LSASS) and the Windows logon service (winlogon) as well as others. Many of these services are crucial for the operating system to function, but others are only as important as an administrator deems. Services such as SQL Server and data backup are not necessary for the successful running of the operating system but may be necessary to provide appropriate services for the network. Not all services, however, are shrink-wrapped and available at the local computer store.

Considering that every network administrator manages her network just a little differently from others and every network has its own idiosyncrasies, you might not be able to find a service that fits some need. In these cases, you can use Perl to satisfy such niche service needs.

Controlling Services

The operating system permits users and processes to control services. You can manually do this by using the Services control panel applet or the NET.EXE command-line application. You also can do so programmatically by using Perl (among other languages). Two extensions in particular can control services: `Win32::Service` and `Win32::Lanman`. Both of these extensions do an admirable job of controlling services; however, the `Win32::Service` extension is very small and provides only service-related functions. For this reason alone, that extension is the focus for this section.

Lists of Services

You can find the list of services installed on a machine by using the `Win32::Service::GetServices()` function. As Example 8.1 shows, obtaining this list of services is trivial. The second parameter passed into the `GetServices()` function is a hash reference that is populated with the display names as keys and their service names as values. This reference is quite important because `Win32::Service` functions expect only the service name as a parameter. Passing in the display name will cause a function to fail.

Example 8.1 *Discovering Which Services Exist on a Machine*

```
01. use Win32::Service;
02.
03. foreach my $Machine ( @ARGV )
04. {
05.   local %List;
06.   print "Available services on $Machine:\n";
07.   if( Win32::Service::GetServices( $Machine, \%List ) )
08.   {
```

continues ▶

Example 8.1 *continued*

```
09.      $~ = FormatHeader;
10.      write;
11.      $~ = FormatData;
12.      foreach $Service ( sort( keys( %List ) ) )
13.      {
14.        write;
15.      }
16.    }
17.    else
18.    {
19.      print Win32::FormatMessage( Win32::GetLastError() ), "\n";
20.    }
21.    print "\n" x 3;
22.  }
23.
24.  format FormatHeader =
25.  @<<<<<<<<<<<<<<<< @<<<<<<<<<<<<<<<<<<<<<<<<<<<<<<<<<<<<<<<<<<<<<<<
26.  "Service Name", "Service Display Name"
27.  ----------------  ----------------------------------------------------
28.  .
29.
30.  format FormatData =
31.  @<<<<<<<<<<<<<<<< @<<<<<<<<<<<<<<<<<<<<<<<<<<<<<<<<<<<<<<<<<<<<<<<
32.  $List{$Service}, $Service
33.  .
```

Starting, Stopping, Pausing, and Resuming

Now that you can get a list of services from a machine, you can start, stop, pause, and resume these services by using these functions:

```
Win32::Service::StartService()
Win32::Service::StopService()
Win32::Service::PauseService()
Win32::Service::ResumeService()
```

Example 8.2 shows how you can use two of these functions to remotely pause a service for 10 seconds. Notice that lines 12 and 16 both refer to the service name, not the service's display name (the %List hash indexes service names by their display names). This point is important because if you pass the display name into one of these functions, it will fail. This means that you need to pass in the service display name "World Wide Web Publishing Service" into the script to pause the Web service (whose service name is "w3svc").

Example 8.2 *Pausing a Service*

```
01.  use Win32::Service;
02.  $Timeout = 5;
03.  $DisplayName = shift @ARGV || die;
04.  $Machine = Win32::NodeName() unless( $Machine = shift @ARGV );
```

```
05. $Machine = "\\\\$Machine";
06. $Machine =~ s/^\\{2,}/\\\\/;
07. if( Win32::Service::GetServices( $Machine, \%List ) )
08. {
09.   if( defined $List{$DisplayName} )
10.   {
11.     print "Pausing the $DisplayName service on $Machine.\n";
12.     Win32::Service::PauseService( $Machine, $List{$DisplayName} );
13.     print "Sleeping for $Timeout seconds...\n";
14.     sleep( $Timeout );
15.     print "Resuming the $DisplayName service on $Machine.\n";
16.     Win32::Service::ResumeService( $Machine, $List{$DisplayName} );
17.   }
18.   else
19.   {
20.     print "There is no '$DisplayName' service on $Machine.\n";
21.   }
22. }
23. else
24. {
25.   print "Could not connect to $Machine: ";
26.   print Win32::FormatMessage( Win32::GetLastError() ), "\n";
27. }
```

Service Status

One other function is also quite useful: the Win32::Service::Status() function. It reports the current status of a given service, either locally or remotely. Example 8.3 does exactly that. Notice that Win32::Service does not export the various status constants. This oversight almost defeats the usefulness of the Status() function because it returns only a numeric value, which means nothing to a typical user. Table 8.1 describes each value that Win32::Service::Status() returns.

Table 8.1   Service Status Values

Status Constant	Value	Description
SERVICE_STOPPED	0x01	The service is not running.
SERVICE_START_PENDING	0x02	The service is starting.
SERVICE_STOP_PENDING	0x03	The service is stopping.
SERVICE_RUNNING	0x04	The service is running.
SERVICE_CONTINUE_PENDING	0x05	The service continue is pending.
SERVICE_PAUSE_PENDING	0x06	The service pause is pending.
SERVICE_PAUSED	0x07	The service is paused.

To use the script in Example 8.3, use the following syntax:

```
perl servicestatus.pl ServiceDisplayName [MachineName]
```

Simply pass the display name of the service into the script. Use Example 8.3 to determine which services exist and what their display names are. You can optionally pass in a machine name to discover the state of the service on a remote computer.

The following shows how to use this script:

```
perl servicestatus.pl "World Wide Web Publishing Service" \\WebServer
```

Example 8.3   *Reporting the Status of a Service on a Remote Machine*

```
01. use Win32::Service;
02.
03. %STATE = (
04.    0  => 'unknown',
05.    1  => 'stopped',
06.    2  => 'starting',
07.    3  => 'stopping',
08.    4  => 'running',
09.    5  => 'resuming',
10.    6  => 'pausing',
11.    7  => 'paused',
12. );
13.
14. $DisplayName = shift @ARGV || die;
15. $Machine = Win32::NodeName() unless( $Machine = shift @ARGV );
16. $Machine = "\\\\$Machine";
17. $Machine =~ s/^\\{2,}/\\\\/;
18. if( Win32::Service::GetServices( $Machine, \%List ) )
19. {
20.    if( defined $List{$DisplayName} )
21.    {
22.      if( Win32::Service::GetStatus( $Machine,
                                        $List{$DisplayName},
                                        \%Status ) )
23.      {
24.        print "The $DisplayName service on $Machine is " .
                 $STATE{$Status{CurrentState}} . "\n";
25.      }
26.      else
27.      {
28.        print "Could not find the '$DisplayName' service.\n";
29.        print "Names are case sensitive.\n";
30.      }
31.    }
32. }
33. else
34. {
35.    print "Could not connect to $Machine: ";
36.    print Win32::FormatMessage( Win32::GetLastError() ), "\n";
37. }
```

Creating and Removing Services

Different techniques are available to install, modify, or remove services. The two prominent ones use either the Win32::Daemon or the Win32::Lanman extensions. They both do a splendid job. Most administrators, however, don't need to install services using Perl because almost all professional services come with some form of setup application that performs the installation. If you need to install some service, it is usually because a script that runs as a service itself has been made. Many administrators write Win32 services using Perl, so they typically use the Win32::Daemon extension; therefore, they rely on its installation and removal functions. Other, nonservice, scripts may instead rely on the functions that Win32::Lanman provides if the extension is already used for other networking-related reasons.

Alternatively, some third-party utilities provide such functionality, such as Microsoft's SC.EXE that comes with the Windows NT/2000 Resource Kit.

Installing Services

To install a service using Win32::Daemon, a call is made to the CreateService() function.

Example 8.4 shows how this can be done. Line 2 configures a hash that describes the service to be installed. The different values available to this hash are listed in Table 8.2.

> *Tip*
>
> *When using the* Win32::Daemon::CreateService() *function, the only hash key you must specify is the* name *key. All other values will default to a value that is common for most services.* ◆

Example 8.4   *Installing a Service*

```
01. use Win32::Daemon;
02. %ServiceConfig = (
03.    name    => 'MyServiceName',
04.    display => 'My Service Display Name',
05.    path    => $^X,
06.    user    => '',
07.    password    => '',
08.    parameters => 'c:\scripts\MyService.pl',
09.    dependencies => [],
10. );
11. if( Win32::Daemon::CreateService( \%ServiceConfig ) )
12. {
13.    print "The '$ServiceConfig{display}' service ";
14.    print "was successfully installed.\n";
15. }
16. else
```

continues ▶

Example 8.4   *continued*

```
17. {
18.    print "Failed to add the '$ServiceConfig{display}' service.\n";
19.    print "Error: ";
20.    print Win32::FormatMessage( Win32::Daemon::GetLastError() ), "\n";
21. }
```

Table 8.2   Configuration Values for a Service

Value	Description
name	The name of the service, such as
	• w3svc
	• scheduler
	• RemoteServerMonitor
display	The display name of the service. This name is displayed in the Service Manager, such as
	• World Wide Web Publishing Service
	• Task Scheduler
	• Remote Server Monitoring service
path	The path to the service program. For Perl scripts that run as a service, it is normally the path to PERL.EXE. It must be a full (not relative) path.
	A perl script can use the $^X variable for this parameter because it represents the full path to the Perl executable.
user	The user ID that the service runs under. It can include a domain such as
	Accounting\Joel
	The account must have the Logon as a Service privilege.
	The default account is Local System.
password	The password that the user account logs on with. This field is not needed if the user account is Local System.
parameters	Any parameters you need to pass into the service when it starts. They are just like command-line parameters. For example, a Perl script acting as a Win32 service specifies the full path to PERL.EXE as the path and specifies (at least) the full path to the Perl script as the parameters followed by any options that the script accepts.

Value	Description
service_type	The type of service being configured. It can be any one value from Table 8.3. For Perl-based services, this value should be SERVICE_WIN32_OWN_PROCESS.
	The default for this value is SERVICE_WIN32_OWN_PROCESS | SERVICE_INTERACTIVE_PROCESS.
start_type	The time the service starts. It can be any one value from Table 8.4.
	The default for this value is SERVICE_AUTO_START.
error_control	The way the system handles a service that reports an error when starting. It can be any one value from Table 8.5.
	The default value is SERVICE_ERROR_IGNORE.
load_order	The name of a load order group that the service is associated with.
	This value is optional and either is not specified or is left as an empty string.
dependencies	A reference to an array. Each element in this array is a string that represents which other services and device drivers the service depends on. The service does not start until at least one member of each dependent group has started.
	There are two types of dependencies: services/device drivers and groups. Prepend a + sign to the name of each group; otherwise, it is assumed to be a name of a service or device driver.
	This value is optional and is usually not specified.

Table 8.3 *Different Service Types*

Service Type	Description
SERVICE_WIN32_OWN_PROCESS	Specifies a service application that runs in its own process. You specify this option when adding a Perl-based service.
SERVICE_WIN32_SHARE_PROCESS	Specifies a service application that shares a process with other services. Many services can be packaged into one binary executable file. In this case, each service runs as a separate thread in the same process space.
SERVICE_INTERACTIVE_PROCESS	Indicates that the service may interact with a user (thus have the ability to accept input and display information onscreen).
	This particular value is a special flag that must be logically OR'ed with either the SERVICE_WIN32_OWN_PROCESS or the SERVICE_WIN32_SHARE_PROCESS constants. This approach works only if the user for the service is Local System.

Table 8.4   Service Start Options

Option	Description
SERVICE_AUTO_START	Specifies that the service will be started automatically by the Service Control Manager during system startup.
SERVICE_DEMAND_START	Specifies that the service will start when it is explicitly told to do so. Either an application starts the service (such as with the net start command), or an administrator starts it from the Service Manager.
SERVICE_DISABLED	Specifies that the service cannot be started. To start the service, you must change its start option to one of the other two options: SERVICE_AUTO_START or SERVICE_DEMAND_START.

Table 8.5   Service Error Control Options

Option	Description
SERVICE_ERROR_IGNORE	An error is recorded in the Win32 Event Log, but the service continues to start.
SERVICE_ERROR_NORMAL	An error is recorded in the Win32 Event Log, and a message box is displayed on the screen, but the service continues to start.
SERVICE_ERROR_SEVERE	An error is recorded in the Win32 Event Log and if the last-known good configuration is being started, the startup operation continues. Otherwise, the system is restarted with the last-known good configuration.
SERVICE_ERROR_CRITICAL	An error is recorded in the Win32 Event Log and if the last-known good configuration is being started, the startup operation fails. Otherwise, the system is restarted with the last-known good configuration.

Previously in Example 8.4, the name key is the name of the service. The Service Manager uses this name to refer to the service. When you're controlling the service using the Win32::Service extension's functions (such as StartService()), you use this name to identify the service. For example, Microsoft's Web Server service's name is w3svc.

The display key is the service's display name. It is what you would see in the Services control panel applet. This value is simply a nicely formatted name that is easier for humans to read than the service name—for example, World Wide Web Publishing Service.

The path key is the *full* path to the service executable file. It *must* be a full path, and it must be to an executable program. If you are using a Perl script as your service, this key is the full path to the PERL.EXE program, such as c:\perl\bin\perl.exe.

The user and password keys represent the user and password to use when the service starts. This is the account that the service will run under. The account must have the Logon as a Service privilege before the service is started (refer to Chapter 2, "Account Maintenance," for a tool to set privileges on user accounts). The privilege is required only to start the service, not to install it. If no username is specified, the Local System is used.

Specifying a full account name for the user key is very important. This name includes the domain that the user account belongs to. The reason for using the full name is to resolve ambiguity. If the local machine has a Joel account and the default domain has a Joel account, the service may not know which account to use and default to the local computer account. An example of a full account name is Accounting\Joel.

The parameters key is a string of values to pass into the service. It is like any parameter list that you might specify on a command line. If the service is a Perl script, this key contains the name of the Perl script to run and any optional switches. For example, assuming that the path points to PERL.EXE, the parameters key may be c:\perl\scripts\myservice.pl -someswitch Some Parameters To Pass In.

The service_type key represents what type of service you are installing. Refer to Table 8.3 for a description of the various service types.

The start_type key indicates when the service will start. Refer to Table 8.4 for the various options.

The error_control key describes what Win32 does if the service starts but ends in an error. Refer to Table 8.5 for the different error control options.

The load_order key is the name of a load order group that the service belongs to. Services are started in groups, so all the services that belong to a particular *load order group* are started at the same time. This way, one group can be loaded after another group, which it may be dependent upon. Usually, you don't need to associate a service with a group, so this key is left blank.

The dependencies key is an array of service names and load order groups. If a service is dependent upon another service to run (such as an email server is dependent upon the TCP/IP protocols), the service specifies its dependencies with this key. The service does not start until each specified service/device driver and at least one member of each specified group has started.

The two types of dependencies are services/device drivers and groups. To specify that a dependency is a group, simply prepend the + (plus) character to the name of each group; otherwise, it is assumed to be a name of a service or device driver.

Reconfiguring a Service

From time to time, you might need to reconfigure a service. If, for example, a service account's password has changed, the service must be reconfigured to use the new password. The Win32::Daemon::ConfigureService() function performs this task. This function works just like the CreateService() function. A hash reference is passed into the function. This hash, however, needs to contain only keys that represent configuration changes.

In Example 8.5, only the service's user and password are changed; therefore, they are the only two keys in the hash. Of course, the name key is included; otherwise, the function would not know what service to modify. Needless to say, the service name is the only aspect of the service that cannot be modified.

Example 8.5   *Configuring a Service*

```
01. use Win32::Daemon;
02. %ServiceConfig = (
03.     name     =>  'w3svc',
04.     user     =>  'MyDomain\WebServerAccount',
05.     password    =>  MyPassword,
06.     machine =>   "\\\\" . Win32::NodeName(),
07. );
08. if( Win32::Daemon::ConfigureService( \%ServiceConfig ) )
09. {
10.   print "The '$ServiceConfig{name}' service ";
11.   print "was successfully re-configured.\n";
12. }
13. else
14. {
15.   print "Failed to configure the '$ServiceConfig{name}' service.\n";
16.   print "Error: ";
17.   print Win32::FormatMessage( Win32::Daemon::GetLastError() ), "\n";
18. }
```

Removing Services

Removing a service is similar to installing the service. The only real difference is that the service name is passed into the DeleteService() function as opposed to a hash reference that is passed into the CreateService() function when installing a service.

Example 8.6 shows how you can remove a service. Notice that the biggest difference between this code and Example 8.4 is that no hash is needed to remove the service.

Example 8.6 *Removing a Service*

```
01. use Win32::Daemon;
02. $ServiceName = 'MyServiceName';
03. $Machine = "\\\\" . Win32::NodeName();
04. if( Win32::Daemon::DeleteService( $Machine, $ServiceName ) )
05. {
06.   print "The '$ServiceName' service was successfully removed.\n";
07. }
08. else
09. {
10.   print "Failed to remove the '$ServiceName' service.\n";
11.   print "Error: ";
12.   print Win32::FormatMessage( Win32::Daemon::GetLastError() ), "\n";
13. }
```

Running Perl Scripts as Win32 Services

You can resolve many problems by writing Perl scripts. Some of these types of problems, however, require that a script is running at all times. On a Windows 2000 or Windows NT machine, programs are run by a user executing them, or they can be automatically run when a user logs on. Either way such execution requires that a user log on. This solution is not always acceptable, however, which is why many administrators create Perl scripts and register them to run as a Win32 service. You can choose from two ways to run a script in such a way: the SRVANY.EXE program and the Win32::Daemon extension. Other applications are similar to SVRANY.EXE, but they are not as widely used.

You can use either of these techniques to effectively run a Perl script from computer boot time until shutdown. The SRVANY.EXE technique can be implemented quickly but lacks the control an administrator may require. Using the Win32::Daemon, on the other hand, requires a bit more thought and coding; however, it implements a Perl script as a true Win32 service, allowing for true Win32 service control.

Services Using *SRVANY.EXE*

The Windows NT/2000 Resource Kit contains a small executable program called SRVANY.EXE. This application enables any program to run as if it were a service—hence its name. The SRVANY.EXE program runs as a service, and its only task is to create a new process, which could be another program or even a Perl script. The SRVANY process manages all service control messages on behalf of the new process it started.

The relatively tiny amount of CPU processing time and memory that it requires does not impose any serious impact on a machine's performance. Therefore, it can be installed to run as different services.

Installing *SRVANY.EXE* Services

Because SRVANY.EXE is a very simple service application, it, unfortunately, cannot install itself as a service. For this function, it relies on other techniques, such as its companion program INSTSRV.EXE. As you can guess, this program is designed to install a service. Actually, just like SRVANY.EXE, it is generic and does not require any other particular application. It can install SRVANY.EXE as a service, but likewise it can install WINWORD.EXE or NETSCAPE.EXE as a service, although you may be hard-pressed to come up with a good reason for doing that. Refer to the earlier section, "Creating and Removing Services," for alternative techniques to install and configure services.

To install SRVANY.EXE (or any other service) using INSTSRV.EXE, simply pass in the name of the service and a full path to the executable as follows:

```
instsrv.exe "MyNewService" c:\tools\srvany.exe
```

That's it. Notice that, unlike using `Win32::Lanman` or `Win32::Daemon`, you don't have much control over how the service is configured. To configure the service, you either can use Regedit to modify the service's Registry key values or configure the service using `Win32::Lanman` or `Win32::Daemon`, even though they were not used to install the service.

After SRVANY.EXE is installed as a service, you need to modify the Registry to configure it. Even if you have already configured the service using `Win32::Lanman` or `Win32::Daemon`, you still need to configure SRVANY.EXE so that it knows what program to run when it starts.

You need to create a Parameters Registry key to hold the SRVANY.EXE configuration. The key must be created under the Services key as follows:

```
HKEY_LOCAL_MACHINE\SYSTEM\CurrentControlSet\Services\MyNewService\
Parameters
```

Notice that the Registry key's path reflects the name you used when installing the service (in this case MyNewService). The values that you need to modify are listed in Table 8.6.

Table 8.6 *SRVANY.EXE Registry Values*

Value Name	Value Type	Description

`Application`	REG_SZ	The path to the application that will be run.
		
		Example:
		`c:\tools\SomeService.exe`
		
		or
		
		`c:\perl\bin\perl.exe`

`AppParameters`	REG_SZ	Any parameters that must be passed into the service specified in the `Application` value. If you're running PERL.EXE as the service, this value is the full path to the Perl script and any parameters to be passed in. Example: `c:\Perl\scripts\MyService.pl` This value is optional.
`AppDirectory`	REG_SZ	The full path to a directory that will be the default directory for the created process. This is an optional value.

You can use INSTSRV.EXE to remove a service as well by passing in the name of the service followed by the keyword `remove`. For example, you can use the following:

```
instsrv.exe "MyNewService" remove
```

Problems with *SRVANY.EXE*

When the computer boots up, all services configured for autostart are started, including services based on SRVANY.EXE. Because SRVANY.EXE acts as a true Win32 service, it can be paused, resumed, and stopped from Perl (using the `Win32::Service` or `Win32::Lanman` extensions), from a command line using the `net` command or from the Services control panel applet. However, pausing and resuming the service will not affect the process that it started.

Consider an example: An administrator has written a clever Perl script that indexes all text files on your hard drive and submits the results to a network database engine. This script is started at bootup when the SRVANY.EXE service starts, and it runs the Perl script as a new process. At this point, the computer is correctly indexing files. However, because you are updating files on your computer, you need to temporarily pause the indexing script. If you pause the service, the SRVANY.EXE service is affected, but the Perl script continues processing. The only way to pause the process is to fully stop the service or terminate it by using the Task Manager or some `kill` utility. However, because the Perl script does not intercept the Service Manager's request to stop, it does not know that it must begin to shut down. Therefore, SRVANY.EXE stops the Perl process by killing it. This is quite drastic and can leave files in a vulnerable state as well as leave database connections open.

If you need to create a process at boot time, the SRVANY.EXE utility can be quite a powerful ally to quickly perform this feat. However, the `Win32::Daemon` provides more control from the Perl script itself and can interact with the Service Manager directly.

Services Using *Win32::Daemon*

The `Win32::Daemon` extension provides a Perl script with all the functionality it needs to run as a true Win32 service. It enables a script to respond to service control requests as a real service would and enables you to control the process as you would expect from any Win32 service.

Because a `Win32::Daemon`–based script does interact with the Service Manager, it is naturally more complicated than a simple script that is launched by SRVANY.EXE. Exactly how complicated such a script must be is a matter of what it needs to do. The simplest form of a `Win32::Daemon` script can be quite simple, as long as a basic framework is observed.

The Service Control Loop

All `Win32::Daemon` scripts must occasionally poll the current service control state. This state may change from time to time, depending on what the Service Manager requires. For example, if the administrator decides to pause the Perl-based service, the script would poll the service control state and discover that it is entering the paused state. It performs whatever task it must to pause itself and then reports to the Service Manager that the service has officially paused itself. Even while the service is in the paused state, however, it must continue to poll the current service control state in case a request is made to resume or stop the service.

Such polling is typically performed in the *service control loop*. This loop calls the `Win32::Daemon::State()` function to query the current control state. The loop must have code to handle the pending states listed in Table 8.7.

Table 8.8 shows optional control states that a service script does not need to process. Most services should process all states (from both tables). These control states must be responded to in a timely manner; otherwise, the Service Manager assumes the service has crashed or is in some nonfunctional state. The rule of thumb is that the service should respond within 20 seconds.

One other set of control states is described in Table 8.9. These states are new to Windows 2000, and responding to them is not necessary. These particular states represent events that a service might want to know about.

Table 8.7   Pending Windows Service Control States

Control State	Description
SERVICE_START_PENDING	The service is starting.
SERVICE_STOP_PENDING	The service is preparing to stop.
SERVICE_CONTINUE_PENDING	The service is resuming from the paused state.
SERVICE_PAUSE_PENDING	The service is preparing to pause.

Table 8.8   Optional Windows Service Control States

Control State	Description
SERVICE_RUNNING	The service is running This is the typical control state.
SERVICE_PAUSED	The service is paused.
SERVICE_STOPPED	The service has stopped.
SERVICE_CONTROL_SHUTDOWN	The system is shutting down. You should prepare to terminate.
SERVICE_CONTROL_USER_DEFINED	This is the first of 128 user-defined states. These values are SERVICE_CONTROL_USER_DEFINED + 0 SERVICE_CONTROL_USER_DEFINED + 1 ... SERVICE_CONTROL_USER_DEFINED + 127

Table 8.9   Service Control States New to Windows 2000

Control State	Description
SERVICE_CONTROL_PARAMCHANGE	A parameter change has been made to the service.
SERVICE_CONTROL_NETBINDADD	A network binding has been added.
SERVICE_CONTROL_NETBINDREMOVE	A network binding has been removed.
SERVICE_CONTROL_NETBINDENABLE	A network binding has been enabled.
SERVICE_CONTROL_NETBINDDISABLE	A network binding has been disabled.

The *Win32::Daemon* Framework

The service control loop begins after the service is officially started. To officially start the service, the script calls the Win32::Daemon::StartService() function. If the function is successful, the service control loop begins. The loop continues until the service enters the SERVICE_STOPPED state. At that point, the script stops the service control loop and calls the Win32::Daemon::StopService() function to instruct the Service Manager to stop interacting with the script. This step is the prelude to ending the service. Example 8.7 shows a very simple skeleton for a Win32 service script. If this code is installed as a service, it works but does not accomplish anything.

Example 8.7   *A Minimal Win32 Service Script*

```
01. use Win32::Daemon;
02. Win32::Daemon::StartService();
03. while( SERVICE_STOPPED != ( $State = Win32::Daemon::State() ) )
04. {
05.   if( SERVICE_START_PENDING == $State )
06.   {
07.     # Add initialization code here
08.     Win32::Daemon::State( SERVICE_RUNNING );
09.   }
10.   elsif( SERVICE_PAUSE_PENDING == $State )
11.   {
12.     # Add pausing code here
13.     Win32::Daemon::State( SERVICE_PAUSED );
14.   }
15.   elsif( SERVICE_CONTINUE_PENDING == $State )
16.   {
17.     # Add resuming code here
18.     Win32::Daemon::State( SERVICE_RUNNING );
19.   }
20.   elsif( SERVICE_STOP_PENDING == $State )
21.   {
22.     # Add stopping code here
23.     Win32::Daemon::State( SERVICE_STOPPED );
24.   }
25.   elsif( SERVICE_RUNNING == $State )
26.   {
27.     # This is the core functionality of the service
28.     # Add code here to perform whatever work the
29.     # service must accomplish. Avoid any code that
30.     # blocks for long durations of time
31.   }
32.   sleep( 5 );
33. }
34. Win32::Daemon::StopService();
```

A few aspects of this example are worth noting. Each code block that deals with a pending state change ends by calling the Win32::Daemon::State() function passing in the new state (lines 8, 13, 18, and 23). Calling this function is imperative so that the script can update the Service Manager with the new state change; otherwise, the service gives up trying to control the service. If that occurs, the service cannot be stopped, paused, or resumed.

Line 32 is especially important; this line simply causes the script to fall asleep for a brief period of time. For most service scripts, such a pause is required; otherwise, it is processed so quickly that it may threaten to suck up CPU processing time needlessly.

Finally, the SERVICE_RUNNING block (lines 25 through 31) contains the code that performs the actual work of the service. When you put the actual processing code in this block, the code is not run if the service enters the SERVICE_PAUSED state, which is exactly what a service should do in the paused state.

What is most important to know regarding this service control loop is that it must periodically loop. That is, it must not enter some race condition that blocks it from looping. An example of a bad-coding practice would be to listen on a socket for a client connection. Unless the listening is non-blocking, it could prevent the service from responding to the Service Manager, risking becoming an abandoned service.

If you are running a version of Perl that supports threads, it is quite possible to create a new thread that performs the processing work. In this way, the thread can be controlled by the service control loop—pausing and resuming as needed.

Registering a *Win32::Daemon* Service on the Network

Often a service is designed to work with outside processes. Examples of such processes may be a time service that provides an "official" time of day that other computers synchronize to, a database engine to which other computers must connect and submit updates, or maybe an antivirus update service in which virus services can connect to and retrieve the latest virus signatures. These types of services may want to announce themselves on the network. Doing so allows other machines to easily locate which machines these processes are running on.

A service can *announce* itself by associating with one of 32 announcement flags. If anyone on the network requests a list of machines running a service, the service specifies one of these flags. The query results in a list of all machines that have a service associated with the specified flag. A machine can query services by calling the Win32::NetAdmin::GetServers() or Win32::Lanman::EnumServers() functions.

A service also announces itself by calling the
Win32::Daemon::SetServiceBits() function. It passes in a bitmask that represents the bits (or flags) that it is associating itself with. For example, Microsoft's SQL Server service announces itself as the SV_TYPE_SQLSERVER service. This constant equates to 0x00000004 or bit number 2.

As you can see in Example 8.8, a call into Win32::NetAdmin::GetServers() actually requests all machines to report whether they are running a service that has registered with bit number 2 (0x04). Microsoft reserves several bits, one of which represents its SQL Server service.

Example 8.8   *Looking for SQL Server Machines*

```
01. use Win32::NetAdmin;
02. $Domain = Win32::DomainName();
03. Win32::NetAdmin::GetDomainController( '', $Domain, $Pdc );
04. if( Win32::NetAdmin::GetServers( $Pdc, $Domain, 0x04, \@List ) )
05. {
06.   foreach my $Machine ( @List )
07.   {
08.     print "\\\\$Machine is a SQL Server.\n";
09.   }
10. }
```

So, when would you actually use this announcement mechanism? Say that you're running a Perl paging service on a machine. This service can accept incoming socket requests to send a text message to someone's pager and register itself on the network so that the client program can simply look up which machines are running this service. This way, you never need to hard-code addresses into the client script, allowing your network to be outfitted with several paging servers throughout the enterprise network.

Microsoft has reserved 22 of the 32 bits for its own purposes, leaving all other services only 10 bits. For all practical purposes, having only 10 bits is not too bad because most machines don't run services that need to announce themselves.

The Win32::Daemon extension exposes these 10 bits as constants:

```
USER_SERVICE_BITS_1
USER_SERVICE_BITS_2
...
USER_SERVICE_BITS_10
```

The Win32::Daemon extension permits only the 10 available bits to be set, so efforts to set other bits will fail. Each call to the SetServiceBits() function clears any previously set bits and then applies the new ones.

Line 63 of the next example, Example 8.9, sets the service bit (using USER_SERVICE_BITS_1) only if a named pipe is successfully created; otherwise, the service terminates. This code is a full-fledged Win32 service that accepts named pipe input and sends pages out on the client's behalf. It makes use of the Net::Pager module available on CPAN. The service has some obvious limitations, such as assuming all pages will go to the AT&T wireless network through the Internet, but it is a terrific example on how a Perl script can be a full Win32 service.

Lines 24–32 open and initialize a log file because most services are better suited to output data to a log file than to a screen. Line 35 officially starts the service; it begins a conversation with the Service Manager and begins to receive service control messages.

Line 40 attempts to display the service because services, by default, are hidden. If it can be displayed, the service switches to the user's main desktop and shows itself. However, due to limitations on how the Perl script's console works, you need to create a new console buffer using Win32::Console, which is what lines 42–45 do. All output to the screen requires printing to the console buffer instead.

Lines 46–155 constitute the main service control loop. At the beginning of the loop (line 46), the service state is queried. As long as the service has not stopped (SERVICE_STOPPED), the script continues to loop. Each iteration of the loop checks if the service is being paused, resumed, or stopped. The heart of the loop, however, falls into two sections: initialization and running.

The *initialization loop* (lines 48–71), where the state is SERVICE_START_PENDING, creates a named pipe with any applicable security. In this case, security is set such that administrators and members of a Pager Users group are allowed to connect to the named pipe to submit a page request. Next, the named pipe is created. Notice that it specifies the PIPE_NOWAIT flag, which puts the pipe into nonblocking mode. This mode prevents the script from waiting until a client connects to the named pipe. Without this nonblocking mode, the service could end up waiting until a client connects before continuing to process the service control loop. This would prevent the service from responding to any service control requests. If the named pipe is successfully created, line 63 announces to the network that the service is running.

The second important part of the service control loop is the *running loop* (between lines 103 and 148). In this loop, the logic is to wait for a client connection, receive the client request, and submit the request in the form of a page.

Finally, the block from lines 7 through 19 and the InstallService() (lines 183-195), RemoveService() (lines 167-209), and GetServiceConfig() (lines 169-181) functions enable you to run the script from a command line to either install or remove the service.

The sister code to this service is shown in Example 8.10, which contains the client code that connects to the Pager service and submits a page request. The real power of this client is that lines 7 through 9 perform the task of autodiscovering which machines are the Pager Service. Notice that line 9 looks up all machines running the Pager service. If at least one machine is returned in the list, a named pipe is created with the service, and the page is submitted.

This client is pretty simple and expects three input parameters:

```
pageclnt.pl "1234567890" "My Subject" "My Message"
```

The first is the pager number, the second is the subject of the page, and the third is the message.

Example 8.9   *A Paging Service*

```perl
01. use Win32::Daemon;
02. use Win32::Console;
03. use Win32::Pipe;
04. use Win32::Perms;
05. use Net::Pager;
06.
07. if( scalar @ARGV )
08. {
09.   if( $ARGV[0] =~ /install/i )
10.   {
11.     InstallService();
12.     exit();
13.   }
14.   elsif( $ARGV[0] =~ /remove/i )
15.   {
16.     RemoveService();
17.     exit();
18.   }
19. }
20.
21. # How much time do we sleep between polling?
22. $SERVICE_SLEEP_TIME = 1;
23. $PIPE_NAME = "PagerService";
24. my $DB_FILE =
25.   ( Win32::GetFullPathName( $0 ) =~ /(.*?)\..*?$/ )[0] . ".log";
26. if( open( LOG, "> $DB_FILE" ) )
27. {
28.   my $Handle = select( LOG );
29.   $| = 1;
30.   select( $Handle );
```

```perl
31.    print LOG "Started: " . localtime() . "\n\n";
32. }
33.
34. # Start the service...
35. if( ! Win32::Daemon::StartService() )
36. {
37.    exit();
38. }
39. # Register the service
40. Win32::Daemon::ShowService();
41.
42. $Buffer = new Win32::Console();
43. $Buffer->Display();
44. $Buffer->Title( "Perl based Pager service" );
45. Write( "Service started\n" );
46. while( SERVICE_STOPPED != ( $State = Win32::Daemon::State() ) )
47. {
48.    if( SERVICE_START_PENDING == $State )
49.    {
50.      # Initialization code
51.      my $Perm;
52.      if( $Perm = new Win32::Perms() )
53.      {
54.        $Perm->Allow( "administrators", FULL );
55.      }
56.
57.      # Now create the pipe and specify to use the permissions above
58.      if( $Pipe = new Win32::Pipe( $PIPE_NAME, 1000,
59.                                   PIPE_NOWAIT | PIPE_READMODE_BYTE,
60.                                   $Perm ) )
61.      {
62.        Win32::Daemon::State( SERVICE_RUNNING );
63.        Win32::Daemon::SetServiceBits( USER_SERVICE_BITS_1 );
64.        Write( "Service is running\n" );
65.      }
66.      else
67.      {
68.        Win32::Daemon::State( SERVICE_STOPPED );
69.        Write( "Service stopping\n" );
70.      }
71.    }
72.    elsif( SERVICE_PAUSE_PENDING == $State )
73.    {
74.      # "Pausing...";
75.      if( $Connected )
76.      {
77.        $Pipe->Disconnect();
78.        $Connected = 0;
79.      }
80.      Win32::Daemon::State( SERVICE_PAUSED );
81.      Write( "Paused\n" );
82.      next;
83.    }
```

continues ▶

Example 8.9   *continued*

```
84.   elsif( SERVICE_CONTINUE_PENDING == $State )
85.   {
86.     # "Resuming...";
87.     Win32::Daemon::State( SERVICE_RUNNING );
88.     Write( "Resumed\n" );
89.     next;
90.   }
91.   elsif( SERVICE_STOP_PENDING == $State )
92.   {
93.     # "Stopping...";
94.     if( $Connected )
95.     {
96.       $Pipe->Disconnect();
97.       $Connected = 0;
98.     }
99.     Win32::Daemon::State( SERVICE_STOPPED );
100.    Write( "Stopped\n" );
101.    next;
102.  }
103.  elsif( SERVICE_RUNNING == $State )
104.  {
105.    # The service is running as normal...
106.    if( ! $Connected )
107.    {
108.      $Connected = Connect( $Pipe );
109.    }
110.    if( $Connected )
111.    {
112.      if( $Pipe->Peek() )
113.      {
114.        my $Result = 0;
115.        my $Data = $Pipe->Read();
116.        if( my $Pager = new Net::Pager )
117.        {
118.          my( $To, $Message ) = split( /\t/, $Data );
119.          # AT&T PCS services has a service number of 7.
120.          # Check with the Net::Pager documentation to
121.          # discover other paging service values.
122.          # This script assumes everyone uses AT&T PCS services.
123.          my $SERVICE = 7;
124.          my $FROM = "Perl Pager";
125.          Write( "Sending page to $To...\n" );
126.          if( $Pager->sendPage( $SERVICE,
127.                                $To,
128.                                $FROM,
129.                                $Message,
130.                                undef ) )
131.          {
132.            Write( "Page was sent\n" );
133.          }
134.          else
```

```
135.            {
136.              Write( "Page failed to send\n" );
137.            }
138.          }
139.          else
140.          {
141.            Write( "Unable to create a pager object\n" );
142.          }
143.          $Pipe->Disconnect();
144.          Write( "Waiting for connection\n" );
145.          $Connected = 0;
146.        }
147.      }
148.    }
149.    else
150.    {
151.    # Got an unhandled control message
152.      Win32::Daemon::State( SERVICE_RUNNING );
153.    }
154.    sleep( $SERVICE_SLEEP_TIME );
155. }
156.
157. sub Connect
158. {
159.    my( $Pipe ) = @_;
160.    my $Connected = 0;
161.    if( $Pipe->Connect() )
162.    {
163.      $Connected = 1;
164.      Write( "Connected by " . ( $Pipe->GetInfo() )[2] . "\n" );
165.    }
166.    return( $Connected );
167. }
168.
169. sub GetServiceConfig
170. {
171.    my $ScriptPath = join( "", Win32::GetFullPathName( $0 ) );
172.    my %Hash = (
173.      name => 'Pager',
174.      display => 'Pager Service',
175.      path    =>   $^X,
176.      user    => '',
177.      password   => '',
178.      parameters => "$ScriptPath",
179.    );
180.    return( \%Hash );
181. }
182.
183. sub InstallService
184. {
185.    my $ServiceConfig = GetServiceConfig();
186.    if( Win32::Daemon::CreateService( $ServiceConfig ) )
187.    {
```

continues ▶

Example 8.9 *continued*

```perl
188.      print "The $ServiceConfig->{display} was successfully installed.\n";
189.    }
190.    else
191.    {
192.      print "Failed to add the $ServiceConfig->{display} ";
193.      print "service.\nError: " . GetError() . "\n";
194.    }
195. }
196.
197. sub RemoveService
198. {
199.    my $ServiceConfig = GetServiceConfig();
200.    if( Win32::Daemon::DeleteService( $ServiceConfig->{name} ) )
201.    {
202.      print "The $ServiceConfig->{display} was successfully removed.\n";
203.    }
204.    else
205.    {
206.      print "Failed to remove the $ServiceConfig->{display} ";
207.      print "service.\nError: " . GetError() . "\n";
208.    }
209. }
210.
211. sub GetError
212. {
213.    return( Win32::FormatMessage( Win32::Daemon::GetLastError() ) );
214. }
215.
216. sub Write
217. {
218.    my( $Message ) = @_;
219.    $Message = "[" . scalar( localtime() ) . "] $Message";
220.    if( defined $Buffer )
221.    {
222.      $Buffer->Write( $Message );
223.    }
224.    else
225.    {
226.      print $Message;
227.    }
228.    if( fileno( LOG ) )
229.    {
230.      print LOG $Message;
231.    }
232. }
```

Example 8.10   *Client to the Pager Service in Example 8.9*

```
01. use Win32::NetAdmin;
02.
03. # The equivalent to USER_SERVICE_BITS_1
04. $Service = 0x00004000;
05.
06. $Domain = Win32::DomainName();
07. Win32::NetAdmin::GetDomainController( '', $Domain, $Pdc );
08. if( Win32::NetAdmin::GetServers( $Pdc, $Domain, $Service, \@List )
09.    && ( scalar @List ) )
10. {
11.    # Just try the first server in the list
12.    if( open( PAGER, "> \\\\$List[0]\\pipe\\PagerService" ) )
13.    {
14.      my $BackupHandle = select( PAGER );
15.      $| = 1;
16.      select( $BackupHandle );
17.      print "Submitting page...\n";
18.      print PAGER "$ARGV[0]\t$ARGV[1]\n";
19.      close( PAGER );
20.    }
21. }
```

Detecting System Shutdown

The Win32::Daemon service control loop can receive a SERVICE_CONTROL_SHUTDOWN message. When the operating system is shutting down, it sends this message to all services. This message gives the service roughly 20 seconds to perform any shutdown tasks, such as closing files, updating databases, or doing whatever else a service may want to perform. When the 20 seconds have expired, the service is terminated by the Service Manager, possibly while the service is still performing shutdown tasks.

If the service requires more time to shut down, it can call the Win32::Daemon::State() function to update the Service Manager with the SERVICE_STOP_PENDING control message and a second parameter with the number of seconds needed to completely finish its shutdown tasks. The Service Manager extends the life span of the service by the time submitted. After that time has expired, the service is terminated. If the service finishes before the time allotted, it can submit the SERVICE_STOPPED control message, and the service is allowed to end on its own.

This scenario is illustrated in Example 8.11. Lines 21 through 27 manage the SERVICE_CONTROL_SHUTDOWN control message. Notice that line 24 informs the Service Manager that not only does the service acknowledge that it is beginning the process of stopping, but it also requests 45 seconds to perform all its shutdown tasks. If it does not successfully set the state to SERVICE_STOPPED within these 45 seconds, the Service Manager will forcibly shut down the service by terminating the process.

Example 8.11   *A* `Win32::Daemon` *Service with Shutdown Handler*

```
01. use Win32::Daemon;
02. Win32::Daemon::StartService();
03. while( SERVICE_STOPPED != ( $State = Win32::Daemon::State() ) )
04. {                          _PENDING
05.   if( SERVICE_STARTING == $State )
06.   {
07.     Win32::Daemon::State( SERVICE_RUNNING );
08.   }
09.   elsif( SERVICE_PAUSE_PENDING == $State )
10.   {
11.     Win32::Daemon::State( SERVICE_PAUSED );
12.   }
13.   elsif( SERVICE_CONTINUE_PENDING == $State )
14.   {
15.     Win32::Daemon::State( SERVICE_RUNNING );
16.   }
17.   elsif( SERVICE_STOP_PENDING == $State )
18.   {
19.     Win32::Daemon::State( SERVICE_STOPPED );
20.   }
21.   elsif( SERVICE_CONTROL_SHUTDOWN == $State )
22.   {
23.     # Request 45 seconds to shut down...
24.     Win32::Daemon::State( SERVICE_STOP_PENDING, 45 );
25.     # Add code here to shut down
26.     Win32::Daemon::State( SERVICE_STOPPED );
27.   }
28.   elsif( SERVICE_RUNNING == $State )
29.   {
30.     # Add code for the running state
31.   }
32.   else
33.   {
34.     # Un-handled control messages
35.   }
36. }
37. Win32::Daemon::StopService();
```

Issues with Perl-Based Services

Perl-based services are wonderful, but they are not without their own hazards. To be fair, it is not as much Perl-based services that can be problematic as it is how Win32 services themselves work. This section discusses how to get around some of Win32 service-related problems.

Debugging

Services are designed to be a lights-out approach to program running; that is, the program starts and eventually terminates without ever having to interact with a user. This means that services rarely need to present information to a user; therefore, most services never expose any windows. Not having any windows, of course, makes it very difficult to debug.

With some creative thinking on your part, this problem quickly becomes manageable. Example 8.9, shown earlier, takes two different approaches to solving this problem. First, it opens a log file (refer to lines 24 through 32). This technique is used for archiving purposes so that a log of the service's activity is created. However, the log can just as easily be used for debugging. The service uses its own Write() function instead of calling Perl's print function. This function is used to redirect information to the log file.

Lines 42 through 45 illustrate another technique to debugging services. In this block of code, the service attempts to show itself by exposing its console window with the ShowService() function. Typically this only works when the service logs on as the local system. It then creates a new console buffer and displays it in the console (lines 42 and 43). When this step is done, anything that is passed into $Buffer->Write() is displayed in the console window. In addition to saving to the log file, this is what the Write() function does, thus enabling the programmer to quickly see what is being logged at the time it is being logged, easing the burden of debugging. This particular method of debugging is useful as long as the service runs under the Local System account. Otherwise, you might not see the created console.

A service can just as easily implement the capability to log entries to the Win32 Event Log (refer to Chapter 5, "Monitoring and Reporting"). Another useful debugging tool is to run a Perl script that creates a named pipe and dumps any incoming data to the screen. This enables the service to connect to the named pipe when it starts and print debug messages into the pipe. This approach provides a programmer with instant debugging information. It also enables you to debug from across the network. This is one of the single most useful tools that can be used when you're debugging services.

Example 8.12 is a named pipe server application that can be used to receive debugging messages from Win32 services (or any other script for that matter). To use this functionality, all you need to do is incorporate the two functions from Example 8.13 into your service script. Then, at the beginning of the service, call the startLog() function, passing in the name of the machine the named pipe server script is running on. If you pass in nothing, the local machine is assumed. Any time the script needs to dump debug information, pass in the data to the Log() function. As long as Example 8.12 is running prior to the service starting, it dumps all the debug information.

Ideally, both service and named pipe scripts are run on the same machine to prevent network access errors if the service is running under the Local System account. You'll learn more about this issue in the next section.

Example 8.12   *Debugging a Win32 Service Using Named Pipes*

```
01. use Win32::Pipe;
02.
03. $PIPE_NAME = "Debug Logging";
04. if( $Pipe = new Win32::Pipe( $PIPE_NAME,
05.                              DEFAULT_WAIT_TIME,
06.                              PIPE_READMODE_BYTE ) )
07. {
08.     Announce();
09.     while( $Pipe->Connect() )
10.     {
11.         my $User = ($Pipe->GetInfo())[2];
12.         print "Pipe opened by $User at " . localtime(). "\n\n";
13.         while( my $In = $Pipe->Read() )
14.         {
15.             print $In;
16.         }
17.         print "\nDisconnecting...\n";
18.         $Pipe->Disconnect();
19.         Announce();
20.     }
21.     $Pipe->Close();
22. }
23. else
24. {
25.     print "\nCould not create pipe\n";
26.     print "Error: " . Win32::FormatMessage( $Win32::Pipe::Error ) . "\n";
27. }
28.
29. sub Announce
30. {
31.     my $PipeName = "\\\\" . Win32::NodeName() . "\\pipe\\$PIPE_NAME";
32.     print "---------------------------------\n";
33.     print "R e a d y   f o r   r e a d i n g :\n";
34.     print "$PipeName is waiting for a client to connect...\n";
35. }
```

Example 8.13   *Named Pipe Debugging Client Routines*

```
01. sub StartLog
02. {
03.     my $Machine;
04.     $Machine = "." unless( $Machine = shift @_ );
05.     if( open( DEBUG_LOG, "> \\\\$Machine\\pipe\\Debug Logging" ) )
06.     {
07.         my $OutputHandle = select( DEBUG_LOG );
08.         $| = 1;
```

```
09.          select( $OutputHandle );
10.     }
11. }
12.
13. sub Log
14. {
15.     my( $Message ) = @_;
16.     print DEBUG_LOG "$Message\n" if( fileno( DEBUG_LOG ) );
17. }
```

Child Processes

Because services are usually not expected to interact with a user, they are automatically run in a hidden environment; this is called a *windows station*. Imagine a windows station to be a virtual computer environment. Because this environment is hidden from the user, it is never seen even though the service is running. You can use the Win32::Daemon extension to reveal the service by moving it from this hidden windows station to the user's windows station, which is always seen by the current user. This is what the ShowService() function does. It is not required to call this function; the only time you would want to call it would be to show the service itself, maybe for debugging purposes. However, there is a catch. If a service is to create new processes, such as spawning another program that will interact with the user, these processes appear only in the service's windows station. If the service is hidden, the new processes are hidden as well.

If you show the service, all processes that it spawns are displayed to the user. The user then not only can see the processes, but can also interact with them by using the mouse and keyboard.

You also can manage these windows stations by using the Win32::AdminMisc extension. Refer to the extension's documentation for more information.

Accounts

As most administrators know, a service must run under an account. Typically most services run under the Local System account. This account is special because it refers not to a user, but to the operating system itself. It is similar to the Administrator account in that it is granted many privileges that most other accounts do not have. It therefore is ideal for running services, but there is a catch. The Local System account does not have network access.

This means that if a service is configured to run as the Local System, it cannot access shared resources over the network. It can open files locally but cannot open them as a UNC or over a network-mapped drive. Access to mapped drives will fail even if the drive is mapped by an administrator with full access before the service attempts to access it.

The two exceptions to this situation are using sockets and acting as the server end of a named pipe. A service running under the Local System account can open, close, and access data through TCP sockets—presumably because there is no inherit security with such network connections. Likewise, a Local System service can create server-side named pipes. Creating such a named pipe does not really involve accessing resources over the network; it is simply creating a file that the system shares with other processes and machines. Such a service, however, cannot create the client end of a named pipe that connects across the network.

Any account that will be used to run a service must be granted the Logon as a Service privilege. There is no exception to this rule.

CASE STUDY   **Creating a Reminder Service**

Jamie has discovered that her Outlook email program has become quite an indispensable tool. Every day she comes to work and checks Outlook to see what meetings she has for the day. Quite Often her schedule is loaded with meetings that take her away from her real job of administering her network. Her peers always seem to be requesting her presence at one meeting after another. Often her computer receives requests while she is away at another meeting. She has found that this is a trick that many of her coworkers have used to avoid having to confront her directly. After all, if she is busy in a meeting across town, it would be nearly impossible for her to know that she has just been invited to another meeting.

One day Jamie decided to sit down and write a Perl script that would check her schedule for her. Because she does not always have access to email, she wanted the script to send her a page whenever a meeting reminder occurs. Because she cannot always guarantee that she will be at her computer in the morning to log on and start up the Perl script, she wrote it as a Win32 service. She also knows that some-times she might need to pause and stop the service, so she wrote it using Win32::Daemon.

She decided to use COM and directly talk with her Outlook email program. However, after some experimentation, Jamie discovered that Outlook can be run in only one process at a time. This meant that either the service can run and integrate with Outlook, or she can log on and run Outlook, but not both at the same time. This solution was quite unacceptable, so she turned to Collaboration Data Objects (CDO).

CDO is a COM-based API that allows a program or script to interact with collaboration services such as Outlook and Microsoft Exchange. Outlook comes with CDO version 1.21, which solved Jamie's problems. Using CDO, Jamie can bypass Outlook altogether and talk directly to her Exchange server, where her schedule resides. It became clear to her that this was the ideal approach.

Example 8.14, shown later in the section "Using the Service," shows the code that she used.

Obtaining CDO

Jamie poked around in the Registry to see whether she already had CDO installed, and much to her surprise, she did. However, her version was CDONTS, which comes with Windows 2000 and provides SMTP and NNTP support. This version does not talk with an Exchange server the way she needed. Therefore, she ran the Microsoft Office setup program and selected the CDO components to install the correct version for her.

Installing and Removing the Service

To make installation and removal simple, Jamie wrote her script to accept installation and removal switches. This way, she never needs to rely on separate applications to install or remove the script as a service. She can install the script by calling

```
perl reminder.pl -install
```

Likewise, she can remove the script by calling

```
perl reminder.pl -remove
```

When installing, she can specify an account and password to run under. For example, this command line installs the script to run under Jamie's account in debug mode (which logs much more information than it normally would):

```
perl reminder.pl -install -account "MyDomain\Jamie"
    -password "MyPassword" -debug
```

continues ▶

▶ *continued*

Several different options can be configured. You can pass in the `-help` switch for a list of options.

Using the Service

The script in Example 8.14 is configured to work for Jamie's Exchange mailbox only. She therefore had to run the script under her user ID and password. This required that she grant her account the privilege to "log on as a service" (refer to Chapter 2 for a tool to set such privileges). Because her Exchange server uses Windows 2000/NT user accounts, she had to make sure that the account running the service not only had permissions to talk with the Exchange server but also had permissions to read her mailbox.

Lines 54 through 61 configure the script to access Jamie's pager. In this example, she uses AT&T's SMS paging service using the `Net::Pager` module. She could just as well have configured it to use another paging service or use SMTP to send email instead. This configuration hash also identifies her Exchange server as well as her mailbox. You can easily modify these values to reflect your own configuration.

Line 70 is important because it determines which file the service will write its log to. This log file shows when pages have been sent out. By default, the log file is placed in the same directory as the script file itself. It also is named the same as the script, with the exception that its file extension is .log. By modifying line 70, you can direct the log to anywhere—as long as the account running the service has permissions to write to the file. For example, you can modify this line as follows:

```
my $DB_FILE = "\\\\.\\pipe\\Debug Logging";
```

This log path would log data to a named pipe created by Example 8.12. This approach is a terrific way to monitor the progress of the service because the named pipe script will display all information that the reminder service logs, in real time. Notice that if the named pipe server script runs on another machine, you can replace the `"\\\\."` with `"\\\\MachineName"`, where `MachineName` is the name of the computer running the named pipe script. So, line 70 might look like this:

```
my $DB_FILE = "\\\\MachineName\\pipe\\Debug Logging";
```

The meat of the script is the `ProcessEvents()` function. Here, CDO queries any appointments and tasks. All tasks are examined, and only appointments that occur between the current time of day and one day later (this time span can be modified by changing the $TIME_CONSIDERATION_INTERVAL variable on line 14). If any of these tasks or appointments have a reminder set, they are examined to see whether the user should be paged.

You can easily modify this script to check multiple users' schedules—provided that the account running the script has permissions to access the mailboxes. A good book on CDO can provide information on other tasks this script can accomplish.

Example 8.14   *The Appointment Reminder Service*

```
01. use Win32::OLE qw( EVENTS HRESULT );
02. use Win32::OLE::Const 'Microsoft CDO 1.21 Library';
03. use Win32::Daemon;
04. use Win32::Console;
05. use Time::Local;
06. use Net::Pager;
07. use Getopt::Long;
08.
09. $SCRIPT_PATH = Win32::GetFullPathName( $0 );
10. $VERSION = 20000619;
11.
12. # How far ahead do we look at calendar events?
13. # In seconds
14. $TIME_CONSIDERATION_INTERVAL = 60 * 60 * 24;
15.
16. # How much time do we sleep between polling the service manager?
17. # In seconds.
18. $SERVICE_SLEEP_TIME = 2;
19.
20. # How often do we actually process calendars?
21. # In seconds.
22. $CALENDAR_PROCESS_TIME_INTERVAL = 60;
23.
24. # Default values
25. %$Config = (
26.    account   => '',
27.    password  => '',
28.    name      => 'Reminder',
29.    display   => 'Reminder Service',
30. );
31.
32. Configure( \%Config );
33. if( $Config{help} || scalar @ARGV )
34. {
35.    Syntax();
36.    exit();
37. }
38. elsif( $Config{install} )
39. {
40.    InstallService();
```

continues ▶

Example 8.14 *continued*

```
41.   exit();
42. }
43. elsif( $Config{remove} )
44. {
45.   RemoveService();
46.   exit();
47. }
48.
49. @FOLDERS = (
50.   CdoDefaultFolderCalendar,
51.   CdoDefaultFolderTasks
52. );
53.
54. %PROFILES = (
55.   "Jamie Smith's Mailbox" => {
56.     pager_service  => '7',  # Service value of 7 represents AT&T PCS
57.     pager_id       => '123 456 7890',
58.     mailbox        => 'Jamie Smith',
59.     server         => 'ExchangeServer',
60.   },
61. );
62.
63. $CLASS = "MAPI.Session";
64. %PROPERTY = (
65.   task_reminder_flag => CdoPidReminderSet,
66.   task_reminder_date => CdoPidReminderTime,
67.   task_due_date      => -2144796608,
68. );
69.
70. my ( $DB_FILE ) = ( $SCRIPT_PATH =~ /(.*?)\..*?$/ )[0] . ".log";
71. if( open( LOG, "> $DB_FILE" ) )
72. {
73.   my $Handle = select( LOG );
74.   $| = 1;
75.   select( $Handle );
76.   print LOG "Software: $0\n";
77.   print LOG "Version: $VERSION\n";
78.   print LOG "Started: " . localtime() . "\n\n";
79. }
80.
81. if( ! $Config{console} )
82. {
83.   # Start the service...
84.   if( ! Win32::Daemon::StartService() )
85.   {
86.     exit();
87.   }
88.   Win32::Daemon::ShowService();
89.
90.   $Buffer = new Win32::Console();
91.   $Buffer->Display();
92.   $Buffer->Title( $Config{display} );
```

```perl
93.   Write( "Service started\n" );
94.  }
95.
96.  Debug( " With debugging mode turned on.\n" );
97.
98.  $NextTime = time();
99.  $PrevState = SERVICE_STARTING;
100. $AppState = 0;
101. while( SERVICE_STOPPED != ( $State = Win32::Daemon::State() ) )
102. {
103.   if( $Config{console} )
104.   {
105.     # Fake out the service control loop if we are running
106.     # as a console application instead of a service
107.     $State = ( $AppState++ )? SERVICE_RUNNING : SERVICE_START_PENDING;
108.   }
109.   Debug( "Service State: $State\n" );
110.   if( SERVICE_START_PENDING == $State )
111.   {
112.     # Initialization code
113.     my $iTotal = 0;
114.     foreach my $ProfileName ( keys( %PROFILES ) )
115.     {
116.       my $Profile = $PROFILES{$ProfileName};
117.       my $Mapi = Win32::OLE->new( $CLASS, \&Quit );
118.       if( defined $Mapi )
119.       {
120.         $Mapi->Logoff();
121.         $Mapi->Logon( {
122.           NoMail => 1,
123.           ProfileInfo => "$Profile->{server}\n$Profile->{mailbox}",
124.         } );
125.         if( Win32::OLE->LastError() != HRESULT( 0x00000000 ) )
126.         {
127.           my $ComError = Win32::OLE->LastError();
128.           Write( "Unable to logon $ProfileName. (Error: $ComError)\n" );
129.           undef $Mapi;
130.         }
131.         else
132.         {
133.           $PROFILES{$ProfileName}->{mapi} = $Mapi;
134.           Write( "$ProfileName has logged on.\n" );
135.           $iTotal++;
136.         }
137.       }
138.     }
139.     if( $iTotal )
140.     {
141.       Win32::Daemon::State( SERVICE_RUNNING );
142.       $PrevState = SERVICE_RUNNING;
143.       Write( "Running\n" );
144.     }
145.     else
146.     {
```

continues ▶

Example 8.14 *continued*

```perl
147.        Write( "Unable to logon any profiles. Stopping\n" );
148.        Win32::Daemon::State( SERVICE_STOPPED );
149.        $PrevState = SERVICE_STOPPED;
150.      }
151.    }
152.    elsif( SERVICE_PAUSE_PENDING == $State )
153.    {
154.      # "Pausing...";
155.      Win32::Daemon::State( SERVICE_PAUSED );
156.      $PrevState = SERVICE_PAUSED;
157.      Write( "Paused\n" );
158.      next;
159.    }
160.    elsif( SERVICE_CONTINUE_PENDING == $State )
161.    {
162.      # "Resuming...";
163.      Win32::Daemon::State( SERVICE_RUNNING );
164.      $PrevState = SERVICE_RUNNING;
165.      Write( "Resumed\n" );
166.      next;
167.    }
168.    elsif( SERVICE_STOP_PENDING == $State )
169.    {
170.      # "Stopping...";
171.      Win32::Daemon::State( SERVICE_STOPPED );
172.      $PrevState = SERVICE_STOPPED;
173.      Write( "Stopped\n" );
174.      next;
175.    }
176.    elsif( SERVICE_PAUSED == $State )
177.    {
178.      # The service is paused so don't do anything
179.      $PrevState = SERVICE_PAUSED;
180.    }
181.    elsif( SERVICE_RUNNING == $State )
182.    {
183.      # The service is running as normal...
184.      my $Time = time();
185.      if( $Time >= $NextTime )
186.      {
187.        ProcessEvents( $Time );
188.        $NextTime = $Time + $CALENDAR_PROCESS_TIME_INTERVAL;
189.      }
190.      $PrevState = SERVICE_RUNNING;
191.    }
192.    else
193.    {
194.      Write( "Received unknown state: $State\n" );
195.      Win32::Daemon::State( $PrevState );
196.    }
197.    sleep( $SERVICE_SLEEP_TIME );
198. }
```

```
199.
200. Win32::Daemon::StopService() unless( $Config{console} );
201.
202. sub ProcessEvents
203. {
204.   my( $Time ) = @_;
205.   my %TimeLimit = (
206.      earliest=> GetTimestringFromArray( GetTimeFromStamp( $Time ) ),
207.      latest => GetTimestringFromArray(
208.                   GetTimeFromStamp( $Time
209.                   + $TIME_CONSIDERATION_INTERVAL ) )
210.   );
211.
212.   Debug( " Processing events\n" );
213.   foreach my $Profile ( keys( %PROFILES ) )
214.   {
215.     my $Mapi = $PROFILES{$Profile}->{mapi};
216.
217.     next if( ! defined $Mapi );
218.     foreach my $FolderType ( @FOLDERS )
219.     {
220.       my $Folder = $Mapi->GetDefaultFolder( $FolderType );
221.       my $Messages = $Folder->Messages();
222.       my $Filter = $Messages->{Filter};
223.       my $Fields = $Filter->{Fields};
224.
225.       # Remove any filters
226.       $Fields->Delete();
227.       $Filter->{Not} = 0;
228.       $Filter->{Or} = 0;
229.
230.       # Filter only on calendar messages (there are usually many
231.       # more of them than tasks)
232.       if( CdoDefaultFolderCalendar == $FolderType )
233.       {
234.         # Note: The End and Start dates are backward. CDO bug.
235.         # Note2: Both dates must be specified. CDO bug.
236.         # Note3: Only both dates can be set. Setting other filter
237.         #     properties causes a "Too complex" error. CDO bug.
238.         #
239.         # If the beginning time AND the ending time are between
240.         # these timestamps then the message will be presented to
241.         # us.
242.
243.         Debug( " Start date: $TimeLimit{earliest}\n" );
244.         Debug( " Stop date: $TimeLimit{latest}\n" );
245.
246.         $Fields->Add( CdoPR_START_DATE, $TimeLimit{latest} );
247.         $Fields->Add( CdoPR_END_DATE, $TimeLimit{earliest} );
248.         Debug( " Processing Calendar...\n" );
249.       }
250.       elsif( CdoDefaultFolderTasks == $FolderType )
251.       {
```

continues ▶

Example 8.14   *continued*

```
252.          Debug( " Processing Tasks...\n" );
253.        }
254.
255.        # Cycle through and consider each message
256.        Debug( " Total messages to consider: '"
257.              . $Messages->Count() . "'\n" );
258.        foreach my $Message ( in $Messages )
259.        {
260.          my @NotifyDate;
261.          my $ID = $Message->{ID};
262.          my $MessageContent;
263.
264.
265.          # If we have already processed this message then
266.          # don't bother trying again.
267.          next if( $PROCESSED{$ID} );
268.
269.          Debug( " Considering: $Message->{Subject}\n" );
270.          if( 1 == scalar ( @NotifyDate = GetNotifyDate( $Message ) ) )
271.          {
272.            # We could not find a reminder date/time for the message
273.            next;
274.          }
275.
276.          # Figure out when the event is scheduled for
277.          my $NotifyTime;
278.          $NotifyTime = timelocal( @NotifyDate );
279.
280.          Debug( "  Notify on " . localtime( $NotifyTime ) . "'\n" );
281.
282.          # If the reminder notification time has not yet come
283.          # then skip to the next message
284.          next if( $NotifyTime > $Time );
285.
286.          $MessageContent = GetMessageContent( $Message );
287.          DisplayMessage( $MessageContent );
288.
289.          # Send out a page
290.          if( ( ! $Config{nopage} )
291.                && ( SendMessage($PROFILES{$Profile},
292.                $MessageContent ) ) )
293.          {
294.            # This block is dangerous. It is here to show
295.            # what can be done but it's commented out to
296.            # prevent accidental modifications to the
297.            # scheduled events on the Exchange server.
298.            # Uncomment at your own risk!
299.
300.            # Turn off this message's reminder
301.            # $Message->{ReminderSet} = 0;
302.
303.            # Update the message with the new reminder state,
```

```perl
304.             # make it permanent and refresh the message
305.             # $Message->Update( 1, 1 );
306.
307.             Write( "   Page was sent on " . localtime() . ".\n" );
308.         }
309.         else
310.         {
311.             # The page failed so leave the reminder set
312.             # so we have another chance at it
313.             Write( "   No page was sent out on" . localtime() . ".\n" );
314.         }
315.
316.         # Remember that the message has been successfully processed
317.         $PROCESSED{$ID} = time();
318.         Write( "\n" );
319.         }
320.     }
321.   }
322.   Debug( " End of processing.\n" );
323. }
324.
325. sub GetMessageContent
326. {
327.   my( $Message ) = @_;
328.   my %Content = (
329.     subject => $Message->{Subject},
330.   );
331.   ( $Content{type} ) = ( $Message->{Type} =~ /([^.]*)$/ );
332.
333.   if( $Message->{Type} eq "IPM.Appointment" )
334.   {
335.     $Content{location} = $Message->{Location};
336.     $Content{time} = $Message->{StartTime};
337.
338.   }
339.   elsif( $Message->{Type} eq "IPM.Task" )
340.   {
341.     my $Date = $Message->{Fields}->Item( $PROPERTY{task_due_date} );
342.     if( defined $Date )
343.     {
344.       $Content{time} = $Date->{Value};
345.     }
346.   }
347.   $Content{name} = $Message->{Session}->{CurrentUser}->{Name};
348.   $Content{profile} = $Message->{Session}->{Name};
349.   return( \%Content );
350. }
351.
352. # Determine the notify date (in an localtime array format)
353. # for a message
354. sub GetNotifyDate
355. {
```

continues ▶

Example 8.14 *continued*

```
356.    my( $Message ) = @_;
357.    my( $Time, @Date );
358.
359.    if( $Message->{Type} eq "IPM.Appointment" )
360.    {
361.      if( $Message->{ReminderSet} )
362.      {
363.        Debug( "  Reminder flag is set.\n" );
364.        @Date = GetTimeFromString( $Message->{StartTime} );
365.        $Time = timelocal( @Date )
366.                  - ( $Message->{ReminderMinutesBeforeStart} * 60 );
367.        @Date = localtime( $Time );
368.      }
369.    }
370.    elsif( $Message->{Type} eq "IPM.Task" )
371.    {
372.      my $ReminderFlag = $Message->{Fields}->Item(
373.                         $PROPERTY{task_reminder_flag} );
374.      my $ReminderDate = $Message->{Fields}->Item(
375.                         $PROPERTY{task_reminder_date} );
376.
377.      next unless( defined $ReminderDate && defined $ReminderFlag );
378.      if( $ReminderFlag->{Value} )
379.      {
380.        Debug( "  Reminder flag is set.\n" );
381.        @Date = GetTimeFromString( $ReminderDate->{Value} );
382.      }
383.    }
384.    return( ( scalar @Date )? @Date : undef );
385. }
386.
387.
388. # Convert a MAPI date/time stamp into a date array
389. sub GetTimeFromString
390. {
391.    my( $Time ) = @_;
392.    my @Temp =
393.      ( $Time =~ m#(\d+)/(\d+)/(\d+)\s+(\d+):(\d+):(\d+)\s+(AM|PM)#i );
394.    my @Date = (
395.      0,
396.      $Temp[4],        # Minute
397.      $Temp[3],        # Hour
398.      $Temp[1],        # Day
399.      $Temp[0] - 1,    # Month
400.      $Temp[2] - 1900, # Year
401.    );
402.    # Convert from 12 to 24 hour time formats
403.    $Date[2] -= 12;
404.    $Date[2] += 12 if( $Date[2] < 0 );
405.    $Date[2] += 12 if( uc $Temp[6] eq "PM" );
406.
407.    return( @Date );
```

```perl
408. }
409.
410. # Convert from a Perl timestamp to a date array
411. sub GetTimeFromStamp
412. {
413.    my( $Time ) = @_;
414.    my @Date = localtime( $Time );
415.
416.    # Month
417.    $Date[4]++;
418.    # Year
419.    $Date[5] += 1900;
420.    return( @Date );
421. }
422.
423. sub GetTimestringFromArray
424. {
425.    my( @Date ) = @_;
426.    return( sprintf( "%2d/%02d/%04d %2d:%02d:00 %s",
427.            $Date[4],
428.            $Date[3],
429.            $Date[5],
430.            $Date[2],
431.            $Date[1],
432.            ( ( $Date[2] < 12)? "AM" : "PM" ) ) );
433. }
434.
435. sub DisplayMessage
436. {
437.    my( $Message ) = @_;
438.    Write( " $Message->{type} Reminder: $Message->{time}\n" );
439.    Write( "   User: $Message->{name}\n" );
440.    Write( "   Subject: $Message->{subject}\n" );
441. }
442.
443. sub SendMessage
444. {
445.    my( $Profile, $MessageContent ) = @_;
446.    my $Result = 0;
447.
448.    if( my $Pager = new Net::Pager )
449.    {
450.      my $Body = "";
451.
452.      $Body .= "T: $MessageContent->{time}"
453.                     if( defined $MessageContent->{time} );
454.      $Body .= " L: $MessageContent->{location}"
455.                     if( defined $MessageContent->{location} );
456.
457.      $Result = $Pager->sendPage(
458.                  $Profile->{pager_service},
459.                  $Profile->{pager_id},
460.                  $Config{display},
```

continues ▶

Example 8.14   *continued*

```
461.                $Body,
462.                undef );
463.   }
464.   return( $Result );
465. }
466.
467. sub GetServiceConfig
468. {
469.   my $ScriptPath = join( "", Win32::GetFullPathName( $0 ) );
470.   my %Hash = (
471.     name    =>  $Config{service},
472.     display =>  $Config{display},
473.     path    =>  $^X,
474.     user    =>  $Config{account},
475.     password =>  $Config{password},
476.     parameters => "\"$ScriptPath\"",
477.     description => "Send out pages to remind you of scheduled events.",
478.   );
479.   $Hash{parameters} .= " -debug" if( $Config{debug} );
480.   $Hash{parameters} .= " -console" if( $Config{console} );
481.   $Hash{parameters} .= " -nopage" if( $Config{nopage} );
482.   return( \%Hash );
483. }
484.
485. sub InstallService
486. {
487.   my $ServiceConfig = GetServiceConfig();
488.
489.   if( Win32::Daemon::CreateService( $ServiceConfig ) )
490.   {
491.     print "The $ServiceConfig->{display} was successfully installed.\n";
492.   }
493.   else
494.   {
495.     print "Failed to add the $ServiceConfig->{display} service.\n";
496.     print "Error: " . GetError() . "\n";
497.   }
498. }
499.
500. sub RemoveService
501. {
502.   my $ServiceConfig = GetServiceConfig();
503.
504.   if( Win32::Daemon::DeleteService( $ServiceConfig->{name} ) )
505.   {
506.     print "The $ServiceConfig->{display} was successfully removed.\n";
507.   }
508.   else
509.   {
510.     print "Failed to remove the $ServiceConfig->{display} service.\n";
511.             print "Error: " . GetError() . "\n";
512.   }
```

```
513. }
514.
515. sub GetError
516. {
517.   return( Win32::FormatMessage( Win32::Daemon::GetLastError() ) );
518. }
519.
520. sub Debug
521. {
522.   Write( @_ ) if( $Config{debug} );
523. }
524.
525. sub Write
526. {
527.   my( $Message ) = @_;
528.   if( defined $Buffer )
529.   {
530.     $Buffer->Write( $Message );
531.   }
532.   else
533.   {
534.     print $Message;
535.   }
536.   if( fileno( LOG ) )
537.   {
538.     print LOG $Message;
539.   }
540. }
541.
542. sub Configure
543. {
544.   my( $Config ) = @_;
545.   my $WarnSub = $SIG{__WARN__};
546.   undef $SIG{__WARN__};
547.   Getopt::Long::Configure( "prefix_pattern=(-|\/)" );
548.   GetOptions( $Config,
549.     qw(
550.       install
551.       remove
552.       account=s
553.       password=s
554.       display=s
555.       name=s
556.       debug
557.       console
558.       nopage
559.       help
560.     )
561.   );
562.   $SIG{__WARN__} = $WarnSub;
563. }
564.
```

continues ▶

Example 8.14 *continued*

```
565. sub Syntax
566. {
567.   my( $Script ) = ( $0 =~ /([^\\]*?)$/ );
568.   my $Whitespace = " " x length( $Script );
569.   print<< "EOT";
570.
571. Syntax:
572. $Script [-install [-account Account] [-password Password]
573. $Whitespace [-display DisplayName] [-name ServiceName] ]
574. $Whitespace [-remove]
575. $Whitespace [-debug]
576. $Whitespace [-console]
577. $Whitespace [-help]
578.
579.     -install..........Installs the service.
580.         -account.......Specifies what account the service runs under.
581.                        Default: Local System
582.         -password......Specifies the password the service uses.
583.         -display......Specifies the display name of the service.
584.                        Default: $Config{display_name}
585.         -name.........Specifies the name of the service.
586.                        Default: $Config{service_name}
587.     -remove...........Removes the service.
588.     -debug............Show debug info. The log file will grow
589.                        quite large
590.     -console..........Run as a console application (not as a
591.                        service).
592.     -nopage...........Do not send out pages.
593. EOT
594. }
595.
596. sub Quit
597. {
598.   foreach my $Profile ( keys( %PROFILES ) )
599.   {
600.     if( defined $PROFILES{$Profile}->{mapi} )
601.     {
602.       my $Mapi = $PROFILES{$Profile}->{mapi};
603.       Write( "Logging out $Mapi->{Name}\n" );
604.       $Mapi->Logoff();
605.       undef $PROFILES{$Profile}->{mapi};
606.     }
607.   }
608. }
609.
610. END
611. {
612.   Quit();
611. }
```

Conclusion

Win32 services have always been an important aspect of the successful operation of Windows machines. These services can perform functions that are active from boot time till shutdown and without requiring any user intervention.

This chapter provided sample scripts that install, remove, and reconfigure services. It also explained how services work and some problems that services face.

9

ADSI and WMI

Microsoft has introduced two rather exciting technologies: the Active
Directory Services Interface (ADSI) and Windows Management
Instrumentation (WMI). Even though they are related, they are also radi-
cally different and have different purposes. These technologies are tightly
integrated with Windows 2000 but are available on the Windows NT 4.0
platform as well. Learning to use these technologies will not be wasted
effort because they will be around for a long time to come.

ADSI and WMI are actually abstractions of other technologies—that is,
they provide functionality that sits on top of other technologies and that
provides an abstracted interface into them. Although this sounds quite chal-
lenging, the truth of the matter is that both ADSI and WMI are extremely
simple to understand and use. This is good news because you can leverage
ADSI and WMI to seriously simplify your network administration activities.

Active Directory Services Interface

The concept of *Directory Services* has always been a part of Microsoft operating systems. A Directory Service (DS) is a type of repository where information is stored. You can think of it as a large database that you fill with
information relevant to your network. You might use a DS to associate a
printer with a particular name or user account with a set of permissions.
A program could then query the database to discover what permissions that
particular user has.

Consider a Web proxy server. Say that all users must go through this
proxy server to surf Web sites on the Internet. The proxy server could query
the DS database to discover whether users are authorized to access the
Internet, thus preventing unauthorized users from accessing Web sites.

Several different variations of DSs are available, ranging from X.500 to Novell's NDS to Lotus Notes. Not to be left out of the rush to directory service nirvana, Microsoft rolled out its own version. The marketing wizards dubbed it the *Active Directory Services* (ADS). Simply stated, ADS is Microsoft's version of a DS.

The problem, however, is that each DS has its own unique interface. Therefore, it is difficult for a program to interact with different DSs without having to be intimate with each DS interface. It also makes it difficult for a program to be "open-ended." As new DSs become available, a program has to be redesigned to incorporate the new DS interfaces.

In an attempt to untangle the mess of DS interfaces, Microsoft implemented the Active Directory Services Interface, which is essentially an abstract interface into various directory services. ADSI provides an architecture that exposes simple functions that are common to most directory services. It provides a simple API that a program can use to interact with any DS.

ADSI has the type of architecture that other DSs can "plug" into. The DS therefore can expose its services to any program willing to interact with ADSI. Each DS must supply a "provider" component that acts as a bridge between ADSI and the DS, which enables a program to speak ADSI yet still interact with various different directory services through their respective provider components. Other abstraction APIs, such as ODBC, work similarly.

One of the inviting aspects of ADSI is that it is automation-compliant. This means that any program that can interact with the IDispatch COM interface can use ADSI. It therefore is a perfect Perl technology. When you use the Win32::OLE extension, any Perl script can interact with any DS that has an installed ADSI provider.

It is important to draw a distinction between ADS and ADSI. Active Directory Services is just a DS, whereas the Active Directory Services Interface is an abstract interface into any one of many different DSs (including ADS) through their providers. It is possible for a machine to have ADSI installed but not ADS.

How Do You Get ADSI?

Windows 2000 and Windows ME both come with ADSI components already installed. However, the ADS runs only on the Windows 2000 Server platforms (Server, Advanced Server, and Data Center).

Microsoft also provides ADSI for Windows NT 4.0, Windows 98, and Windows 95. You can download it from the MS Web site at `http://www.microsoft.com/adsi/`.

Learning About ADSI

Learning the ADSI interface is fairly easy. However, doing so without a good guide can be a bit daunting at first. I find two resources particularly useful for learning about ADSI. The first resource is the ADSI help files. You can download them from Microsoft's ADSI site. Check out `http://www.microsoft.com/adsi/` and look around for the ADSI Help Files download link.

Another good place to find documentation is Microsoft's Developer Network (MSDN). Its ADSI documentation is online under the MSDN Win32 API documentation at `http://msdn.microsoft.com/library/`.

After you access this link, you need to drill down in the table of contents (in the left frame). Select Platform SDK and then Network and Directory Services. Finally, select the Active Directory, ADSI, and Directory Services link.

For a hard-copy version of ADSI documentation, check out the book *Windows NT/2000: ADSI Scripting for System Administration* by Thomas Eck (New Riders). Not only does it cover the history of ADSI, but it also explains how ADSI works in real-world settings. It includes many sample scripts that illustrate how ADSI works and are useful for any administrator. All the scripts are coded in Visual Basic, but converting them into Perl is a trivial task. Many of the ADSI scripts in this chapter are Perl versions of those found in Thomas's book.

Namespaces

ADSI defines unique scopes for a given DS provider called a *namespace*. Consider a namespace to be a context in which functionality is related. For example, if a DS provider called MyDS allows you to modify printer settings, those printer settings are located in the MyDS namespace.

Each namespace defines its own way to represent data. For example, one DS provider may refer to a user by a username, whereas another provider may refer to a user by a user ID. When a program interacts with different namespaces, it needs to know how each namespace manages its own data.

ADSI allows a program to specify which namespace (or DS provider) it wants to interact with by defining an *ADsPath* (Active Directory Services Path) string. All ADsPath strings must begin with the name of an ADSI provider. Some of the standard provider prefix strings are listed in Table 9.1.

Table 9.1   Common ADSI Provider ADsPath Prefixes

ADsPath String (Provider Namespace)	Description
ADs:	Active Directory Service. This provider interacts with Windows 2000's Active Directory Services. It can also interact with Active Directory installed on a non-Windows 2000 machine (such as Microsoft Exchange and Site servers).
WinNT:	Windows NT directory service. This provider interacts with the Windows NT domain and user account managers. It can also interact with Windows 2000 directory services, although it doesn't take full advantage of Windows 2000's Active Directory Services.
LDAP:	Lightweight Directory Access Protocol (LDAP). This provider uses the LDAP protocol to interact with any LDAP-enabled directory service (including Active Directory Services).
NDS:	Novell Directory Service.
IIS:	The IIS metabase configuration database. This provides access into IIS's configuration database (called the *metabase*).

The ADsPath is case-sensitive, and its syntax changes depending on what provider is specified. A programmer has to refer to the provider's documentation to determine how to use it.

Because each provider performs functions that relate only to its namespace, understanding what information and functionality each namespace can provide is important. Additionally, understanding the meaning of a namespace's properties and what syntax to use is imperative. This is where the schema comes in.

Schemas

A *schema* is a sort of dictionary of terms that a particular DS provider uses. Each property that a DS exposes is accessed as an ADSI COM object. The schema enables an application to learn what each object represents. The schema for a provider describes each class that the provider implements.

Classes

ADSI providers expose a series of different *classes*. These classes are similar to object-oriented C++ or Perl classes. An ADSI class is simply a group of properties and methods. One class, for example, may represent a user account in a domain. This particular class has a property for the username and password. It also may have a method for renaming the user account.

Binding

A Perl script interacts with ADSI classes by *binding* to a particular object. This binding simply means that ADSI produced a COM object that represents a particular class. The ADsPath string is also known as a *binding string*. This string represents the path an ADSI provider will use to bind to a particular ADSI object. Each object is based on an ADSI class that exists in an ADSI namespace.

When a script requests such an ADSI COM object, the ADSI provider must determine what type of class the script is attempting to bind to, which can result in time delays. Say that a Perl script implements the following line:

```
$ADSIObj = Win32::OLE->GetObject( "WinNT://SomeName" );
```

The WinNT: provider must determine what SomeName is—a computer or a domain name. It might do so by first querying for a domain called SomeName. If that query fails, then it tries to access a machine called \\SomeName. Of course, this entire process could impose a blocking delay. In this case, the binding to the domain or computer class is very inefficient. The WinNT: provider allows a request to specify what class to bind to. You make this request by specifying a comma followed by the class name like this:

```
$ADSIObj = Win32::OLE->GetObject( "WinNT://SomeName,computer" );
```

In this case, the ADSI provider knows that the script is attempting to bind to the computer class. The provider can quickly instantiate the appropriate class.

In the previous example, the AdsPath referred to a particular object that is interpreted as either a network domain or a network machine. Either way, the provider component recognizes that the path is to something that is a networked object. Sometimes, however, a provider's syntax can make a request vague and undecipherable. Consider this request:

```
$ADSIObj = Win32::OLE->GetObject( "WinNT://SomeName/JOEL" );
```

In this case, it is not clear what SomeName and JOEL are. SomeName could be either a domain or a computer. JOEL could be a computer in the SomeName domain, or it could be a user, local group, or global group in either the SomeName domain or the SomeName computer.

You can clarify this ambiguity by specifying which class the object refers to:

```
$ADSIObj = Win32::OLE->GetObject( "WinNT://SomeName/JOEL,user" );
```

Or you can break out the request into multiple requests:

```
$ADSIObj = Win32::OLE->GetObject( "WinNT://SomeName,computer" );
$User = $ADSIObj->GetObject( "User", "JOEL" );
```

In the previous example, notice that the ADsPath string specified the computer class. This string was used to resolve any naming conflicts that might arise if both a SomeName domain and a SomeName computer exist. Likewise, you usually can discover the correct ADSI object faster if you specify the class.

Using ADSI

When a Perl script uses ADSI, it must load the Win32::OLE extension. The script requests an ADSI COM object by calling the extension's GetObject() function. If the request is valid, the resulting ADSI COM object represents the namespace from the specified ADSI provider. The following is an example of such a request:

```
$AdsiObject = Win32::OLE->GetObject( "WinNT://MyDomain" );
```

Notice that the ADsPath ("WinNT://MyDomain") in this case represents the WinNT: provider. It could have just as well been another provider such as LDAP: or IIS:.

For the sake of simplicity, the ADSI examples in this chapter use the WinNT: and IIS: providers.

Discovering the ADSI providers

One of the easiest tasks that ADSI can perform is to enumerate the different ADSI providers installed on a local machine. Example 9.1 demonstrates this capability by binding to the ADs: namespace and then enumerating each provider.

Example 9.1   *Displaying the ADSI Providers*

```
01. use Win32::OLE qw( in );
02.
03. $ADsPath = "ADs:";
04. if( $DS = Win32::OLE->GetObject( $ADsPath ) )
05. {
06.   my $iCount = 0;
07.   print "This machine has the following ADSI providers installed:\n";
08.   foreach my $Provider ( in( $DS ) )
09.   {
10.     print ++$iCount . ") $Provider->{Name}\n";
11.   }
12. }
```

Discovering Classes and Properties

Reading the documentation that comes with an ADSI provider can go a long way toward helping you discover what classes and properties it exposes. However, in some situations, a function might return an unknown ADSI object.

Example 9.2 demonstrates how a Perl script can programmatically discover what classes and properties an ADSI provider exposes. The script starts by requesting an ADSI COM object. By default, it requests a WinNT: bound domain class object. However, you can pass in any valid ADSI path. Line 5 decides what ADSI path to use.

Next, line 6 binds to the ADSI COM object. Line 9 binds to the ADSI COM object's class schema. Now that you have the schema object, you can interrogate it to discover what properties and subclasses it exposes. You do so by calling into the script's ProcessClass() function. The ProcessClass() function starts by requesting a schema object that represents the passed-in schema's parent. It does so because a class' schema describes what properties the class has, but each property's syntax is defined in the class' parent class. For this reason, line 20 requests the schema object's parent object.

Lines 22 through 25 get the class' list of mandatory and optional parameters. Line 27 discovers what subclasses the ADSI COM object can hold (what ADSI refers to as "containment"). Lines 35 through 38 then enumerate each of these subclasses and print them.

Lines 47 through 59 enumerate each of the class' properties and request the respective property object from the parent schema object (line 54). The property object's name and syntax are then written to the screen. Finally, lines 62 through 73 walk through all the subclasses and repeats the entire process on each one.

Tip

It is not uncommon for one ADSI class to contain subclasses that are of the same type. For example, you might have a directory class that can contain directory subclasses. This is why lines 28 and 67 were added to Example 9.2. They keep track of which classes have been processed. This prevents endless recursion on such classes. ◆

Example 9.2 *Programmatically Discovering ADSI Class Properties*

```
01. use Win32;
02. use Win32::OLE qw( in );
03.
04. $Domain = Win32::DomainName();
05. $ADsPath = "WinNT://$Domain" unless( $ADsPath = shift @ARGV );
06. if( my $ADSIObject = Win32::OLE->GetObject( $ADsPath ) )
07. {
08.   print "Examining the '$ADsPath' ADSI class...\n";
09.   if( my $DSSchema = Win32::OLE->GetObject( $ADSIObject->{Schema} ) )
10.   {
11.     ProcessClass( $DSSchema );
12.   }
```

continues ▶

Example 9.2   *continued*

```
13. }
14.
15. sub ProcessClass
16. {
17.   my( $DSSchema ) = @_;
18.   local $PropType;
19.   # Get the class' parent class...
20.   my $ParentClass = Win32::OLE->GetObject( $DSSchema->{Parent} );
21.   # Get this class' properties...
22.   my %Properties = (
23.         mandatory   => $DSSchema->{MandatoryProperties},
24.         optional    => $DSSchema->{OptionalProperties}
25.   );
26.   # Go and get all sub classes that this class may have...
27.   my $SubClasses = $DSSchema->{Containment};
28.   $ClassList{$DSSchema->{Name}} = 1;
29.   print "Class:  $DSSchema->{Name}\n";
30.   if( scalar @{$SubClasses} )
31.   {
32.     $~ = SUBCLASS_HEADER_FORMAT;
33.     write;
34.     $~ = SUBCLASS_FORMAT;
35.     map
36.     {
37.       write;
38.     } @{$SubClasses};
39.     print "\n";
40.   }
41.
42.   $~ = PROPERTY_HEADER_FORMAT;
43.   write;
44.   $~ = PROPERTY_FORMAT;
45.
46.   # Display all properties...
47.   foreach $PropType ( keys( %Properties ) )
48.   {
49.     my $PropList = $Properties{$PropType};
50.     next unless( scalar @{$PropList} );
51.     foreach my $PropName ( @{$PropList} )
52.     {
53.       local $Property;
54.       if( $Property = $ParentClass->GetObject( "Property", $PropName ) )
55.       {
56.         write;
57.       }
58.     }
59.   }
60.   print "\n";
61.
62.   if( scalar @{$SubClasses} )
63.   {
```

```
64.    foreach my $Class ( @{$SubClasses} )
65.    {
66.      my $ADsPath = $DSSchema->{Parent} . "/$Class";
67.      next if( defined $ClassList{$Class} );
68.      if( my $ADSIObj = Win32::OLE->GetObject( $ADsPath ) )
69.      {
70.        ProcessClass( $ADSIObj );
71.      }
72.    }
73.  }
74.  print "\n";
75. }
76.
77. format SUBCLASS_HEADER_FORMAT =
78.    Subclasses
79.    --------------------------
80. .
81. format SUBCLASS_FORMAT =
82.    @<<<<<<<<<<<<<<<<<<<<<<<<<<<
83.    $_
84. .
85. format PROPERTY_HEADER_FORMAT =
86.    Property    Name                                Type
87.    ----------  ------------------------------      ----------
88. .
89. format PROPERTY_FORMAT =
90.    @<<<<<<<<< @<<<<<<<<<<<<<<<<<<<<<<<<<<<<<< @<<<<<<<<<
91.    $PropType, $Property->{Name}, $Property->{Syntax}
92. .
```

Discovering Domains

Procuring the list of available domains that a machine can see is relatively simple. To do so, you bind to the root of the WinNT: ADSI provider's name-space and then enumerate each object. Example 9.3 does exactly this.

Line 4 requests an ADSI COM object that is bound to the WinNT: name-space. Lines 8 through 11 perform the actual enumeration, and line 10 has the distinction of printing the name of the domain.

Note

The WinNT: *provider does not seem to differentiate between NT domains and workgroups. Example 9.3 will print out all available domains as well as all available workgroups. There does not seem to be any simple way to determine whether a domain reported by* WinNT: *is indeed a domain or a workgroup, other than testing for valid domain properties (see Example 9.4).* ◆

Example 9.3 *Displaying Available Domains*

```
01. use Win32::OLE qw( in );
02.
03. $ADsPath = "WinNT:";
04. if( $AD = Win32::OLE->GetObject( $ADsPath ) )
05. {
06.   my $iCount = 0;
07.   print "This machine can see the following domains:\n";
08.   foreach my $Domain ( in( $AD ) )
09.   {
10.     print ++$iCount . ") $Domain->{Name}\n";
11.   }
12. }
```

In the case of Example 9.3, only the domain names are displayed. Although this script displays only the names of each domain, the Domain class contains several other properties that can be printed as well.

If you don't know what properties the Domain object has, you can use a script to discover them. Example 9.4 does this by adding a GetProperties() subroutine. The routine, which is defined in lines 30 through 44, works much like Example 9.2's ProcessClass() function. It obtains the schema for the given ADSI COM object (line 35). It then accesses the array of mandatory and optional properties that the schema defines. Lines 15 through 26 enumerate each property and display their values. Lines 19 through 24 check to see if the domain object represents the valid NT domain or a workgroup.

Example 9.4 *Displaying Available Domains and Their Properties*

```
01. use Win32::OLE qw( in );
02.
03. $ADsPath = "WinNT:";
04. if( $AD = Win32::OLE->GetObject( $ADsPath ) )
05. {
06.   my $iCount = 0;
07.   my $Schema;
08.   my $PropertyList;
09.
10.   print "This machine can see the following domains:\n";
11.   foreach my $Domain ( in( $AD ) )
12.   {
13.     $PropertyList = GetProperties( $Domain ) unless( ref $PropertyList );
14.     print ++$iCount . ") $Domain->{Name}\n";
15.     foreach my $Property ( @{$PropertyList} )
16.     {
17.       # Check that $Domain is indeed a domain and not
18.       # a workgroup.
19.       if( ! defined $Domain->{$Property} )
20.       {
```

```
21.          print "\tCan not query domain properties.\n";
22.          print "\tThis must be a workgroup.\n";
23.          last;
24.        }
25.      print "\t $Property: $Domain->{$Property}\n";
26.    }
27.  }
28. }
29.
30. sub GetProperties
31. {
32.   my( $Obj ) = @_;
33.   my @Properties;
34.
35.   if( my $Schema = Win32::OLE->GetObject( $Obj->{Schema} ) )
36.   {
37.     foreach my $PropList ( $Schema->{MandatoryProperties},
38.                            $Schema->{OptionalProperties} )
39.     {
40.       push( @Properties, @{$PropList} ) if( defined $PropList );
41.     }
42.   }
43.   return( \@Properties );
44. }
```

Impersonation

So far, the examples in this chapter have been pretty straightforward. However, they all assume that the user running the Perl script has permission to interact with the ADSI COM object. If the user is an administrator, this assessment is probably accurate. However, when a different user account is required, ADSI provides a mechanism that enables the user to impersonate another user, provided that she has the correct credentials.

A Perl script can request an ADSI COM object bound to the top class in a given ADSI provider namespace. The resulting class object exposes a method called OpenDSObject(). This method accepts an ADSI path, along with a user ID, password, and options.

Example 9.5 displays all ADSI objects found within a specified ADSI path. By default, the path is WinNT://DOMAINNAME, where DOMAINNAME is the name of the local machine's domain. You can change the ADSI path by passing one in from the command line. For example,

```
perl DisplayADSIObject.pl WinNT://MyDomain
```

In this case, the MyDomain domain is specified. Any valid ADSI path can be passed in such as:

```
perl DisplayADSIObject.pl WinNT://MyDomain/MyComputer/Browser,service
```

This would select the Browser service from the computer called MyComputer in the domain called MyDomain.

This script displays all objects that the specified path contains. For example, if you pass in a path to a domain (as in WinNT://MyDomain), it returns a list of all users, groups, and machines that make up the domain.

The interesting thing about this script is that it enables a user to impersonate another user. The user can do so by specifying the -u and -p switches, as in this example:

```
perl DisplayADSIObject.pl -u Administrator -p MyPassword
```

Optionally, the user can pass in a list of filters using the -f switches. If any filters are specified, only objects that match one of these filters are displayed. For example, the following command displays only user accounts and local groups from the computer called MyMachine:

```
perl DisplayADSIObject.pl -f user -f localgroup WinNT://MyMachine,computer
```

The first thing to notice about Example 9.5 is that line 4 loads the Win32::OLE::Const module, which loads the ADSI type library and all constants associated with it. This point is important because the script uses some of these constants to perform any user impersonation.

The script performs its impersonation magic by providing a GetADSIObject() subroutine. The script calls this function in line 13. Notice that it passes in a reference to the %Config hash. The hash contains all configuration options such as the ADSI path, username, and password.

Line 16 binds to the schema object that represents the ADSI COM object requested in line 13. The binding to the schema object allows the script to discover class information, such as if the object is a container. A container can hold other objects (a directory is a container because it holds files and other directories). If it is a container, a filter can be applied to it.

When a container's objects are enumerated, all the objects are referenced. However, if a filter has been applied to a container, an enumeration of its objects results in only those objects that are of the type specified by the filter. For example, enumerating a domain's objects can yield users, local groups, global groups, and computers. However, if a filter is applied to a domain object that specifies only users and computers, only user and computer objects are enumerated.

Line 24 applies a filter to the ADSI COM object if the user specifies a list of classes to filter. Note that the filter accepts only an array reference. It can be either an anonymous array or (in this case) a reference to an array.

Lines 28 through 31 perform the actual enumeration and display each object held within the ADSI COM object.

Lines 39 through 67 define the GetADSIObject() subroutine. Line 45 tests whether the user specified another user to impersonate. If not, line 64 requests the ADSI object as a script normally would. However, if a user was specified, line 47 determines what ADSI provider was specified and binds to that provider's namespace (line 49). Lines 51 through 56 then call the resulting ADSI provider object's OpenDSObject() method, passing in the ADSI path, username, password, and any parameters. In this case, the ADS_SECURE_AUTHENTICATION, ADS_USE_ENCRYPTION, and ADS_READONLY_SERVER flags are all OR'ed together and are passed in. This results in an attempt to impersonate the specified user using an encrypted and secure (such as Kerberos or NTLM) connection to a domain controller (either primary or backup). If the impersonation fails, line 58 prints out the resulting error.

Example 9.5   *Impersonating Another User with ADSI*

```
01. use Getopt::Long;
02. use Win32;
03. use Win32::OLE qw( in );
04. use Win32::OLE::Const 'Active DS Type Library';
05.
06. $Config{path} = "WinNT://" . Win32::DomainName();
07. Configure( \%Config );
08. if( $Config{help} )
09. {
10.   Syntax();
11.   exit;
12. }
13. if( $AD = GetADSIObject( \%Config ) )
14. {
15.   my $iCount = 0;
16.   my $Schema = Win32::OLE->GetObject( $AD->{Schema} );
17.
18.   # The schema object's Container property shows if we are a container.
19.   if( $Schema->{Container} )
20.   {
21.     if( scalar @{$Config{filter}} )
22.     {
23.       # Apply a filter
24.       $AD->{Filter} = $Config{filter} ;
25.     }
26.     print "This '$AD->{ADsPath}' $AD->{Class} object contains ";
27.     print "the following objects:\n";
28.     foreach my $Object ( in( $AD ) )
29.     {
30.       print ++$iCount . ") $Object->{Name} ($Object->{Class})\n";
31.     }
32.   }
33.   else
34.   {
35.     print "The '$AD->{ADsPath}' is a $AD->{Class} object.\n";
```

continues ▶

Example 9.5 *continued*

```
36.  }
37. }
38.
39. sub GetADSIObject
40. {
41.   my( $Config ) = @_;
42.   my $ADSIObject;
43.   my $ADsPath = $Config->{path};
44.
45.   if( defined $Config->{user} )
46.   {
47.     my( $ADProvider, $Path ) = ( $ADsPath =~ m#^([^/]*)(.*)# );
48.
49.     if( my $AD = Win32::OLE->GetObject( $ADProvider ) )
50.     {
51.       if( ! ( $ADSIObject = $AD->OpenDSObject( $ADsPath,
52.                               $Config->{user},
53.                               $Config->{password},
54.                               ADS_SECURE_AUTHENTICATION
55.                               | ADS_USE_ENCRYPTION
56.                               | ADS_READONLY_SERVER ) ) )
57.       {
58.         print "Error:\n" . Win32::OLE->LastError();
59.       }
60.     }
61.   }
62.   else
63.   {
64.     $ADSIObject = Win32::OLE->GetObject( $ADsPath );
65.   }
66.   return( $ADSIObject );
67. }
68.
69. sub Configure
70. {
71.   my( $Config ) = @_;
72.   my $Result;
73.   Getopt::Long::Configure( "prefix_pattern=(-|\/)" );
74.   $Result = GetOptions( $Config,
75.                         qw(
76.                             user|u=s
77.                             password|p=s
78.                             filter|f=s@
79.                             help|?|h
80.                         ) );
81.   $Config{path} = shift @ARGV if( scalar @ARGV );
82.   $Config{help} = 1 if( ! $Result );
83.   return();
84. }
85.
86. sub Syntax
```

```
87. {
88.    my( $Script ) = ( Win32::GetLongPathName( $0 ) =~ /([^\\]*?)$/ );
89.    my $Whitespace = " " x length( $Script );
90.    print<< "EOT";
91.
92. Syntax:
93.    $Script [-f filter] [-u User] [-p Password] [ADSI Path]
94.       -f Filter.......Name of an ADSI class to filter.  If any filters
95.                       are specified then only objects that are of the
96.                       specified filter types will be displayed.
97.                       This switch can be specified multiple times.
98.       -u User........Name of a user account to impersonate.
99.       -p Password.....Password of the specified user.
100.      ADSI Path.......This is the ADSI path to use.
101.                      Default is WinNT://DOMAIN
102. EOT
103. }
```

User Account Information

To see just how you can use ADSI to query DSs, look at Example 9.6, which displays user configuration information. Just pass in any number of computer, user, or group names. The names passed in can take one of these three formats:

```
account
Domain\account
\\machine\account
```

The account can be the name of a user account or a group name. If you specify a domain, account can be a computer name as well.
For example, the command

```
perl ADSIDumpAccount.pl joel
```

displays information about the default domain's account joel. However, the command

```
perl ADSIDumpAccount.pl \\ServerA\joel
```

displays information about the joel account on the machine \\ServerA—just as the command

```
perl ADSIDumpAccount.pl "MyDomain\Domain Admins"
```

displays information about the Domain Admins group in the MyDomain domain. The script will also interpret other, nonuser accounts, such as:

```
perl ADSIDumpAccount.pl MyDomain\ServerA
```

This will display information for the machine \\ServerA in the MyDomain domain.

Example 9.6   *Using ADSI to Retrieve User Information*

```
01. use Win32;
02. use Win32::OLE;
03.
04. foreach my $Account ( @ARGV )
05. {
06.    my( undef,
07.       $fMachine,
08.       $Domain,
09.       $AccountName ) = ( $Account =~ /((\\\\)?(.*)\\\)?(.*)?$/ );
10.    my $Class = ( "" eq $fMachine )? "domain" : "computer";
11.    $Domain = Win32::DomainName() if( "" eq $Domain );
12.    if( my $AD = Win32::OLE->GetObject( "WinNT://$Domain,$Class" ) )
13.    {
14.       my $User = $AD->GetObject( "", $AccountName ) || next;
15.       my $PropertyList = GetProperties( $User );
16.
17.       print "$User->{Name}\n";
18.       foreach my $Property ( sort( @{$PropertyList} ) )
19.       {
20.         next if( "" eq $Property );
21.         print "\t $Property: $User->{$Property}\n";
22.       }
23.    }
24. }
25.
26. sub GetProperties
27. {
28.    my( $Obj ) = @_;
29.    my @Properties;
30.
31.    if( my $Schema = Win32::OLE->GetObject( $Obj->{Schema} ) )
32.    {
33.       foreach my $PropList ( $Schema->{MandatoryProperties},
34.                              $Schema->{OptionalProperties} )
35.       {
36.         push( @Properties, @{$PropList} ) if( defined $PropList );
37.       }
38.    }
39.    return( \@Properties );
40. }
```

Enabling Accounts

So far, you have learned how to query information by using ADSI. Here, I turn the tables a bit and illustrate how a script can modify settings. At first, you might think that this procedure should be as simple as modifying the parameters on an ADSI COM object. Actually, this assumption is incorrect.

If a script requests an ADSI object, it can query its properties over and over again. This is relatively painless when the ADSI object represents something on the local machine. Every time the script accesses a property, the ADSI provider talks to the local machine, discovers the value of the property, and then returns it to the script. However, if the ADSI object represents, say, a user on a remote machine, the ADSI provider has to request the property's value from across the network. This could have serious performance ramifications, especially if a script processes many objects and properties.

To lessen the impact on a network, ADSI caches various objects and properties. Having this cache means that the provider has to query across the network only once—to get the object the first time it is referenced. This strategy greatly improves network and script performance.

This approach does have one slight problem, though. If you modify an object's properties, they are modified to the cached object. This, again, improves performance, not having to write across the network every time modifications are made. However, a burden is placed on the script to commit any changes that are made.

Committing changes made to an ADSI object is simple. You can commit an ADSI object that has properties by calling the object's SetInfo() method, which forces ADSI to submit the cached object to its repository. This repository can either be a local machine or a remote machine across the network.

Example 9.7 illustrates how an object can be committed from cache. This script enables or disables specified accounts. The magic of this script occurs in line 25, which calls the user object's SetInfo() method. Here, the modifications made to the user account are committed to the user database where the account resides.

Line 26 is for those of us who are paranoid that method calls don't always work. It calls the GetInfo() method, which refreshes the user object in the cache. It forces ADSI to go out across the network and procure the latest properties for the user account. Lines 27 and 28 then check to see whether the property was successfully set.

The script takes any number of accounts in one of the following formats:

```
account
domain\account
\\machine\account
```

The script, by default, enables the specified accounts. If the -d switch is passed in, the accounts are disabled.

Example 9.7   *Enabling and Disabling Accounts*

```
01. use Getopt::Long;
02. use Win32;
03. use Win32::OLE;
04.
05. %Config = (
06.    disable => 0,
07. );
08. Configure( \%Config );
09. print (( $Config{disable} )? "Disabling" : "Enabling" );
10. print " the following accounts:\n";
11.
12. foreach my $Account ( @ARGV )
13. {
14.   my( undef,
15.       $fMachine,
16.       $Domain,
17.       $UserName ) = ( $Account =~ /((\\\\)?(.*)\\\)?(.*)?$/ );
18.   my $Class = ( "" eq $fMachine )? "domain" : "computer";
19.   $Domain = Win32::DomainName() if( "" eq $Domain );
20.   if( my $AD = Win32::OLE->GetObject( "WinNT://$Domain,$Class" ) )
21.   {
22.     my $User = $AD->GetObject( "User", $UserName ) || next;
23.     print "  $Account ";
24.     $User->{AccountDisabled} = $Config{disable};
25.     $User->SetInfo();
26.     $User->GetInfo();
27.     print (( $User->{AccountDisabled} == $Config{disable} )?
28.           "(successful)" : "(failed)" );
29.     print "\n";
30.   }
31. }
32.
33. sub Configure
34. {
35.   my( $Config ) = @_;
36.   my $Result;
37.   Getopt::Long::Configure( "prefix_pattern=(-|\/)" );
38.   $Result = GetOptions( $Config, "disable|d" );
39.   return();
40. }
```

Because administrators will most likely play with Example 9.7, I have included Example 9.8, which displays all disabled user accounts. Line 19 uses the filtering discussed earlier (refer to Example 9.5).

The script can be passed in any number of domain or machine names. By default the script displays accounts that are enabled. You pass in the -d switch to show only disabled accounts. For example,

```
perl ShowEnabled.pl MyDomain \\MyMachine -d
```

displays all accounts that are disabled in the MyDomain domain as well as the
\\MyMachine machine.

Example 9.8   *Displaying All Enabled or Disabled Accounts*

```
01. use Getopt::Long;
02. use Win32;
03. use Win32::OLE qw( in );
04.
05. Configure( \%Config );
06. print "The following accounts are ";
07. print (( $Config{disable} )? "disabled" : "enabled" );
08. print ":\n";
09.
10. push( @ARGV, Win32::DomainName() ) if( ! scalar @ARGV );
11. foreach my $Domain ( @ARGV )
12. {
13.    my( $fMachine,
14.      $Name ) = ( $Domain =~ /(\\\\)?(.*)$/ );
15.    my $Class = ( "" eq $fMachine )? "domain" : "computer";
16.    if( my $AD = Win32::OLE->GetObject( "WinNT://$Name,$Class" ) )
17.    {
18.      # We only want user accounts.
19.      $AD->{Filter} = [ "User" ];
20.      foreach my $User ( in( $AD ) )
21.      {
22.        if( $User->{AccountDisabled} == $Config{disable} )
23.        {
24.          print "  $Domain\\$User->{Name}\n"
25.        }
26.      }
27.    }
28. }
29.
30. sub Configure
31. {
32.    my( $Config ) = @_;
33.    my $Result;
34.    Getopt::Long::Configure( "prefix_pattern=(-|\/)" );
35.    $Result = GetOptions( $Config, "disable|d" );
36.    return();
37. }
```

Disconnecting Network Sessions

ADSI can be a powerful tool for system administrators. Example 9.9 uses
ADSI to display all connected user sessions to a remote machine. This script
accepts machine names in one of the following formats:

```
machine
domain\machine
```

For example,

```
perl ADSIDisplaySessions.pl ServerA MyDomain\ServerB
```

displays all resources on the two specified machines that have been opened remotely.

If a -d switch is passed in, *all* the user sessions are disconnected. This capability can be useful when you're taking down a server, renaming public directories and files, or modifying share properties.

Example 9.9   *Disconnecting Network Sessions*

```
01. use Getopt::Long;
02. use Win32;
03. use Win32::OLE qw( in );
04.
05. Configure( \%Config );
06. foreach my $MachineName ( @ARGV )
07. {
08.   my $ADsPath;
09.   my $Machine;
10.   print "\n$MachineName:\n";
11.   $MachineName =~ s#\\#/#g;
12.   $ADsPath = "WinNT://$MachineName,computer";
13.   next unless( $Machine = Win32::OLE->GetObject( $ADsPath ) );
14.
15.   if( my $FileService = $Machine->GetObject( "FileService",
16.                                              "LanmanServer" ) )
17.   {
18.     my $Sessions = $FileService->{Sessions};
19.     local $Session;
20.
21.     $~ = SESSION_HEADER_FORMAT;
22.     write;
23.     $~ = SESSION_FORMAT;
24.     foreach $Session ( in( $Sessions ) )
25.     {
26.       local %Time = (
27.         connect => FormatTime( $Session->{ConnectTime} ),
28.         idle    => FormatTime( $Session->{IdleTime} )
29.       );
30.       $Sessions->Remove( $Session->{Name} ) if( $Config{disconnect} );
31.       write;
32.     }
33.   }
34. }
35.
36. sub Configure
37. {
38.   my( $Config ) = @_;
39.   my $Result;
40.   Getopt::Long::Configure( "prefix_pattern=(-|\/)" );
41.   $Result = GetOptions( $Config, "disconnect| d" );
```

```
42.    return();
43. }
44.
45. sub FormatTime
46. {
47.     my( $Seconds ) = @_;
48.     my( $Day, $Hour, $Min, $Sec, $Delta );
49.     $Day = int( $Seconds / ( 3600 * 24 ) );
50.     $Delta = $Seconds % ( 3600 * 24 );
51.     $Hour = int( $Delta / 3600 );
52.     $Delta = $Delta % 3600;
53.     $Min = int( $Delta / 60 );
54.     $Sec = int( $Delta % 60 );
55.     return( sprintf( "%02d:%02d:%02d:%02d",
56.                       $Day, $Hour, $Min, $Sec ) );
57. }
58.
59. format SESSION_HEADER_FORMAT =
60. User            Computer         Connection Time Idle Time
61. -------------   --------------   --------------- ----------
62. .
63. format SESSION_FORMAT =
64. @<<<<<<<<<<<<< @<<<<<<<<<<<<<< @<<<<<<<<<<<<<< @<<<<<<<<<<
65. $Session->{User}, $Session->{Computer}, $Time{connect}, $Time{idle}
66. .
```

The IIS ADSI Provider

ADSI comes with several default providers. The provider that interfaces with Microsoft's Internet Information Server (IIS) is called IIS:. Using this particular provider is the only way a Perl script can interact with IIS.

The IIS service has quite a large object model with an impressive number of properties. You can see this for yourself by running Example 9.2 and passing in an ADsPath string that points to a valid IIS server like this:

```
perl DisplayADSIProviderClasses2
```

```
.pl IIS://localmachine
```

This command displays all the IIS classes and properties stemming from the specified path. If you want to examine only the IIS Web server classes, you can specify an ADSI ADsPath of IIS://localmachine/W3SVC. To examine only the FTP classes, use IIS://localmachine/MSFTVSVC.

Discovering IIS Properties

Just like any other ADSI-based class, a script can bind to the ADSI schema object to discover the names of the properties for a particular class. Example 9.10 starts at the path the user specified and displays all the object's properties. It then recurses into each subobject.

This script enables you to specify a particular path. When you pass in the name of a machine, the top-level class and *all* subclasses are displayed. You use the script like this:

```
perl IISWebDump.pl webserver
```

This command displays all properties for the *entire* IIS site on the machine webserver. Here's another example:

```
perl IISWebDump.pl webserver/W3SVC/1
```

This will examine only the properties for the first virtual Web server on the machine webserver.

Note

Interestingly enough, Example 9.10 will not work correctly if it is run on a Windows 2000 machine and attempts to connect to a Windows NT 4.0 machine (or vice versa). This is due to schema differences between the Windows 2000 and NT 4.0 versions of the IIS: metabase. The Microsoft KnowledgeBase article that discusses this can be found at http://support.microsoft.com/support/kb/articles/Q246/5/75.ASP. ◆

This script is surprisingly similar to Example 9.2. The real difference between the two is that Example 9.10 displays each property value. This enables an administrator to quickly see what values his Web server has set.

Example 9.10   *IIS Property Value Dump*

```
01. use Win32;
02. use Win32::OLE qw( in );
03.
04. push( @ARGV, Win32::NodeName() ) if( ! scalar @ARGV );
05. foreach my $Machine ( @ARGV )
06. {
07.   my $ADsPath = "IIS://$Machine";
08.   if( my $IIS = Win32::OLE->GetObject( $ADsPath ) )
09.   {
10.     ProcessObject( $IIS );
11.   }
12. }
13.
14. sub ProcessObject
15. {
16.   my( $Object ) = @_;
17.   local $PropertyName;
18.   my $iCount = 0;
19.
20.   print "\nName:  $Object->{Name}\n";
21.   print "Class: $Object->{Class}\n";
22.   print "Path:  $Object->{ADsPath}\n";
```

```
23.    print "    This object contains the following sub objects:\n";
24.    print "    ---------------------------------------------\n";
25.    foreach my $Sub ( in( $Object ) )
26.    {
27.      print "   ", ++$iCount, ") ";
28.      print "$Sub->{Name} ($Sub->{Class}) $Sub->{ADsPath}\n";
29.    }
30.    print "\n";
31.
32.    $~ = PROPERTY_HEADER_FORMAT;
33.    write;
34.    $~ = PROPERTY_FORMAT;
35.    foreach $PropertyName ( sort( @{GetProperties( $Object )} ) )
36.    {
37.      next if( "" eq $PropertyName );
38.      local( $Value ) = $Object->{$PropertyName};
39.      if( "ARRAY" eq ref $Value )
40.      {
41.        $Value = join( "\n", @{$Value} );
42.      }
43.      write;
44.    }
45.
46.    # Recursively process each sub object
47.    foreach my $Sub ( in( $Object ) )
48.    {
49.      ProcessObject( $Sub );
50.    }
51. }
52.
53. sub GetProperties
54. {
55.    my( $Obj ) = @_;
56.    my @Properties;
57.
58.    if( my $Schema = Win32::OLE->GetObject( $Obj->{Schema} ) )
59.    {
60.      foreach my $PropList ( $Schema->{MandatoryProperties},
61.                             $Schema->{OptionalProperties} )
62.      {
63.        push( @Properties, @{$PropList} ) if( defined $PropList );
64.      }
65.    }
66.    return( \@Properties );
67. }
68.
69. format PROPERTY_HEADER_FORMAT =
70.    Property                      Value
71.    ----------------------------  ------------------------------------
72. .
73. format PROPERTY_FORMAT =
74.    @<<<<<<<<<<<<<<<<<<<<<<<<<<<<  ^<<<<<<<<<<<<<<<<<<<<<<<<<<<<<<<<<<<<
75.    $PropertyName,                $Value
```

continues ▶

Example 9.10   *continued*

```
76. ~                        ^<<<<<<<<<<<<<<<<<<<<<<<<<<<<<<<<<<<<<
77.                          $Value
78. ~                        ^<<<<<<<<<<<<<<<<<<<<<<<<<<<<<<<<<<<<<
79.                          $Value
80. ~                        ^<<<<<<<<<<<<<<<<<<<<<<<<<<<<<<<<<<<<<
81.                          $Value
82. ~                        ^<<<<<<<<<<<<<<<<<<<<<<<<<<<<<<<<<<<<<
83.                          $Value
84. ~                        ^<<<<<<<<<<<<<<<<<<<<<<<<<<<<<<<<<<<<<
85.                          $Value
86. ~                        ^<<<<<<<<<<<<<<<<<<<<<<<<<<<<<<<<<<<<<
87.                          $Value
88. ~                        ^<<<<<<<<<<<<<<<<<<<<<<<<<<<<<<<<<<<<<
89.                          $Value
90. ~                        ^<<<<<<<<<<<<<<<<<<<<<<<<<<<<<<<<<<<<<
91.                          $Value
92. ~                        ^<<<<<<<<<<<<<<<<<<<<<<<<<<<<<<<<<<<<<
93.                          $Value
94. ~                        ^<<<<<<<<<<<<<<<<<<<<<<<<<<<<<<<<<<<<<
95.                          $Value
96. .
```

Modifying IIS Properties

Often you simply need to modify properties on an IIS machine. If you have several different machines to perform this task, using a GUI-based application can be quite time-consuming. Example 9.11 enables you to query or set properties on multiple machines or virtual servers at one time.

The script takes any number of IIS: relative paths that you want to modify. It also takes any number of -p switches, which indicate what properties to query or set. Check out this example:

```
perl IISProperty.pl localhost/W3Svc/1 server2/W3Svc/1
/p ServerComment /p AuthAnonymous
```

This command displays the ServerComment and AuthAnonymous properties for the first virtual Web server on the machine's localhost and server2.

If you specify a -set switch, the script sets the specified properties. In this case, each -p switch needs to specify a format of PropertyName=NewValue. Now consider this example:

```
perl IISProperty.pl localhost/W3Svc/1 server2/MSFTPSvc/1
/p "ServerComment=This is a test!!!" /p AuthAnonymous=0 /set
```

This command sets the ServerComment property on the first virtual Web server on localhost and the first virtual FTP server on server2. However, the AuthAnonymous property is set to 0 (thus turning off anonymous authentication) only on the first virtual Web server on localhost because the property does not exist on FTP servers. (A virtual FTP server's anonymous property is `AllowAnonymous`.)

Example 9.11 *Displaying and Modifying IIS Properties*

```
01. use Getopt::Long;
02. use Win32;
03. use Win32::OLE qw( in );
04.
05. Configure( \%Config );
06. push( @ARGV, Win32::DomainName() ) if( ! scalar @ARGV );
07. foreach my $Machine ( @ARGV )
08. {
09.   my $ADsPath = "IIS://$Machine";
10.   if( my $IIS = Win32::OLE->GetObject( $ADsPath ) )
11.   {
12.     ProcessObject( $IIS );
13.   }
14. }
15.
16. sub ProcessObject
17. {
18.   my( $Object ) = @_;
19.   local $PropertyName;
20.   my $fDirty = 0;
21.
22.   print "\n$Object->{ADsPath}\n";
23.   foreach my $Property ( sort( keys( %{$Config{prop}} ) ) )
24.   {
25.     my $Value = $Config{prop}->{$Property};
26.     next unless( defined $Object->{$Property} );
27.
28.     if( $Config{set} )
29.     {
30.       print " Setting '$Property' => '$Value'\n";
31.       $Object->{$Property} = $Value;
32.       $fDirty = 1;
33.     }
34.     else
35.     {
36.       print " $Property: $Object->{$Property}\n";
37.     }
38.   }
39.   $Object->SetInfo() if( $fDirty );
40. }
41.
42. sub Configure
43. {
44.   my( $Config ) = @_;
45.   my $Result;
46.   Getopt::Long::Configure( "prefix_pattern=(-|\/)" );
47.   $Result = GetOptions( $Config,
48.           qw(
```

continues ▶

Example 9.11 *continued*

```
49.                    propl p=s%
50.                    setl s
51.              ) );
52.  return();
53. }
```

Displaying an IIS Tree

As virtual Web directories and real file system directories are created, renamed, and removed, making sure that a given Web site has all its directories can be difficult. Because Win32 has the TREE.EXE command, it only seems reasonable that something similar would be available for an IIS server.

Conceptually, Figure 9.1 illustrates how such an IIS tree would look. Each node is broken out and displayed relative to its parent node. In this case, the first virtual Web server is displayed. The top-level node is the virtual Web server number 1. Notice that the virtual Web server's comment is displayed in parentheses.

```
---1 (This is a test!!!)
   +---Root
   |   +---Scripts
   |   |   \---Proxy
   |   |        \---w3proxy.dll
   |   +---localstart.asp
   |   +---IISAdmin
   |   +---IISSamples
   |   +---MSADC
   |   +---IISHelp
   |   +---Webpub
   |   +---_vti_pvt
   |   +---_vti_log
   |   +---_private
   |   +---_vti_txt
   |   +---_vti_script
   |   +---_vti_cnf
   |   +---_vti_bin
   |   \---Printers
   +---IIsCertMapper
   \---Filters
        \----Home ISAPI Home Filter
```

Figure 9.1 *An IIS tree dump of the first virtual Web server.*

Example 9.12 displays the IIS tree. You run this script by passing in a path relative to the IIS: provider like this:

```
perl IISTreeDump.pl webserver/W3SVC
```

This command displays the tree for all virtual Web servers on the webserver computer.

Here's another example:

```
perl IISTreeDump.pl webserver
```

This command displays the entire IIS tree on the webserver computer. All IIS services would be displayed including the web, ftp, nntp, and any other service that has been configured.

By default, the IIS tree is displayed using graphic characters. Under certain circumstances, however, these graphic characters may not display correctly, such as if the display font does not support them. To correct this, pass in the -a switch. This will display the tree in ASCII-only characters.

Example 9.12   *Displaying an IIS Tree*

```
01. use Getopt::Long;
02. use Win32;
03. use Win32::OLE qw( in );
04.
05. %CHAR = (
06.   graphic => {
07.     horizontal  =>  "\xc4",
08.     vertical    =>  "\xb3",
09.     tee         =>  "\xc3",
10.     corner      =>  "\xc0"
11.   },
12.   ascii  => {
13.     horizontal  =>  "-",
14.     vertical    =>  "|",
15.     tee         =>  "+",
16.     corner      =>  "\\"
17.   }
18. );
19.
20. Configure( \%Config );
21. if( $Config{help} )
22. {
23.   Syntax();
24.   exit();
25. }
26. $CharSet = ($Config{ascii})? $CHAR{ascii} : $CHAR{graphic};
27. push( @ARGV, Win32::NodeName() ) if( ! scalar @ARGV );
28. foreach my $Machine ( @ARGV )
29. {
30.   my $ADsPath = "IIS://$Machine";
31.   if( my $IIS = Win32::OLE->GetObject( $ADsPath ) )
```

continues ▶

Example 9.12   *continued*

```
32.    {
33.      ProcessDir( $IIS );
34.    }
35. }
36.
37. sub ProcessDir
38. {
39.    my( $Object, $IndentString ) = @_;
40.    local $PropertyName;
41.    my @SubDirList = in( $Object );
42.    my $iCount = scalar @SubDirList;
43.
44.    print $CharSet->{horizontal} x 3, $Object->{Name};
45.    if( ( "IIsWebServer" eq $Object->{Class} )
46.        || ( "IIsFtpServer" eq $Object->{Class} )
47.        || ( "IIsSmtpServer" eq $Object->{Class} )
48.        || ( "IIsNntpServer" eq $Object->{Class} ) )
49.    {
50.      print " ($Object->{ServerComment})";
51.    }
52.    print "\n";
53.    foreach my $Sub ( @SubDirList )
54.    {
55.      my $String;
56.
57.      if( --$iCount )
58.      {
59.        $String .= "  $CharSet->{vertical}";
60.        print $IndentString, "  $CharSet->{tee}";
61.      }
62.      else
63.      {
64.        $String .= "    ";
65.        print $IndentString, "  $CharSet->{corner}";
66.      }
67.      ProcessDir( $Sub, $IndentString . $String );
68.    }
69. }
70.
71.
72. sub Configure
73. {
74.    my( $Config ) = @_;
75.    my $Result;
76.
77.    Getopt::Long::Configure( "prefix_pattern=(-|\/)" );
78.    $Result = GetOptions( $Config,
79.                          qw(
80.                            asciil a
81.                            helpl ?l h
82.                          )
```

```
83.   );
84.   push( @{$Config->{servers}}, @ARGV );
85.   if( ! scalar @{$Config->{servers}} )
86.   {
87.     push( @{$Config->{servers}}, Win32::NodeName() );
88.   }
89.   $Config->{help} = 1 unless( $Result );
90. }
91.
92. sub Syntax
93. {
94.   my( $Script ) = ( Win32::GetLongPathName( $0 ) =~ /([^\\\/]*?)$/ );
95.   my( $Line ) = "-" x length( $Script );
96.
97.   print <<EOT;
98.
99. $Script
100. $Line
101. Displays an IIS server tree.
102.
103. Syntax:
104.     perl $Script [-a] Server [ Server2 ... ]
105.           -a.........Uses ascii characters to display the IIS tree.
106.           Server......The name of an IIS server.
107.                       If no servers are specified then the local
108.                       machine is used.
109. EOT
110. }
```

Windows Management Instrumentation

The computer industry has been trying to develop a standard way to access management information from across the network. This work has led to the Web-Based Enterprise Management (WBEM) initiative. This initiative uses the industry standard Common Information Model (CIM), which defines what information is accessible. These standards work together and enable you to connect to remote machines to query and manage settings and processes.

Microsoft's implementation of WBEM is called Windows Management Instrumentation (WMI). Any program can integrate with WMI to expose events, properties, and other settings. If you're willing to learn WMI, you can quickly bring your network under control. WMI is a serious force that every Win32 administrator should become familiar with.

Whereas using ADSI is a fantastic way to query settings bound to a database (such as the user database), WMI provides access into running processes, hardware, and events, just to name a few items.

Microsoft also provides ADSI for Windows NT 4.0, Windows 98, and Windows 95. You can download it from the MS Web site at `http://msdn.microsoft.com/downloads/sdks/wmi/`.

WMI Details

Just like ADSI, WMI works with *providers*. A provider acts as a bridge between WMI and some process or database. For example, by default, there are WMI providers for SNMP objects, Registry objects, and Win32 objects. If a third party writes a new program or service, it can ship a WMI provider, which enables you to use WMI to interact with the program or service. WMI also shares the concepts of *namespace* and *classes* with ADSI.

Generally, to request a WMI object, you must construct a path string that specifies the `WinMgmts:` provider. This provider accesses the WMI service (`WinMgmts.exe`). When specifying a WMI path, you can declare a security level immediately after the provider. Generally, you use the `{impersonationLevel=impersonate}` string to indicate that you want to represent yourself on a remote machine (this would attempt to impersonate yourself on the remote machine). It is not needed when you use WMI on Windows 2000 machines but should always be specified for backward compatibility with Windows NT and Windows 95/98.

Next, you need to specify the bang (`!` character) in the path followed by double slashes (`//`) and the machine name, as in this example:

```
WinMgmts:{impersonationLevel=impersonate}!//MachineName
```

This path returns a WMI object that represents the specified machine (`MachineName` in this case). This particular path returns an `SWbemServices` class object. This object can be used either to retrieve other WMI objects or instantiate a WMI object. For example,

```
$Path = "WinMgmts:{impersonationLevel=impersonate}!//MyMachine";
$WMI = Win32::OLE->GetObject( $Path );
```

results in an `SWbemServices` object: `$WMI`.

The `SWbemServices` class defines several methods, two of which are of importance to Perl: `Get()` and `InstancesOf()`. The `Get()` method returns a class or a collection of objects (refer to Example 9.16). The `InstancesOf()` method returns all instances of a specified class (see Example 9.13). Both of these functions are described in the next few sections.

Discovering Disks on Remote Machines

Example 9.13 uses WMI to obtain a remote machine's drive information. Line 21 requests an `SWbemService` object from the remote machine. Line 28 then calls into the `InstancesOf()` method, requesting all instances of the `Win32_LogicalDisk` class.

This script accepts any number of machine names. The disks from each of the specified machines are enumerated and displayed. For example, you could call the script using:

```
perl WMIDisks.pl \\ServerA \\ServerB
```

This would display information regarding all drives (floppy, CD-ROM, hard drive, and mapped network drives) for the machines \\ServerA and \\ServerB.

Example 9.13   *Discovering Drive Information on Remote Machines*

```perl
01. use Win32;
02. use Win32::OLE qw( in );
03.
04. %TYPE = (
05.   0   =>  'Unknown',
06.   1   =>  'No root',
07.   2   =>  'Removable',
08.   3   =>  'Local',
09.   4   =>  'Network',
10.   5   =>  'CDRom',
11.   6   =>  'RAM Disk'
12. );
13.
14. push( @ARGV, Win32::NodeName() ) if( ! scalar @ARGV );
15. foreach my $Machine ( @ARGV )
16. {
17.   # Remove any backslashes
18.   $Machine =~ s/\\+//;
19.   my $CLASS = "WinMgmts:{impersonationLevel=impersonate}!//$Machine";
20.   print "\\\\$Machine\n";
21.   if( my $WMI = Win32::OLE->GetObject( $CLASS ) )
22.   {
23.     local $Disk;
24.
25.     $~ = DISK_HEADER_FORMAT;
26.     write;
27.     $~ = DISK_FORMAT;
28.     foreach $Disk ( in( $WMI->InstancesOf( "Win32_LogicalDisk" ) ) )
29.     {
30.       local $Drive = $TYPE{$Disk->{DriveType}};
31.       local %Size = (
32.         total =>  FormatNumber( $Disk->{Size} ),
33.         free  =>  FormatNumber( $Disk->{FreeSpace} )
34.       );
35.       write;
36.     }
37.   }
38.   print "\n";
39. }
40.
41. sub FormatNumber
```

continues ▶

Example 9.13 *continued*

```
42. {
43.   my( $Number ) =@_;
44.   while( $Number =~ s/^(-?\d+)(\d{3})/$1,$2/ ){};
45.   return( $Number );
46. }
47.
48. format DISK_HEADER_FORMAT =
49.    FS    Type     Size                     Free
50. ... ..... .......... ...................... ......................
51. .
52. format DISK_FORMAT =
53. @<< @<<<< @<<<<<<<< @>>>>>>>>>>>>>>>>>>> @>>>>>>>>>>>>>>>>>>>
54. $Disk->{Name}, $Disk->{FileSystem}, $Drive, $Size{total}, $Size{free}
55. .
```

Process Lists

In Chapter 7, "Processes," you learned a few techniques to procure a process list. Example 9.14 is another example of a script displaying a process list using WMI. The list can be from a local or remote machine.

The script accepts a machine name as a parameter indicating the machine from which the process list should be retrieved. If no machine name is passed in, the local machine is assumed.

Example 9.14 *Displaying a WMI-Based Process List*

```
01. use Win32::OLE qw( in );
02.
03. $Machine = "." unless( $Machine = shift @ARGV );
04. $Machine =~ s#^[\\/]+## if( $ARGV[0] =~ m#^[\\/]{2}# );
05.
06. # This is the WMI moniker that will connect to a machine's
07. # CIM (Common Information Model) repository
08. $CLASS = "WinMgmts:{impersonationLevel=impersonate}!//$Machine";
09.
10. # Get the WMI (Microsoft's implementation of WBEM) interface
11. $WMI = Win32::OLE->GetObject( $CLASS )
12.    || die "Unable to connect to \\$Machine" . Win32::OLE->LastError();
13.
14. # Get the collection of Win32_Process objects
15. $ProcList = $WMI->InstancesOf( "Win32_Process" );
16.
17. $~ = PROCESS_HEADER;
18. write;
19. $~ = PROCESS_INFO;
20.
21. # Cycle through each Win32_Process object
22. # and write out its details...
23. foreach $Proc ( sort( SortProcs ( in( $ProcList ) ) ) )
```

```
24. {
25.     write;
26. }
27.
28. sub SortProcs
29. {
30.   lc $a->{Name} cmp lc $b->{Name};
31. }
32.
33. sub FormatNumber
34. {
35.     my( $Number ) = @_;
36.     my( $Suffix ) = "";
37.     my $K = 1024;
38.     my $M = 1024 * $K;
39.
40.     if( $M <= $Number )
41.     {
42.         $Suffix = "M";
43.         $Number /= $M;
44.     }
45.     elsif( $K <= $Number )
46.     {
47.         $Suffix = "K";
48.         $Number /= $K;
49.     }
50.
51.     $Number =~ s/(\.\d{0,2})\d*$/$1/;
52.
53.     {} while ($Number =~ s/^(-?\d+)(\d{3})/$1,$2/);
54.
55.     return( $Number . $Suffix );
56. }
57.
58. sub FormatDate
59. {
60.     my( $Date ) = @_;
61.     $Date =~ s/(\d{4})(\d{2})(\d{2})(\d{2})(\d{2})(\d{2}).*/$1.$2.$3 $4:$5:$6/;
62.     return( $Date );
63. }
64.
65. format PROCESS_HEADER =
66. @||| @||||| @||||||||||||||||| @|||| @|||||| @||||||| @||||||||||||||||||||
67. PID, Parent, "Process Name", "Thrds", "Memory", "Mem Peak", "Created"
68. ---- ------ ----------------- ----- ------- -------- --------------------
69. .
70.
71. format PROCESS_INFO =
72. @||| @||||| @<<<<<<<<<<<<<<<< @>>>> @>>>>>> @>>>>>>> @>>>>>>>>>>>>>>>>>>>>
73. $Proc->{'ProcessID'}, $Proc->{'ParentProcessID'}, $Proc->{Name},
    $Proc->{'ThreadCount'}, FormatNumber( $Proc->{'WorkingSetSize'} ),
    FormatNumber( $Proc->{'PeakWorkingSetSize'} ),
    FormatDate( $Proc->{'CreationDate'} )
74. .
```

Killing Processes

Just as with the previous example (refer to Example 9.14), this section revisits a script that was covered in Chapter 7's task killing script (refer to Example 7.19). Using WMI, however, Example 9.15 is not only able to terminate a process on the local machine, but it can also terminate processes on remote machines.

If a machine name is passed in as the first parameter (denoted by prepending a machine name with double backslashes), all process termination takes place on the specified machine. All additional parameters are either considered to be process ID (PID) numbers or the name of a process.

If a process name is passed in, all processes matching the name are terminated. If the name contains wildcards such as * and ?, it is used as a regular expression. For example,

```
perl WMI_Kill.pl \\server 415 .*word
```

terminates a process with PID 415 and any process that has word in its name on the machine \\server.

Example 9.15 *Using WMI to Kill Processes*

```
01. use Win32::OLE qw( in );
02.
03. $Machine = "." unless( $Machine = shift @ARGV );
04. $Machine =~ s#^[\\/]+## if( $ARGV[0] =~ m#^[\\/]{2}# );
05.
06. # This is the WMI moniker that will connect to a machine's
07. # CIM (Common Information Model) repository
08. $CLASS = "WinMgmts:{impersonationLevel=impersonate}!//$Machine";
09.
10. # Get the WMI (Microsoft's implementation of WBEM) interface
11. $WMI = Win32::OLE->GetObject( $CLASS )
12.    || die "Unable to connect to \\$Machine:" . Win32::OLE->LastError();
13.
14. # Get the collection of Win32_Process objects
15. $ProcList = $WMI->InstancesOf( "Win32_Process" );
16.
17. # Try to kill each PID passed in
18. foreach $Pid ( @ARGV )
19. {
20.   my $KillList = GetProc( $Pid, $ProcList );
21.   if( scalar @$KillList )
22.   {
23.     foreach my $Proc ( @$KillList )
24.     {
25.       print "Killing $Proc->{Name} ($Proc->{ProcessID})...";
26.
27.       # We found the correct Win32_Process object so
28.       # call its Terminate method
29.       $Result = $Proc->Terminate( 0 );
```

```
30.        if( 0 == $Result )
31.        {
32.          print "Successfully terminated";
33.        }
34.        else
35.        {
36.          print "Failed to terminate";
37.        }
38.        print "\n";
39.      }
40.    }
41.    else
42.    {
43.      print "$Pid not found.";
44.    }
45. }
46.
47. sub GetProc
48. {
49.    my( $Pid, $ProcList ) = @_;
50.    if( $Pid =~ /^\d+$/ )
51.    {
52.      $List = GetProcByPid( $Pid, $ProcList );
53.    }
54.    else
55.    {
56.      $List = GetProcByName( $Pid, $ProcList );
57.    }
58.    return( $List );
59. }
60.
61. sub GetProcByPid
62. {
63.    my( $Pid, $ProcList ) = @_;
64.
65.    # Cycle through each Win32_Process object
66.    # until you find the right one
67.    foreach my $Proc ( in( $ProcList ) )
68.    {
69.      return( [ $Proc ] ) if( $Pid == $Proc->{ProcessID} );
70.    }
71.    return( [] );
72. }
73.
74. sub GetProcByName
75. {
76.    my( $Name, $ProcList ) = @_;
77.    my( @Procs );
78.    my( $Regex ) = ( $Name =~ m#[$^\\/*?{}\[\]]+# );
79.
80.    # Cycle through each Win32_Process object
81.    # until you find the right one
82.    foreach my $Proc ( in( $ProcList ) )
```

continues ▶

Example 9.15   *continued*

```
83.  {
84.    if( $Regex )
85.    {
86.      push( @Procs, $Proc ) if( $Proc->{Name} =~ /$Name/i );
87.    }
88.    else
89.    {
90.      push( @Procs, $Proc ) if( lc $Name eq lc $Proc->{Name} );
91.    }
92.  }
93.  return( \@Procs );
94. }
```

Creating Remote Processes

Example 9.16 creates a process on a remote machine. You just pass in parameters that you would normally use on the command line. For example, if you want to run the NOTEPAD.EXE program loading in a particular file, you can call the script like this:

```
perl WMI_Run.pl notepad.exe c:\temp\MyFile.txt
```

This command starts the Notepad program loading in the specified file.

If you want to run a program on a remote machine, simply pass in the remote machine name as the first parameter. The following uses the same example:

```
perl WMI_Run.pl \\server notepad.exe c:\temp\MyFile.txt
```

This command runs the Notepad program on the machine \\Server. Note that the file loaded is relative to the remote machine. Therefore, c:\temp\MyFile.txt refers to the C:\ drive on the remote machine.

Both the local and the remote machine must have WMI installed for this script to work.

Example 9.16   *Creating Remote Processes*

```
01. use Win32::OLE qw( in );
02. use Win32::OLE::Variant;
03.
04. $Machine = "." unless( $Machine = shift @ARGV );    $MACHINE = SHIFT @ARGV ;
05. $Machine =~ s#^[\\/]+## if( $ARGV[0] =~ m#^[\\/]{2}# );
06.
07. # This is the WMI moniker that will connect to a machine's
08. # CIM (Common Information Model) repository
09. $CLASS = "WinMgmts:{impersonationLevel=impersonate}!//$Machine";
10.
11. # Get the WMI (Microsoft's implementation of WBEM) interface
12. $WMI = Win32::OLE->GetObject( $CLASS )
```

```
13.   || die "Unable to connect to \\$Machine:" . Win32::OLE->LastError();
14.
15. # Now get a Win32_Process class object...
16. $Process = $WMI->Get( "Win32_Process" )
17.   || die "Unable to get the process list:" . Win32::OLE->LastError();
18.
19. # Create a BYREF variant so a COM object can modify its value and
20. # return it to us.
21. $vPid = Variant( VT_I4 | VT_BYREF, 0 );
22.
23. # Now go ahead and create the new process using the Create() method
24. # off of the Win32_Process object
25. if( 0 == $Process->Create( join( " ", @ARGV ), undef, undef, $vPid ) )
26. {
27.     print "Process successfully created with PID $vPid\n";
28. }
29. else
30. {
31.     print "Failed to create process.\n";
31. }
```

Conclusion

With the alphabet soup of technologies that are coming of age, you have a plethora of tools at your disposal. The ADSI and WMI technologies are available for all Win32 platforms, thus enabling you to automate your networks.

This chapter just covered the tip of the ADSI and WMI iceberg. Reading more information on these technologies either online or in book form is worthwhile. Either way, the knowledge you gain will become indispensable because these tools will mature and become more prevalent in every Win32 network.

Example Code and Online Book Discussions

There are bound to be bugs and typos that creep up. When they do, we will squash them on this book's Web site, which can be found at www.newriders.com. This site will include sample code and errata.

Roth Consulting's Web site hosts a Usenet group (news://news.roth.net/Books.AdminHandbook) where you can participate in an ongoing discussion related to the topics covered in this book. While you are there, you can check into the other Win32 Perl-related groups. The Web site also maintains a page dedicated to this book (http://www.roth.net/books/handbook/) where you can find reviews, information, example code, and any errata.

Modules Used in This Book

There are many modules and extensions used throughout this book. Some do not come standard with ActivePerl. The following table indicates where you can find the modules and extensions used in this book.

Extension	Where to Obtain It
Getopt::Long	http://www.cpan.com
Net::Pager	http://www.simplewire.com/
Net::Ping	http://www.cpan.org/
	Part of the libnet package
Net::SMTP	http://www.cpan.org/
	Part of the libnet package
IO::Socket	http://www.activestate.com/ or
	http://www.cpan.org/
	Comes as part of ActivePerl
Time::Local	http://www.cpan.org/
	Comes with Perl; also available on CPAN

continues ▶

Extension	Where to Obtain It
Win32::AdminMisc	http://www.activestate.com/
	Part of Win32lib, which comes with ActivePerl or http://www.roth.net/perl/packages/ for updated versions
Win32::API	http://www.activestate.com/
	Part of Win32lib, which comes with ActivePerl
	or http://dada.perl.it/ at Aldo Calpini's site
Win32::API::Prototype	http://www.roth.net/perl/packages/
Win32::Daemon	http://www.roth.net/perl/packages/
Win32::Console	http://www.activestate.com/
	Part of Win32lib, which comes with ActivePerl
	or http://dada.perl.it/ at Aldo Calpini's site
Win32::EventLog	http://www.activestate.com/
	Part of Win32lib, which comes with ActivePerl
Win32::EventLog::Message	http://www.roth.net/perl/packages/
Win32::GUI	http://dada.perl.it/
Win32::Lanman	http://jenda.krynicky.cz/ or
	ftp://ftp.roth.net/pub/ntperl/others/Lanman/
Win32::NetAdmin	http://www.activestate.com/
	Part of Win32lib, which comes with ActivePerl
Win32::ODBC	http://www.activestate.com/
	Part of Win32lib, which comes with ActivePerl
	or http://www.roth.net/perl/packages/ for updated versions
Win32::OLE	http://www.activestate.com/
	Part of Win32lib, which comes with ActivePerl
Win32::OLE::Const	http://www.activestate.com/
	Part of Win32lib, which comes with ActivePerl
Win32::Perms	http://www.roth.net/perl/packages/
Win32::Pipe	http://www.activestate.com/
	Part of Win32lib, which comes with ActivePerl
	or http://www.roth.net/perl/packages/ for updated versions
Win32::Registry	http://www.activestate.com/
	Part of Win32lib, which comes with ActivePerl
Win32::Service	http://www.activestate.com/
	Part of Win32lib, which comes with ActivePerl
Win32::WinError	http://www.activestate.com/
	Part of Win32lib, which comes with ActivePerl
Win32API::Registry	http://www.activestate.com/
	Part of Win32lib, which comes with ActivePerl

Installing Extensions

By far the easiest way to install an extension is by using the PPM Perl script. You typically can use this by specifying the following command from a DOS box:

```
ppm install win32-api
```

This particular command will attempt to download and install the Win32::API extension. Notice that you need to replace the Perl namespace delimiter :: (double colons) with a dash. By default, the PPM script will contact ActiveState.com to retrieve the requested extension. In some cases, however, updated versions of extensions can be found in other locations. Such locations can be specified with a --location switch. For example, to install Win32::EventLog::Message try

```
ppm install win32-eventlog-message --
location=http://www.roth.net/perl/packages/
```

If you are located behind a firewall or proxy server, you need to read the documentation for PPM.

Perl Information

After you have digested all the information in this book, you may be wondering where to go next. That is easily answered—you go online! In this section you will find a small sampling of Internet sites you can check out to find more information on Win32 Perl. These particular sites are well-suited to act as a springboard, thrusting you headlong into the world of Perl programming.

Web Sites

The Official Perl Web Site

http://www.perl.com/

Make no mistake about it—this is the *official* Perl Web site. You can depend on finding the real scoop on Perl here.

CPAN

http://www.cpan.org/

The Comprehensive Perl Archive Network (CPAN) is the global network of Perl code. Authors post modules, scripts, and extensions here, and they are replicated around the world. Chances are that someone has already written code to do what you need. You would look for it here.

ActiveState Tool Corp.

http://www.activestate.com/

These are the guys you can thank for porting Perl to Win32. Sure, there have been many Win32 ports, but this team has been championing it for years. Drop them an email thanking them for all their hard work!

Microsoft Developer Network

http://msdn.microsoft.com/

You might not expect it, but this site has a few articles on Perl. More importantly, they have *the entire Win32 API documented online!* When you are struggling with the Win32::API extension, you can check your syntax and values with this Web site.

This site also empowers you with the ability to search all of the KnowledgeBase articles. This can quickly solve some headaches for more than just Win32 Perl-related woes.

Perl for Win32

http://www.netaxs.com/~joc/perlwin32.html

This is *the* place for Win32 Perl administrators. If you have not yet visited this site, then do so, *now!* Not only that, but bookmark it as well. Here you can find everything from the latest modules to book reviews. This site is a perfect jumping point with tons of links to various Perl-related sites.

Dada's perl lab

http://dada.perl.it/

This is Aldo Calpini's Perl site. He has produced some of the more influential Win32 extensions—Win32::API and Win32::GUI in particular.

Roth Consulting

http://www.roth.net/

This is the home for many Win32 extensions, book guide, Win32::ODBC FAQ, and other Perl-related information.

Jutta Klebe's Web Site

http://www.bybyte.de/jmk/

This is where you can find Jutta's Win32::PerfLib extension.

SimpleWire

http://www.simplewire.com/

This is where you can pick up the latest copy of the Net::Pager module.

Amine Moulay Ramdane's Perl for Win32 Modules Site

http://www.generation.net/~aminer/Perl/

Amine has contributed a flurry of exciting hard-core modules.

Piedmont Professional Services

http://www.ppservices.com/default_prog_perl.htm

This Web page has a slew of Perl-related links.

Carvdawg's Perl Page

http://patriot.net/~carvdawg/perl.html

Here you can find a bundle of Perl scripts that mostly center around Win32 and security issues.

WebRing

http://www.netaxs.com/~joc/perlring.html

For those who are not familiar with WebRings, they are basically a ring of Web sites all linked together. Each WebRing shares a common theme; this one has the Perl theme, of course.

Usenet

The Usenet is just a smorgasbord of information waiting to be consumed. Here you can read what people have written, or you can post a message yourself. You may have to check with your Internet service provider to discover which Usenet server to access.

If you don't have direct access to the Usenet, you can access it through a Usenet Web site such as Deja.com (http://www.deja.com/usenet).

The following table lists the Usenet groups monitored by Perl folks the most:

Usenet Group	Description
comp.lang.perl	This is a now-defunct general Perl discussion group. Even though some postings still are made to this group, most serious Perl users frequent the comp.lang.perl.misc group.
comp.lang.perl.announce	Here's a good place to read what new modules and extensions are being introduced.
comp.lang.perl.misc	This is a miscellaneous Perl discussion group. This is where most people post messages.
comp.lang.perl.modules	This group is where you can post messages regarding Perl modules and extensions.
comp.lang.perl.moderated	This useful group discusses most any Perl topic. Because it's moderated, don't be surprised if traffic is low and the messages are concise and well thought-out.

continues ▶

Usenet Group	Description
alt.perl	This is an alternative Perl discussion group. You can find some pretty interesting stuff here.
alt.perl.sockets	This group discusses networking and socket-related Perl issues.

Alternatively, you can access the Roth Consulting Usenet >server at news.roth.net. There are several groups on this server covering various Win32 Perl extensions:

```
Win32::AdminMisc              Win32::ODBC
Win32::API::Prototype         Win32::OLE
Win32::Daemon                 Win32::Perms
Win32::EventLog::Message      Win32::Pipe
Win32::Lanman                 Win32::RASAdmin
Win32::Message                Win32::Tie::Ini
```

List Servers

Another very popular way to communicate among fellow Perl administrators is to participate in one of the various listserv lists. These lists are basically email-based lists that resend mail messages to a group.

ActiveState
http://www.activestate.com/Support/Mailing_Lists/index.html
ActiveState has their own listserver where Win32 Perl folks participate.

Topica.com
http://www.topica.com/
Topica is a listserver portal site that defines what they call *channels* (their equivalent for a list). Hop over to their site and run a search on the keyword "perl". There are many Perl-related lists to choose from.

Electronic Magazines and Journals

The Perl Journal
http://www.itknowledge.com/tpj/
TPJ is a tried and true mainstay that is an absolute *must* for any administrator.

Perl Month
http://www.perlmonth.com/
This is an ongoing journal that has interesting articles and features.

Web Techniques Magazine

`http://www.webtechniques.com`

Although this is not a Perl-only magazine, it does cover Perl topics from time to time. Either way, it is interesting reading.

Worthwhile Win32 Perl Administration Books

Aeleen Frisch, *Essential Windows NT System Administration*, O'Reilly & Associates, 1998.

Dave Roth, *Win32 Perl Programming: The Standard Extensions*, New Riders, 1999.

Randal L. Schwartz, Tom Christiansen, Erik Olson, *Learning Perl on Win32 Systems*, O'Reilly & Associates, 1997.

David N. Blank-Edelman, *Perl for System Administration*, O'Reilly & Associates, 2000.

Scott McMahan, *Automating Windows with Perl*, CMP Books, 1999.

Tim Bunce and Alligator Descartes, *Programming the Perl DBI*, O'Reilly & Associates, 2000.

Index

A

E

Windows 2000 Answers

New Riders proudly offers something unique for Windows 2000 administrators—an interesting and discriminating book on Windows 2000 Server, written by someone in the trenches who can anticipate your situation and provide answers you can trust.

INSIDE
Windows 2000 Server

William Boswell

ISBN: 1-56205-929-7

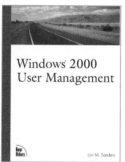

Windows 2000 User Management

Lori M. Sanders

ISBN: 1-56205-886-X

Managing the user and the user's desktop environment is a critical component in administering Windows 2000. *Windows 2000 User Management* provides you with the real-world tips and examples you need to get the job done.

Windows 2000 Active Directory is just one of several Windows 2000 titles from New Riders' acclaimed *Landmark Series*. Perfect for network architects and administrators, this book describes the intricacies of Active Directory to help you plan, deploy, and manage Active Directory in an enterprise setting.

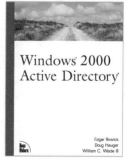

Windows 2000 Active Directory

Edgar Brovick
Doug Hauger
William C. Wade III

ISBN: 0-7357-0870-3

Advanced Information on Networking Technologies

New Riders Books Offer Advice and Experience

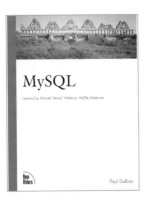

LANDMARK

We know how important it is to have access to detailed, solution-oriented information on core technologies. *Landmark Series* books contain the essential information you need to solve technical problems. Written by experts and subjected to rigorous peer and technical reviews, our *Landmark* books are hard-core resources for practitioners like you.

ESSENTIAL REFERENCE

The *Essential Reference* series from New Riders provides answers when you know what you want to do but need to know how to do it. Each title skips extraneous material and assumes a strong base of knowledge. These are indispensable books for the practitioner who wants to find specific features of a technology quickly. Avoiding fluff and basic material, these books present solutions in an innovative, clean format—and at a great value.

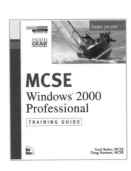

CERTIFICATION

New Riders offers a complete line of test preparation materials to help you achieve your certification. With books like the *Training Guide* and software like the revolutionary *ExamGear*, New Riders offers comprehensive products built by experienced professionals who have passed the exams and instructed hundreds of candidates.

Microsoft Technologies

Inside Windows 2000 Server
By William Boswell
1st Edition
1515 pages, $49.99
ISBN: 1-56205-929-7

Taking the author-driven, no-nonsense approach we pioneered with our *Landmark* books, New Riders proudly offers something unique for Windows 2000 administrators—an interesting, discriminating book on Windows 2000 Server written by someone who can anticipate your situation and give you workarounds that won't leave a system unstable or sluggish.

Windows 2000 Active Directory
By Ed Brovick, Doug Hauger, and William Wade III
1st Edition
416 pages, $29.99
ISBN: 0-7357-0870-3

Written by three of Microsoft's key premium partners, with high-level access to people, information, and resources, this book offers a concise, focused, and informative *Landmark* format, filled with case studies and real-world experience for Windows 2000's most anticipated and most complex feature—the Active Directory.

Windows 2000 Essential Reference
By Steven Tate, et al.
1st Edition
670 pages, $35.00
ISBN: 0-7357-0869-X

Architected to be the most navigable, useful and value-packed reference for Windows 2000, this book uses a creative "telescoping" design that you can adapt to your style of learning. The authors give you answers based on their hands-on experience with Windows 2000 and apply their formidable credentials toward giving you the answers you won't find anywhere else.

Windows 2000 Routing and Remote Access Service

By Kackie Charles
1st Edition
400 pages, $34.99
ISBN: 0-7357-0951-3

Ideal for system administrators looking to create cost-effective and secure remote access across the network. Author Kackie Charles uses concrete examples to demonstrate how to smoothly integrate Windows 2000 routing with your existing routing infrastructure, and connect users to the network while maxmizing available bandwidth. Featured coverage includes new authentication models, routing protocols, configuration of the Windows 2000 router, design issues, security, and troubleshooting.

Windows 2000 Deployment & Desktop Management

By Jeffrey A. Ferris
1st Edition
408 pages, $34.99
ISBN: 0-7357-0975-0

More than a simple overview of new features and tools, this solutions-driven book is a thorough reference to deploying Windows 2000 Professional to corporate workstations. The expert real-world advice and detailed exercises make this a one-stop, easy-to-use resource for any system administrator, integrator, engineer, or other IT professional planning rollout of Windows 2000 clients.

Windows 2000 DNS

By Herman Knief, Jeffrey Graham, Andrew Daniels, and Roger Abell
2nd Edition
480 pages, $39.99
ISBN: 0-7357-0973-4

Focusing on such key topics as designing and securing DNS services, planning for interoperation, and installing and using DHCP and WINS services, *Windows 2000 DNS* is a comprehensive guide to the newest iteration of Microsoft's DNS. The authors provide you with real-world advice, best practices, and strategies you will need to design and administer DNS for optimal performance.

Windows 2000 User Management

By Lori Sanders
1st Edition
240 pages, $34.99
ISBN: 1-56205-886-X

With the dawn of Windows 2000, it has become even more difficult to draw a clear line between managing the user and managing the user's environment and desktop. This book, written by a noted trainer and consultant, provides a comprehensive, practical guide to managing users and their desktop environments with Windows 2000.

Windows 2000
Professional

Windows 2000 Professional

By Jerry Honeycutt
1st Edition
330 pages, $34.99
ISBN: 0-7357-0950-5

Windows 2000 Professional explores the power available to the Windows workstation user on the corporate network and Internet. The book is aimed directly at the power user who values the security, stability, and networking capabilities of NT alongside the ease and familiarity of the Windows 9X user interface. This book covers both user and administration topics, with a dose of networking content added for connectivity.

Planning for
Windows 2000

Planning for Windows 2000

By Eric K. Cone,
Jon Boggs, and
Sergio Perez
1st Edition
448 pages, $29.99
ISBN: 0-7357-0048-6

Are you ready for Windows 2000? This book explains the steps involved in preparing your Windows NT-based heterogeneous network for Windows 2000. Rollout procedures are presented in detail as the authors draw from their own experiences and scenarios to explain an otherwise tangled series of procedures. *Planning for Windows 2000* is an indispensable companion to anyone considering migration.

Windows 2000
Server
PROFESSIONAL
REFERENCE

Windows 2000 Server Professional Reference

By Karanjit Siyan,
Ph.D.
3rd Edition
1848 pages, $75.00
ISBN: 0-7357-0952-1

Windows 2000 Professional Reference is the benchmark of references available for Windows 2000. Although other titles take you through the setup and implementation phase of the product, no other book provides the user with detailed answers to day-to-day administration problems and tasks. Solid content shows administrators how to manage, troubleshoot, and fix problems that are specific to heterogeneous Windows networks, as well as Internet features and functionality.

Windows 2000
Security

Windows 2000 Security

By Roberta Bragg
1st Edition
608 pages, $39.99
ISBN: 0-7357-0991-2

No single authoritative reference on security exists for serious network system administrators. The primary directive of this title is to assist the Windows networking professional in understanding and implementing Windows 2000 security in his organization. Included are Best Practices sections, which make recommendations for settings and security practices.

Windows NT/2000 Network Security

By Eugene Schultz
1st Edition
440 pages, $45.00
ISBN 1-57870-253-4

Windows NT/2000 Network Security provides a framework that will promote genuine understanding of the Windows security model and associated capabilities. The goal is to acquaint readers with the major types of Windows security exposures when used in both peer-to-peer and client-server settings. This book teachs readers the specific security controls and settings that address each exposure, and shows them how to evaluate tradeoffs to determine which control (if any) to apply.

Windows NT/2000 Thin Client Solutions

By Todd Mathers
2nd Edition
840 pages, $45.00
ISBN: 1-57870-239-9

A practical and comprehensive reference to MetaFrame 1.8 and Terminal Server Edition, this book should be the first source for answers to the tough questions on the TSE/MetaFrame platform. Building on the quality of the previous edition, additional coverage of installation of Terminal Services and MetaFrame on a Windows 2000 Server, as well as chapters on TSE management, remote access, and application integration, are included.

Windows 2000 Virtual Private Networking

By Thaddeus Fortenberry
1st Edition
350 pages, $45.00
ISBN 1-57870-246-1
January 2001

Because of the ongoing push for a distributed workforce, administrators must support laptop users, home LAN environments, complex branch offices, and more—all within a secure and effective network design. The way an administrator implements VPNs in Windows 2000 is different than that of any other operating system. In addition to discussions about Windows 2000 tunneling, new VPN features that can affect Active Directory replication and Network Address Translation are also covered.

Windows 2000 Active Directory Design & Deployment

By Gary Olsen
1st Edition
648 pages, $45.00
ISBN: 1-57870-242-9

This book focuses on the design of a Windows 2000 Active Directory environment, and how to develop an effective design and migration plan. The reader is lead through the process of developing a design plan by reviewing each pertinent issue, and then provided expert advice on how to evaluate each issue as it applies to the reader's particular environment. Practical examples illustrate all of these issues.

Windows 2000 and Mainframe Integration
By William Zack
1st Edition
390 pages, $40.00
ISBN:1-57870-200-3

Windows 2000 and Mainframe Integration provides mainframe computing professionals with the practical know-how to build and integrate Windows 2000 technologies into their current environment.

Windows 2000 Server: Planning and Migration
By Sean Deuby
1st Edition
480 pages, $40.00
ISBN:1-57870-023-X

Windows 2000 Server: Planning and Migration can quickly save the NT professional thousands of dollars and hundreds of hours. This title includes authoritative information on key features of Windows 2000 and offers recommendations on how to best position your NT network for Windows 2000.

Windows 2000 Quality of Service
By David Iseminger
1st Edition
264 pages, $45.00
ISBN:1-57870-115-5

As the traffic on networks continues to increase, the strain on network infrastructure and available resources has also grown. *Windows 2000 Quality of Service* teaches network engineers and administrators to how to define traffic control patterns and utilize bandwidth on their networks.

Windows NT Power Toolkit
By Stu Sjouwerman and Ed Tittel
1st Edition
848 pages, $49.99
ISBN: 0-7357-0922-X

A unique offering from New Riders, this book covers the analysis, tuning, optimization, automation, enhancement, maintenance, and troubleshooting of both Windows NT Server 4.0 and Windows NT Workstation 4.0. *Windows NT Power Toolkit* includes comprehensive coverage of all service packs and security updates, IE5 upgrade issues, recent product additions, third-party tools and utilities.

Windows NT Terminal Server and Citrix MetaFrame
By Ted Harwood
1st Edition
46 pages, $29.99
ISBN: 1-56205-944-0

This technical reference details all aspects of planning, installing, administering, and troubleshooting Microsoft Terminal Server and Citrix MetaFrame systems. MetaFrame greatly enhances the usability of NT as a thin-client solution, but the heterogeneous networking issues involved in its integration will be a significant source of information pain. *Windows NT Terminal Server and Citrix Metaframe* is one of only two books available on this technology.

Windows NT Performance Monitoring, Benchmarking, and Tuning
By Mark Edmead and Paul Hinsberg
1st Edition
288 pages, $29.99
ISBN: 1-56205-942-4

Windows NT Performance Monitoring, Benchmarking, and Tuning provides a one-stop source for sound technical information on doing everything necessary to fine-tune your network. From benchmarking to analyzing performance numbers to isolating and solving resource bottlenecks, the authors provide a reliable blueprint for ensuring optimal Windows NT performance.

Windows 2000 TCP/IP
By Karanjit S. Siyan, Ph.D.
2nd Edition
920 pages, $39.99
ISBN 0-7357-0992-0

Focusing on ways to administer networks using Microsoft TCP/IP, this book is for professionals who want to read about best practices on using the technology. Without spending time on basics that readers already understand, *Windows 2000 TCP/IP* presents advanced solutions and is a must-have for any system administrator.

Windows NT Registry: A Settings Reference
By Sandra Osborne
1st Edition
576 pages, $29.99
ISBN:1-56205-941-6

More than a simple troubleshooting or optimization book, this solutions-driven guide shows you how to manage hardware, Windows NT Workstation and other clients, notebook computers, application software, and Internet settings using the Registry in the most efficient and cost-effective manner possible. If you're a network developer, system engineer, server administrator, or workstation technician, you'll come to rely on the expert advice contained in this comprehensive reference.

Windows NT Domain Architecture
By Gregg Branham
1st Edition
312 pages, $39.95
ISBN: 1-57870-112-0

As Windows NT continues to be deployed more and more in the enterprise, the domain architecture for the network becomes critical as the complexity increases. This book contains the in-depth expertise that is necessary to truly plan a complex enterprise domain.

Windows NT Device Driver Development
By Peter Viscarola and W. Anthony Mason
1st Edition
704 pages, $50.00
ISBN: 1-57870-058-2

This title begins with an introduction to the general Windows NT operating system concepts relevant to drivers, then progresses to more detailed information about the operating system, such as interrupt management, synchronization issues, the I/O Subsystem, standard kernel mode drivers, and more.

Windows NT/2000 Native API Reference
By Gary Nebbett
1st Edition
528 pages, $50.00
ISBN: 1-57870-199-6

This book is the first complete reference to the API functions native to Windows NT and covers the set of services that are offered by the Windows NT to both kernel- and user-mode programs. Coverage consists of documentation of the 210 routines included in the NT Native API, and the functions that will be added in Windows 2000. Routines that are either not directly accessible via the Win32 API or offer substantial additional functionality are described in especially great detail. Services offered by the NT kernel—mainly the support for debugging user mode applications—are also included.

DCE/RPC over SMB: Samba and Windows NT Domain Internals
By Luke Leighton
1st Edition
312 pages, $45.00
ISBN: 1-57870-150-3

Security people, system and network administrators, and those writing tools for them all need to be familiar with the packets flowing across their networks. Authored by a key member of the Samba team, this book describes how Microsoft has taken DCE/RPC and implemented it over SMB and TCP/IP.

Delphi COM Programming
By Eric Harmon
1st Edition
500 pages, $45.00
ISBN: 1-57870-221-6

Delphi COM Programming is for all Delphi 3, 4, and 5 programmers. After providing readers with an understanding of the COM framework, it offers a practical exploration of COM to enable Delphi developers to program component-based applications. Typical real-world scenarios, such as Windows Shell programming, automating Microsoft Agent, and creating and using ActiveX controls, are explored. Discussions of each topic are illustrated with detailed examples.

Applying COM+
By Gregory Brill
1st Edition
450 pages, $49.99
ISBN: 0-7357-0978-5

By pulling a number of disparate services into one unified technology, COM+ holds the promise of greater efficiency and more diverse capabilities for developers who are creating applications—either enterprise or commercial software—to run on a Windows 2000 system. *Applying COM+* covers the features of the new tool, as well as how to implement them in a real case study. Features are demonstrated in all three of the major languages used in the Windows environment: C++, VB, and VJ++.

Windows NT Applications: Measuring and Optimizing Performance
By Paul Hinsberg
1st Edition
288 pages, $40.00
ISBN: 1-57870-176-7

This book offers developers crucial insight into the underlying structure of Windows NT, as well as the methodology and tools for measuring and ultimately optimizing code performance.

Exchange & Outlook: Constructing Collaborative Solutions
By Joel Semeniuk and Duncan Mackenzie
1st Edition
576 pages, $40.00
ISBN 1-57870-252-6

The authors of this book are responsible for building custom messaging applications for some of the biggest Fortune 100 companies in the world. They share their expertise to help administrators and designers use Microsoft technology to establish a base for their messaging system and to lay out the tools that can be used to help build those collaborative solutions. Actual planning and design solutions are included along with typical workflow/collaborative solutions.

Windows Script Host
By Tim Hill
1st Edition
448 pages, $35.00
ISBN: 1-57870-139-2

Windows Script Host is one of the first books published about this powerful tool. The text focuses on system scripting and the VBScript language, using objects, server scriptlets, and ready-to-use script solutions.

Windows NT Shell Scripting
By Tim Hill
1st Edition
400 pages, $32.00
ISBN: 1-57870-047-7

A complete reference for Windows NT scripting, this book guides you through a high-level introduction to the Shell language itself and the Shell commands that are useful for controlling or managing different components of a network.

Win32 Perl Programming: The Standard Extensions
By Dave Roth
1st Edition
640 pages, $40.00
ISBN:1-57870-067-1

Discover numerous proven examples and practical uses of Perl in solving everyday Win32 problems. This is the only book available with comprehensive coverage of Win32 extensions, where most of the Perl functionality resides in Windows settings.

Windows NT/2000 ADSI Scripting for System Administration
By Thomas Eck
1st Edition
700 pages, $45.00
ISBN: 1-57870-219-4

Active Directory Scripting Interfaces (ADSI) allow administrators to automate administrative tasks across their Windows networks. This title fills a gap in the current ADSI documentation by including coverage of its interaction with LDAP and provides administrators with proven code samples that they can adopt to effectively configure and manage user accounts and other usually time-consuming tasks.

Windows NT Automated Deployment and Customization
By Richard Puckett
1st Editon
300 pages, $32.00
ISBN: 1-57870-045-0

This title offers time-saving advice that helps you install, update and configure software on each of your clients, without having to visit each client. Learn how to control all clients remotely for tasks, such as security and legal software use. Reference material on native NT tools, registry edits, and third-party tools is included.

SMS 2
Administration

By Darshan Doshi
and Mike Lubanski
1st Edition
448 pages, $39.99
ISBN: 0-7357-0082-6

SMS 2 Administration offers comprehensive coverage of how to design, deploy, and manage SMS 2.0 in an enterprise environment. This book follows the evolution of a software management system from the initial design through the implementation life cycle, to day-to-day management and usage of the system. Packed with case studies and examples pulled from the author's extensive experience, this book makes this complex product seem almost simple.

SQL Server
System
Administration

By Sean Baird and
Chris Miller, et al.
1st Edition
352 pages, $29.99
ISBN: 1-56205-955-6

Assuming that the reader is familiar with the fundamentals of database administration and has worked with SQL Server in some capacity, this book focuses on the topics of interest to most administrators: keeping data consistently available to users. Unlike other SQL Server books that have little relevance to the serious SQL Server DBA, *SQL Server System Administration* provides a hands-on approach that administrators won't find elsewhere.

Internet
Information
Services
Administration

By Kelli Adam
1st Edition
192 pages, $29.99
ISBN: 0-7357-0022-2

Administrators who know IIS from previous versions need this book to show them in concrete detail how to configure the new protocols, authenticate users with the new Certificate Server, and implement and manage the new e-commerce features that are part of IIS 5. This book gives you all of that: a quick read that provides real-world solutions, and doubles as a portable reference.

SQL Server 7
Essential Reference

By Sharon Dooley
1st Edition
400 pages, $35.00
ISBN: 0-7357-0864-9

SQL Server 7 Essential Reference is a comprehensive reference of advanced how-tos and techniques for developing with SQL Server. In particular, the book addresses advanced development techniques used in large application efforts with multiple users developing Web applications for intranets, extranets, or the Internet. Each section includes details on how each component is developed and then integrated into a real-life application.

Linux/UNIX

Linux System Administration

By M. Carling, James T. Dennis, and Stephen Degler
1st Edition
368 pages, $29.99
ISBN: 1-56205-934-3

Today's overworked sysadmins are looking for ways to keep their networks running smoothly and achieve enhanced performance. Users are always looking for more storage, more services, and more Speed. *Linux System Administration* guides the reader in the many intricacies of maintaining a secure, stable system.

Linux Firewalls

By Robert Ziegler
1st Edition
496 pages, $39.99
ISBN: 0-7357-0900-9

This book details security steps that a small, non-enterprise business user might take to protect his system. These steps include packet-level firewall filtering, IP masquerading, proxies, tcp wrappers, system integrity checking, and system security monitoring with an overall emphasis on filtering and protection. The goal of *Linux Firewalls* is to help people get their Internet security measures in place quickly, without the need to become experts in security or firewalls.

Linux Essential Reference

By Ed Petron
1st Edition
368 pages, $24.95
ISBN: 0-7357-0852-5

This title is all about getting things done by providing structured organization to the plethora of available Linux information. Providing clear and concise instructions on how to perform important administration and management tasks, as well as how to use some of the more powerful commands and more advanced topics, the scope of *Linux Essential Reference* includes the best way to implement the most frequently used commands, manage shell scripting, administer your own system, and utilize effective security.

UnixWare 7 System Administration

By Gene Henriksen
and Melissa Henriksen
1st Edition
560 pages, $39.99
ISBN: 1-57870-080-9

In great technical detail, this title presents the latest version of SCO UnixWare and is the definitive operating system resource for SCO engineers and administrators. SCO troubleshooting notes and tips are integrated throughout the text, as are tips specifically designed for those who are familiar with other UNIX variants.

Solaris Advanced System Administrator's Guide

By Janice Winsor
2nd Edition
587 pages, $39.99
ISBN: 1-57870-039-6

This officially authorized tutorial provides indispensable tips, advice, and quick-reference tables to help you add system components, improve service access, and automate routine tasks. this book also includes updated information on Solaris 2.6 topics.

Solaris System Administrator's Guide

By Janice Winsor
2nd Edition
324 pages, $34.99
ISBN: 1-57870-040-X

Designed to work as both a practical tutorial and quick reference, this book provides UNIX administrators complete, detailed descriptions of the most frequently performed tasks for Solaris. Learn how to employ the features of Solaris to meet these needs of your users, and get tips on how to make administration easier.

Solaris Essential Reference

By John Mulligan
1st Edition
304 pages, $24.95
ISBN: 0-7357-0023-0

A great companion to the solarisguide.com website, *Solaris Essential Reference* assumes readers are well-versed in general UNIX skills and simply need some pointers on how to get the most out of Solaris. This book provides clear and concise instructions on how to perform important administration and management tasks.

Networking

Cisco Router Configuration &Troubleshooting

By Mark Tripod
2nd Edition
330 pages, $39.99
ISBN: 0-7357-0999-8

A reference for the network and system administrator who finds himself having to configure and maintain existing Cisco routers, as well as get new hardware up and running. By providing advice and preferred practices, instead of just rehashing Cisco documentation, this book gives networking professionals information they can start using today.

Understanding Directory Services

By Beth Sheresh and Doug Sheresh
1st Edition
390 pages, $39.99
ISBN: 0-7357-0910-6

Understanding Directory Services provides the reader with a thorough knowledge of the fundamentals of directory services: what Directory Services are, how they are designed, and what functionality they can provide to an IT infrastructure. This book provides a framework to the exploding market of directory services by placing the technology in context and helping people understand what directories can, and can't, do for their networks.

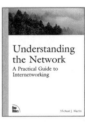

Understanding the Network: A Practical Guide to Internetworking

By Michael Martin
1st Edition
690 pages, $39.99
ISBN: 0-7357-0977-7

Understanding the Network addresses the audience in practical terminology, and describes the most essential information and tools required to build high-availability networks in a step-by-step implementation format. Each chapter could be read as a standalone, but the book builds progressively toward a summary of the essential concepts needed to put together a wide-area network.

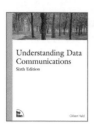

Understanding Data Communications
By Gilbert Held
6th Edition
620 pages, $39.99
ISBN: 0-7357-0036-2

Gil Held's book is ideal for those who want to get up to speed on technological advances as well as those who want a primer on networking concepts. This book is intended to explain how data communications actually work. It contains updated coverage on hot topics like thin client technology, x2 and 56Kbps modems, voice digitization, and wireless data transmission. Whatever your needs, this title puts perspective and expertise in your hands.

LDAP: Programming Directory Enabled Applications
By Tim Howes and Mark Smith
1st Edition
480 pages, $44.99
ISBN: 1-57870-000-0

This overview of the LDAP standard discusses its creation and history with the Internet Engineering Task Force, as well as the original RFC standard. LDAP also covers compliance trends, implementation, data packet handling in C++, client/server responsibilities and more.

Gigabit Ethernet Networking
By David Cunningham and William Lane
1st Edition
560 pages, $50.00
ISBN: 1-57870-062-0

Gigabit Ethernet is the next step for speed on the majority of installed networks. Explore how this technology will allow high-bandwidth applications, such as the integration of telephone and data services, real-time applications, thin client applications, such as Windows NT Terminal Server, and corporate teleconferencing.

Supporting Service Level Agreements on IP Networks
By Dinesh Verma
1st Edition
270 pages, $50.00
ISBN: 1-57870-146-5

An essential resource for network engineers and architects, *Supporting Service Level Agreements on IP Networks* will help you build a core network capable of supporting a range of service. Learn how to create SLA solutions using off-the-shelf components in both best-effort and DiffServ/IntServ networks. Learn how to verify the performance of your SLA, as either a customer or network services provider, and use SLAs to support IPv6 networks.

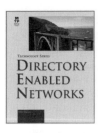

Directory Enabled Networks

By John Strassner
1st Edition
752 pages, $50.00
ISBN: 1-57870-140-6

Directory Enabled Networks is a comprehensive resource on the design and use of DEN. This book provides practical examples side-by-side with a detailed introduction to the theory of building a new class of network-enabled applications that will solve networking problems. DEN is a critical tool for network architects, administrators, and application developers.

Quality of Service in IP Networks

By Grenville Armitage
1st Edition
310 pages, $50.00
ISBN: 1-57870-189-9

Quality of Service in IP Networks presents a clear understanding of the architectural issues surrounding delivering QoS in an IP network, and positions the emerging technologies within a framework of solutions. The motivation for QoS is explained with reference to emerging real-time applications, such as Voice/Video over IP, VPN services, and supporting Service Level Agreements.

Differentiated Services for the Internet

By Kalevi Kilkki
1st Edition
400 pages, $50.00
ISBN: 1-57870-132-5

This book offers network architects, engineers, and managers of packet networks critical insight into the continuing development of Differentiated Services. It addresses the particular needs of a network environment as well as issues that must be considered in its implementation. Coverage allows networkers to implement DiffServ on a variety of networking technologies, including ATM, and to solve common problems related to TCP, UDP, and other networking protocols.

Designing Addressing Architectures for Routing and Switching

By Howard Berkowitz
1st Edition
500 pages, $45.00
ISBN: 1-57870-059-0

One of the greatest challenges for a network design professional is making the users, servers, files, printers, and other resources visible on their network. This title equips the network engineer or architect with a systematic methodology for planning the wide area and local area network "streets" on which users and servers live.

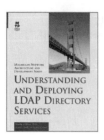

Understanding and Deploying LDAP Directory Services

By Tim Howes, Mark Smith, and Gordon Good
1st Edition
850 pages, $50.00
ISBN: 1-57870-070-1

This comprehensive tutorial provides the reader with a thorough treatment of LDAP directory services. Minimal knowledge of general networking and administration is assumed, making the material accessible to intermediate and advanced readers alike. The text is full of practical implementation advice and real-world deployment examples to help the reader choose the path that makes the most sense for his specific organization.

Switched, Fast, and Gigabit Ethernet

By Sean Riley and Robert Breyer
3rd Edition
615 pages, $50.00
ISBN: 1-57870-073-6

Switched, Fast, and Gigabit Ethernet, Third Edition is the one and only solution needed to understand and fully implement this entire range of Ethernet innovations. Acting both as an overview of current technologies and hardware requirements as well as a hands-on, comprehensive tutorial for deploying and managing switched, fast, and gigabit ethernet networks, this guide covers the most prominent present and future challenges network administrators face.

Wide Area High Speed Networks

By Dr. Sidnie Feit
1st Edition
624 pages, $50.00
ISBN: 1-57870-114-7

Networking is in a transitional phase between long-standing conventional wide area services and new technologies and services. This book presents current and emerging wide area technologies and services, makes them understandable, and puts them into perspective so that their merits and disadvantages are clear.

Local Area High Speed Networks

By Dr. Sidnie Feit
1st Edition
655 pages, $50.00
ISBN: 1-57870-113-9

There is a great deal of change happening in the technology being used for local area networks. As Web intranets have driven bandwidth needs through the ceiling, inexpensive Ethernet NICs and switches have come into the market. As a result, many network professionals are interested in evaluating these new technologies for implementation. This book provides real-world implementation expertise for these technologies, including traces, so that users can realistically compare and decide how to use them.

The DHCP Handbook

By Ralph Droms
and Ted Lemon
1st Edition
535 pages, $55.00
ISBN: 1-57870-137-6

The DHCP Handbook is an authoritative overview and expert guide to the setup and management of a DHCP server. This title discusses how DHCP was developed and its interaction with other protocols. Learn how DHCP operates, its use in different environments, and the interaction between DHCP servers and clients. Network hardware, inter-server communication, security, SNMP, and IP mobility are also discussed. Also, included in the book are several appendices that provide a rich resource for networking professionals working with DHCP.

Designing Routing and Switching Architectures for Enterprise Networks

By Howard
Berkowitz
1st Edition
992 pages, $55.00
ISBN: 1-57870-060-4

This title provides a fundamental understanding of how switches and routers operate, enabling the reader to use them effectively to build networks. The book walks the network designer through all aspects of requirements, analysis, and deployment strategies, strengthens readers' professional abilities, and helps them develop skills necessary to advance in their profession.

Wireless LANs: Implementing Interoperable Networks

By Jim Geier
1st Edition
432 pages, $40.00
ISBN: 1-57870-081-7

Wireless LANs covers how and why to migrate from proprietary solutions to the 802.11 standard, and explains how to realize significant cost savings through wireless LAN implementation for data collection systems.

Network Performance Baselining

By Daniel Nassar
1st Edition
736 pages, $50.00
ISBN: 1-57870-240-2

Network Performance Baselining focuses on the real-world implementation of network baselining principles and shows not only how to measure and rate a network's performance, but also how to improve the network performance. This book includes chapters that give a real "how-to" approach for standard baseline methodologies along with actual steps and processes to perform network baseline measurements. In addition, the proper way to document and build a baseline report will be provided.

The Economics of Electronic Commerce

By Soon-Yong Choi,
Andrew Whinston,
Dale Stahl
1st Edition
656 pages, $49.99
ISBN: 1-57870-014-0

This is the first electronic commerce title to focus on traditional topics of economics applied to the electronic commerce arena. While all other electronic commerce titles take a "how-to" approach, this focuses on what it means from an economic perspective.

Intrusion Detection

By Rebecca Gurley Bace
1st Edition
340 pages, $50.00
ISBN: 1-57870-185-6

Intrusion detection is a critical new area of technology within network security. This comprehensive guide to the field of intrusion detection covers the foundations of intrusion detection and system audit. *Intrusion Detection* provides a wealth of information, ranging from design considerations to how to evaluate and choose the optimal commercial intrusion detection products for a particular networking environment.

Understanding Public-Key Infrastructure

By Carlisle Adams
and Steve Lloyd
1st Edition
300 pages, $50.00
ISBN: 1-57870-166-X

This book is a tutorial on, and a guide to the deployment of, Public-Key Infrastructures. It covers a broad range of material related to PKIs, including certification, operational considerations and standardization efforts, as well as deployment issues and considerations. Emphasis is placed on explaining the interrelated fields within the topic area, to assist those who will be responsible for making deployment decisions and architecting a PKI within an organization.

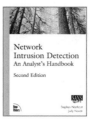

Network Intrusion Detection: An Analyst's Handbook

By Stephen Northcutt and
Judy Novak
2nd Edition
480 pages, $45.00
ISBN: 0-7357-1008-2

Get answers and solutions from someone who has been in the trenches. Author Stephen Northcutt, original developer of the Shadow intrusion detection system and former Director of the United States Navy's Information System Security Office, gives his expertise to intrusion detection specialists, security analysts, and consultants responsible for setting up and maintaining an effective defense against network security attacks.

Domino System Administration

By Rob Kirkland
1st Edition
860 pages, $49.99
ISBN: 1-56205-948-3

Need a concise, practical explanation about the new features of Domino, and how to make some of the advanced stuff really work? *Domino System Administration* is the first book on Domino that attacks the technology at the professional level, with practical, hands-on assistance to get Domino 5 running in your organization.

Lotus Notes & Domino Essential Reference

By Dave Hatter and Tim Bankes
1st Edition
675 pages, $45.00
ISBN: 0-7357-0007-9

If you need something to facilitate your creative and technical abilities—something to perfect your Lotus Notes and Domino programming skills—this is the book for you. This title includes all of the objects, classes, functions, and methods found if you work with Lotus Notes and Domino. It shows the object hierarchy and the overlying relationship between each one, organized the way the language is designed.

Other Books By New Riders

Professional Certification

TRAINING GUIDES

MCSE Training Guide:
Networking Essentials, 2nd Ed.
156205919X • $49.99

MCSE Training Guide: Windows
NT Server 4, 2nd Ed.
1562059165 • $49.99

MCSE Training Guide: Windows
NT Workstation 4, 2nd Ed.
1562059181 • $49.99

MCSE Training Guide: Windows
NT Server 4 Enterprise, 2nd Ed.
1562059173 • $49.99

MCSE Training Guide: Core
Exams Bundle, 2nd Ed.
1562059262 • $149.99

MCSE Training Guide: TCP/IP,
2nd Ed.
1562059203 • $49.99

MCSE Training Guide: IIS 4,
2nd Ed.
0735708657 • $49.99

MCSE Training Guide: SQL Server
7 Administration
0735700036 • $49.99

MCSE Training Guide: SQL Server
7 Database Design
0735700044 • $49.99

CLP Training Guide: Lotus
Notes 4
0789715058 • $59.99

MCSD Training Guide: Visual
Basic 6 Exams
0735700028 • $69.99

MCSD Training Guide: Solution
Architectures
0735700265 • $49.99

MCSD Training Guide: 4-in-1
Bundle
0735709122 • $149.99

A+ Certification Training Guide,
2nd Ed.
0735709076 • $49.99

Network+ Certification Guide
073570077X • $49.99

Solaris 2.6 Administrator
Certification Training Guide,
Part I
157870085X • $40.00

Solaris 2.6 Administrator
Certification Training Guide,
Part II
1578700868 • $40.00

Solaris 7 Administrator
Certification Training Guide, Part I
and II
1578702496 • $49.99

MCSE Training Guide: Windows
2000 Professional
0735709653 • $49.99

MCSE Training Guide:
Windows 2000 Server
0735709688 • $49.99

MCSE Training Guide: Windows
2000 Network Infrastructure
0735709661 • $49.99

MCSE Training Guide: Windows
2000 Network Security Design
073570984X • $49.99

MCSE Training Guide: Windows
2000 Network Infrastructure
Design
0735709823 • $49.99

MCSE Training Guide: Windows
2000 Directory Services.
Infrastructure
0735709769 • $49.99

MCSE Training Guide: Windows
2000 Directory Services Design
0735709831 • $49.99

MCSE Training Guide: Windows
2000 Accelerated Exam
0735709793 • $69.99

MCSE Training Guide: Windows
2000 Core Exams Bundle
0735709882 • $149.99

Java 2 Certification Training Guide
1562059505 • $39.99

FAST TRACKS

CLP Fast Track: Lotus
Notes/Domino 5 System
Administration.
0735708789 • $39.99

CLP Fast Track: Lotus
Notes/Domino 5 Application
Development
0735708789 • $39.99

MCSD Fast Track: Solution
Architectures
073570029X • $29.99

MCSD Fast Track: Visual Basic 6,
Exam 70-175
0735700184 • $19.99

MCSD Fast Track: Visual Basic 6,
Exam 70-176
0735700192 • $19.99

# How to Contact Us

Visit Our Web Site

`www.newriders.com`

On our Web site you'll find information about our other books, authors, tables of contents, indexes, and book errata.

Email Us

Contact us at this address:

`nrfeedback@newriders.com`

- If you have comments or questions about this book
- To report errors that you have found in this book
- If you have a book proposal to submit or are interested in writing for New Riders
- If you would like to have an author kit sent to you
- If you are an expert in a computer topic or technology and are interested in being a technical editor who reviews manuscripts for technical accuracy

- To find a distributor in your area, please contact our international department at this address.

`nrmedia@newriders.com`

- For instructors from educational institutions who want to preview New Riders books for classroom use. Email should include your name, title, school, department, address, phone number, office days/hours, text in use, and enrollment, along with your request for desk/examination copies and/or additional information.
- For members of the media who are interested in reviewing copies of New Riders books. Send your name, mailing address, and email address, along with the name of the publication or Web site you work for.

Write to Us

New Riders Publishing

201 W. 103rd St.

Indianapolis, IN 46290-1097

Call Us

Toll-free (800) 571-5840 + 9 + 7477

If outside U.S. (317) 581-3500. Ask for New Riders.

Fax Us

(317) 581-4663

We Want to Know What You Think

To better serve you, we would like your opinion on the content and quality of this book. Please complete this card and mail it to us or fax it to 317-581-4663.

Name_____

Address _____

City_____State_____Zip_____

Email Address _____

Occupation _____

What influenced your purchase of this book?
❑ Recommendation
❑ Cover Design
❑ Table of Contents
❑ Index
❑ Magazine Review
❑ Advertisement
❑ New Rider's Reputation
❑ Author Name

How would you rate the contents of this book?
❑ Excellent
❑ Very Good
❑ Good
❑ Fair
❑ Below Average
❑ Poor

How do you plan to use this book?
❑ Quick reference
❑ Self-training
❑ Classroom
❑ Other

What do you like most about this book?
Check all that apply.
❑ Content
❑ Writing Style
❑ Accuracy
❑ Examples
❑ Listings
❑ Design
❑ Index
❑ Page Count
❑ Price
❑ Illustrations

What do you like least about this book?
Check all that apply.
❑ Content
❑ Writing Style
❑ Accuracy
❑ Examples
❑ Listings
❑ Design
❑ Index
❑ Page Count
❑ Price
❑ Illustrations

Can you name a similar book that you like better than this one, or one that is as good? Why?

_____

_____

How many New Riders books do you own? _____

What are your favorite computer books? _____

_____

What other titles would you like to see us develop? _____

_____

Any comments for us? _____

_____

_____

_____

_____

Win32 Perl Scripting, 1-57870-215-1

www.newriders.com • Fax 317-581-4663

Fold here and tape to mail

New Riders Publishing
201 W. 103rd St.
Indianapolis, IN 46290